*Christian Ritual
and the World of
Shakespeare's Tragedies*

Other books by Herbert R. Coursen, Jr.:

"The Rarer Action": Hamlet's Mousetrap
As Up They Grew
Storm in April
Survivor
Lookout Point
Shaping the Self: Style and Technique in the Narrative

Christian Ritual
and the World of
Shakespeare's Tragedies

Herbert R. Coursen, Jr.

Lewisburg
Bucknell University Press
London: Associated University Presses

Associated University Presses, Inc.
Cranbury, New Jersey 08512

Associated University Presses
108 New Bond Street
London W1Y OQX, England

Library of Congress Cataloging in Publication Data

Coursen, Herbert R
  Christian ritual and the world of Shakespeare's tragedies.

  Bibliography: p.
  Includes index.
  1. Shakespeare, William, 1564-1616—Tragedies. 2. Shakespeare, William, 1564-1616—Religion and ethics. 3. Christianity in literature. I. Title.
PR2983.C69   822.3′3   74-201   ISBN 0-8387-1518-4

PRINTED IN THE UNITED STATES OF AMERICA

This book is for Susan, Elizabeth,
Leigh, and Virginia

Contents

Preface

The plays I discuss in this book seem to me to have profoundly Christian overtones and ramifications. But they are primarily great drama, neither bound in by some "Christian doctrine," encompassed within some broad concept of "Christian humanism," nor, indeed, ultimately expressing some explicit "Christian meaning." That *Macbeth* occurs within a Christian world, is, to me, inescapable. That *King Lear* begins and ends in a non-Christian context seems equally inescapable, although the beginning trembles with Christian possibility and the ending is rendered more deeply painful by memory of that possibility lost. This book, then, does not attempt to defend the questionable thesis that Shakespeare's is "Christian tragedy."

What Shakespeare may have believed as a man is irrelevant, as well as undiscoverable. But that he employed received religious tradition as one of the sources of his drama is relevant, and that tradition is discoverable. The alternatives faced by the major characters in these plays include a possible decision *against* individual will, *in accord with* a power consonant with the Christian deity, and *in harmony with* the healing and fulfilling force celebrated in the Holy Communion as practiced within the English Church, with only slight alterations of rubric, ritual, or doctrine during Shakespeare's lifetime. That the major character—or tragic hero—makes the anti-sacramental decision in each play suggests, for example, that *Macbeth* and *King Lear* imitate similar anti-sacramental actions within different worlds.

The study of these plays is not, I hope, artificially centered on some esoteric theory of the Eucharist, nor does it impose the Eucharist upon dramatic movement. Rather, I hope to show that sacrament, particularly the Eucharist, informs the distinct rhythms of each play, and is central to an under-standing of why these plays are tragedies, of why Richard, Hamlet, Othello, Lear, and Macbeth must each die amid the wreckage of the world he had helped destroy. I try here to pursue the dramatic curve of the plays, attempting to define the world of each play and suggesting how ritual informs the play at its most profound moments, particularly how ritual deepens an audience's response to what happens on stage. That the imitation of sacrament within a play would have created deep and probably unperceived resonances within the spectator is an implicit thesis of the discussion of each play. It should not be ignored, however, because it helps ex-plain the elusive mystery that we feel we have almost grasped, even in our postsacramental world, during great perfor-mances of these profound plays. And it helps explain why Shakespeare dominated his own age, the greatest few years of English drama.

Folger Shakespeare Library, 1971

Note: Unless otherwise noted, biblical quotations are from the Geneva Bible (Geneva, 1560), undoubtedly the most popular Bible of Shakespeare's lifetime. Quotations from *The Book of Common Prayer* are from the Queen Elizabeth Edi-tion, which controlled the ritual of the Church from 1559 to 1604. Quotations from the Homilies are from the 1623 Folio, which brought the two books of Homilies issued under Elizabeth into one volume, in a form identical, except for spelling and punctuation, to that of Shakespeare's lifetime. Quotations from Shakespeare accord with the Neilson-Hill *Complete Plays and Poems* (Cambridge, Mass., 1942), al-though my lineation of prose passages does not always pre-cisely follow Neilson-Hill.

Acknowledgments

I have been fortunate enough to have been taught by many superb Shakespeareans: John Shannon, Dorothy Dromeshauser, C. L. Barber, Theodore Baird, John Moore, Davis Harding, J. A. S. McPeek, William Rosen, and Leonard F. Dean. The staff of the Folger Library, particularly O. B. Hardison and Richard Schoeck, were tremendously helpful to me, not only in opening to me the resources of that fine facility, but in offering constructive criticism to me whenever I requested it, which was often. Saranne Thomke listened with rare patience to every word of the manuscript (excluding footnotes) and provided an encouragement and a momentum toward its completion that I will always appreciate. Professor Naomi Diamond heard both the *Richard II* and the *Othello* chapters and fought me every inch of the way on things I "hadn't earned." Whatever I have earned in those chapters is a result of her keen understanding of what I was trying to do. Other Folger colleagues who proved helpful, in one way or another, were Professors Stephen Smith, Kay Michael, Ruth Widman, and J. Leeds Barroll. Professor Roy W. Battenhouse corrected several sheer "errors of judgment" in the *Othello* chapter, and has kindly allowed me to incorporate several of his penciled marginal notations as footnotes in that chapter. I am indebted to colleagues at Bowdoin College—Professors James Fisher, Peter Friend,

Abbott Ikeler, Franklin Burroughs, Edward Pols, Lawrence Hall, and Louis Coxe—for a variety of assists rendered along the way. My gratitude extends as well to Bowdoin's President, Roger Howell, a fine Elizabethan scholar, who has consistently encouraged my own scholarship and research. I would be remiss were I not to recognize my wonderful parents, Herbert and Mildred Coursen, who made it possible for me to become an elderly graduate student, and Susan Coursen, who saw me through those years, keeping the children tranquil while I tried to study. To Nancy March, Paula Burnett, Joanne Homer, and Cynthia Little my thanks for nursing my ailing back through the notes and bibliography. To Mrs. Mathilde E. Finch my gratitude for a meticulous job of copy editing what must have seemed at times an incomprehensible mishmash. And, finally, financial gratitude to The Bowdoin College Research Fund, The Ford Foundation, and the Folger Library Fellowship Program, administered by the Trustees of Amherst College. Amen.

Introduction:
The Communion as Comedy

Sin consists in the act by which man wills himself for himself.
—St. Bernard

The Elizabethan Communion Service resembles the "comedy of the Christian life" described by Northrop Frye: "We first encounter the law in its harsh tyrannical form of an external barrier to action, a series of negative commands, and we are eventually set free of this law, not by breaking it, but by internalizing it: it becomes an inner condition of behavior, not an external antagonist as it is to the criminal."[1] At the same time, many Shakespearean comedies resemble the Mass described by O. B. Hardison: "The mythic event celebrated is rebirth, not death, although it is a rebirth that requires death as its prelude. The experience of the participants is transition from guilt to innocence, from separation to communion."[2] The "deaths" of Hero, Sebastian, and "drown'd Viola" (*Twelfth Night*, V.i.248); of Marina and of Thasia "supposed dead/ And drown'd" (*Pericles*, V.iii.35-36); of the sons of Cymbeline, "for many years thought dead" (V.v.456); and of Hermione, precede the reconciliation of these characters with those from whom they have been separated and, often, alienated. The psychic death of Lear is a necessary prelude to his reunion with Cordelia in perhaps Shakespeare's greatest comic scene.

The opening rubrics of the Communion Service enjoin law in its harshest terms:

> And if any of those be an open and notorious evil liver, so that ye congregacion by him is offended, or have done any wrong to hys neighbours by word or dede: ye Curate havyng knowledge therof, shal cal hym, and advertyse hym, in any wise not to presume to the Lordes table, until he have openly declared him self to have truely repented and amended his former naughty lyfe, that the Congregation may therby be satisfyed, which afore were offended. . . .
>
> The same order shall the Curate use with those, betwixt whome he perceyveth malice and hatred to raigne, not suffering them to be partakers of the Lordes table, untyll he know them to be reconciled. And if one of the parties so at variance, be content to forgeve from the bottome of hys hart, that he hym self hath offended: and the other partye wyll not be perswaded to a godly unity, but remain stil in his forwardnes and malice: The Minister in that case, ought to admit the penitent person to the holy Communyon, and not hym that is obstinate.

In each case, the pattern for readmission to the sacred ritual is clearly outlined, and, in each case, the pattern is "comic." One incapable of the cleansing of personal vice or frailty which, in comedy, precedes a rejoining of society, is prohibited from attendance at the celebration. We can understand immediately why an Oliver must undergo a "conversion" (IV.iii.137) in *As You Like It* to participate in the play's final "rites" (V.iv.203), and why a Don John must be excluded from the ceremonies lying just beyond the end of *Much Ado About Nothing*, indeed faces "brave punishments" (V.iv.130). To Antonio, the law is not a continuing external antagonist at the end of *The Tempest;* Prospero leaves him to his "inward pinches" (V.i.77). The law has become internalized as a guilt that Antonio refuses to release through contrition.

To be eligible to attend a Communion Service, not to be a notorious evil liver, not to be malicious or hateful, is a negative precondition for the movement toward the oneness with Christ that *completes* the comic pattern of Communion and that usually lies just beyond the end of a comedy in a feast or a marriage. Even those who satisfy the requirements of the initial rubrics must have the "thoughtes of [their] hartes [cleansed] by the inspiracion [inbreathing] of [God's] holy spirite," and, as part of that process, must "knelying . . . aske Goddes mercye for their transgressyon of" each of the Ten Commandments. After each Commandment, the congregation prays that God "incline [bend] our hartes to kepe this lawe." The rehearsal of the Mosaic Law involves primarily legal rather than spiritual transgression, emphasizing formal external observance rather than internalization through faith. Thus the congregation responds collectively, with a common voice speaking of "*our* hartes." The movement of the Communion is toward the "New Testament," therefore inward, toward the spiritual status of the individual parishioner:

> Ye that mynde to come to the holye Communion of the bodye and bloude of our savioure Christe, must consyder what saincte Paul writeth unto the Corinthiens, how he exhorteth all persons diligently to trye and examyne them selves, before they presume to eate of that breade and drinke of that cuppe. For as the benefyte is greate, yf wyth a trulye penitente herte and lyvely faith we receive that holy sacrament (for then we spiritually eate the fleshe of Christ, and drincke his bloude, then we dwell in Christe and Christe in us, we be one wyth Christ, and Christ with us) so is the danger great, if we receyve the same unworthely.

The admonition reflects Christ's extension of the Ten Commandments to the realm of the spirit in the Sermon on the Mount.

The Priest's invitation reiterates the comic pattern embodied within the Communion and repeated in many of its components:

> You that do truly and ernestly repente you of youre sinnes, and be in love, and charite with your neighbors and entende to lede a newe lyfe, folowing the commaundementes of God, and walkynge from hence furthe in his holy waies: Draw nere and take this holy Sacrament to your comforte, make your humble confession to almighty God, before this congregation here gathered together in his holye name, mekely knelynge upon your knees.

Here the rhythms are more positive than in the opening rubrics: sins are repented, love and charity replace hatred and malice; the thrust toward the new life beyond the sacrament is emphasized; community of God and congregation is implied.

While the General Confession *is* "general" and does not, as in the rehearsal of the Ten Commandments, specify crimes, its emphasis is on internal guilt, not external transgression, and on inward pain, not the legal retribution more prominent in the law-giving of the Old Testament:

Almighty God, father of oure Lorde Jesus Christe, maker of all thynges, Judge of all menne, we acknowledge and bewayle our manifolde synnes and wyckednesse, which we from tyme to tyme moste grevously have committed, by thoughte woorde and deede, against thy divine Majestie, provokynge mooste justlye thy wrathe and indignation againste us: we do earnestly repente, and bee hartely sorye for these our misdoinges, the remembraunce of them is grevous unto us: the burthen of theim is intollerable: have mercy upon us, have mercye upon us, mooste mercyfull father, for thy sonne oure Lorde Jesus Christes sake, forgeve us all that is paste, and graunte that we may ever hereafter serve and please the, in newenes of lyfe, to the honour and glorye of thy name throughe Jesus Christe our Lorde.

The Confession imitates what Hardison calls the three phases of the Christian pattern: Pathos ("oure manifolde synnes and wyckednesse," whose burden is "intollerable"), Peripety ("we do earnestly repente"), and Theophany ("forgeve us all that is paste, and graunte that we may ever hereafter serve and please the, in newenes of lyfe").[3]

The secular comedy might be expected to close with the Absolution, which occurs after the Confession, but before the Transmission of the Host:

Almightye God, oure heavenly father, who of his great mercy hathe promised forgevenes of sinnes, to al them, which with hartye repentaunce and true faithe turne to hym: have mercye upon you, pardon and deliver you from all your sinnes, confirme and strengthen you in all goodnes, and bring you to everlastyng lyfe; through Jesus Christe our Lorde.

The Absolution reemphasizes the necessity for individual preparedness prior to Communion. Its "promise" signals a further stage in the process of stripping away of sin prior to reception of the host.

The lifting up of hearts that follows is vital to the Elizabethan conception of Communion, because if Christ is not *in* the elements, but bodily in heaven, as the Creed asserts, the communicants must elevate their hearts *to* Him to participate in His power:

Lift up your hartes.
We lyfte them up unto the Lorde.

With impending matrimony and pledges toward newness of life, a comedy ends. The Gentlemen of *Love's Labour's Lost,* on completion of their year's "purgation" (Biron "must be purg'd" [V.ii.829] to achieve his "reformation" [V.ii.879]), also Orlando, Beatrice, and Benedick, who have moved themselves past the barriers that separated them from the truths of their own natures and hence separated them from others, have cleansed themselves of error and affectation, and are ready to participate in a spiritual reenactment of their "conversions." The Communion beyond the comedy will do for individual souls in the context of eternity which, within the play, has been done for the characters in the context of society. The Communion begins where the comedy ends, excluding the Don Johns and Antonios who have not translated themselves into the "new society" that the reformed characters of comedy enter at the end of the play. The initial application of the law, rubrical and Mosaic, is social ("*open* and *notorious* evil liver, so that ye *congregacion* by him is offended . . . ," "*those betwixt whome* he perceyveth malice and hatred to raigne. . ."), but gives way to the spiritual interior of the law, to the invisible reality within each heart. The Eucharist fulfills the promise of comedy by incorporating the act of oneness itself.

The importance of the moment of Communion for the Elizabethan cannot be overemphasized, for it is in the receiving of the sacraments and not in the consecration of the elements that the fusion of Christ and communicant, blood and wine occurs. The 1559 Prayer Book confirms for the Elizabethan Cranmer's 1549 Prayer Book, and thus confirms for England the basic tenets of the Reformation. Hooker's discussion is the culmination of the long debate regarding transubstantiation, "substance" and "presence," and underlines the Prayer Book's enforcement of the individual reception of the elements, even while Hooker rationalizes or even dodges the terms of the debate. The Prayer Book, of course, does not descend to the debate, since liturgy reflects doctrine. It is more important, says Hooker, to "meditate with silence what we have by the sacrament, and less to dispute of the matter how." "What these elements are in themselves it skilleth not. It is enough that to me which take them they are the body and blood of Christ." The Communion is a "mystical participation" and "the soul of man is the receptacle of Christ's presence."[4] The individual becomes, then, part of the sacramental action—his inner state is vital to it, his own faith in the mystery is basic, his heart does the feeding and so participates in the profound incorporation with Christ.

The debate that Hooker summarizes for the divines of the English Church is summarized for the churchgoer in "An Homilie of the Worthy receiving and reverent esteeming of the Sacrament of the body and blood of Christ." Predictably, the Homily emphasizes the individual requirements for participation. Though a fallen being, man can still accept Communion, "which although it seeme of smale vertue to some, yet being rightly done by the faythfull, it doeth not onely helpe their weakeness (who be by their poysoned nature readier to remember injuries than benefits) but strengtheneth and comforteth their inward man with peace and gladness and maketh them thankeful to their redeemer." For the "inward man" to receive such comfort he must participate directly "in the institution of [Christ's] heavenly Supper, where every one of us must be ghestes, and not gazers, eaters and not lookers, feeding ourselves, and not hiring others to feed for us." Man's ability to create *of* himself a sacrament *by* himself is asserted: "this is to stike fast to Christs promise made in his Institution, to make Christ thine own, and to apply his merits unto thy selfe. Herein thou needest no other mans helpe."

The taking of the bread and wine removes the participants from the temporal pattern, taking them back in time to the Last Supper, making them symbolic disciples. The intersection of the individual spirit with Christ and of temporal life with eternity, and the movement of the heart up to body and blood (a transcendence of space as well as of time), mark a step beyond secular comedy. The reception of the host imitates the final movement of the divine comedy promised the soul of the faithful communicant:

> The bodie of our lord Jesu Christ, which was geven for the, preserve thy body and soule into everlastinge life. . . .
> The bloude of our lorde Jesu Christ, which was shedd for the, preserve thy body and soule into everlastinge life. . . .

The moment of temporal, spatial, and spiritual intersection passed, the individual is sent into the world again, his sacramental potentiality confirmed in a mystical instant, his "inward man" cleansed and refreshed, asked essentially to retain the oneness achieved at the moment of his reception of the bread and wine:

> we be very membres incorporate in thy mistical body, whiche is the blessed company of al faithful people, and be also heyres through hope of thy everlasting kingdom, by the merites of the most precious death and passion of thy deere sone.

And he is asked, existentially, to continue in the practice of all Christian virtues:

> We now most humbly beseche the, O hevenly father, so to assist us with thy grace, that we may continue in that holy felowship, and do all suche good workes as thou has prepared for us to walke in, throughe Jesus Christe our Lorde.

The Communion fulfills the two stages in the creation of a "holy object," as defined by K. D. MacKenzie, having transferred to the communicant the properties of the consecrated and received elements. A "holy object is one which is purified from all lower associations"; a "holy object is one which is sanctified for a religious purpose."[5] Presumably, "all suche good workes" will qualify the individual for the next Communion, preventing his notorious evil living, forestalling hatred and malice, permitting him to enter again into the ritual cleansing, the ceremony of admission of guilt, awareness of the need for forgiveness, achievement of oneness with Christ, of thanksgiving, and of movement again onto the pathways of the secular world and ultimately into the next.

That the individual becomes a sacramental component,

that he is not merely receiving already consecrated elements or observing their reception by a priestly representative, has profound implications for drama. By providing the individual a dynamic role in Communion, giving him a psychological and moral *choice,* and, above all, by creating of him a sacramental element at the instant of reception, he becomes not only a character in the drama of Communion, but potentially a character in secular drama, complete with a concomitant *theory* of character. If, as Hardison argues, the medieval Mass was the "sacred phase of parallel elements turned to secular use on the profane stage,"[6] Elizabethan drama, particularly Shakespeare's, represents the same mimesis, exploring the sacramental possibilities of characters within worlds predicated on the Christian dynamic and represented most profoundly by the Communion Service. Hardison's translation of the Mass into secular drama applies with equal weight to Elizabethan drama:

> Just as the Mass is a sacred drama encompassing all history and embodying in its structure the central pattern of Christian life on which all Christian drama must draw, the celebration of the Mass contains all elements necessary to secular performances. The Mass is the general case—for Christian culture, the archetype. Individual dramas are shaped in its mold.[7]

The 1559 Prayer Book's confirmation of the individual role in Communion was bound to affect, if not determine, the drama that emerged in the late sixteenth and early seventeenth centuries. To explain Marlowe, for example, strictly on the basis of the morality tradition is simplistic, because the morality does not explain the greater complexity and individuality of a Dr. Faustus, as contrasted with an Everyman. The very difference in names captures the individual emphasis reflected profoundly in the Prayer Book. To add to the morality inheritance the Protestant insistence on the individual decision to believe is to add a vital element to an understanding of the dimensions of Faustus. To claim that the confirming of the individual as *himself* sacramental is the matrix for the great drama that ensued is also simplistic, because it ignores dramatic tradition. The 1559 Prayer Book, however, was a vital document in the cultural flow from which great dramatic art emerged, perhaps inevitably, from no less profound religious ritual. The Prayer Book marks a moment of definition within the flow of history, one of the agents whereby history is transformed into culture. The Communion Service at once encourages that drama by emphasizing the individual's sacramental possibilities and potential disasters, hence his dramatic potentiality, and allows members of the culture to share in secular drama as they shared as individuals in the sacred drama of Communion. Communion was their cultural heritage, their individual experience, and thus one of the forms a dramatist could employ to evoke a deep response from his spectator.

The Elizabethan went to the theater with a ritual knowledge based on the Eucharist, whether he was a disgruntled Catholic, who preferred his version of the Mass, a dissenting Puritan, who may have used a modified form of worship contained in versions of the Geneva Bible, or a devout or passive Protestant. He was preconditioned to respond on a level deeper than that of mere entertainment to the movement of Shakespeare's comedies, which imitated a deeper ritualistic archetype shared to some degree by every member of the audience. If comedy imitates the progress of an individual from error to insight, from alienation to reunion with society in this world, Communion is a deeper comedy: the dramatic issue of the character is his soul, his destination eternity. The spectator's experience of a comedy would have involved the deepest of resonances. In the progress of the comic character toward self-knowledge and a "new society," the Elizabethan would have witnessed the mimesis of the journey of his own soul toward salvation.

Shakespeare achieves what Norman Holland calls a "continuum": "By projecting what is in the characters outward into external visible events and actions, a play paves the way for the audience's own act of projection. We find in the external reality of a play what is hidden in ourselves. Drama shows virtue her own feature, scorn her own image, and the very age and body of the time his form and pressure. Watching a set of events in a play feels, for this reason, very different from reading them in a novel."[8] Holland predicates his continuum on psychoanalytic grounds, seeing the play as re-creating the infantile fears of its auditor in dramatic terms, involving him profoundly and achieving for him a psychic purgation. A continuum based on ritualistic premises seems equally valid—the Eucharist as dramatic archetype for the comedy, creating within the spectator a deep response that returns to the stage in an increasingly more profound interaction between play and auditor. The action is being imitated not merely "on stage," but within a theater wrapped within a single experience of participation. It is one thing to notice "feasting" in Shakespeare's plays, as does G. Wilson Knight,[9] but another to recognize the archetype of feasting, which would have evoked profound reverberations within the single spectator, making him a communicant in a secular sacrament, a guilty creature sitting at a comedy, vibrating with the deeper rhythms of the Eucharist.

NOTES TO INTRODUCTION

1. Northrop Frye, *A Natural Perspective* (New York, 1965), p. 133.
2. O. B. Hardison, *Christian Rite and Christian Drama in the Middle Ages* (Baltimore, Md., 1965), p. 284.
3. *Ibid.*, p. 285.
4. For valuable recent discussions of the seventeenth-century religious background, see A. G. Dickens, *The English Reformation* (London, 1964), Peter Brook, *Thomas Cranmer's Doctrine of the Eucharist* (London, 1965), W. R. Trimble, *The Catholic Laity in Elizabethan England* (London, 1964), P. E. Hughes, *Theology of the English Reformers* (London, 1965), and W. A. Clebsch, *England's Earliest Protestants: 1520-1535* (London, 1964).
5. K. D. MacKenzie, *Liturgy and Worship*, ed. W. K. Lowther Clarke (London, 1932), p. 473.
6. Hardison, *Christian Rite*, p. 285.
7. *Ibid.*, p. 79.
8. Norman Holland, *Psychoanalysis and Shakespeare* (New York, 1964), pp. 347-49.
9. G. Wilson Knight, "The Milk of Concord," in *The Imperial Theme* (Oxford, 1931), pp. 124-54.

1
Richard II

th' inconstant people
Love many princes merely for their faces
And outward shows; and they do covet more
To have a sight of these than of their virtues.
Yet thus much let the great ones still conceal:
When they observe not Heaven's imposed conditions
They are no Kings, but forfeit their commissions.

Altofronto, in Marston's *The Malcontent* (V.vi.153-59)

Characters in comedy move toward self-recognization and a "new society" created of characters who have been educated or reformed during the course of the play. Comedy imitates the deeper rhythms of the Communion Service and moves *toward* Communion, specifically toward the intersection of the lines of comedy and the Communion of the marriages at the play's end. The tragic hero tends to move away from the creative and healing power of the supernature and pulls his world with him, so that the world itself plunges away from the possibilities of Communion, further and further away from the positive potentiality of social and religious ritual. Any "new society" emerging at the play's end does so only over the hero's dead body. The new society may be better than the old, as Malcolm's will be compared to Macbeth's; it may be different from the old, as Bolingbroke's will be compared to Richard's; or the end of the play can question whether *any* society can be built upon tragic wreckage, as in *King Lear*. Tragedy tends to pursue the irrational rhythm defined by Paul Tillich: "man's resistance against reuniting love, his estrangement from himself, from other beings, and from the ground of his being."[1] In a Christian world, the action of the tragic hero resembles the process Richard Sewell ascribes to Faustus: "What he is learning is the truth of his own nature—a truth which it was his peculiar Renaissance compulsion to forget or deny: that he is creature as well as creator; a man and not a god; a dependent, responsible part of a greater whole."[2] Shakespeare employs medieval heritage as he received it from the Elizabethan Communion Service, not as proven fact but as *potential* truth to be perceived by his tragic hero and, inevitably, as the truth against which the fall of that hero must be measured. Whether he perceives the truth or not, he invariably denies it, to discover in his own way "the paradox of Christian doctrine, that nature without grace is unnatural."[3] The tragic pattern is neatly defined by Roy W. Battenhouse:

> The Shakespearean hero's defective action shadows Christian paradigm in the same sense that falsehood inevitably depends upon truth, or the corruption of anything depends upon the good it corrupts.[4]

The inevitable contrast between potential comedy and actual tragedy that Shakespeare structures into his tragedies creates the response Auden defines: "at the end of a Greek tragedy we say, 'What a pity it had to be this way'; at the end of a Christian tragedy, 'What a pity it had to be this way when it might have been otherwise.' "[5]

A brief examination of Shakespeare's comic pattern will define that "otherwise," the context against which to measure the very different movement of the tragedies.

Love's Labour's Lost offers an instructive commentary on the process of purgation necessary before an individual can participate in the Communion beyond the comedy, in this case before the marriages of the Ladies and the Gentlemen can occur. In Elizabethan practice, of course, the marriage would have occurred within a Communion Service.

Having watched their own charade as Muscovites dashed "like a Christmas comedy" (V.iii.462) within the Ladies' more comprehensive production, the Gentlemen ridicule the Play of the Nine Worthies. Unlike the shallower Demetrius and Lysander, however, they perceive the parallel between what they have been and what they now observe. "Though my mocks come home by me," Dumain says, "I will now be merry" (V.ii.637-38). The past pretensions of the Gentlemen are reflected at them when Holofernes appears for Judas Maccabaeus. "A Judas!" Dumain cries (V.ii.600). "Not Iscariot, sir," the pedant protests (V.ii.601). But Holofernes is not allowed to play Maccabaeus; he becomes for Biron "A kissing traitor" (V.ii.603). Biron defines his own career, of course; he abandoned vows of sobriety for love. Judas here is not the Maccabaeus of unrelenting faith, but the betraying Iscariot. The equation is lightly intended, but Biron's confession shows that it is not unintended:

> For your fair sakes have we neglected time
> Play'd foul with our oaths. Your beauty, ladies,
> Hath much deform'd us, fashioning our humours
> Even to the opposed end of our intents.
>
> (V.ii.765-68)

The Worthies are dispersed by the intrusion of the somber Mercade with his message of death—another example in *Love's Labour's Lost* of a play overwhelmed by a greater comprehensiveness, this time by the reality of the world beyond plays. As the play of the Nine Worthies surrenders to the truth of Mercade's message, so the men are finally asked to face the reality they have evaded throughout *Love's Labour's Lost.* Biron's admission that he is "blown . . . full of maggot ostentation" (V.ii.409) had been a fit of rhyme against rhyme, as he had admitted when Rosaline had chided him for using "sans":

> Yet I have a trick
> Of the old rage. Bear with me, I am sick;
> I'll leave it by degrees.
>
> (V.ii.416-18)

In this analogue to the awakening of Lear, Biron recognizes

that the process of erasing his pretentious mask is only just begun. Recognition of folly is one thing, purgation another. The princess consigns the king "to some forlorn and naked hermitage" (V.ii.805) for a year's testing of his "offer made in heat of blood" (V.ii.810). The king, she charges, is "perjur'd much,/ Full of dear guiltiness" (V.ii.800-801). Biron is also "attaint with faults and perjury"; he "must be purged too" (V.ii.828-29). Rosaline's command to Biron anticipates Hamlet's injunction to the skull of Yorick:

> You shall this twelvemonth term from day to day
> Visit the speechless sick and still converse
> With groaning wretches; and your task shall be,
> With all the fierce endeavour of your wit
> To enforce the pained impotent to smile.
>
>   (V.ii.860-64)

One way of divorcing oneself from pretense is to face truth. The wisdom of Rosaline's prescription is proved by Biron's inability to grasp its intent:

> To move wild laughter in the throat of death?
> It cannot be; it is impossible;
> Mirth cannot move a soul in agony.
>
>   (V.ii.865-67)

Mere wit, like mere asceticism or mere romanticism, is an inadequate antidote to the complexities and pain of the world, an inappropriate prelude to the "world-without-end" bargain of marriage (V.ii.799). Rosaline's reply reveals the inadequacy of even the most skilled manipulators, and thus anticipates Prospero's Epilogue:

> Why, that's the way to choke a gibing spirit,
> Whole influence is begot of that loose grace
> Which shallow laughing hearers give to fools.
> A jest's prosperity lies in the ear
> Of him that hears it, never in the tongue
> Of him that makes it.
>
>   (V.ii.868-873)

The prosperity of a reformation lies not in the reformer. What Francis Fergusson says of Prospero applies here: "His power is limited; all he can do is *show* them, he cannot directly produce a change of heart in any of them."[6] While Rosaline may initiate a change of heart in Biron, only he can complete it. That Biron's wit exists primarily for *his* gratification suggests that more layers of self-love must be stripped away, more "wormwood" be weeded from his "fruitful brain" (V.ii.857) before he will be fit for marriage, which is not, after all, to be entered "unadvisedly, lightly, or wantonly." Rosaline's weeding metaphor echoes the Homily on Matrimony, which defines her project with Biron: "if thou wouldst use . . . diligence to instruct and order the minde of thy spouse, if thou wouldst diligently apply thy selfe to weede out by little and little the noysome weedes of uncomely maners out of [his] minde, with wholesome precepts, it could not bee, but in time thou shouldest feele the pleasant fruit thereof to both your comforts."

Biron recognizes that although he has produced and has been the butt of comedies, the larger play will not be a comedy:

Our wooing doth not end like an old play;
Jack hath not Jill: These ladies' courtesy
Might well have made our sport a comedy.

(V.ii.884-86)

The King replies "it wants a twelvemonth and a day" (V.ii.887) and Biron rhymes back, "that's too long for a play" (V.ii.888), reiterating by *using* rhyme that the process of purgation must extend beyond "the play." As part of the pattern of overthrowing convention in *Love's Labour's Lost,* its own potential pat ending is denied.

The Gentlemen's temporary exile to barren cells or hospitals will have as its goal the winning of the Ladies' hands. The "Sixth Act," then, will repeat the Gentlemen's alternatives of asceticism and love. Now, however, the alternatives are more than shallow formulae. In the play, the self-deception of asceticism preceded a sudden shift to another deception, the superficial code of courtly love. In the "Sixth Act," self-knowledge will precede a further fulfillment, love for another and marriage. Instead of the exclusive alternatives of retreat from the world and of affected love, opposite extremes will be harmonized, true asceticism becoming the avenue toward true rite.

Love's Labour's Lost itself, like the smaller plays within it, is absorbed into a larger reality, by a world outside the play in which Biron and the other gentlemen will be able by losing themselves to find themselves. Their own pretensions will be superseded, by more real selves. The movement toward personal validity, of course, must precede the union of marriage *and* the Communion within which the marriage would be performed. "Throw away that spirit," Rosalind tells Biron, "And I shall find you empty of that fault,/ Right joyful of your reformation" (V.ii.877-79).

While comedy imitates on a secular plane the deeper rhythms of Communion, at times in comedy ritual does not work. The contrast between the malfunction of ritual in comedy and in tragedy is instructive. The former represents a "correctable error," the latter a surface manifestation of a deeper cosmic problem that must be resolved before true rite can occur, before ceremony and the truth it embodies can be reunited.

Perhaps the most obvious example in a Shakespearean comedy of a sacramental model for a scene is the interrupted marriage of Claudio and Hero in *Much Ado About Nothing*. Even as Beatrice and Benedick, the "round" characters (as Forster uses the term in *Aspects of the Novel*), are deceived into truth, finding their deeper selves suddenly resonating to the conversations on which they are allowed to eavesdrop, the shallow Claudio is deceived into falsehood. With no *inner* sense of Hero's worth, he is prey for Don John's stratagem.

The scene represents an explicit marriage, unlike many of the imitations of ritual in tragedy, whose links with their archetype are more implicit. The spectator of *Much Ado About Nothing* knows that the ceremony will be interrupted and that the error will be corrected once Dogberry manages to transmit his report to Leonato. Thus, while we experience the scene with shock, perhaps, at Claudio's vehemence, its impact has been defused in advance, and we fear no fatal consequences.

In *Othello,* no Dogberry will arrive in time to dispel the Moor's radical delusion. His actions are not qualified by any counterpointed movement toward correction of error, and without that reassurance in *Othello,* we respond with deepening terror as we gradually realize that Othello's recognition of his error will come only, if it comes, on the far side of tragedy, after Desdemona has been sacrificed to his delusion. The comic countermovement, most apparent in *Much Ado About Nothing* and *Measure for Measure,* is rigidly excluded from *Othello,* but not necessarily from other tragedies. In *King Lear* we hear several times of Cordelia's return to Britain on Lear's behalf. We witness her concern, her reconciliation with her father, *and* the failure of her crusade, which leads to her death. The comic countermovement in *King Lear* fails, as it does in *Romeo and Juliet,* thus pressing the larger dramatic pattern toward the death of youth, virtue, and innocence that is one of the consistent concomitants of Shakespeare's tragedies. But such possibilities do not shadow the interrupted ritual of *Much Ado About Nothing.*

From Leonato's request for "only the plain form of marriage" (IV.i.2) to Friar Francis's questioning of "any inward impediment" to prevent marriage (IV.i.12), the ceremony follows the outlines of the "solemnizacion of Matrimonye" in the Prayer Book. Claudio indeed pursues the proper format in disclosing Hero's "impediment"; he is nothing if not an observer of proper forms; indeed, his tendency toward routine observance is one of the traits that make him susceptible to appearances that contradict their reality. The ceremony, which should confirm "an honorable state, instytuted of God In Paradise, in the time of mannes innocencie," and should signify "the mystical union that is betwixt Christ and his Churche," is suddenly transformed into an event which, as Benedick says, "looks not like a nuptual" (IV.i.69). Hero is accused of possessing the "carnall lustes and appetytes, like brute beastes that have no understandying," which the opening rubrics proscribe: "She knows the heat of a luxurious bed . . . [is] more intemperate in [her] blood/ Than Venus or those pamp'red animals/ That rage in savage sensuality" (IV.i.42-62). In attempting to uncover the "biting error"

(IV.i.172), the "strange misprision in the princes" (IV.i.187) that led to the accusation, Friar Francis pursues the prescribed course: "The solempnization must be deferred unto suche tyme as the truthe be tried": "This wedding-day," he says, "Perhaps is but prolong'd" (IV.i.255-56).

The scene really shows Claudio denying *himself* the sacrament. By defaming Hero he commits an anti-sacramental act and thus makes himself ineligible for the ceremony. His repentence is shallowly demonstrated by his willingness to marry an unknown, and although it may be, as Northrop Frye says, that "in his second marriage ceremony he pledges his loyalty first before he has seen the bride, and this releases him from his humorous bondage,"[7] Claudio demonstrates no change in his "inward man." But then, there is no inward man to discover. A Claudio can say "yet sinn'd I not/ But in mistaking" (V.i.284-85). Lacking an inward dimension of truth against which to measure the validity of appearances, he could not say with Beatrice, "I/ Believe it better than reportingly" (III.i.115-16). Claudio returns to some sort of readiness for the sacrament, but one must question whether he has learned anything as a result of his destruction of the first.

The primary function of the Claudio-Hero story, with all of its mechanism of the rebirth archetype is to demonstrate in its shallowness and hyperbole the vitality and "naturalness" of the Beatrice-Benedick relationship, which does not rely on forms and ceremonies whose inner reality seems to refute its outward shows, as Hero's did for the misinformed Claudio:

> O Hero, what a Hero hadst thou been,
> If half thy outward graces had been plac'd
> About thy thoughts and counsels of thy heart!
>
> (IV.i.101-3)

Friar Francis's interpretation contradicts Claudio's and coincides with that of Beatrice and Benedick, who would not have been deceived into disrupting the ceremony, whose own self-deceptions have been cleared away to reveal the deeper truths of their own natures, preparing them more completely for participation in the "holy rites" to be conducted in "the chapel presently" (V.iv.68-71). While Benedick's "A miracle!" (V.iv.91) parodies the miraculous resurrection of Hero, Claudio's last speech glances not at what Benedick might have done, but, indeed, at what Claudio himself has done in the play:

> I had well hop'd thou wouldst have denied Beatrice, that I might have cudgell'd thee out of thy single life, to make thee a double-dealer. (V.iv.114-16)

The broken ritual in *Much Ado About Nothing* is an overt and superficial mechanism that produces its effect primarily *on stage.* It does not resonate within the spectator by appealing to his own ritual experience, as does the larger comic rhythm of the play, which includes the interrupted marriage. Nor, perhaps, is it intended to, since it works within the context of the shallow and formal Claudio and the idealized Hero. Claudio is incapable of the deeper reformations achieved by Beatrice and Benedick, and his union with Hero only superficially predicts the more profound and hard-earned reconciliation of Leontes and Hermione. The interrupted marriage, then, is a temporary delay within a comic movement toward the very goal delayed by Claudio's accusation, but it is through Beatrice and Benedick that we appreciate the validity of the "holy rites" just beyond the play's last line.*

In tragedy, however, ritual fails for deeper reasons. The forces embodied in the tragic world cannot be propitiated through mere recognition of a "mistake." In *King Lear,* as I will suggest, the potential comedy is not rejected gratuitously by a Shakespeare intent upon shocking a Dr. Johnson, but fails because of elements that Lear's initial mistakes have made part of the world Cordelia would redeem, elements that, though finally recognized by Lear, cannot be erased by recognition. The challenge to the deep creative and energizing forces of the cosmos is more profound in tragedy than in

---

* A similar configuration in *Twelfth Night* is Caesario's denial of Olivia, quickly resolved by the arrival of Sebastian, Olivia's true husband. In *Twelfth Night* the complication works out *without* the indictment we must attach to Claudio, although Sebastian capitulates as quickly to Olivia as Claudio does to Hero's "cousin," although perhaps not so quickly as Oliver to Celia (cf. *As You Like It,* V.ii.1-11).

comedy, hence the chances for true rite are more remote once the challenge is launched—once a king is murdered, a Desdemona or a Cordelia rejected. The opportunities for realignment of the world of the play with the positive supernature—the "outer mystery," as Professor West calls it[8]—usually become less and less within the power of the tragic hero as he tries every way except the *only* way to rectify the situation into which he has plunged himself and his world. As comedy tends to move *toward* Communion, tragedy usually drives further and further away from it, until, often, only the death of the hero and the destruction of his world restore *the* world to harmony with the encompassing supernature. And it is questionable in the case of *King Lear* whether any positive restoration occurs.

Without debating the case of *Richard II* as "tragedy," we can perceive there how ritual works—or, more correctly, does *not* work—in the tragic world.

The tragic world divorces itself from the unifying powers expressed in Communion. The "notorious evil" is committed either before the play begins (as in the murder of King Hamlet) or within the play (as in the murder of Duncan). *Richard II* provides examples of both the crime before and the crime within the play: first, Richard's complicity in Gloucester's murder, a secret crime that causes suspicion and recrimination to permeate the opening scenes and gives Bolingbroke the pretext for shaking the seemingly firm foundations of Richard's kingship; second, Richard's seizing of the Lancastrian estates, allowing Bolingbroke to return to England and completing the division in the kingdom suggested by the Bolingbroke-Mowbray conflict.

Whether the England imaged in Gaunt's great speech ever existed, or whether his words are merely the first example of the looking-back-to-past-and-better-times so pervasive in the Second Henriad is dramatically irrelevant. *Richard II* imitates the profound transition from an England alive only in the memories of Gaunt and York to "this new world" in which Fitzwater and his ambitious colleagues hope to "thrive" (IV.i.78) in emulation of Bolingbroke. Gaunt's premises are easily defined, but require caution, because the "medieval" world of this play is framed primarily of Elizabethan commonplaces. Gaunt's admonishment of the duchess that "God's is the quarrel" (I.ii.37) is sound sixteenth-century doctrine, as the "Homily on Disobedience" attests. England's freedom from invasion and its heroic character in battle had been validated some seven years prior to the first performance of *Richard II*. And regardless of the similarities that Elizabeth and Essex may have glimpsed between Richard and the Virgin Queen, the Elizabeth of 1595 could scarcely be accused of unroyal crimes. Yet, as if Shakespeare felt the old century and the aging queen swinging toward a different ordering of things, he makes the sixteenth-century tenets —absolute loyalty to a monarch, patriotism and heroism, and a stainless throne—the virtues John of Gaunt mourns.* To these Gaunt adds an underlying religiosity, to which Richard subscribes only as he dies, and to which Bolingbroke supplies only lip service. York adds, of course, the fine speech on "degree." Medieval England in this play was chivalric and heroic, whether imaged in York's recollection of the Black Prince at Crecy ("that young Mars of men") (II.iii.101) ** or Gaunt's of "this seat of Mars" (II.i.41), generator of Crusades to "stubborn Jewry" (II.i.55), a memory that will reverberate against Bolingbroke's "crusade" and prophetically against the civil wars that will encumber Bolingbroke's England. England may have been a "teeming womb of royal kings" (II.i.51), but the Duchess of York, another figure of the dying order, tells us of something more than her own aging body when she says that her "teeming date [is] drunk up with time" (V.ii.91).

Gaunt's England was a generator of sacred energy emerging from a "blessed plot" (II.i.50), a land and a people in harmony with God and His universe, at enmity only with "stubborn" foes, with those against whom Mowbray is to fight: "black pagans, Turks, and Saracens" (IV.i.95), or against French combatants engaged within the rules of chivalry. Combined with these elements of medieval England

---

*The "Tudor Myth of History," of course, would have viewed Elizabethan England as a *return* to the virtues John of Gaunt celebrates.
**The Black Prince haunts this play much as Richard I haunts *King John*.

are architectural details: "a moat defensive to a house"
(II.i.48).* Moat and house are typical of the microcosm-
macrocosm habit of Gaunt's mind; they stand for an England
free for these many years from "infection and the hand of
war" (II.i.44), haven for a "happy breed of men" (II.i.45), a
"little world" (II.i.45), an "other Eden, demi-paradise"
(II.i.42). England as Eden can be over-stressed, of course,
pressed into an archetypal configuration that can manipulate
dramatic meanings to its own designs. But the association in
this play is hardly random—the imagery of a garden defiled
runs consistently through the play and coalesces into archetype. It is not that England *was* an "other Eden," but that
the transition from one England to another is profound
enough to be equated to the movement from Eden to the
different, more dangerous, and obviously less coherent world
beyond. Gaunt's England is not merely a garden, resting
under God's beneficent aegis, but a progenitor of value, the
condition concomitant with God's grace. Gaunt's England is a
model of the perfect world designed by God for man, a
world "charged with the grandeur of God," that is, infused
with it *and* held responsible for it. But Gaunt's words occur
within a periodic sentence of Miltonic scope. The main clause
tells us that his living land has been leased out, "is now
bound in with shame,/ With inky blots and rotten parchment
bonds" (II.i.63-64). Sacredness has been reduced to com-
merce, idealism to commodity.** And upon this negative
note, Richard enters the sick chamber, to hear not Gaunt's
eulogy for England but an admonition that enrages him.

The world in which Gaunt lived, then, was static ("a moat
defensive"), ceremonial, based on religious premises (an
"other Eden"), and essentially timeless. Time existed to be
observed, as York tells Richard, as one of the grand rhythms
of the supernature, reflecting the orderly sequence of man's
world:

*Imagery of ruined buildings comments on Gaunt's words: "empty lodgings an
unfurnished walls." (I.ii.68), "the rude ribs of that ancient castle" (III.iii.32), and
"this castle's tattered battlements" (III.iii.52).

**Gaunt's speech can be read as describing the interim between King John's trou-
bled reign and the advent of troublesome King Richard II. As the Bastard says at
the end of *King John:* "Naught shall make us rue/ If England to itself do rest but
true" (V.vii.117-18).

    take from Time
His charters and his customary rights;
Let not tomorrow then ensue to-day;
Be not thyself; for how art thou a king
But by fair sequence and succession?

                                                        (II.i.195-99)

Richard "wasted time" (V.v.49)—as king he *laid* waste to
time; and time as it emerges into the plays that follow will be
either a device for men to use advantageously or a force driving man toward a fate devoid of spiritual significance. Time
set free becomes "modern time," saving daylight perhaps, but
never assisting men toward the ultimate light, which sustained the old order of *Richard II* as re-created in the dying
minds of its inhabitants. It is not that mere anarchy has been
loosed upon the world by Richard's defection from
sovereignty, but that the prime elements of the world
change; time becomes a medium for a Prince Hal to exploit,
although, ironically, time exploits him both as prince (cf.
II Henry IV:II.ii), and as a king doomed to an early death.
    The world in which Gaunt survives briefly has lost its con-
tact with the deeper energizing forces of the universe, as has
Claudius's Denmark and Macbeth's Scotland. In the later
tragedies the divorce from the supernature imposes an immediate divorce from positive higher values, imaged in the
return of a kingly ghost or in horrible hallucinations. In
Richard II, the transition from edenic premises to a postedenic world is the dramatic issue to be imitated. Its imitation
requires not merely the majestic vision of a John of Gaunt,
but a king who should be, but is not, the embodiment of that
vision. It requires, as well, a nemesis, in this case a man without his father's vision, who will be pulled toward the empty
zone of command. In the process, the old vision must vanish.
Bolingbroke will never lead his "crusade." His son's war will
culminate in the miracle of Agincourt, and will absorb, in
rhetoric, at least, some of the grandeur of Gaunt's England.
But that war and its gains will become bitter to the next generation.
    Richard's hand in Gloucester's murder denies him the
support to his kingship that ritual should provide. He cannot

reconcile Bolingbroke and Mowbray, "betwixt whome," as the
Communion rubrics say, "he perceyveth malice and hatred to
raigne." Richard is disqualified from the priestly role and can
only preside over the anti-rituals the play will present as a reflection of what has happened in the kingdom.*

Bolingbroke's indictment of Mowbray endows the crime
with the most universal implications:

> That he. . . like a traitor coward,
> Sluic'd out [Gloucester's] innocent soul through streams of blood;
> Which blood, like sacrificing Abel's, cries
> Even from the tongueless caverns of the earth,
> To me for justice and rough chastisement.
>
> (I.i.100-106)

While Bolingbroke may find hyperbole his most convenient
vehicle here, the crime is hardly a casual slaughter; rather, it
"hath the primal eldest curse upon it." If Richard *is*
responsible for it (and we can't be sure until John of Gaunt
tells us he is), he has committed an archetypal crime which,
like the murder of King Hamlet, must have deep negative
reverberations within his kingdom. That Bolingbroke is aiming at Richard is suggested by the Abel-Gloucester equation.
Mowbray was not Gloucester's close relative—but Richard
was, as York reiterates in contrasting Richard with his father,
whose "hands were guilty of no kindred blood,/ But bloody
with the enemies of his kin" (II.i.182-83).

Richard cannot allow either Bolingbroke *or* Mowbray to
win the trial by combat. Bolingbroke's accusation aims at
Richard. An ambitious duke trapped in a medieval hierarchy, Bolingbroke can pose as defender of the right, but his
resolution has a more specific pitch, as Richard knows and
Mowbray reiterates:

> What thou art, God, thou, and I do know;
> And all too soon, I fear, the King shall rue.
>
> (I.iii.204-5)

Bolingbroke's victory would vindicate him as the kingdom's

*Richard's line "Our doctors say this is no month to bleed" (I.i.154) reminds us
ironically of the healing power of one of Shakespeare's most neglected kings, Edward the Confessor, in *Macbeth*.

prime exponent of justice (the king's role), enhance his already obvious popularity with the people, and greatly increase his strength as Richard's rival. The consummate
pragmatist would be in a position to develop deeper threats
to Richard's crown. As Westmoreland later makes clear, a
Mowbray victory would hardly have cemented Richard's
kingship:

> But if your father had been victor there,
> He ne'er had borne it out of Coventry;
> For all the country in a general voice
> Cried hate upon him; and all their prayers and love
> Were set on Hereford, whom they doted on
> And bless'd and grac'd and did, more than the King.
>
> (*II Henry IV*:IV.i.134-39)

While Westmoreland may be a biased interpreter of
Bolingbroke's popularity (he could hardly say otherwise of
the man who became king), the point he is making is irrelevant to his debate with the rebels, therefore acceptable as an
objective version of the relative popularity of the two antagonists, and, by extension, of Richard's uneasy position between them.

Richard must intercede. Goddard is right to find Richard's
interrupting speech self-refuting; the refutation derives from
Richard's participation in a crime that destroys his role as
impartial magistrate, which, indeed, permits Bolingbroke to
assume the role of justicer for the kingdom. Richard cannot
permit "the rites of knighthood" (I.i.75) to fulfill themselves
because he, "God's substitute/ His deputy anointed in His
sight,/ Hath caused [Gloucester's] death" (I.ii.37-39).
Richard's personal involvement prohibits him, however "impartial" (I.i.114) he may try to seem, from allowing the pattern of medieval justice to complete itself.

The language describing the trial by combat suggests that
the ceremony represented a valid fusion of word and action,
the inviolate linkage of things visible and invisible:

> And, by the grace of God and this mine arm,
> To prove him, in defending of myself,
> A traitor to my God, my King, and me.
>
> (I.iii.22-24)

To prove, by God's grace and my body's valour
In lists on Thomas Mowbray, Duke of Norfolk,
That he's a traitor, foul and dangerous,
To God of heaven, King Richard, and to me.

(I.iii.37-40)

Mowbray and Bolingbroke claim that arm will match word,
yet both can not be right: "yet one but flatters us," says
Richard (I.i.25). In a deeper sense, *neither* can be right.
Richard's decision for a trial by combat is the final echo of a
world no longer capable of such arbitration. There simply
can not be any intrinsic justice done by the trial.

Richard's conclusion of the opening scene is neatly self-
refuting: "We were not born to sue, but to command"
(I.i.196). His next line admits that his royal command "cannot do to make you friends" (I.i.197). Indeed, he can do little
within the scene, except to try to ascertain the extent of
Bolingbroke's knowledge and the concomitant insecurity of
his own position:

Tell me, moreover, hast thou sounded him
If he appeal the Duke on ancient malice,
Or worthily, as a good subject should,
On some known ground of treachery in him?

(I.i.8-11)

Cousin of Hereford, what dost thou object
Against the Duke of Norfolk, Thomas Mowbray?

(I.i.28-29)

What doth our cousin lay to Mowbray's charge?

(I.i.84)

Thomas of Norfolk, what say'st thou to this?

(I.i.110)

He can claim impartiality (I.i.115), and can warn Bolingbroke
not to go too far:

How high a pitch his resolution soars!

(I.i.109)

Were he my brother, nay, my kingdom's heir,
As he is but my father's brother's son. . . .

(I.i.116-17)

The scene, however, is dominated by the accuser and defendant, the accuser assuming the king's role, with Richard helpless to insist that the "wrath-kindled gentlemen be rul'd by" him (I.i.152). Richard's untenable position is emphasized both by the aspiring Bolingbroke and by Mowbray, who responds convincingly to the accusations dealing with the funds Richard sent him, and who apologizes again to Gaunt. He dismisses the main charge, however, with less than three ambiguous lines:

> For Gloucester's death,
> I slew him not; but to my own disgrace
> Neglected my sworn duty in that case.
>
> (I.i.132-34)

Does he mean that he ignored the order to protect Gloucester or to slay him? In Holinshed, but not here, Mowbray claims to have saved Gloucester's life "contrarie to the will of the king." Richard subsequently "appointed one of his own servants" to kill Gloucester. Perhaps the latter appointment was Aumerle.

Mowbray is perhaps intentionally brief and vague. He is looking at the guilty man, and hoping perhaps that Richard will resolve the debate. Richard can do so only by exiling a Mowbray involved in guilt of commission or omission. But that guilt is subordinate to Richard's guilt, as are all the crimes within the play, including Bolingbroke's—that is, until the murder of Richard, when Bolingbroke will be forced, like the early Richard, into the role of banisher for his own willed crime.

Prior to Richard's plea of impartiality, Bolingbroke has already disclaimed "the kindred of the king" (I.i.70) and his "high blood's royalty" (I.i.71). To do so, however, is to assume the king's prerogative, as Richard admits:

> Now, by my sceptre's awe, I make a vow,
> Such neighbour nearness to our sacred blood
> Should nothing privilege him, nor partialize
> The unstooping firmness of my upright soul.
>
> (I.i.118-21)

Farewell, my blood; which if to-day thou shed,
Lament we may, but not revenge thee dead.

(I.iii.57-58)

Bolingbroke's anticipation of Richard's dispensation emphasizes the role the duke is playing, that of the extirpator
of "all the treasons for these eighteen years/ Complotted and
contrived in this land" (I.i.95-96), a role he will continue to
play (cf. IV.i). His assumption of the right to determine the
fate of royal blood predicts what will follow, when he, too,
will be compromised by the blood he has contrived to shed.

A final element emerging from the opening scene is that
of Richard's instinctive yielding to power, shown here in the
reiteration of the disclaiming of kindred that Bolingbroke introduces, and, soon, by his reduction of Bolingbroke's sentence, when Richard is faced with Gaunt's regret as father
for what Gaunt as judge has decreed. Richard is unafraid of
power only when it is not facing him. Once Bolingbroke is
gone, he can laugh at the duke's courtship of the populace.
Once Gaunt is dead, he can seize the estate with a snap of his
fingers. One of the deepest ironies emerging from the opening scene is that Richard, dead, will be far more powerful
than Richard, king. Richard's power lies within a future he
will not see, as the past, pressing onward, informs the future
of its meaning.

While the interrupted duel is a good example of the
"broken ritual" so prevalent in Shakespearean tragedy, and
while the trail has clear religious sanctioning, it is not precisely sacramental in the strict religious sense. Mowbray does,
however, "celebrate/ This feast of battle" (I.iii.91-92) and has
already defended himself against Bolingbroke's charges by
citing his religious observances:

But for you, my noble Lord of Lancaster,
The honourable father to my foe,
Once did I lay an ambush for your life,
A trespass that doth vex my grieved soul;
But ere I last receiv'd the sacrament
I did confess it, and exactly begg'd
Your Grace's pardon; and I hope I had it.

(I.i.135-41)

Mowbray describes here the comic pattern embodied in Communion—guilt, repentence, pardon. The irony, however, is that the world of this play cannot *complete* the external forms that signify inward spiritual health. Pardoned by the father, Mowbray is indicted by the son. Indicted by Bolingbroke. Mowbray is banished by the king, a banishment dictated by political considerations, which, in turn, emerge from the king's abandonment of the religious premises Mowbray had embraced.

The murder of Gloucester, as described by his widow, carries forward the profound implications of Bolingbroke's accusation, this time with strong sacramental overtones:

> Finds brotherhood in thee no sharper spur?
> Hath love in thy old blood no living fire?
> Edward's seven sons, whereof thyself art one,
> Were as seven vials of his sacred blood,
> Or seven fair branches springing from one root.
> Some of those seven are dried by nature's course,
> Some of those branches by the Destinies cut;
> But Thomas, my dear lord, my life, my Gloucester,
> One vial full of Edward's sacred blood,
> One flourishing branch of his most royal root,
> Is crack'd, and all the precious liquor spilt,
> Is hack'd down, and his summer leaves all faded,
> By Envy's hand and Murder's bloody axe.
> Ah, Gaunt, his blood was thine!
>
> (I.ii.9-22)

The destruction of a tree of life (the Jesse Tree) is the first of the play's many metaphors of a garden defiled or destroyed, a garden whose edenic associations grow stronger as they become less applicable, as blood becomes *anti*-sacramental, a staining of the realm, not a sustaining of the living land and the souls within it. The spilling of "sacred blood," of "precious liquor," is a sacrilege to be repeated in various contexts throughout the play until, inevitably Richard's royal blood itself is spilt. The duchess images a desecrated shrine—the seven branches springing from one root combine with the earlier "fire" to suggest a candelabra. And the "crack'd" and "hack'd" symbolic tree will echo ultimately against "those hands/ Which made the fault" as Richard looks

upon his mirror, broken image of his kingship, now "crack'd
in an hundred shivers" (IV.i.289). While Bolingbroke has
disclaimed kindred earlier, the duchess's appeal to Gaunt is
the first of many such pleas made in the play, most of them
indexes of the divided loyalties a divided world must engender. The Duke of York, for example, is torn between
Richard and Bolingbroke, once the latter returns, and later,
between his wife's appeals for her son (and his) and his loyalty to Bolingbroke. York vehemently insists upon the latter,
perhaps betraying a guilt for not having more vigorously defended his former king.

Richard has introduced *division* into his kingdom, represented by the antagonists whose own true motives, in turn,
are separated from their challenges and retorts, as is
Richard's motive beneath his magisterial pose. The kingdom's
split is reflected even in the contrast between scenes—public
accusation followed by a private scene between Gaunt and
the Duchess of Gloucester revealing one of the meanings of
the previous scene, the pageantry of the combat followed by
the cynicism of Richard, Aumerle, and Green, and, later, the
contrast between the brisk efficiency of Bolingbroke (III.i)
and the mournful retreat to personal grief of Richard (III.ii).
The Duchess of Gloucester has been separated from "[her]
life, [her] Gloucester," has only her "companion grief"
(I.ii.55). According to her accusation, Gaunt has also suffered
a basic alienation:

> and though thou liv'st and breath'st,
> Yet art thou slain in him. Thou dost consent
> In some measure to thy father's death,
> In that thou see'st thy wretched brother die,
> Who was the model of thy father's life.
>
> (I.ii.24-28)

Her rhythm becomes liturgical, her meaning, clearly, is that
Gaunt has committed a crime against *himself* as sacrament,
since he shares the sacred blood spilled in Gloucester's murder, and thus is "slain in him," in contrast to the hopes expressed for the "most precious bloud" of Christ in the Prayer
of Humble Access, where blood helps create a unity of *life*:
"that we may evermore dwell in him, and he in us." Gaunt

must also suffer the division between judge and father, must
consent to his own son's banishment:

> You urg'd me as a judge; but I had rather
> You would have bid me argue like a father. . .
> A partial slander sought I to avoid,
> And in the sentence my own life destroyed.
>
> (I.iii.237-42)

Here, the "word" is inconsistent with the "act." The "sentence" (both utterance and judgment) destroys the "life."

Gaunt and Bolingbroke reveal a further division, one suggestive of the two worlds of the play splitting apart under
Richard's destructive kingship:

> Bolingbroke. How long a time lies in one little word!
> Four lagging winters and four wanton springs
> End in a word: such is the breath of kings.
>
> (I.iii.213-15)

> Gaunt. Thou canst help Time to furrow me with age,
> But stop no wrinkle in his pilgrimage.
> Thy word is current with him for my death,
> But dead, thy kingdom cannot buy my breath.
>
> (I.iii.229-32)

Gaunt emphasizes the limitations Richard has ignored, allowing his power to dissipate. Bolingbroke equates Richard's
capriciousness with power. Richard's willfulness *will* be
Bolingbroke's path to power, and at the same time be one of
the elements that will greatly mitigate that power once
Bolingbroke attains it. Richard "breathless" (V.vi.31) will in
some ways be stronger than Richard breathing. Richard will
be remembered by the dying Henry IV in "the very latest
counsel/ That ever I shall breathe" (*II Henry IV,* IV.v.183-84).
Bolingbroke, looking perhaps to his future, is impressed with
strength, with what the king *can* do. Gaunt, looking to the
past, deplores the ignoring of the *limits* of the king's power,
which has cut the king off *from* power and so cut England off
from its past, when the nation was a sacrament vibrating with
a deeper spiritual reality. The king is *not* God, but, as Gaunt
says, His "substitute,/ His deputy." Father and son: one con-

servative, the other eager to plunge to the future that the
father will predict but not see. England's transition is reflected in their contradictory views of kingship, a contradiction focused in the unconscious architect of the shift from
medieval to modern England—Richard, whose power is ca-
price, whose ignorance of the limits of his power destroys it
for him, and for Bolingbroke.

Mowbray and Bolingbroke must divorce themselves from
England. Mowbray is banished even from its language:

> My native English, now I must forgo. . .
> What is thy sentence then but speechless death,
> Which robs my tongue from breathing native breath?
>
> (I.iii.160-73)

Bolingbroke describes his sentence as a separation from his
nativity and nature:

> Then, England's ground, farewell; sweet soil, adieu;
> My mother and my nurse, that bears me yet!
>
> (I.iii.306-7)

Richard intervenes to prevent Bolingbroke's marriage
(II.i.167-68), and the duke suffers further divorces between
himself and his station during his absence. He is "bereft and
gelded of his patrimony" (II.i.237). Not only is his inheritance seized, but if his charges against Bushy and Green are
accurate, they have tried to erase all evidence of him:

> you have. . . .
> From my own windows torn my household coat,
> Raz'd out my imprese, leaving me no sign,
> Save men's opinions and my living blood,
> To show the world I am a gentleman.
>
> (III.i.22-27)

Bolingbroke's response is to part the souls of Bushy and
Green from their bodies (III.i.3). Such a process might indeed rid the kingdom of its caterpillars were Bolingbroke the
king. But not the least of the kingdom's problems is his
perhaps inevitable arrogation of the role Richard should fill.

Richard's defection from sovereignty, indeed his physical
departure for Ireland (creating "the absent time" [II.iii.79]),
has left England in a power vacuum, similar to that of Rome

after Caesar's assassination. England is cut loose from legality, and York, the man left in charge, who would like to assert order, is helpless, within "an inextricable tangle of right and unright," to use Bradley's useful phrase:[10]

> Both are my kinsmen:
> Th' one is my sovereign, whom both my oath
> And duty bids defend; t'other again
> Is my kinsman, whom the King hath wrong'd,
> Whom conscience and my kindred bids to right.
>
> (II.ii.111-15)

This model for Macbeth's debate with himself before the murder of Duncan is, for York, a prelude to paralysis.* He can only be "as neuter," with all distinctions that he *could* make divorced from meaningful contexts:

> I may be I will go with you; but yet I'll pause,
> For I am loath to break our country's laws.
> Nor friends nor foes, to me welcome you are.
> Things past redress are now with me past care.
>
> (II.iii.168-71)

One of the operative words for the condition Richard has engendered is "hollow." Ritual is without its spiritual core, so Aumerle's parting from Bolingbroke must be "hollow" (I.iv.9); Northumberland must see in the face of England "the hollow eyes of death" (II.i.270); Gaunt must find a "grave,/ Whose hollow womb inherits naught but bones" (II.i.82-83); and Bushy and Green, followers of Richard, must be "grav'd in the hollow ground" (III.ii.140). The only unhollow element in a world where positive value has no substance must be "grief," which "boundeth where it falls,/ Not with the empty hollowness, but weight" (I.ii.59). Grief is the inward condition of both the queen for whom birth creates another negative metaphor, and Richard:

> Yet again, methinks,
> Some unborn sorrow, ripe in fortune's womb,
> Is coming towards me, and my inward soul
> With nothing trembles.
>
> (II.ii.9-12)

---

*York is a precursor of *King Lear*'s Gloucester, also trapped between the factions combating for control of the island empire.

And these external manners of laments
Are merely shadows to the unseen grief
That swells with silence in the tortur'd soul.
There lies the substance.

(IV.i.295-98)

England, surrounded by a "moat defensive" (II.i.48), has
been invaded not from without but by forces emerging from
within the crown, which, in Gaunt's metaphor, is a model of
a kingdom being destroyed from the very place which should
confirm the protection granted "this precious stone set in the
silver sea" (II.i.46). The destiny of such a king as Richard
must be the divorce of his kingdom from meaning. Shakespeare has the pattern of hollowness culminate in a double
metaphor capturing both of the tendencies of this strand of
imagery—Bolingbroke inherits a crown empty of significance,
while Richard's crown is filled only with his self-pity, one of
the elements of willfulness that have deprived the crown of
substance:

    Here, cousin,
On this side my hand, and on that side thine.
Now is this golden crown like a deep well
That owes two buckets, filling one another,
The emptier ever dancing in the air,
The other down, unseen, and full of water.
That bucket down and full of tears am I,
Drinking my griefs, whilst you mount up on high.

(IV.i.182-89)

Death, too, is substance, "for within the hollow crown/
That rounds the mortal temples of a king/ Keeps Death his
court" (III.ii.160-62), as Richard says, lamenting his "body
natural." But within the same round stretches the larger entity of the "body politic," as John of Gaunt attempts to suggest to Richard:

A thousand flatterers sit within thy crown,
Whose compass is no bigger than thy head;
And yet incaged in so small a verge,
The waste is no whit lesser than thy land.

(II.i.100-103)

If the king is hollow, so must his kingdom be. Richard has
divorced himself from his role, hence from his kingdom:

The commons hath he pill'd with grievous taxes,
And quite lost their hearts; the nobles hath he fin'd
For ancient quarrels, and quite lost their hearts.

(II.i.246-48)

"Thy death-bed," says Gaunt, extending his own microcosm to Richard's realm, "is no lesser than thy land. . . . Landlord of England art thou now, not King" (II.i.95-113). Richard, he suggests prophetically, is "possess'd now to depose [himself]" (II.i.108). Gaunt's "Convey me to my bed, then to my grave" (II.i.137) foreshadows Bolingbroke's command, prelude to Richard's inevitable movement toward his grave: "Go, some of you convey him to the tower" (IV.i.316). Richard responds to Gaunt with fury, threatening to separate Gaunt's "head from [his] unreverent shoulders" (II.i.123). The indictment of the king as "body politic" has merely evoked the rage of Richard as "body natural."

Richard, as king, is deaf to counsel:

[his ear] is stopp'd with other flattering sounds,
As praises, of whose taste the wise are fond,
Lacivious metres, to whose venom sound
The open ear of youth doth always listen.

(II.i.17-20)

His imitation of "fashions in proud Italy" (II.i.8) draws his attention from the deeper English heritage that Gaunt celebrates, but Gaunt's great words, ironically, reach only York, who already agrees (an example of words separated from their proper audience):

This other Eden, demi-paradise,
This fortress built by Nature for herself
Against infection and the hand of war,
This happy breed of men. . .
Renowned for their deeds as far from home,
For Christian service and true chivalry,
As is the sepulchre in stubborn Jewry,
Of the world's ransom, blessed Mary's Son. . .

(II.i.42-56)

Later we discover that the only character in the play able to translate this conception of England's heritage into reality is Mowbray, who does it not in England but in some corner of a foreign field:

Many a time hath banish'd Norfolk fought
For Jesu Christ in glorious Christian field,
Streaming the ensign of the Christian cross
Against black pagans, Turks, and Saracens;
And, toil'd with works of war, retir'd himself
To Italy; and there at Venice gave
His body to that pleasant country's earth,
And his pure soul into his captain Christ,
Under whose colours he had fought so long.

(IV.i.92-100)

Mowbray has exported the English virtues described by Gaunt, has, it would seem, taken with him the country's chivalric quality, leaving England devoid of medieval glory and ready for the myriad skulls Carlisle envisions as the island's future.

Richard's thrusts against order impose upon him the inevitability of similar actions, dictated by an individual will becoming increasingly removed from a kingly role and thus becoming increasingly desperate, compulsive, and, of course, willful. The point is neatly made when Richard hears of Gaunt's illness:

Rich. Now put it, God, in the physician's mind
      To help him to his grave immediately!
      The lining of his coffers shall make coats
      To deck our soldiers for these Irish wars.
      Come, gentlemen, let's all go visit him.
      Pray God we may make haste, and come too late!
All. Amen.

(I.iv.59-65)

This parody of prayer, dictated by Richard's will and revealing an impiety that blocks his vision of the true role of king, reverses, of course, the opening prayers of the Elizabethan Visitation of the Sicke:

most mercifull God, and saviour, extend thy accustomed goodness, to this thy servaunt whiche is greved with syckenesse, visit him O Lorde, as thou diddest visit, Peters wifes mother, and the capiteines servaunt. So visit and restore unto this sicke person his former health (if it bee thy wil) or els geve him grace so to take thy visitation, that after this painful life [is] ended, he may dwell with the in life everlastyng.

As Richard becomes less and less a king, anti-ritual must become his mode. It is true, as Traversi says, that "when Richard desires [Gaunt's] death it is his own vocation that he is in fact setting aside,"[11] and the parody prayer illustrates the point. But his wish for Gaunt must be referred back to his original crime against Gaunt's brother. The incident within the play reminds us of the murder before the play; and the consequences of the murder are to be extended in Richard's further crime against his own kingship, his seizing of Bolingbroke's inheritance:

> Take Hereford's rights away, and take from Time
> His charters and his customary rights;
> Let not to-morrow then ensue to-day;
> Be not thyself; for how art thou a king
> But by fair sequence and succession?
>
> (II.i.195-99)

Richard removes himself and his kingship from the natural rhythms of control and continuity. Later, to underline the perversion of roles that must occur within a kingdom whose king has violated his role, Scroop tells Richard that "The very beadsmen learn to bend their bows/ Of double-fatal yew against thy state" (III.ii.116-17). Almsmen who should pray for the king take up arms against him.

It is impossible to overemphasize the significance of Richard's defection from true kingship. Since, as Kantorowicz points out, Richard represents "the mystic body of his subjects and the nation,"[12] his sacramental function is profound. His body politic is like the elements of the Communion Service at the moment they become functional, that is, at the moment of transmission. The king "was 'liturgical' as a king because, and in so far as, he represented and 'imitated' the image of the living Christ."[13] He was "human by nature, divine by grace,"[14] thus imitating the dual nature of the elements—Christ and bread, body politic and body natural, the latter, like the bread and wine, the medium within which incarnation occurs (and it is an occurrence, *not* a residence). The king imitates as well, of course, the dual nature of Christ (divine and human, body politic and body natural). The "doctrine of theology and canon law," says Kantorowicz, "that the Church and Christian society in general, was a '*corpus mysticum* the head of which is Christ' has been transferred by the jurists from the theological sphere to that of the state the head of which is the king."[15]

The equation between body politic and Christ is obvious, that between body politic and Communion perhaps less obvious. Like the Communion, "this Christ-imitating king was pictured and expounded also as the 'mediator' between heaven and earth."[16] The king is the medium through which his subjects and his nation participate in the larger spiritual mysteries of the cosmos. The king imitates Christ; his subjects imitate Christ's disciples within the kingdom as within the Communion. But like the individual communicant, the king must *understand* his role and understand that its efficacy depends upon the choices he makes, choices that either confirm or undermine it. As with the elements, the sacramental fusion must *occur* within the king. It does not merely *reside* there, as Richard tries to insist. The complex equation of monarch with sacrament is underlined by the "Collectes . . . for the Quene" in the Prayer Book. In each, Elizabeth's position between God and subject is made clear, her authority as God's surrogate is enunciated, and her dual responsibility as receiver of sacrament and transmitter of it to her people is emphasized:

> so rule the heart of thy chosen servant, Elizabeth our Quene and governoure that she (knowing whose minister she is) may above all things, seke thy honoure and glory: and that we her subjects (duely considering whose authority she hath) may faithfully serve, honour, and humblye obey her in the and for the, according to thy blessed worde, and ordinance.

(In other words, "We obey Thee in her, and her in Thee.")

> we be taughte by thy holy word, that the hartes of Princes are in thy rule and governaunce, and that thou doest dispose, and turne them as it semeth best to thy Godly wysedome: we humbly beseche thee, so to dispose and governe the harte of Elizabeth, thy servaunte, our Quene and governor, that in all her thoughtes, wordes, and workes she may ever seke thy honoure and glorye, and studye to preserve thy people committed to her charge, in welth, peace, and godlyness.

If the individual becomes a sacramental component during the transmission, he does so in relation to his own soul. The king is the visible embodiment of the invisible mysteries of his nation, and his participation in "notorious evil" threatens the soul of that nation. England, of course, is seen as sacramental in *Richard II,* seen as much more than what Reese calls the "sentient being,"[17] as a land once resonating with the health derived from its union with spiritual forces. This is John of Gaunt's England, which plunges away from its edenic premises to become stained with blood, sprinkled with skulls. It is not true, as Kantorowicz says, that "there is as yet no split in Richard when, on his return from Ireland, he kisses the soil of his kingdom and renders that famous . . . account of the loftiness of his royal estate."[18] The split may be barely perceptible as yet, like that in the House of Usher or the Golden Bowl, but it is there. Richard has separated himself from his role as king, and removed his realm from the sources of health:

Dear earth, I do salute thee with my hand,
Though rebels wound thee with their horses' hoofs.
As a long-parted mother with her child . . .
Greet I thee, my earth.

(III.ii.6-10)

Richard himself has "leased out" (II.i.59) his realm, "hath [put] the realm in farm" (II.i.256), has, as he admits, "Made glory base, a sovereignty a slave,/ Proud majesty a subject, state a peasant" (IV.i.251-52), has "grown bankrout like a broken man" (II.i.257). His "commercial exploitation of a sacred trust"[19] creates the condition whereby traitors wound the living earth, "march . . . upon her peaceful bosom,/ Frighting her pale-fac'd villages with war" (II.iii.92-94) because, as Reese suggests, Richard "has been guilty of an unroyal crime . . . and when the ruler is a guilty man, rebellion is one of the manifestations of his guilt."[20]

In the simplest terms, England and Richard have fallen from God. "He that hath suffer'd this disordered spring," says the Gardener, "Hath now himself met with the fall of leaf" (III.iv.48-49). The play's garden imagery is most concentrated, of course, in the allegorical garden scene, with its emphasis on binding "up yon dangling apricocks" (III.iv.29), supporting "the bending twigs" (III.iv.32), cutting "off the heads of too fast growing sprays" (III.iv.34), rooting "away/ The noisome weeds" (III.iv.37-38); "the whole land," complains the Servant,

> Is full of weeds, her fairest flowers chok'd up,
> Her fruit trees all unprun'd, her hedges ruined,
> Her knots disorder'd and her wholesome herbs
> Swarming with caterpillars.

(III.iv.43-47)

"O, what pity is it," the Gardener continues,

> That he had not so trimm'd and dress'd his land
> As we his garden! We at time of year
> Do wound the bark, the skin of our fruit-trees,
> Lest being over-proud in sap and blood,
> With too much riches it confound itself;
> Had he done so to great and growing men,
> They might have liv'd to bear and he to taste
> Their fruits of duty. Superfluous branches
> We lop away, that bearing boughs may live;
> Had he done so, himself had borne the crown,
> Which waste of idle hours hath quite thrown down.

(III.iv.55-66)

While the Homilies abound, as does the Bible, in garden imagery that almost inevitably conveys an allegorical sense of Eden, it is perhaps not accidental that the Homily "of falling from God" should employ garden imagery more abundantly than any other, dealing as it does, and as *Richard II* does, with "a second fall of cursed man" (III.iv.76). The Homily illuminates the garden imagery of the play by suggesting that what happens to the individual who falls from God must extend automatically to the kingdom of the king who falls from God. "As long as a man doeth prune his vines, doeth dig at the rootes, and doeth lay fresh earth to them, hee hath a mind to them, he perceiveth some token of fruitfulness that may be recovered in them." But once he falls from God, "as by pride and sinne wee goe from God, so shall God and all goodnesse with him goe from us . . . he will let us lie waste, he will give us over, he will turne away from us, he will dig and delve no more about us, hee will let us alone, and suffer us to bring foorth even such fruite as wee will, to bring foorth brambles, bryers, and thornes, all naughtinesse, all vice, and that so abundantly, that they shall cleane overgrow us, choke, strangle, and utterly destroy us." The Homily images its garden as John of Gaunt and the Servant describe England: Gaunt sees his country as an "other Eden, demi-paradise" (II.i.41) served by the sea "in the office of a wall" (II.i.42), as "This blessed plot, this earth, this realm, this England" (II.i.50). The Servant talks of "our sea-walled garden" (IV.iii.43). The Homily talks of "a goodly vineyard" made by God "for his beloved children":

> hee hedged it, he walled it round about, he planted it with chosen vines, and made a Turret in the middest thereof, and therein also a vine-press. And when he looked that it should bring him foorth good grapes, it brought forth wild graps: and after it followeth, Now shall I shew you (saith God) what I wil doe with my vineyard: I will plucke downe the hedges, that it may perish: I will breake downe the walles that it may bee troden under foot: I will let it lie wast, it shall not be cut, it shall not bee digged, but briers and thornes shall overgrowe it, and I shall command the cloudes that they shall no more raine upon it. . . . God at length doeth so forsake his unfruitfull vineyard, that hee will not onely suffer it to bring foorth weedes, bryers, and thornes, but also further to punish the unfruitfulness of it. Hee saith hee will not cut it, hee will not delve it, and hee will commaund the cloudes that they shall not raine upon it.

Richard, clearly, is responsible for the transition from the garden Gaunt celebrated to an England where only "blood . . . shall manure the ground" (IV.i.137), where "blood" will be the only medium of growth (V.vi.46).

Richard's comparisons of himself to Christ, valid within the *concept* of his kingship, represent false ritual because of his *practice* of his kingship. Richard, says Eric La Guardia, "is unable to perceive a categorical distinction between word and deed, the symbolic and the actual, ceremony and history."[21] This is true, of course, but it is Richard who has created the dichotomy he can no longer resolve. "The sacred state," continues LaGuardia, "is a symbolic conception, sustained by the operation of its elaborate forms"[22] and it is precisely the *spirit* of these forms that Richard had violated and cannot

reinstitute. It is not so much that Richard *confuses* mortality
and divinity, history and ceremony, body natural and body
politic, as LaGuardia suggests, but that he destroys their fusion, so that they, like his kingdom, are inevitably in conflict.
If the state is sacred, a fusion of secular with spiritual,
Richard is the keeper of the holy metaphor. He must preserve it, not merely use it as his license. What he does not
recognize is his responsibility for the destruction of the equation that makes ceremony a "higher reality," allowing secular
pageantry to intersect divinity, which makes ceremony part
of the patterned movement of history—not a contradiction to
invisible powers as is a trial by combat undercut by historical
facts that make it a pretense. The point is not that "the
mythical embodiment of the word must not be taken too literally, at least if one is mortal," nor is it that Richard's "tragic
error" is the taking "upon himself the power of transforming
word into flesh,"[23] it is that Richard has destroyed the links
between myth and secular reality, between the king as sacrament and as person, between the kingdom as consecration
and as land.

The play's "garden" imagery has been treated by a number
of critics,[24] as has the imagery of "the sun" in the Second Henriad. An element seems to have been neglected, however, in
this complex symbolic construct. Citing Newbolt's edition of
1912, Matthew Black's Variorum Edition says that "Richard's
badge was a sun obscured by or breaking from clouds."[25]
Shakespeare seems to have seized upon the emblem as a
means of expressing what happens to Richard. Its ambiguity
is neat—is the sun emerging or becoming obscured? By the
time Richard insists on the former, the latter has become the
meaning of his badge, a central "blot" of the many mentioned in the play and noted accurately by Altick.[26] Richard's
metaphor is rhetoric divorced from political reality:

> know'st thou not
> That when the searching eye of heaven is hid
> Behind the Globe, that lights the lower world,
> Then thieves and robbers range abroad unseen
> In murders and in outrage boldly here;
> But when from under this terrestrial ball
> He fires the proud tops of the eastern pines

And darts his light through every guilty hole,
Then murders, treasons, and detested sins,
The cloak of night being pluck'd from off their backs,
Stand bare and naked, trembling at themselves?

(III,ii,36-46)

Richard employs the full symbolism of dawn, not merely the
sun peeping out of clouds; but the world he would illuminate
is gone, as Salisbury, himself a doomed figure, has already
predicted:

Ah, Richard, with the eyes of heavy mind
I see thy glory like a shooting star
Fall to the base earth from the firmament.
Thy sun sits weeping in the lowly west,
Witnessing storms to come, woe, and unrest.

(II.iv.18-22)

A gravitational force seems to dominate the "nature" of the
play, pulling Richard's sun downward into the western
clouds. The "eastern pines" lie in Richard's past. His future is
to "go to Flint castle; there I'll pine away" (III.ii.209).
Richard's union with the ultimate visible manifestation of the
cosmos is no longer valid. We know that Salisbury's is the
choric voice, although it is not until later (V.vi.8), that we
learn that his prophecy, like Gaunt's, is uttered with the
tongue of a doomed man. Both noblemen fall, for different
reasons, with the star that descends to the "base earth," the
inevitable "grave" of the play, on which Richard dwells at
length a few lines after his desperate comparison of himself
to the sun. Richard extends Salisbury's "star-earth" collision
with more magnificent lines:

Down, down I come; like glist'ring Phaethon,
Wanting the manage of unruly jades.

(III.iii.178-79)

The lines intersect a minor thread of imagery with which
Shakespeare illuminates the world of this play, the several references to the management of horses, culminating in
Richard's affected anger at the horse that would not stumble
under Bolingbroke (V.v.84-89). Although Bolingbroke will
later compare himself to a "comet" (*I Henry IV*: III.i.47), his

decline will not be that of a star. Richard is the last to make
the plunge. Bolingbroke will die gradually, like diseased
modern man, and will die because he has inherited the world
Richard has given him:

> A king of beasts indeed, if aught but beasts,
> I had been still a happy king of men.
>
> (V.i.35-36)

Richard points not only at his political ineptitude (he *was* a
king of men, and failed), but at the future. To insure the
world Bolingbroke gives *him,* Henry V must insist that his
men "imitate the action of the tiger" (*Henry V*: III.i.6).
His metaphor shows what Richard lost, and suggests the con-
trivances that politicians in this new world must practice:

> Yet herein will I imitate the sun,
> Which doth permit the base contagious clouds
> To smother up his beauty from the world,
> That when he please again to be himself
> Being wanted, he may be more wonder'd at
> By breaking through the foul and ugly mists
> Of vapours that did seem to strangle him.
>
> (*I Henry IV*: I.ii.220-26)

Richard lost the fusion between metaphor and truth. Hal
re-creates it through a diminished political mimesis. England
after Richard comes to resemble the Britain that Lear abandons to ambition, calculation, and dismemberment. Bolingbroke inherits not a garden, but a jungle.

England's basic departure from deeper meanings has occurred before the play begins. Guilty of Gloucester's blood,
Richard cannot control "nature," as he suggests in the first of
the fire-water (sun-cloud) contrasts. He extends the natures
of the two antagonists into the elements, and, indeed, they
become elemental forces without a true king to control them:

> High-stomach'd are they both and full of ire,
> In rage deaf as the sea, hasty as fire.
>
> (I.i.18-19)

While the elements of sea and fire are contrasted, as they
should be in a well-ordered scheme of nature, Richard's ina-

bility to control them suggests that they will collide as they
should not in a well-ordered kingdom—unless in a trial by
combat, which does not occur. But the kingdom is compromised by the disorder of its king, anticipated in the badge
of sun emerging from or being obscured by cloud. Richard
has already determined that the contact of the alien elements
of fire and water must occur, and that the contact must be
collision. Gaunt reiterates the imagery of fire and water
(linked with growing) in the confrontation with the duchess:

> . . .when they see the hours ripe on earth,
> Will rain hot vengeance on offenders' heads.
>
> (I.ii.7-8)

The duchess, arguing an immediate, temporal cause, fails to
recognize his image of heat, or his faith in a universe more
comprehensive than familial ties:

> Finds brotherhood in thee no sharper spur?
> Hath love in thy old blood no living fire?
> Edward's seven sons, whereof thyself art one,
> Were as seven vials of his sacred blood,
> Or seven fair branches springing from one root.
>
> (I.ii.9-13)

The linkage of fire and moisture suggests a confusion deep
in the nature of things, where alien elements war in more
than metaphor. Bolingbroke, however, possesses that literal
mind which sees things as they are:

> O, who can hold a fire in his hand
> By thinking on the frosty Caucasus? . . .
> Or wallow naked in December snow
> By thinking on fantastic summer's heat?
>
> (I.iii.294-99)

Richard believes *he* can, not recognizing on his return from
Ireland that his badge no longer images reality, but instead
emblematizes the "louring tempest" (I.iii.187) and "the de-
vouring pestilence" (I.iii.283), the "violent fires" and "sudden
storms" (II.i.34-35) that have "clouded all [his] happy days on
earth" (III.ii.68), "the tidings of calamity" that ride over the
kingdom

> Like an unseasonable stormy day
> Which makes the silver rivers drown their shores
> As if the world were all dissolv'd to tears.
>
> (III.ii.106-9)

Scroop's pun on "tide" is obvious, as is the link between the storm over England and the tears of Richard that encourage it. "What a tide of woes," moans York, "Comes rushing on this woeful land at once!" (II.ii.98-99).

The symbolism of Richard's badge achieves its culmination in a brilliant series of phrases. Bolingbroke claims that he comes but for his own:

> Provided that my banishment repeal'd
> And lands restor'd again be freely granted.
> If not, I'll use the advantage of my power
> And lay the summer's dust with showers of blood
> Rain'd from the wounds of slaughtered Englishmen.
>
> (III.iii.40-44)

His threat to "bedrench" with a "crimson tempest" "The fresh green lap of fair King Richard's land" (III.iii.46-47) is paralleled by his command to his army to display its power. His words suggest a collision of elements that can not occur naturally:

> Methinks King Richard and myself should meet
> With no less terror than the elements
> Of fire and water, when their thund'ring shock
> At meeting tears the cloudy cheeks of heaven.
> Be he the fire, I'll be the yielding water;
> The rage be his, whilst on the earth I rain
> My waters—on the earth, and not on him.
>
> (III.iii.54-60)

Bolingbroke images a "terrorless" storm. Water douses fire, does not yield before it. Paradox, perhaps, veils intent. Possibly Bolingbroke admits as much, if we take "rain" as a pun on "reign."

Immediately, Richard appears. Bolingbroke is captivated by the tableau, as if viewing a superb illumination full of symbolic reverberations:

See, see, King Richard doth himself appear,
As doth the blushing discontented sun
From out the fiery portal of the east,
When he perceives the envious clouds are bent
To dim his glory and to stain the track
Of his bright passage to the occident.

Bolingbroke demonstrates some appreciation of the very
symbolism he is in the process of exiling from the world-
—and he expresses his own role in that exile. Down comes
the weeping sun, and with the movement occurs the transition "from Richard's night to Bolingbroke's fair day"
(III.ii.218). The transfer of power is conveyed cynically by
Richard, as he wishes his successor "many years of sunshine
days" (IV.i.221), and more magnificently, later in the deposition scene:

O that I were a mockery king of snow,
Standing before the sun of Bolingbroke,
To melt myself away in water-drops!

(IV.i.260-62)

He has been a "mockery king," like a monument of snow
("Alack, alack, for woe/ That any harm should stain so fair a
show" [III.iii.70-71]), without intrinsic reality, permitting his
tears to melt his kingdom away, indeed to wash away his
balm (the "moisture imagery" relates as well to the several
images of washing, and to the Pilate suggestions, of course).
He has melted himself away. Here, Richard *is* the yielding
water, as he will reiterate in the last of his weeping images,
his hope that his queen's sad story will cause its hearers "in
compassion [to] weep the fire out" (V.i.48).

Bolingbroke reigns on the earth, having become the sun.
But the sun is, at best, a metaphor now. Richard has squandered whatever reality might have inhered in the sun *qua*
king, the fusion Chaucer celebrates in "the younge sunne."
That world goes with Richard to Pomfret, and the new world
finds a prince who will translate Richard's badge into political
strategy.

England may have been "too much in the sun" under

Richard, but it will experience the fusion of sun and royalty
only in isolated similes hereafter, not in principle: "gorgeous
at the sun at midsummer," says Vernon of Hal (*I Henry
IV*:IV.i.102). The words, however, refer to Hal's premature
emergence to save his inheritance at Shrewsbury, and are
consistent, although Vernon can not know this, with Hal's
controlling device for instant reformation. Gaunt's reflection
on his own demise reflects England's as well: "The setting
sun, and music at the close" (I.i.12). The sun's descent to a
mere factor of man's manipulation results from Richard's
inept translation of its power:

> His rash fierce blaze of riot cannot last,
> For violent fires soon burn out themselves.

(II.i.33-34)

> Soon kindled and soon burnt.

(I Henry IV: III.ii.62)

Finally, of course, Richard "weep [s] the fire out" (V.i.48).

While Richard's deposition of himself is the logical consequence and indeed the inevitable destiny of his decisions, he
states the truth only once: "I wasted time, and now doth time
waste me" (V.v.49). By defying one of nature's great
rhythms, an emanation of supernature, Richard becomes its
subject, as will Macbeth more profoundly.

> One day too late, I fear me, noble lord
> Hath clouded all thy happy days on earth.
> O, call back yesterday, bid time return,
> And thou shalt have twelve thousand fighting men!
> To-day, to-day, unhappy day, too late,
> O'erthrows thy joys, friends, fortune, and thy state.

(III.ii.67-72)

Richard's creation of "the absent time" (II.iii.79) leads to
his own complicated metaphor of time:

> now hath Time made me his numb'ring clock.
> My thoughts are minutes; and with sighs they jar
> Their watches on unto mine eyes, the outward watch,
> Whereto my finger, like a dial's point,
> Is pointing still, in cleansing them from tears.

Now sir, the sound that tells what hour it is
Are clamorous groans, which strike upon my heart,
Which is the bell. So sighs and tears and groans
Show minutes, times, and hours; but my time
Runs posting on in Bolingbroke's proud joy,
While I stand fooling here, his Jack o'th' clock.

(V.v.50-60)

Richard has been reduced to a timepiece, a means whereby Bolingbroke achieves time's meaning. Richard's self-pitying metaphor finds its ultimate dramatic point much later, in the insomnia of Henry IV:

O thou dull god, why liest thou with the vile
In loathsome beds, and leav'st the kingly couch
A watch-case or a common 'larum-bell?

(*II Henry IV:* III.i.15-17)

Henry sees himself as no better than the movement of a watch, which must be working even when it should be still, **and as residing at the center of a bell, the focal point for the** reporting of emergencies. His plight and that of his son ("What watch the King keeps..." [*Henry V:* IV.ii.300]) are products of Richard's wasting of time. Kings become subject to time rather than mediators between the positive rhythms of time and their kingdoms, a point Gaunt attempted to make in warning Richard of the limits of a king's command over the great rhythms of the cosmos:

Shorten my days thou canst with sullen sorrow,
And pluck nights from me, but not lend a morrow.
Thou canst help Time to furrow me with age,
But stop no wrinkle in his pilgrimage.
Thy word is current with him for my death,
But dead, thy kingdom cannot buy my breath.

(I.iii.227-32)

"Time goes upright with his carriage" only when it is observed, when a king keeps proper watch over his dispensation. Henry IV cannot—and not merely because he is a usurper. Usurpation is a manifestation of the deeper and prior disorders Richard has engendered. The wasted Gaunt can only lecture on true kingship. He cannot effect it, since "correction lieth" (I.ii.4) in Richard's hands. Once Richard confirms his earlier crime by taking "from Time/ His charters and his customary rights" (II.i.195-96), no restoration can occur. Even Henry V, that bright exception within the Tudor myth of history, is "too famous to live long" (*I Henry VI:* I.i.5).

Yet even in his approach to "self awareness," Richard plays with his fate in what Traversi aptly terms "an academic exercise in poetic pessimism."[27] Richard tries to translate word into flesh:

> My brain I'll prove the female to my soul,
> My soul the father; and these two beget
> A generation of still-breeding thoughts,
> And these same thoughts people this little world,
> In humours like the people of this world.
> For no thought is contented. The better sort,
> As thoughts of things divine, are intermix'd
> With scruples and do set the word itself
> Against the word:
> As thus, "Come little ones," and then again,
> "It is as hard to come as for a camel
> To thread the postern of a small needle's eye."
>
> (V.v.6-17)

Richard neglects the crucial qualification that Christ makes: it is a "riche man" (in Matthew, Mark, and Luke [Geneva Version]) who cannot "enter the Kingdome of God." Richard's omission suggests not only that he is careless of his text, but that he has yet to "[shake] off the regal thoughts/ With which [he] reigned" (IV.i.163-64), as his soliloquy later confirms (V.v.32-36). Richard's inclusion of "riche man" would resolve the seeming paradox between the "little one"—symbol of spiritual innocence—and the "riche man"—symbol of worldliness and impiety. Christ, indeed, goes further, in the tenth chapter of Mark, a passage that was very familiar to the Elizabethan by dint of its incorporation into the Sacrament of Baptism: "whosoever doeth not receive the kyngdome of God, as a lytle chylde: he shall not entre therin." For Richard to penetrate the paradox would be for him to see himself at last, to see the impiety that brought him down and to recognize that he must *become* a little one, must be born again, to achieve spiritual health in his body natural, which is all he has left. Had Richard penetrated the paradox, he would have seen why he, "the proud king," is excluded from his own kingdom, a paradigm of God's Kingdom, and why his own incarnation failed. Another proud king, Lear, is similarly unable to translate word into reality, but does struggle back to his "own kingdom," as Kent says (IV.vii.76). It is perhaps not too much to say that the Elizabethan audience would have been disturbed enough by Richard's omission of "Riche man" to recognize that he does not achieve self-understanding in this soliloquy.

Instead, he sets the word against the word, and his own inability to *fuse* the words, to be a pious king, ramifies explicitly into his kingdom. Richard's own name is "usurp'd," as he tells us (IV.i.257), another incidence of the loss of identity suffered by the characters of the play, the dark indistinguishable world into which they plunge, no matter what they do, no matter which of the play's kings they follow. Mowbray's is the choric voice:

> Then thus I turn me from my country's light,
> To dwell in solemn shades of endless night.
>
> (I.iii.176-77)

Bolingbroke exiles Exton with similar words:

> With Cain go wander through shades of night,
> **And never show thy head by day nor light.**
>
> (V.vi.43-44)

Richard becomes "lesser than [his] name" (III.iii.136) even as his kingdom lapses toward the vague destiny the queen perceives:

> **But what it is, that is not yet known; what,**
> I cannot name; 'tis nameless woe, I wot.
>
> (II.ii.39-40)

Aumerle becomes

> Aumerle that was
> But that is lost for being Richard's friend,
> And, Madam, you must call him Rutland now.
>
> (V.ii.41-43)

Northumberland's "Richard" (III.iii.6) draws a rebuke from
York. Northumberland protests "only to be brief/ Left I his
title out" (III.iii.10-11). "The time hath been," York responds, that "your whole head's length" would have answered for such brevity (III.iii.11-14). Between that time and
this has come the erasure of Bolingbroke's "imprese"
(III.i.25), an act predicting the elimination of Richard's title.
Gaunt has defined Richard's activity: "thou dost seek to kill
my name in me" (II.i.86). The king cannot deal in such activities with impunity. Northumberland suggests that words
are to be measured in the context of efficiency. The word as
index to ceremonial value is lost, but the principal "traitor"
(V.i.248) is Richard, not Northumberland. The kingdom
does not plunge into total namelessness, but some names are
lost, others are changed, and many become negative—
Richard a "traitor with the rest" (IV.i.248). Nobles loyal to
the king-that-was become, in the new dispensation, "dangerous consorted traitors" (V.vi.15), a churchman becomes a
"grand conspirator (V.vi.19), Exton becomes "Cain" (V.vi.43),
even as Bolingbroke attempts to assign him "the guilt of conscience" (V.vi.41).

The deep schism the world of *Richard II* experiences is
suggested by the constant "appeal to ancestry" and to familial
ties made by characters who oppose Richard. The Duchess of
Gloucester makes the appeal to Gaunt, as the Duchess of
York does to York. Gaunt berates Richard for dividing father
and son (II.i.80) and for refuting his ancestry:

> O, had thy grandsire with a prophet's eye
> Seen how his son's son should destroy his sons,
> From forth thy reach he would have laid thy shame,
> Deposing thee . . .

>   (II.i.104-6)

York extends the argument, invoking Richard's father and
grandfather:

> when [thy father] frown'd, it was against the French
> And not against his friends. His noble hand
> Did win what he did spend and spent not that

Which his triumphant father's hand had won.
His hands were guilty of no kindred blood,
But bloody with the enemies of his kin.

(II.i.178-83)

York goes on, of course, to suggest that Richard compounds
his own defection from ancestry by denying Bolingbroke the
rights of inheritance. Richard, typically, plays with the idea,
expressing his awareness of the altered lines of inheritance
he has encouraged by disrupting the sequence of
Bolingbroke's succession:

Cousin, I am too young to be your father,
Though you are old enough to be my heir.

(III.iii.202-3)

York, painfully aware that Bolingbroke is his "kinsman . . .
Whom conscience and my kindred bids to right"
(II.ii.114-15), is therefore susceptible to Bolingbroke's at-
tempt to rouse York's "father instinct":

You are my father, for methinks in you
I see old Gaunt alive. O, then, my father,
Will you permit that I shall stand condemn'd
A wandering vagabond. . . ?

(II.iii.117-20)

You have a son, Aumerle, my noble cousin;
Had you first died, and he had been thus trod down,
He should have found his uncle Gaunt a father
To rouse his wrongs and chase them to the bay.

(II.iii.125-28)

Having acquiesced to this argument, or, perhaps, to the impossibility of his situation, York, in turn, must attempt to
condemn his own son and rob his wife of *her* identity:

wilt thou pluck my fair son from mine age,
And rob me of a happy mother's name?
Is he not like thee? Is he not thine own?

(V.ii.92-94)

York's actions, she suggests, reflect a denial of all levels of
meaning in marriage, ultimately a denial of York himself:

> thou dost suspect
> That I have been disloyal to thy bed,
> And that he is a bastard, not thy son.
> Sweet York, sweet husband, be not of that mind.
> He is as like thee as a man may be. . . .
>
> (V.ii.104-8)

York can be loyal to the new king only by betraying his
son. He too "set'st the word itself against the word"
(V.iii.116-19). According to his duchess, a wife divided
against her husband, York engages in false prayers, in the
linguistic contradiction that the divided world forces upon
those who would endow their words with religious relevance:

> He prays but faintly and would be deni'd;
> We pray with heart and soul and all beside . . .
> His prayers are full of false hypocrisy;
> Ours of true zeal and deep integrity.
> Our prayers do out-pray his; then let them have
> That mercy which true prayer ought to have.
>
> (V.iii.103-10)

While her prayer is granted, its granting does not make of
Bolingbroke a "true king." The plot was planned by
Richard's party, representing a deposed king still alive, and
thus emphasizing Bolingbroke's dilemma. The Duchess of
York praying for pardon creates a disjunctive analogue to
the Duchess of Gloucester begging for revenge, but both
imply the *unnatural* choices that Gaunt and York have made:

> and though thou liv'st and breath'st,
> Yet art thou slain in him.
>
> (I.ii.24-25)

> Is he not like thee? Is he not thine own? . . .
> He is as like thee as any man may be.
>
> (V.ii.94-108)

To be loyal to one king is to ignore a brother's murder; to be
loyal to another is to demand a son's death. And York's indictment of Aumerle is a distant echo of Gaunt's judgment
against Bolingbroke. The word *against* the flesh—into such
dilemmas are the characters thrust who inhabit the world
Richard has divided. The placement of Carlisle's speech as a

dramatic interruption of Bolingbroke's seemingly effortless ascent to the throne, and the power of the speech, tell us that this is the voice of a prophet uttering truths reaching further than do the predictions of Bolingbroke or the party conspiring against him:

> Come, lords, away,
> To fight with Glendower and his complices.
> A while to work, and after holiday.
>
> (III.i.42-44)

> Come home with me to supper: I will lay
> A plot shall show us all a merry day.
>
> (IV.i.332-33)

The "word against the word" is but a prelude to the internecine struggle Carlisle predicts for what was "a Christian climate" (IV.i.130):

> O, if you raise this house against this house,
> It will the woefullest division prove
> That ever fell upon this cursed earth.
>
> (IV.i.145-47)

A fallen world can only fall further. The sacrament that Mowbray took as a medium toward the pardon of John of Gaunt becomes a sanction for regicide:

> Before I freely speak my mind herein,
> You shall not only take the Sacrament
> To bury mine intents, but also to effect
> **Whatever I shall happen to devise** . . .
>
> (IV.i.326-34)

> A dozen of them here have ta'en the Sacrament,
> **And interchangeably set down their hands,**
> To kill the King at Oxford.
>
> (V.ii.97-99)

Such an oath is, according to the Homily against Swearing and Perjury, "unlawfull and ungodly," but it represents the setting of one word against another, of religion against allegiance to the monarch—precisely the "woeful division" Richard engenders and Carlisle describes.

As chief victim of his own defection, Richard's role in de-

posing himself is inevitable. Not only is the momentum of
Richard's downfall abetted by his eager cooperation with the
forces pulling him down ("We must to London . . . I must not
say no" [III.iii.208-9]), but Richard, as at once keeper of and
destroyer of the validity of ritual in the realm, is the only
figure who can employ it against himself, since as John of
Gaunt says, "correction lieth in those hands/ Which made the
fault" (I.ii.4-5). The Deposition is the anti-ritualistic fulfillment of Richard's anti-sacramental actions, as Richard himself predicts in a moment of false confidence:

> Not all the water in the rough rude sea
> Can wash the balm off from an anointed king;
> The breath of worldly men cannot depose
> The deputy elected by the Lord.

                                                    (III.ii.54-57)

Richard seems far less concerned, however, with the symbolic appropriateness, indeed the necessity of deposing
himself—necessary because he alone can do it, and because
deposition fulfills the pattern of anti-sacrament he has imposed upon his realm—than with embarrassing Bolingbroke.
Thus the scene is a fulfillment of an anti-ritualistic destiny
that Richard never fully grasps, *and* of his own will. Richard's
will merges neatly with the role of anti-king, as it had
clashed with his role as king. And, in being his own
anti-king, Richard revenges himself against the new king, by
reminding Bolingbroke of the premises of kingship. Richard
will not read the part set down for him, specifically the indictment Northumberland presses upon him, and, instead,
dramatizes his downfall so skillfully and emphasizes the deep
seriousness of deposition so effectively that his last great
scene expresses and helps create the dilemma the new king
inherits. Henry V, fresh from coronation, uses Falstaff to
make the King's first scene a triumph that confirms his new
crown against all the forces threatening it. Richard, as he abdicates, uses Bolingbroke to make the King's last scene a
prediction of all the forces that will threaten Henry IV's new
throne. Bolingbroke will never lead his Crusade, will never
wash Richard's blood from his hands, partly because true

ritual can never occur within *his* guilty kingdom and partly
because of the completely political ethic he introduces—"This
new world," as Fitzwater calls it (IV.i.78).

On his return from Ireland, Richard alternates between
wildly unrealistic hopes and a self-dramatizing despair. He
seeks an army in the sky:

> For every man that Bolingbroke hath press'd
> To lift shrewd steel against our golden crown,
> God for his Richard hath in heavenly pay
> A glorious angel; then, if angels fight,
> Weak men must fall, for Heaven still guards the right.
>
> (III.ii.58-62)

His words ignore not only Carlisle's more practical "The
means that heavens yield must be embraced" (III.ii.29), but
also Gaunt's "Let Heaven revenge" (I.ii.40)—the former ad-
vocating action in conjunction with spiritual powers, the latter suggesting that heaven will be reluctant to leap to battle
on the side of a bad king. Richard continues to assume that
"right" *resides* in kingship, that his role confers privilege but
no concomitant responsibility. His unreal vision of the kingship, of course, helps *make* it unreal.

Alternating with a view of kingship rendered increasingly
insubstantial as reports of defections from Richard's ranks
increase, is the despairing man beneath:

> Cover your heads, and mock not flesh and blood
> With solemn reverence. Throw away respect,
> Tradition, form, and ceremonious duty;
> For you have but mistook me all this while.
> I live with bread like you, feel want,
> Taste grief, need friends: subjected thus,*
> How can you say to me I am a king?
>
> (III.ii.171-77)

This is the man who has seduced Richard from kingship and
who denies him any effective response to Bolingbroke, the
Richard who seduces Bolingbroke *toward* kingship. Henry V
will discuss the man beneath the king in similar terms before
Agincourt, but he will move gradually back into his role as

---

*The line suggests, on a secondary level of meaning, "with subjects like these," i.e.,
"like these who now desert me."

king, leading his men into battle. Richard reverses that process, gradually embracing his role as man, losing the men he might lead. Richard throws away "respect,/ Tradition, form, and ceremonious duty" and pursues "that sweet way . . . into despair" (III.ii.205). His impulse to play the martyr encourages the development of the role and the inevitable movement of Bolingbroke into the vacuum of rule: "A king, woe's slave, shall kingly woe obey" (III.ii.210). Here, Richard makes his body natural, his woe, ruler over his body politic.

Richard's ability to control the two roles rhetorically and histrionically in the Deposition Scene is prefigured in his speech of submission to Bolingbroke's emissary, Northumberland:

> I'll give my jewels for a set of beads,
> My gorgeous palace for a hermitage,
> My gay apparel for an almsman's gown,
> My figur'd goblets for a dish of wood,
> My sceptre for a palmer's walking-staff,
> My subjects for a pair of carved saints . . .
>
> (III.iii.147-52)

Richard's exchange of the implements of kingship for those of religion works ironically to suggest the personal attribute that might have brought him into alignment with his political self, and have allowed true rite to function in his kingdom. The kingly elements represent the will he embraced, and since he does not employ the royal plural (as he had in his opening speech of this scene to Northumberland), it would seem that he looked upon them as *his,* rather than as the outward symbols of an office rightly performed. Neglect of the *spirit* of the religious symbols has drained the spiritual reality from the kingly ones. His indictment of the pride of Bolingbroke and Northumberland, valid enough perhaps if delivered by a York or Carlisle, reverberates in Richard's case more profoundly against the accuser than the accused.

Bolingbroke has offered to submit to Richard's kingship, "Even at [Richard's] feet to lay [his] arms and power/ Provided that my banishment repeal'd/ And lands restor'd again be freely granted" (III.iii.39-41). While the situation *may* be impossible politically, Richard does not wait to hear

Bolingbroke's response to the restoration of his rights. Instead he wishes that he "were as great/ As is [his] grief, or lesser than [his] name" (III.iii.136-39). Obviously, the encouragement of grief has diminished his name, the emotional man has eroded the potential king. The idea that Bolingbroke should be king seems to come from Richard, as he develops the ironic mode he will employ so effectively in the Deposition Scene:

> Most mighty prince, my Lord Northumberland,
> What says King Bolingbroke? Will his Majesty
> Give Richard leave to live till Richard die?
> You make a leg, and Bolingbroke says ay.
>
> (III.iii.172-75)

The Deposition Scene rings with religious references—Judas, Pilate—part of Richard's pageant of betrayal. But the allusions to Judas can only be ironic. Not only was Richard wrong when he flailed his executed cronies, Wiltshire, Bushy, and Green, as "each one thrice worse than Judas!" (III.ii.132), but since Judas was possibly the only disciple to be of Christ's kindred, Richard's allusion points as much at his role in killing Gloucester ("Abel") as at his supposed betrayers. The source invalidates the allusions. Richard, indeed, suggests that *he* is responsible for his deposition and, at the same time, he blames the lesser men around him for his downfall, translating the scene into as much a defeat of them as of himself:

>   Were they not mine?
> Did they not sometime cry, "All Hail!" to me?
> So Judas did to Christ; but He, in twelve,
> Found truth in all but one; I, in twelve thousand, none.
> God save the King!—Will no man say amen?
> Am I both priest and clerk? Well then, amen.
> God save the King! although I be not he;
> And yet, amen, if heaven do think him me.—
> To do what service am I sent for hither?
>
> (IV.i.168-76)

While his indictment admits no complicity in his demise, Richard *must* be both priest and clerk. Since only "the hand of God/. . . [can dismiss] us from our stewardship"

(III.iii.77-78), only Richard can perform the offices of prayer
and response in the anti-"service" of his deposition.

Richard develops the dichotomy between king and man:

> You may my glories and my state dispose,
> But not my griefs; still am I king of those.
>
> (IV.i.192-93)

While Richard makes a clear distinction here, he has previously allowed grief to be king over him personally, hence
politically as well. The king's two bodies interplay subtly;
Richard retains the personality that destroyed the prince; the
despair that was at once a factor within the process of the
loss of the throne and an increasing concomitant of that loss
becomes increasingly a contributor to Richard's downward
movement:

> The cares I give I have, though given away;
> They 'tend the crown, yet still with me they stay.
>
> (IV.i.195-99)

The actual deposition speech is the anti-ritualistic center of
the play, the inevitable result of Richard's defiance of the
premises of his kingship. Again Richard does not assume the
royal plural, emphasizing that he, as man, is undecking himself, not he as king. Ironically, the attributes of kingship are
more emphatically stressed when they are stripped off by an
"I":

> Now mark me, how I will undo myself.
> I give this heavy weight from off my head
> And this unwieldy sceptre from my hand,
> And pride of kingly sway from out my heart.
> With mine own tears I wash away my balm,
> With mine own hands I give away my crown,
> With mine own tongue deny my sacred state,
> With mine own breath release all duteous oaths.
>
> (IV.i.203-10)

The treason of the observers is emphasized by the contradiction Richard skillfully enunciates:

> God pardon all oaths that are broke to me!
> God keep all vows unbroke are made to thee!
>
> (IV.i.214-15)

and by his own contradictory use of the lesser of his persons—his body natural—to erase the greater. He is correct to find himself

> a traitor with the rest;
> For I have given here my soul's consent
> To undeck the pompous body of a king;
> Made glory base, a sovereignty a slave,
> Proud majesty a subject, state a peasant.
>
> (IV.i.248-52)

But it was Richard, of course, who had reduced England to "a pelting farm" (II.i.60). The scene develops inevitably to the eradication of his very identity—precisely what was attempted on Bolingbroke during *his* banishment:

> I have no name, no title;
> No, not that name was given me at the font,
> But 'tis usurp'd.
>
> (IV.i.255-57)

While "water cannot wash away [the] sin" (IV.i.242) of his deposition, his tears wash away his balm and the holy water of his baptism; Richard has been chief traitor to his own identity. Ironically, as he plays out the part of his own treason, his personality grows dominant, magnificent in the role of despair and downfall as it had been despicable and capricious in the role of king:

> Was this face the face
> That every day under his household roof
> Did keep ten thousand men? Was this the face
> That, like the sun, did make beholders wink?
> Is this the face which fac'd so many follies,
> That was at last out-fac'd by Bolingbroke?
>
> (IV.i.281-86)

This echo of Faustus's speech to Helen, later to be repeated by Cordelia, again in the context of the abasement of a proud king, represents another of Richard's approaches to self-knowledge. The mirror image represents the aspects of kingship that now are shadow, no longer his substantial attributes, because Richard, the man holding the mirror, has destroyed them, has made them a mere reflection of his former

position: "How soon my sorrow hath destroyed my face"
(IV.i.291). Richard accepts Bolingbroke's correction:

> The shadow of my sorrow! Ha! let's see.
> 'Tis very true, my grief lies all within;
> And these external manners of laments
> Are merely shadows to the unseen grief
> That swells with silence in the tortur'd soul.
> There lies the substance.
>
> (IV.i.293-99)

Richard's reality lies within, not in the shattered mirror,
fragments of his body politic, of a now insubstantial pageant
signifying nothing. Even the outward signs of grief on the
face of the body natural are but a shadow of the absolute
within.

Richard's apostrophe to the mirror might seem the postur-
ing of a vain man, but his words *mock* vanity, rendering the
mirror image meaningless and thus destroying it before the
fact. "A brittle glory shineth in this face" (IV.i.288) because it
is the face of "unking'd Richard" (IV.i.220). The smashing of
the mirror is a sudden recapitulation of Richard's own career
and the final stroke in the separation of his dual natures.

As Richard's personality dominates the scene, his kingship
diminishes; the scene is the play in microcosm. Yet here his
rhetorical manipulation of his two roles is consummate and
his grandeur greatest even as its premises evaporate in tears
and balm and baptismal water. Forcing himself more and
more into the mode of anti-ritual, Richard aligns himself
with inevitability, develops a magnificent anti-ritual, and so
simultaneously triumphs over and *through* his own destruction. The control of the roles is superb, but that Richard is
playing a part within his own self-destructive production is
obvious. Richard embraces the offer of Eliot's Fourth Temp-
ter, incapable of penetrating further into the premises of
martyrdom, achieving a self-gratification. Yet his "martyrdom" shakes the new king, making *his* body politic as fragile
as the mirror Richard smashed. In deposing Richard,
Bolingbroke wreaks the same destruction on his body politic
as Richard has on his throughout the play. For all his playing
the role of martyr, Richard *does* become one. He had pre-

dicted his burial "in the King's highway" (III.iv.155), a prophecy fulfilled when his subjects throw "dust . . . upon his sacred head" (V.ii.30), and recalled by the Archbishop of York much later, once Richard has achieved martyrdom:

> What trust is in these times?
> They that, when Richard liv'd would have him die,
> Are now become enamour'd on his grave.
> Thou, that threw'st dust upon his goodly head
> When through proud London he came sighing on
> After th' admired heels of Bolingbroke,
> Cri'st now, "O earth, yield us that king again,
> And take thou this!"
>
> (*II Henry IV,* I.iii.100-107)

The dust that lands on unkinged Richard's head, however, is a consequence of an original "dust that hides our sceptre's gilt" (II.i.294).

Richard's parting from his queen illustrates the inevitable anti-rituals that must continue in the world after his deposition. Richard had prevented Bolingbroke's marriage, Bolingbroke had accused Bushy and Green of making "a divorce betwixt [Richard's] queen and him" (III.i.12). The separation of Richard and his queen is more than a divorce, it is an anti-marriage, an analogue to Richard of his "unkinging":

> Doubly divorc'd! Bad men, you violate
> A twofold marriage, 'twixt my crown and me,
> And then betwixt me and my married wife.
> Let me unkiss the oath 'twixt thee and me . . .
>
> (V.i.71-74)

Perhaps "The breath of worldly men cannot depose/ The deputy elected by the Lord" (III.ii.56-57), but here, as in the deposition scene, such injunctions are ignored: "it shoulde never be lawfull to put a sonder those, whome thy by matrimone haddest made one." Perhaps to emphasize that these are "Bad men," Richard refuses to be his own priest in his "unmarrying.":*

---

*Northumberland's "My guilt be on my head, and there an end" (V.i.69) would seem to place him within the "Judas—Pilate" context Richard has attempted to create. He echoes the mob before Pilate's palace: "Then answered all the people, and said, His blood be on us, and on our children" (Matthew 27:25). Northumberland here participates in an anti-sacrament and has been one of the chiefest of the

> And yet not so, for with a kiss 'twas made.
> Part us, Northumberland.

(V.i.75-76)

Their parting represents a ritual separation of what was fused in marriage:

> Queen.   **And must we be divided? Must we part?**
> K. Richard. **Ay, hand from hand, my love, and heart from heart.**

(V.i.81-82)

Instead of becoming one flesh, they, "two together weeping, make one woe" (V.i.86). Again, grief becomes ultimate reality. They marry sorrow and self-destruction, appropriately, since Richard has engendered the inevitable division between king and man, king and kingdom, king and queen, and that union analogous to the fusion of divinity and flesh, "signifying unto us the mistical union that is betwixt Christ and his Churche," between man and wife:

> Come, come, in wooing sorrow let's be brief,
> Since, wedding it, there is such length in grief.
> One kiss shall stop our mouths, and dumbly part;
> Thus give I mine, and thus take I thy heart.

(V.i.93-96)

But hearts once exchanged to create a new union are now returned to enunciate a final separation:

> Give me mine own again; 'twere no good part
> To take on me to keep and kill thy heart.—
> So, now I have mine own again, be gone,
> That I may strive to kill it with a groan.

(V.i.97-100)

The ceremony that joined them hoped that they might

mob demanding Richard's deliverance to his "sour cross" (IV.i.241). Northumberland's guilt will not find an "end" in himself, but in his son, Hotspur, "Second to none, unseconded" by Northumberland (*II Henry IV*, II.iii.34). Northumberland is hardly a participant in any precise analogue to the crucifixion, but his guilt pursues him, as Richard said it would, into the disease-ridden world of *II Henry IV*. Richard's words to Northumberland (*Richard II*, V.i.55-59) are repeated almost verbatim by Henry IV (*II Henry IV*, III.i.70-77), and by then the prophecy of Northumberland's further defections from England's monarch, whoever he is, has been fulfilled. In his recalling of Richard's words, Henry IV suggests that he was a spectator to them, yet he was not on stage during the scene in which Richard spoke them and Northumberland then parted Richard and his queen.

"abide in thy love unto their lives ende." The anti-ritual that
parts them ends with the queen's thoughts of death and
Richard's words "the rest let sorrow say" (V.i.102). Richard
prevented Bolingbroke's marriage; now Bolingbroke must
prevent Richard's—obviously to avoid the claim of Richard's
heir, should Richard produce one. Bolingbroke anticipates
the dilemma of Macbeth—to determine the future as a ratifi-
cation of his past actions. Richard *has* named an heir, of
course, a fact that will ramify into the scene Henry V will
stage for the traitors before sailing for destiny at Agincourt.

Another of the metaphors whereby Shakespeare suggests
the conflict deep within the natural order of the world is that
of music, here a contrast to the harmonious music of *The
Tempest* or *King Lear* (IV.vii.), where music suggests the creation of a new order, tragically temporary in *King Lear,* more
permanent, though heavily qualified, in *The Tempest.*
Banished Mowbray grieves at his loss of language:

> now my tongue's use is to me no more
> Than an unstringed viol or a harp,
> Or like a cunning instrument cas'd up,
> Or, being open, put into his hands
> That knows no touch to tune the harmony.
>
> (I.iii.161-65)

Banished Bolingbroke quickly rejects his father's fancy that
he "Suppose the singing birds musicians . . . and thy steps no
more/ Than a delightful measure or a dance" (I.iii.287-90).
Gaunt hopes that his dying words to Richard will "Enforce
attention like deep harmony" (II.i.6). But York isolates the
less harmonious sounds beguiling Richard's ears:

> Lascivious metres, to whose venom sound
> The open ear of youth doth always listen.
>
> (II.i.19-20)

Soon Gaunt's voice in death joins that of Mowbray in
banishment: "His tongue is now a stringless instrument"
(II.i.149).

After Richard has possessed Bolingbroke's inheritance, "we
hear this fearful tempest sing" (II.i.263), as music merges

with imagery of storm, the reversal of the poetic process in
The Tempest, where storm modulates toward harmony. The
queen's lady-in-waiting offers to "dance" (III.iv.6) and "sing"
(III.iv.19), but neither can cheer a grieving queen:

> My legs can keep no measure in delight,
> When my poor heart no measure keeps in grief;
> Therefore no dancing . . .
>
> (III.iv.7-9)

> 'Tis well that thou hast cause [to sing];
> But thou shouldst please me better wouldst thou weep.
>
> (III.iv.19-20)

Music, finally, like so many other metaphors within this in-
credibly interwoven poetic fabric, finds its locus in Richard,
who interprets it rightly as an echo of his own misgovern-
ment:

> Music do I hear?
> Ha, ha! keep time! How sour sweet music is,
> When time is broke and no proportion kept!
> So is it in the music of men's lives.
> And here have I the daintiness of ear
> To check time broke in a disordered string;
> But for the concord of my state and time
> Had not an ear to hear my true time broke.
>
> (V.v.42-48)

Typically, the truth of Richard's perceptions emerges within
a finger exercise on "the music of men's· lives," a kind of
commencement address. Yet he sees that, regardless of what
metaphor the bad music creates with his kingship, it says two
things to his "body natural"—one to that physical being
aware that he once wore a crown, another to the solitary man
who wishes to be loved:

> This music mads me; let it sound no more;
> For though it have holp madmen to their wits,
> In me it seems it will make wise men mad.
> Yet blessing on his heart that gives it me!
> For 'tis a sign of love; and love to Richard
> Is a strange brooch in this all-hating world.
>
> (V.v.61-66)

As King, Richard was unlovable. As man, parting from his wife, or soliloquizing in prison, he seems suddenly aware of the need for love. He gives it, in an almost unnoticed line, by dismissing the loyal Groom, endangered, as Richard knows: "If thou love me, 'tis time thou wert away" (V.v.96). The Groom exits, with another of those lines expressing the divorce between word and feeling: "What my tongue dares not, that my heart shall say" (V.v.97; cf. Aumerle on "Farewell" [I.iv.11-19]). Richard's gift of life to the Groom is the only gift he bestows, and it comes as his murderer presses toward his cell. For Richard, the perception of harmony comes only after he has wasted the chance to achieve it.

Richard's defection as sacramental king has denied sacrament to his kingdom, has led inevitably to the ritual stripping of his body politic by his body natural and from thence to the sacrilege of Exton's deed:

> Exton, thy fierce hand
> Hath with the King's blood stained the King's own land.
> (V.v.111)

The original murder—"all the precious liquor spilt" (I.ii.19)—culminates in the final murder:

> As full of valor as of royal blood!
> Both have I spilled; O would the deed were good!
> For now the devil, that told me I did well,
> Says that the deed is chronicled in hell.
> (V.v.114-17)

Richard Altick accurately notes the play's frequent use of "tongue," "mouth," "speech," and "word."[28] To his list must be added "breath," a word with perhaps even more profound implications than the others, since its use ranges from "the breath of kings" (I.iii.214) to the "breath of worldly men" (III.i.56). Like so many actions in this changing world, th' mere act of breathing is usually negative, predicting the expiration of the living principle of England, embodied in the transitional figure who will finally lie "all breathless" (V.vi.31):

The hopeless word of "never to return"
Breathe I against thee.

(I.iii.152-53)

What is thy sentence then but speechless death,
Which robs my tongue from breathing native breath.

(I.iii.171-72)

Thy word is current with him from my death,
But dead, thy kingdom cannot buy my breath.

(I.iii.230-31)

To breathe the abundant dolor of the heart.

(I.iii.256)

Gaunt. Will the King come, that I may breathe my last
        In wholesome counsel to his unstaid youth?
York. Vex not yourself, nor strive not with your breath;
        For all in vain comes counsel to his ear.

(II.i.1-4)

And sighed my English breath in foreign clouds,
Eating the bitter bread of banishment . . .

(III.i.20-21)

And fight and die is death destroying death,
Where fearing dying pays death servile breath.

(III.ii.184-85)

Thou kill'st me in his life; giving him breath,
The traitor lives, the true man's put to death.

(V.iii.72-73)

The constant linkage of "breath" with "death" seems more
than a necessary rhyme sounding within isolated parts of the
play. Mowbray, Gaunt, Carlisle, and York all use the rhyme,
reminding us that the kingdom is like the Gaunt described by
the Duchess of Gloucester: "and though thou livest and
breathest/ Yet art thou slain in him" (I.ii.24-25). "Thou dost
consent/ In some large measure to thy father's death," she
continues (I.ii.25-26). Richard can respond to dying Gaunt by
claiming that "I am in health, I breathe, and see thee ill"
(II.i.92), can argue that "the breath of worldly men cannot
depose/ The deputy elected by the Lord" (III.i.56-57), yet

soon says "with mine own breath release all duteous vows . . .
For I have given my soul's consent/ T' undeck the pompous
body of a king" (IV.i.209, 248-49). Yet Richard "all breathless" removes the kingdom's power to breathe again, as
Henry IV will tell us in the ambiguous opening of his play:

> So shaken as we are, so wan with care,
> Find we a time for frighted peace to pant
> And breathe short-winded accents of new broils
> To be commenc'd in strands afar remote.
>
> (*I Henry IV*: I.i.1-4)

Henry's futile effort to mitigate his usurpation will be the
theme of "the very latest counsel/ That ever I shall breathe"
(*II Henry IV*: IV.v.182-83). "Such is the breath of kings," he
had said, long before, of a different king, of a king and a
world he was to help render "breathless."

The play's final scene is the familiar patterned sequence in
which the ruler receives the series of reports that tie up all
loose threads, or in which a quick series of events resolves all
remaining plot complexities. As in *King Lear,* where a series
of events seems to validate "this judgement of the heavens"
(V.iii.231), so in *Richard II* a series of reports seemingly confirms Bolingbroke's security as king. Bolingbroke's mag-
nanimous pardoning of Carlisle further burnishes the new
king's crown. It seems an auspicious beginning, but the scene
represents a series of false codas. As Lear enters with the
body of Cordelia, so Exton enters with the body of Richard,
a "buried fear" (V.vi.31) whose vibrations will shake
Bolingbroke's reign. In the world of *King Lear* the dead
Cordelia is the denial of any positive issue from the profound education of Lear; in Henry IV's world, the dead
Richard represents the resolution of one dilemma through
the introduction of another. Bolingbroke's good fortune and
magnanimity are transformed into condemnation as he at last
enters the guilty world toward which he has been pressing
from the first. Kingly largess suddenly becomes condemnation:

Exton, I thank thee not; for thou hast wrought
A deed of slander with thy fatal hand
Upon my head and all this famous land.*

(V.vi.34-36)

He could preside successfully over a trial (IV.i) similar to that
which Richard had had to mitigate and avoid, because
Bolingbroke was not guilty of Gloucester's blood. He could
oversee a series of quick and crown-confirming victories.
Now the very guilt he assigned to Mowbray at the beginning
("blood, like sacrificing Abel's"[I.i. 104]) and to Exton at the

---

*While Bolingbroke accepts his guilt, since the "deed" materialized from out of
his "own mouth" (V.vi.37), the story of Exton, Richard, and Bolingbroke is clearly
analogous to that of "an Amalekite," Saul and David, as depicted in the Homily on
"Obedience to Rulers and Magistrates":

> When an Amalekite . . . had killed King Saul, hee went to David, supposing to
> have had great thankes for his message that he had killed David's deadly
> enemy, and therefore he made great haste to tell to David the chaunce, bring-
> ing with him King Saul's crowne that was upon his head, and his bracelet that
> was upon his arm, to perswade his tidings to bee true. But godly David was so
> farre from rejoycing at this newes, that immediately and foorthwith hee rent
> his clothes off his backe, hee mourned and wept, and said to the messenger,
> How is it that thou wast not afraid to lay thy hands on the Lords annointed to
> destroy him? And by and by David made one of his servants kill the mes-
> senger, saying, Thy blood bee on thine owne head, for thine own mouth hath
> testified and witnessed against thee, granting that thou hast slaine the Lords
> annointed.

The story reflects the heinousness of killing *any* king: "it is an intolerable ignorance,
madnesse, and wickednesse for subjects to make any murmuring, rebellion, resistance, or withstanding, commotion, or insurrection against their most deare and
most dread Soveraigne Lord and king, ordained and appointed of God's goodnes
for their commodity, peace, and quietnesse." Whatever solution there may be to the
problem of a bad king, Bolingbroke's is not viable. Bolingbroke had been divided
from his body politic—but in assuming the kingship and having Richard killed, he
merely *deepens* the division.
    While Gaunt's reluctance to "lift/ An angry arm against . . . His deputy anointed in
His sight" (I.ii.38-41) is the "medieval" point of view in the play, it is clearly sound
Elizabethan doctrine as well, as the Homily of Obedience makes clear: "David might
have killed his enemie King Saul," but prays instead, "keepe me that I lay not my
hand upon him, seeing he is the anoynted of the Lord." Nothing justifies "any insurrection, sedition, or tumults, either by force of armes (or otherwise) against the
annointed of the Lord, or any of his officers: But wee must in such case patiently
suffer all wrongs, and injuries, referring the judgement onely to God." One must
wonder how Essex's followers could have considered *Richard II* as a justification for
rebellion, particularly since the Homily against Rebellion which, with the Homily of
Obedience, converges so prominently with the doctrinal context of the play, was
written in 1571, specifically to prevent rebellions like those led by Northumberland
and by Westmoreland in 1569. Bolingbroke had been warned by York that "the
heaven's are o'er our heads" (III.iii.17) and had claimed not to "oppose . . ./ Against
their will" (III.iii.18-19). In *one* sense his disclaimer is valid, yet he is a participant in
events that do destroy his country's sacramental vitality, that insist on the development of a new order predicated on necessity, no longer within any supernatural
context, except in the public rhetoric of Henry IV and Henry V. The will of heaven
becomes anachronistic and irrelevant in the new world that pulls Bolingbroke forward even as he presses toward it.

end ("With Cain go wander through the shades of night" [V.vi.42]) is his:

> Lords, I protest, my soul is full of woe
> That blood should sprinkle me to make me grow.
>
> (V.vi.45-46)

The blood that has stained the land now tinges the human embodiment of that land. Bolingbroke is now part of the garden whose corruption began with the murder of Gloucester and is completed with the murder of Richard. But this justice of the heavens echoes in negative overtones of Baptism and the Eucharist. Redemptive rituals bring solace, not "woe" to the "soul." Even for the all-sufficient Bolingbroke, "woe" becomes the sum of his inwardness. In attempting to restore his own body politic, Bolingbroke has been forced to become king and, in the process, has suffered a division deeper than he had as duke. He will grow (he is no Macbeth; although troubled like Macbeth with fits, his line will not be extirpated), but he is forced into the role of a kingly hypocrite:

> Come, mourn with me for what I do lament,
> And put on sullen black incontinent . . .
> March sadly after; grace my mournings here
> In weeping after this untimely bier.
>
> (V.vi.48-52)

The only ritual available to the world of the play is a funeral, whose chief mourner "did wish" for the very death he now sincerely mourns. If this was a tragic world, it now moves toward the ambiguous, dilemma-filled world of the history play, whose dialectic, as Rossiter says, is "ambivalence."[29] Ritual, like Richard, lies "all breathless."

In giving up his throne, Richard achieves a revenge against Bolingbroke. He continues to be revenged, posthumously, throughout the reign of Henry IV and even unto the night before Agincourt. The throne is now Bolingbroke's, but with it go few of the advantages that Richard inherited and squandered. With it go all of the disadvantages attendant on the killing of even a bad king. Although Bolingbroke projects

a crusade, his plight is clearly that which he predicted when
he washed the blood of Bushy and Green "from off [his]
hands" (III.i.5-6)—the plight of Pilate:

> I'll make a voyage to the Holy Land,
> To wash this blood off from my guilty hand.
>
> (V.vi.49-50)

The projected crusade never occurs, of course, and later
we find that even *it* was politically motivated. Bolingbroke's
immediate announcement of a crusade could be considered
as a panicky effort to move back inside the discarded sacramental system. As developed, the crusade is deferred from
political necessity; as finally defined, it is merely another
political device. Whatever it may have been at the moment of
Bolingbroke's announcement, the crusade takes on an inevitably political coloration as it is absorbed within the momentum of Bolingbroke's political world. It moves from sacramental possibilities while the memory of them was still green
to a mere reflex of politics. As the meaning of the world
changes, the meanings of past motivations must also change,
altered or rationalized to conform to the new order pressing
outward from the deposition of the old, reshaping the past as
it creates its future. Piety in the history plays that follow is
subordinate to politics; ritual belongs to the world destroyed
by the strange cooperation of Richard and his rival. Ceremony is empty or worse than empty; it becomes "poison'd
flattery," as Henry V says (IV.i.268).

Richard's defection would have required *some* response, as
even Gaunt admits, and was calculated to pull Bolingbroke's
ambition into the vacuum. That Bolingbroke becomes
Richard's victim suggests that his career will be nontragic, a
king struggling through a bewildering and debilitating world
of deceptive appearances and venomous jealousies. Ritual becomes the invention of men—Hal imitating the sun, Henry
IV projecting a crusade for political purposes, Falstaff imitating a king, or—as in the cases of the corpse of Hotspur and
the capture of Coleville—a military hero, Henry V translating
Falstaff's interruption into the high point of his coronation.
Ritual will no longer be the transmitter of deeper spiritual

mysteries as it was in the world John of Gaunt recalls, before the murder of Gloucester, the leasing out of England, the precedent-destroying seizure of Bolingbroke's inheritance. These events drain the "holy mystery" from England's king and soil, forcing ritual to become negative, a trial by combat to become a perversion of justice, pragmatically necessary perhaps, but a disruption of the deeper necessities inherent in the world order. That order itself is thwarted into irrelevancy by the denial of its ritual expression.

Ritual thus becomes anti-ritual, as in the Deposition scene, a stripping away of meaning toward negation and loss of identity that reverses the Communion Service's stripping away of guilt toward completion of identity in Christ. The world of *Richard II* plunges away from larger, more comprehensive meanings, divorces itself from mystery, and narrows to the sublunary politics of ambitious men. Whether or not *Richard II* qualifies as a tragedy, it suggests how ritual "works" in tragedy. Shakespeare's preoccupation with ritual and its representation in the tragic world, which contacts the supernature negatively, which alienates itself from controlling and more comprehensive orders, visible and invisible, was to wait while he pursued the political careers of Henry IV and Henry V, but was to emerge profoundly in *Hamlet* and the tragedies beyond.

NOTES TO CHAPTER 1: *Richard II*

1. Paul Tillich, *Love, Power, and Justice* (New York, 1954), p. 108. Cf. Pascal, *Pensées:* "The God of the Christians is a God of love and consecration, a God who makes them feel their utter misery and his infinite mercy, who unites himself with the ground of their being and fills them with humility, joy and love." Rudolph Bultmann provides an illuminating summary of the process of alienation *or* reconciliation, suggesting why Christ is not a tragic hero, yet seconding Saint Bernard in suggesting how tragedy can evolve in Christian terms: "Because man is a self who is concerned with his authenticity and can find it (as that of creature) only when he surrenders himself to the claim of God, there is the possibility of sin. Because from the beginning the claim of God has to do with man's authentic existence, there is the possibility of misunderstanding: the man who is called to authenticity falsely wills to be himself." *Existence and Faith* (Cleveland, 1960), pp. 156-57. St. Bernard's theology is discussed in Etienne Gilson, *The Spirit of Mediaeval Philosophy* (New York, 1936). For discussions of *hamartia*, see Roger L. Cox, *Between Earth and Heaven* (New York, 1969) pp. 1-26 and 27-70, Roy W. Battenhouse, *Shakespearean Tragedy: Its Art and Its Chris-*

tian Premises (Bloomington, Ind., 1969), pp. 204-66, and Harold S. Wilson, *On the Design of Shakespearian Tragedy* (Toronto, 1957), pp. 221-27.

2. Richard Sewell, *The Vision of Tragedy* (New Haven, Conn., 1959), p. 64.
3. M. D. H. Parker, *The Slave of Life* (London, 1955), p. 132.
4. Battenhouse, *Shakespearean Tragedy*, p. 264.
5. W. H. Auden, "The Christian Tragic Hero," *New York Times Book Review,* 16 December, 1945.
6. Francis Fergusson, "Introduction," *The Tempest* (New York, 1961), p. 14.
7. Northrop Frye, *A Natural Perspective* (New York, 1965), p. 81.
8. Robert H. West, *Shakespeare and the Outer Mystery* (Lexington, Ky., 1968).
9. Harold Goddard, *The Meaning of Shakespeare* (Chicago, 1951), pp. 151-52.
10. A. C. Bradley, *Oxford Lectures in Poetry* (London, 1909), p. 255.
11. Derek Traversi, *Shakespeare: From Richard II to Henry V* (Stanford, Calif., 1957), p. 20.
12. Ernst H. Kantorowicz, *The King's Two Bodies* (Princeton, N.J., 1957) p. 39.
13. *Ibid.*, p. 43.
14. *Ibid.*, p. 46.
15. *Ibid.*, p. 52.
16. *Ibid.*, p. 47.
17. M. M. Reese, *The Cease of Majesty* (New York, 1961), p. 248.
18. Kantorowicz, *King's Two Bodies*, p. 27.
19. R. J. Dorius, "A Little More than a Little," *SQ* 11 (1960): 19.
20. Reese, *Cease of Majesty*, p. 244.
21. Eric LaGuardia, "Ceremony and History: The Problem of Symbol from *Richard II* to *Henry V*," *Pacific Coast Studies in Shakespeare* (1965), p. 71.
22. *Ibid.*, p. 73.
23. *Ibid.*, p. 74.
24. Notably Dorius, "A Little More than a Little."
25. *Richard II*, ed. Matthew Black, p. 173, n23.
26. Richard D. Altick, "Symphonic Imagery in *Richard II*," *PMLA* 62 (1947), reprinted in *Richard II*, ed. Kenneth Muir (New York, 1963), pp. 199-234.
27. Traversi, *Shakespeare: From Richard II to Henry V*, p. 47.
28. Altick, "Symphonic Imagery."
29. A. P. Rossiter, *Angel with Horns* (London, 1961).

2

Hamlet

The soul was not only created capable, but also desirous, of heavenly things.

—St. Bernard

Our Redeemer held up *His Cross like a mouse-trap* to our captor, and baited it with his Blood.
—Peter Lombard, *Sentences* (III.19) (original italics)

The judgement of conscience [is] the judgement of God.
—William Perkins, *A Discourse of Conscience* (1596)

The world of *Hamlet,* like that of *Richard II,* is haunted by a secret murder committed before the play begins. In *Hamlet,* however, the ghost himself appears and that ghost is a king's. It seems very doubtful, in spite of the efforts of many scholars, that the Ghost can be defined in any precise theological context other than that he provides, but surely what he tells Hamlet about his murder is later corroborated by Claudius. The Ghost is an element of "the outer mystery" impinging upon a moral nature. Regardless of what the Ghost *is,* his effect on Hamlet is the dramatic imperative that must be charted. The Ghost's march along the parapets intersects a troubled human mind, and the question is not the precise identity of the Ghost but what Hamlet *makes* of him. As West suggests, "the dramatic bond in Shakespeare's

89

tragedies between human morality and the cosmic fact becomes uncertain, because we never know precisely what the cosmic fact is."[1] Regardless of what otherworldly visitors may come to Shakespeare's plays, the plays concentrate on the central *human* drama. Dramatically, it is Hamlet's problem—not the critics'—to determine the nature of the Ghost, and the answers he reaches lie within the tragedy, not in research on Elizabethan-Jacobean ghost lore or medieval theology.

The murder of King Hamlet, like Richard's murder of Gloucester, is endowed with the most fundamental of implications: "it hath the primal eldest curse upon it" (III.iii.37). Since it was regicide, and since the killer of the old king is now king, we can expect the world of the play to be cut loose from deeper sources of order. Like the world of *Richard II,* and of *Macbeth* after the murder of Duncan, the world of *Hamlet* has suffered an alienation *beyond* that of a "fallen world." Fallen man, his "poysoned nature," in the words of the Homily on the Sacrament, his "corrupt inclinations of the flesh," in the words of the Homily on Matrimony, his "nature, so corrupt and leavened with the sower bitterness of the poyson which we received by the inheritance of our old father Adam," in the words of the Homily of the Resurrection, his "manifolde synnes and wyckedness," is potentially redeemable through the cleansing and elevating power of the Eucharist. But the worlds of *Richard II, Macbeth,* and *Hamlet* drop below the already severely circumscribed postedenic premises, resembling the "notorious evil liver" who is denied Communion even before it begins. Each world suffers a *further* fall, that attendant on the "tragic world," as Richard continues to destroy the sources of kingship, as Macbeth compounds the sacrilegious murder of Duncan in a bloodbath, and as Hamlet, with a chance to redeem Denmark, fails, to wander toward the bloody destiny of Act V.

Hamlet and *Richard II* are perhaps the two Shakespearean plays most reflective of Keats's term "negative capability"—"when man is capable of being in uncertainties, mysteries, doubts, without any irritable reaching after fact and reason."

As I have suggested, however, judgment seems finally to rest on Richard's shoulders in his play. He is king. Some response was demanded by Richard's failures, whether Bolingbroke was waiting in the wings of history or not. "God's quarrel" descends to the competition of mere men. Richard's soul may "mount . . . on high" while his "gross flesh sinks downward" (V.v.112-13) to the earth to die, but the contrasting movements he describes signal the loss in England of that cosmic contact which he, its last possible exponent, claims to achieve in his dying breath. Richard predicts that "globe of sinful continents," Falstaff (*II Henry IV*: II.iv.309), thus, since Falstaff is a monstrous reflection of illness, the sickness pervading with increasing virulence the reign of Henry IV. That illness, however, is not imaged in the strange withering of bay trees—the natural manifestation of the loss of supernatural contact, or grace, to be reitereated profoundly within Macbeth's Scotland. The illness of Henry IV is focused in his own wasting away, in Falstaff's "water" (*II Henry IV*: I.ii.2), and in the feigned illnesses of such as the "crafty sick" Northumberland (*II Henry IV*: Induction, 37), the "deaf" Falstaff (*II Henry IV*: I.ii.78), Bullcalf with his "whoreson cold" (*II Henry IV*: III.ii.193), and Doll simulating pregnancy with a pillow, indeed "swol'n with some other grief" (*II Henry IV*: Induction, 13). Such efforts at evasion are signs of a sick kingdom, but they are not reflective of a deep natural disorder. The kingdom is sick in the modern sense; illness, real or faked, is part of the syndrome of an ineffective politics. The apparent exception, the portents preceding Henry IV's death, are to be read in the context of the death of kings—any king, even Bolingbroke. His already dying world reflects within itself a further death:

> Gloucester. The people fear me; for they do observe
>> Unfather'd heirs and loathly births of nature:
>> The seasons change their manners, as the year
>> Had found some months asleep and leap'd them over.
> Clarence. The river hath thrice flow'd, no ebb between,
>> And the old folk, time's doting chronicles,
>> Say it did so a little time before
>> That our great-grandsire, Edward, sick'd and died.
>>> (*II Henry IV*: IV.iv.121-28)

The metaphor of the river can be read as a prediction of Henry V's accession, as well as a commentary upon the death of his father:

> The tide of blood in me
> Hath proudly flow'd in vanity till now:
> Now doth it turn and ebb back to the sea,
> Where it shall mingle with the state of floods
> And flow henceforth in formal majesty.
> (*II Henry IV*: V.ii.129-33)

The interpenetration of outer mystery and the microcosm of England is seldom an issue or an image in the world that presses out from Richard's defection and inevitable deposition. Bolingbroke may have "met this crown" through "by-paths and indirect, crook'd ways" (*II Henry IV*: IV.iv.185-186), but those ways seemed inevitable once the sun of kingship veiled itself in the moisture of grief produced by the man within the robes. Henry IV's imagery of merely terrestrial progress and stealth is an accurate description of a world that sees the sun only as device, not as valid metaphor reflective of truth. Richard broke the metaphor.

Hamlet, faced with a world whose bridge between earth and the positive supernature has been shattered by regicide, might seem a victim of his world, as so many critics have claimed. Hamlet, however, might have built the bridge again. Untainted by anything save original sin (of which Hamlet is profoundly aware), his opportunity is greater than that of the doubly-stained Richard. Hamlet, after all, did not murder his father, although Freudian critics suggest that the wish was father to that thought. *Hamlet*, when placed against *Richard II*, shows us, again, a world whose rituals have gone awry. But it shows us further a tragic hero who creates an opportunity to redeem that world, an opportunity Richard never really has. Richard's crime is merely recapitulated and compounded in his play. Hamlet's tragic failure is projected against the potential "comic" ending he might have achieved, the possibilities against which the play that *does* develop must be measured.

Immediately, we discover the status of ritual in Claudius's Elsinore:

Francisco at his post. Enter to him Bernardo.
Ber. Who's there?
Fran. Nay, answer me. Stand, and unfold yourself.
Ber. Long live the king!

(I.i.1-3)

"*I'm* the sentry here—not you!!" says Francisco, who departs with the ominous observation that he is "sick at heart" (I.i.9). Bernardo's password becomes suddenly complicated a few lines later, when a "figure, like the King that's dead" (I.i.41) appears—long live *which* king? The Ghost emerges in defiance of the rites of passage designed to complete the transition from this world into the next:

thy canoniz'd bones, hearsed in death,
Have burst their cerements . . . the sepulchre
Wherein we saw thee quietly inurn'd,
Hath op'd his ponderous and marble jaws
To cast thee up again.

(I.iv.45-51)

The dead king appears not in his winding sheet, but in "complete steel" (I.iv.52), linking him with the ominous preparations for war described by Horatio and telling us that, while the external threat to Denmark may be removed, a man of war still walks within the kingdom, indeed stalks the very battlements of the royal palace.

Hamlet has already hinted that Denmark suffers from something even more fundamental than a "brother's murder" (III.iii.38). He sees the world as "an unweeded garden/ That grows to seed" (I.ii.135). While the image of a corrupted garden might be appropriate to a young man recently initiated into the world's imperfections, gazing back across his adolescence to the happy gardens of his youth, his words suggest a deeper alienation of Denmark from creativity, or, as the Second Part of the Homily, "How dangerous a thing it is to fall from God," suggests:

God at length doeth so forsake his unfruitful vineyard, that he will not onely suffer it to bring foorth weedes, bryers, and thornes, but also further to punish the unfruitfulnesse of it.

Hamlet's metaphor, a product of his "prophetic soul" (I.v.40), is confirmed by the Ghost's even more explicit evocations of Eden:

> It's given out that, sleeping in mine orchard,
> A serpent stung me; so the whole ear of Denmark
> Is by a forged process of my death
> Rankly abus'd; but know, thou noble youth,
> The serpent that did sting thy father's life
> Now wears his crown.
>
> (I.v.35-40)

The real process of old Hamlet's death—the pouring of poison into the ear—is equivalent to the serpent's action in Eden. Claudius's crime, then, is equated with man's first disobedience, the act that created the initial breach between man and God. Like the murder of Gloucester, Claudius's crime not only destroys the harmony of a perfect world, but, since it is also, like the killing of Gloucester, equated to the murder of Abel by Cain, is the first murder within a fallen world. Its fundamental implications could hardly be more emphatic.

Yet, even in this world, certain rhythms continue to function, if only at its outermost edges, at its intersection with "the outer mystery." The Ghost reports that he has been denied the final sacraments:

> Cut off even in the blossoms of my sin,
> Unhousel'd, disappointed, unaneal'd,
> No reck'ning made, but sent to my account
> With all my imperfections on my head.
>
> (I.iv.76-79)

It is hard to believe, with Battenhouse, that this is an "isolated gobbet of sacramental language."[2] The denial of sacrament to King Hamlet is a metaphor for its denial to the Denmark that survives him. The lines help explain the Ghost's emphasis on *his* murder: "But this most foul, strange, and unnatural" (I.iv.28), and suggest why he must "fast in fires/ Till the foul crimes done in [his] days of nature/ Are burnt and purg'd away" (I.iv.11-13). The invisible world of heaven, hell, and purgatory, the bourn lying, for better or for worse, behind the sacraments, works on, modulating its inevitable rhythms. Time, that crucial index of order in Shakespeare's plays, is punctually observed by the Ghost, both in his comings and goings:

> Thus twice before, and jump at this dead hour,
> With martial stalk hath he gone by our watch.
>
> (I.i.65-66)

> Ber. It was about to speak, when the cock crew.
> Hor. And then it started like a guilty thing
>   Upon a fearful summons.
>
> (I.i.147-49)

> And I with them the third night kept the watch;
> When, as they had deliver'd, both in time,
> Form of the thing, each word made true and good,
> The apparition comes.
>
> (I.iii.208-11)

> It lifted up it head and did address
> Itself to motion, like as it would speak;
> But even then the morning cock crew loud,
> And at the sound it shrunk in haste away,
> And vanish'd from our sight.
>
> (I.iii.216-20)

> I am thy father's spirit,
> Doom'd for a certain term to walk the night,
> And for the day confin'd to fast in fires . . .
>
> (I.v.9-11)

> But, soft! methinks I scent the morning's air.
> Brief let me be.
>
> (I.v.58-59)

>   Fare thee well at once!
> The glow-worm shows the matin to be near,
> And 'gins to pale his uneffectual fire.
> Adieu, adieu!
>
> (I.v.88-91)

Assuming the Ghost's version of his daily confinement to be valid, these are the rhythms of the purgatorial system to which he is bound. In the world of Denmark, however, he "usurp[s] this time of night" (I.i.46), and emphasizes the kingdom's removal from its place within the positive supernature:

> Some say that ever 'gainst that season comes
> Wherein our Saviour's birth is celebrated,
> The bird of dawning singeth all night long;
> And then, they say, no spirit can walk abroad;
> The nights are wholesome; then no planets strike,
> No fairy takes, nor witch hath power to charm,
> So hallow'd and so gracious is the time.

$$(\text{I.i.158-64})$$

Majestic as Marcellus's lyric is, it does *not* necessarily "sing . . .
out to suggest a beneficent spirit ruling over all these things,"
as David Daiches claims.[3] That a Ghost *has* appeared suggests that the times are neither hallowed nor gracious. Denmark lies beneath another season, "the season/ Wherein the
spirit held his wont to walk" (I.iv.5-6), and Horatio's is the
choric voice:

> in the gross and scope of my opinion,
> This bodes some strange eruption to our state.

$$(\text{I.i.68-69})$$

> the moist star
> Upon whose influence Neptune's empire stands
> Was sick almost to doomsday with eclipse.
> And even the like precurse of fierce events,
> As harbingers preceding still the fates
> And prologue to the omen coming on,
> Have heaven and earth together demonstrated
> Unto our climatures and countrymen.

$$(\text{I.i.118-25})$$

While an ominous figure walks above, Claudius, below, can
act like a king and call Hamlet's mourning of the king that's
dead a "fault to nature" (I.ii.102). But Claudius's is the prior
and more unnatural fault. He can act like the interpreter and
dispenser of the supernature he should represent—"Take thy
fair hour, Laertes. Time be thine" (I.ii.62)—but his murder
of the former king and usurpation of more than a time of
night has driven "time . . . out of joint" (I.v.189). The disastrous careers of the members of the Polonius family suggest
that ignorance of the king's crime produces no immunity
from its effects. Francisco, the soldier who sees kings only
from the ranks, is "sick at heart" (I.i.9). Those who shiver
through the first night's cold are aware of the disease in the

air, the "strange eruption," of which Horatio speaks. The
hidden "impostume" (IV.iv.27) kills all who adhere to
Claudius. Polonius dies in his service. Rosencrantz and Guildenstern present what they believe to be the king's commandment and find, probably to their brief bewilderment,
that the warrant is for their deaths. In a sense, the commission *is* that of Claudius; his followers are doomed. Rosencrantz himself unwittingly defines the effect of the murder of
a king, one that incorporates him and his twin, Guildenstern:

> The cease of majesty
> Dies not alone, but like a gulf, doth draw
> What's near it with it.
>
> (III.iii.15-17)

Claudius's murder of King Hamlet splits the lines of authority in Denmark, a version of the division typical of the tragic
world, whether in Lear's rending his kingdom asunder even
while retaining his regal additions, in Richard's willful fomenting of competition for his throne, or in the doubts that
gradually gather around Macbeth's crown. To whom does
one report in Elsinore? Horatio chooses to report to the
Prince:

> Break we our watch up; and, by my advice,
> Let us impart what we have seen to-night
> Unto young Hamlet; for, upon my life,
> This spirit, dumb to us, will speak to him.
> Do you consent we shall acquaint him with it,
> As needful in our loves, fitting our duty?
>
> (I.i.168-73)

The Ghost has come to see his son, one king invading the
realm of another. Ophelia reports Hamlet's antic appearance
in her chamber to her father, but thus assures her role as
pawn in Polonius's senile game of chess. Rosencrantz and
Guildenstern report to Claudius, but the fact that they were
"sent for" (II.ii.283) proves embarrassing once they find
Hamlet, whose "trust" (III.iv.203) they never achieve. Their
continued adherence to Claudius fractures their former links
with Hamlet, although it is hard to believe that such ciphers
were ever close to the Prince (Stoppard's play captures accu-

rately their existential inauthenticity). That the kingdom is
out of joint is not the fault of Rosencrantz and Guildenstern,
but the twin nonentities choose Claudius, oblivious to the call
of personal loyalty Horatio heeds. Nor is Horatio alone. Marcellus and Bernardo come to him initially, a prelude to
Horatio's going to Hamlet. Claudius never learns of the
Ghost's appearance, an extraordinary fact considering whose
guards these are.

Hamlet himself is well aware of the discrepancy between a
true king and the "player" king, Claudius. He makes the distinction between the king as body politic and as body natural,
granting Claudius the latter, denying him the former: "The
body is with the King, but the King is not with the body"
(IV.ii.29-30). Hamlet, indeed, finds a player king more
worthy than Claudius. The player, at least, does not *deny* his
fictional representation:

> He that plays the King shall be welcome;
> His majesty shall have tribute of me.
>
> (II.ii.313-14)

The lines point ahead to the "neglected tribute" of England
to Denmark's new King Claudius (III.i.178). King Hamlet
represented the union of the king's two bodies, and his very
appearance denies the fusion to Claudius. The dual lines of
authority are neatly summarized in Gertrude, who, unlike
Hamlet, cannot see the Ghost of her former husband during
the Closet scene, and who is forbidden by her son to go
again to her present husband's bed. In denying the old
king—one meaning of her inability to glimpse his image
—she is denied the new king. Gertrude loves her son, young
Hamlet, but has married this king, and when Hamlet presents her with the alternative of clinging to the memory of
one king or to the body natural of another, her heart is
"cleft . . . in twain" (IV.iv.156). Gertrude suffers the inner
divorce of the other characters—Ophelia "Divided from herself and her fair judgement" (IV.vi.85), Claudius, and ultimately Hamlet, each "a man to double business bound"
(III.iii.41). Claudius cannot fuse his "words" and "thoughts"
(III.iii.47-48). Hamlet is "From himself . . . ta'en away" and

becomes "of the faction that is wrong'd" by his *alter ego,* the non-Hamlet who has "hurt [his] brother" (V.ii.245-55). Gertrude dies by drinking poisoned wine prepared by Claudius for Hamlet. Her rejection of Claudius's "do not drink" (V.ii.301) might signal her allegiance to Hamlet *over* Claudius, but it is grimly appropriate that her toast to Hamlet allows her to be killed by Claudius. Laertes falls in with the king's plot and is killed in its execution; acting "almost 'gainst [his] conscience" (V.ii.306), he finds that "the foul practice [turns] itself on [him]" (V.ii.328-29). Claudius himself is "justly serv'd . . . [with] poison temp'red by himself" (V.ii.338-39). Since he serves himself, he too must die, victim of what he knew to be the deep division between his will and his soul, and of the divorce he has made between Denmark and the creative powers of the universe.

While such an account lays the blame for the tragedy at Claudius's feet, Hamlet clearly has a role in it. At the play's beginning, a representative of the outer mystery solicits his help in setting the time right:

My father's spirit in arms! All is not well . . .

(I.ii.255)

 Foul deeds will rise,
Though all the earth o'er whelm them, to men's eyes.

(I.ii.257-58)

Denmark's perimeters touch larger powers negatively. Things visible are signs of *foul* deeds, not emblems of spiritual health. The kingdom has entered, through the murder of its king, upon the anti-sacramental world of the tragedy:

The time is out of joint;—O cursed spite,
That ever I was born to set it right!

(I.v.189-90)

Hamlet receives not merely an injunction to revenge, but a larger and seemingly incompatible responsibility to realign the kingdom with its invisible spiritual reality. The great surrounding supernature has sent its ghostly emissary to request that Hamlet become a surrogate-king, assuming the role

Claudius can not fulfill. Hamlet is asked not merely to be an intermediary between divine power and the human state, but to *return* the latter to the aegis of the former. Such is the nature of his task as he himself expresses it in his despairing cry about time. Later, he will define himself even more explicitly—if ambiguously—as an instrument of larger forces:

> Heaven hath pleas'd it so,
> To punish me with this and this with me,
> That I must be their scourge and minister.
>
> (III.iv.173-75)

The task imposed upon him by the Ghost, however, would seem impossible, even if we consider merely Hamlet's temporal problem of dealing with Claudius. To move beyond that great problem, Hamlet is asked to restore ceremony's spiritual validity in a world where sacrament *must* be corrupt.

The Ghost's intrusion *would* be anti-sacramental in a Denmark aligned with supernature. As it is, the Ghost's punctuality and the larger issues of his mission indicate *his* alignment with universal rhythms, even if they involve the temporary pains of purgatory. Whatever he may be, the Ghost's appearance it not merely a product of his own volition; his time is controlled by wills other than his, and it is doubtful that they are of hell.

Regardless of the Ghost's residence, and regardless of the potential diabolism Hamlet ascribes to him (I.iv.40-42, II.ii.627-32, III.ii.87-89), corrupted rite in *Hamlet* emerges from the murder of the former king. The primary anti-sacrament within the early world of the play is the marriage of Claudius and Gertrude, tinged as it is by the memory of a recent funeral. Claudius suggests a deep division within his royal person—not between the king's two bodies, but between two extremes of his body politic, which has so recently engaged in a state funeral and a state marriage:

> our sometime sister, now our queen,
> Th' imperial jointress of this warlike state,
> Have we, as 'twere with a defeated joy,—
> With one auspicious, and one dropping eye,

With mirth in funeral and with dirge in marriage,
In equal scale weighing delight and dole,
Taken to wife.

(I.ii.8-14)

Hamlet ascribes the marriage to a cynical economics:

Thrift, thrift, Horatio! The funeral bak'd meats
Did coldly furnish forth the marriage tables.

(I.ii.180-81)

His sentiment is echoed by the Player-Queen:

The instances that second marriage move
Are base respects of thrift, but none of love.

(III.ii.192-93)

Alone and more despairing, Hamlet sees the marriage as an absolute indictment of his mother:

A little month, or e'er those shoes were old
With which she followed my poor father's body,
Like Niobe, all tears,—why she, even she—
O God! a beast, that wants discourse of reason,
Would have mourn'd longer—married with mine uncle.

(I.ii.147-51)

Marriage, to Hamlet, has become bestial, as the Prayer Book admonishes it should not be: "[Matrimonie] is not to be enterprised, nor taken in hande unadvisedly, lightly, or wantonly, to satisfye mennes carnall lustes and appetytes, lyke brute beastes that have no understanding." Gertrude has denied her role as a sacramental component in a ceremony "instytuted of God in Paradise, in the time of mannes innocencie, signifying unto us the mystical union that is betwixt Christ and his Churche." In marrying Claudius, her husband's brother, she commits incest: "our sometime sister, now our queen": "O, most wicked speed, to post/ With such dexterity to incestuous sheets!" (I.ii.156-57). Her adultery represents a sacrilege against her first marriage:

Ay, that incestuous, that adulterate beast . . .
   won to his shameful lust
The will of my most seeming-virtuous queen.
O Hamlet, what a falling-off was there!

From me, whose love was of that dignity
That it went hand in hand even with the vow
I made to her in marriage . . .

(I.v.42-50)

Hence she echoes the Adam-Cain dimension of Claudius's crime—an offense against an institution of "mannes innocencie in Paradise" compounded by further transgression after the Fall. Regardless of Hamlet's psychological involvement with his mother, he is characterized as deeply troubled by her remarriage and seems to recognize that the new marriage imposes upon itself negative vectors dictated by forces deeper than an individual will or wills: "It is not, nor it cannot, come to good" (I.ii.158).

Contemplating the marriage, Hamlet seems to see himself as part of an inevitable flow toward disaster. Soon, the Ghost imposes upon him the task of revenging a "foul, strange, and unnatural" murder, *and* of relieving Denmark of the disease spreading outward from the crime. The dual responsibilities seem contradictory: to extirpate Claudius (an incestous, adulterous, usurping regicide, who also happens to be a king whose legitimacy is unquestioned even to the end of the play, by everyone except the Ghost, Hamlet and, finally perhaps, by Horatio) and to restore Denmark to its sacramental unity. Indeed, Hamlet seems called upon to "take arms against a sea of troubles" (III.i.59)—a metaphor of impossibility—and to "end them" (III.i.60) only through his death. But it is important to note that the Ghost never says "Kill Claudius":

But, howsoever thou pursuest this act,
Taint not thy mind, nor let thy soul contrive
Against thy mother aught. Leave her to heaven,
And to those thorns that in her bosom lodge
To prick and sting her.

(I.v.84-88)

The very words separating Gertrude from Claudius's fate, whatever that may be, give Hamlet wide latitude in the pursuit of "this act." He is enjoined to perform the act while remaining free from guilt.* To rush down and run Claudius

*Most critics see the Ghost's "Taint not thy mind" as part of a parallel construction concerning Hamlet's approach to Gertrude. Folio's punctuation, however, allows

through might not save Hamlet from the tainting of his mind. Hamlet must align the action with the positive world order represented by the Ghost. If the Ghost were a devil out for souls, his emphasis on the perfection of his own marriage vow, his predication of Gertrude's guilt, combined with his hope for her ultimate salvation, would have to be fitted into the most oblique and diabolic of deceptions. But how can Hamlet frame a revenge that meshes with Christian practice? Again, the seeming impossibility of his task is emphasized.

We cannot assume, however, that "act" and "revenge" are necessarily equivalent to the *killing* of Claudius, particularly since the Ghost himself calls "Murder most foul, as in the best it is," even while underlining the deeper horror of his own demise. And, since his murder was regicide, constituted even more specific sacrilege in the denial of last rites, and incorporated the breaking of the most solemn of vows, both to a king and those of matrimony, along with adultery, incest, and usurpation into its motivation, it is hard to write the Ghost off as too vindictive, as Professor Battenhouse does.[4] The Ghost has come to enlist a minister, and must be granted some indignation as he makes his case against Claudius. One has only to suggest that, assuming that this *is* a shape from purgatory (and the Ghost's intimate acquaintance with and aversion to his "prison house" is devastatingly convincing on stage, at least), he has simply not completely purged his earthly effects, hence displays bitter passion in recalling the crimes committed against him. He is undergoing a purgation in the context of eternity similar to that which will be experienced on the temporal plane by, say, the Gentlemen of *Love's Labour's Lost* during their year's exile, designed to prepare them for marriage, as purgatory prepares for heaven.

"Act," indeed, will become operative in a context that fulfills the staggering requirements of Hamlet's task. While he admits that he is hardly Hercules (I.ii.153), he does develop a potential solution to the complex of problems facing him.

the clause to be considered a separate injunction pertaining to Hamlet. See, for example, Roy W. Battenhouse, *Shakespearean Tragedy* (Bloomington, Ind., 1969), pp. 237-45.

"Howsoever thou pursuest this act" becomes "When thou seest that act afoot" (III.ii.83):

>   I have heard
> That guilty creatures sitting at a play
> Have by the very cunning of the scene
> Been struck so to the soul that presently
> They have proclaim'd their malefactions;
> For murder, though it have no tongue, will speak
> With most miraculous organ.
>
> (II.ii.617-23)

Hamlet provides the rationale behind his play—as certain other Shakespearean manipulators do not[5]—thus helping us to recognize the crucial inconsistency between his plans and their execution. In planning "The Murder of Gonzago," Hamlet suggests that revenge is not its ultimate aim. He adumbrates a play whereby Claudius's *soul* ("the conscience of the King" [II.ii.634]) will be so worked that he must confess publicly—"presently" (meaning "at once") to "proclaim" (suggesting public declaration) his "malefactions," not merely reveal his guilt to an intently watching Hamlet. He has designed a play that *will* torture Claudius with guilt, but that will give that guilt release, as outlined in the Homily of Repentence, which defines the first two parts of repentance as "contrition of the heart" and "an unfained confession and acknowledging of our sinnes." Hamlet himself solicits the larger powers that have enlisted him, powers that man alone cannot control. Murder has been revealed to Hamlet; perhaps Claudius's knowledge of it will betray itself as well, no matter how the king tries to overwhelm it before the eyes of man. The Ghost's narrative evokes his own horror in the telling of it, and Hamlet's. Could the same response be predicted in Claudius, observing a dramatic version of the Ghost's story? The inner mystery of the soul of man is the sector coinciding with the outer mystery of the universe from which the Ghost has come. The sacramental possibilities of the play-within are emphasized by Hamlet's use of the word *miraculous* and, later in the soliloquy, *conscience*. But, as Francis Fergusson says, "if [Hamlet] stumbles on the theater as a means of realizing his vision . . . he does not clearly un-

derstand what he has accomplished."⁶ At the end of his so-
liloquy, Hamlet, reduces his conception to a testing of the
Ghost's validity, not a means of fulfilling the mission the
Ghost has imposed on him:

> The spirit that I have seen
> May be the devil; and the devil hath power
> T' assume a pleasing shape; yea, and perhaps
> Out of my weakness and melancholy,
> As he is very potent with such spirits,
> Abuses me to damn me. I'll have grounds
> More relative than this.
>
> (II.ii.627-33)

Hamlet further reduces the play's potentiality to the level of
a duel between himself and Claudius:

> I'll observe his looks.
> I'll tent him to the quick; if he but blench,
> I know my course.
>
> (II.ii.625-27)

His play will suffer at its climactic moment from just such a
reduction. His personal feelings will cancel the higher vision
he himself has defined.

That Hamlet does not clearly understand the potential of
his creation is suggested again in his instructions to Horatio
immediately prior to the play. He speaks of Claudius's "occulted guilt" unkenneling itself (III.ii.85-86), leaping forth
like an animal from a hiding place. The strength of the
metaphor suggests more than a mere private revelation.
Then, however, Hamlet reverts to a belief that the play will
provide not public exposure but mere facial expressions
meaningful to those anticipating them:

> For I mine eyes will rivet to his face,
> And after we will both our judgements join
> To censure of his seeming.
>
> (III.ii.90-92)

The *real* possibility of Claudius's guilt reduces itself to "seeming." Apparently Hamlet believes that Claudius may escape
detection by the uninformed. If so, his play will be a disaster;

if not, if the play can force Claudius publicly to proclaim his malefactions, it will be a triumph. But although he has expressed the latter possibility, Hamlet views the play primarily as a prelude to further action ("If he but blench,/ I know my course"), not as a vehicle relieving him of the *necessity* for further action. We should enter the play scene aware of its possible lines of development: an innocent Claudius, perhaps offended by the subject matter, but observing the complete performance calmly; a guilty Claudius controlling himself under the pressure of the play; a guilty Claudius revealing his guilt by facial expression; or a guilty Claudius, unable to contain his guilt, confessing publicly. The latter two are the operative possibilities, because they have been explicitly predicated by Hamlet. We are prepared also for Hamlet to be a *solely* passive, if intent, observer of Claudius observing the play. Depending on which way the scene develops, it will embrace one of the dichotomies represented in the Ghost, who may be a "spirit of health or goblin damn'd" (I.iv.40), who may bring "airs from heaven or blasts from hell" (I.iv.41), whose intentions may be "wicked or charitable" (I.iv.42). Events following the play suggest that the meaning of the Ghost *is* determined by the play, but not as Hamlet claims it is.

Has Shakespeare shown Claudius's character to be susceptible to open confession? A Iago, a Iachimo, or an Edmund, for example, might be expected to sit through the performance ostensibly unmoved. Shortly before the play, however, Claudius reveals a conscience to be caught. Polonius speaks of "devotion's visage/ And pious action" with which "we do sugar o'er/ The devil himself" (III.i.47-49). The sententiae draw a tortured aside from Claudius:

> How smart a lash that speech doth give my conscience!
> The harlot's cheek, beautied with plast'ring art,
> Is not more ugly to the thing that helps it
> Than is my deed to my most painted word.
> O heavy burden!
>
> (III.i.50-54)

Claudius echos the Communion's General Confession: "The

remembraunce of [our misdoinges] is grevous unto us: the burthen of theim is intollerable." As Harold Goddard says, "The character of Claudius fits the situation [of Hamlet's play] as if explicitly created for it ... a man conscious of his sin and longing to be rid of it—a fit subject for the redemptive power of art"[7]—and, indeed, a fit subject for the sacramental imperative underlying Hamlet's play. To claim that a play cannot have this effect on a guilty creature is to deny not only Hamlet's own words, but the ritual sources and ritual power of drama, the power of which Shakespeare has already shown such an awareness in the comedies, in evoking, for example, the truth resident in the hearts of Beatrice and Benedick through staged scenes on which they are allowed to eavesdrop. It is to ignore what Shakespeare is soon to do with Macbeth in the Banquet scene, where a ghostly pantomime evokes virtual confession of murder from that sin-haunted king: "Thou canst not say I did it" (III.iv.50). Dramatic presentation *per se* partakes of a power more likely to evoke emotional response than other *genre*, as the player's breakdown before a mere speech from a play suggests. Norman Holland defines the psychological response of spectator to play much as Hamlet had in his "guilty creatures" speech; indeed, he paraphrases Hamlet's definition of drama:

> By projecting what is in the characters outward into externally visible events and actions, a play paves the way for the audience's own act of projection. We find in the external reality of a play what is hidden in ourselves. Drama shows virtue her own feature, scorn her own image, and the very age and body of the time his form and pressure. Watching a set of events in a play feels, for this reason, very different from reading them in a novel.[8]

Holland's suggestion would seem to be even *more* applicable to a play specifically designed to represent visually the "occulted guilt" lying beneath the coats of Claudius's "most painted" words. O. B. Hardison, writing of the famous Townswoman of Lynn, who confessed to the murder of her husband during a performance of *Fair Francis*, suggests that "the psychology underlying [such instances] is plain enough. The perpetrator of an undiscovered crime is troubled by a

guilty conscience. He is in torment. Confession, the only way
to relieve the pain, is prevented by his fear of the consequences. Seeing the crime enacted on the stage can make the
pangs of conscience so intense that the need for relief via
confession becomes stronger than the fear of exposure. The
confession has two beneficial results. First, a crime is solved
and a criminal punished. Society is strengthened, if only minutely, by the clearing up of an injustice."[9] In the hypothetical case of Claudius's confession, but in the not hypothetical
play *beyond* the "Murder of Gonzago," the benefits to society
would be immense. The results of delaying the exposure of
an evildoer are outlined in the "Sermon on Charitie," in
words that echo Rosencrantz on kings ("like a gulf, doth
draw/ What's near with it"):

> And such rebukes and punishments of them that offend, must
> be done in due time, lest by delay, the offenders fall headlong
> into all manner of mischiefe, and not onely be evill themselves,
> but also doe hurt unto many man, drawing other by their evill
> example, to sinne and outrage after them.

All the deaths within the play follow the play-within. It is a
potential watershed of Denmark's redemption, even for the
saving of Claudius's soul, or the prelude to bloodshed for
almost all those, guilty or free, who inhabit the world of the
play, except for the impassive Horatio and the distant adven-
turer, Fortinbras.

G. R. Hibbard claims that "no theater audience, surely, has
ever envisaged this possibility [that the play-within could
cause Claudius "to reveal his guilt in public"]."[10] But against
this contention, through which Hibbard assumes the persona
of every spectator of every performance of *Hamlet* since the
dawn of the seventeenth century (how many spectators would
that be?), we must place the contemporary account of the
Townswoman of Lynn from which Hamlet draws in his
"guilty creatures" speech, a speech that does appear in the
received text and that might be available to an alert theater
audience.*

---

*The audience of Sir Laurence Olivier's movie version must be included within
Hibbard's sweeping generalization, but that is because Sir Laurence omitted the so-
liloquy, running instead through a midnight palace, shouting "The play's the thing/
Wherein I'll catch the conscience of the King!"

If Claudius is fit for redemption, what of Hamlet? Has he been shown to be capable of an attitude that might permit his play to redeem rather than revenge? He exhibits such an attitude on the arrival of the players. When news of their approach reaches him, he shows, according to Rosencrantz, "a kind of joy/ To hear of it" (III.i.18). He greets them graciously:

> You're welcome, masters, welcome all. I am glad to see thee well. Welcome, good friends. (II.ii.440-41)

He asks Polonius to "see the players well bestow'd" (II.ii.546), and when the counselor replies that he "will use them according to their desert" (II.ii.552), Hamlet exclaims:

> God's bodykins, man, better. Use every man after his desert and who should scape whipping? Use them after your own honour and dignity. The less they deserve, the more merit is in your bounty. Take them in. (II.ii.553-58)

"God's bodykins"—the bread of the Communion. And while the phrase was an expletive, not necessarily to be construed in its religious context, the words that follow are precisely in the spirit of the sacrament of forgiveness, consonant with the Prayer of Humble Access, which immediately precedes the priest's breaking of the bread, and with the Elizabethan "Prayer for true repentence and mercie": "be not angry with us for ever, for our great and manifold sins, neither deale with us according to our desertes."[11] The amount of "merit" in God's "bounty" is, of course, as the prayer suggests, "great and infinite."

Hamlet has risen above the cynicism and despair that have characterized him thus far. His melancholy drops like a robe from his shoulders; we glimpse him as he might have been had not events in Denmark thwarted his creative drives. Suddenly he is an artist:

> You could for a need, study a speech of some dozen or sixteen lines which I would set down and insert in't, could you not? (II.ii.565-68)

"Aye, my lord" (II.ii.569), replies the First Player. Hamlet tells him to follow Polonius, "and look you, mock him not" (II.ii.571). While the line could be delivered with an ironic wink, it would seem that the man Hamlet has mocked so mercilessly becomes subject to Hamlet's charity. For a moment, free of negation, he follows his own advice about using men better than they deserve. He loses himself in the coming of the players, and, in losing himself, finds himself. He also finds a potential solution to his vast external problems——Claudius and Denmark.

The coming of the players is itself another aspect of the displacement of proper value in the kingdom—"their inhibition comes by means of the late innovation" (II.ii.346-47)—and may hint at Hamlet's substitution in the Play scene of the action of the child actors, who "cry out on the top of the question," for his "wonted place" (II.ii.353-55), the maturity represented by the adult troupe. They have been replaced by children who themselves align their high voices *against* their own interests, for they "exclaim against their own succession" (II.ii.367-68). They are the source of an artistically destructive controversy, which foreshadows Hamlet's conflict before his play: "There was for awhile no money bid for argument unless the poet and player went to cuffs in the question" (II.ii.371-73). The substitution of immaturity for wisdom is exemplified by Polonius, once "accounted a good actor" (III.ii.105), now a "great baby" again (II.ii.399), an emblem of the shortsighted child actor whose voice will deepen and exclude him from his profession. But, again, the equation points at Hamlet as well. He sees the situation of the now itinerant "tragedians of the city" (II.ii.342) as directly analogous to the "late innovation" Denmark has suffered:

> It is not strange; for mine uncle is King of Denmark, and those that would make mows at him while my father lived, give twenty, an hundred ducats apiece for his picture in little. (II.ii.380-83)

Claudius is equated with the children, King Hamlet with the exiled tragedians. The strategy for the "Murder of Gonzago" may have its genesis in the latter equation, but Hamlet, who *still* makes mouths at Claudius, typically draws no lesson for

himself out of the controversy described by Rosencrantz and
Guildenstern.

The Player's speech offers a subtle commentary on the
question of Hamlet and revenge, by showing the spectator
one thing and Hamlet another, thus preparing us for
Hamlet's crucial inability to recognize the soul-coercing potentiality he assigns to "The Murder of Gonzago." Hamlet
begins with a misquotation:

> "The rugged Pyrrhus, like th' Hyrcanian beast,"
> —'tis not so, it begins with Pyrrhus—
> "The rugged Pyrrhus, he whose sable arms. . ."
>
> (II.ii.472-74)

Pyrrhus, as Arthur Johnston says, "unites in his person the
avenger of Paris' double crime of lust and murder of Pyrrhus'
father, as Hamlet is the avenger of Claudius' double
crime."[12] The parallel is unmistakable, and, significantly,
Hamlet's slip at the beginning of the speech likens Pyrrhus to
the tiger, the beast the revenger must become. Both Pyrrhus
and Hamlet are clothed in black. At the play, Hamlet links
himself with the sable-armed Pyrrhus: "Nay then, let the
devil wear black for I'll have a suit of sables" (III.ii.137-38).
By then, Hamlet and Pyrrhus are becoming the same person;
Hamlet is merging with Lucianus's "thoughts black"
(II.ii.266), and reflecting, in his surrender to hatred,
Claudius's "bosom black as death" (III.iv.67), as his conception of his production continues to sink from its initial elevated premises. Hamlet's inability to grasp the equation between himself and Pyrrhus renders him susceptible to it.
Later, when it is too late, he *will* glimpse the parallel between himself and Laertes: "For by the image of my cause, I
see/ The portraiture of his" (V.ii.77-78).

Hamlet wonders whether the speech "live[s] in [the]
memory" of the player. We are reminded, perhaps, of
Hamlet's "Remember thee!/ Ay, thou poor ghost, while
memory holds a seat/ In this distracted globe. Remember
thee!" (I.v.94-96). While a subtle critic might try to create a
further link between the earlier speech and the later (via
"globe," "Hercules," "Hercules and his load," and the actors

themselves), it suffices that the Player's speech is like the
Ghost's revelation—a vivid glimpse of a past moment when a
damned deed was perpetrated. In each narrative, a prone
and defenseless king is killed. The political ramifications for
Denmark in the death of King Hamlet are echoed by the
linked destructions of Priam and Troy:

> Th' unnerved father falls. Then senseless Illium,
> Seeming to feel the blow, with flaming top
> Stoops to his base.
>
> (II.ii.496-98)

Each narrative is associated with a queen who weeps for her
dead husband—Hecuba, "With bisson rheum" (II.ii.529), and
Gertrude, "like Niobe, all tears" (II.ii.149). One of the inferences would seem to be that if Hamlet should pursue
Pyrrhus's course, he will come to resemble *Claudius,* as in
significant ways he will.

Hamlet stops his recitation at the point where Pyrrhus
seeks Priam:

> "Roasted in wrath and fire,
> And thus o'er-sized with coagulate gore,
> With eyes like carbuncles, the hellish Pyrrhus
> Old grandsire Priam seeks."
> So, proceed you.
>
> (II.ii.483-87)

He loves the speech, yet, while he can express the motivation
for the killing of Priam, he does not continue to the portion
paralleling what Pyrrhus does and what Hamlet feels he must
do. Hamlet's halt may result, then, from his intuition that revenge as depicted in the Pyrrhus episode is a devilish activity.
Pyrrhus is "hellish" and Troy is wrapped in a "tyrannous and
damned light" (II.ii.482). As Pyrrhus is about to kill the prostrate Priam, he pauses:

> "So, as a painted tyrant, Pyrrhus stood,
> And like a neutral to his will and matter
> Did nothing."
>
> (II.ii.502-4)

His pause anticipates Hamlet's, standing over the kneeling

Claudius, when Hamlet himself defines the hellish nature of his revenge. Pyrrhus's momentary neutrality also defines the dilemma of Claudius at that later moment—the painted tyrant trapped between will and matter, who must mask his "deed" with his "most painted word" (III.i.53). Finally, as Hamlet lashes through the arras to kill Polonius after restraining his sword against Claudius, "so after Pyrrhus' pause/ Aroused vengeance sets him new awork" (II.ii.509-10). As Johnston says, "what is significant about the episode chosen to mirror the act that Hamlet is called to do is the reversal of emotional sympathy; the deed is one of terror, its perpetrator inhuman and brutalized. 'Roasted in wrath and fire' the 'hellish Pyrrhus' is damned."[13] Indeed, pity is evoked for Pyrrhus's victims, not only in the verse but in the actor's response to it. The death of a defenseless "king" (Hamlet's word for Duke Gonzago [III.ii.254]) is presented yet a third time, of course, in the play-within, precisely at the climax of the play-without. The Ghost's narrative and the Player's speech help focus that later moment, which, in turn, points ahead to Hamlet's killing of Claudius.

While the parallel between Pyrrhus and Hamlet seems clear, and while his stopping of his recitation suggests that intuitively he grasps it, Hamlet chooses to develop a correspondence between himself and the *Player,* a parallel which, as Johnston says, is "less immediately obvious" but which serves as "a spur to his own dulled sense of duty."[14] The Player's speech is itself interrupted as the Player becomes over-involved in his content. While Hamlet interprets the Player's reaction as a "getting into character" (cf. II.ii.579), it disturbs Polonius sufficiently to insist, "Pray you, no more" (II.ii.544), as he will later cry, "Give o'er the play" (III.ii.279). Hamlet might interpret the Player's emotional involvement as calling for *greater* control, but uses it as a mere hint of the hyperbolic response *he* should provide to a murder that his prophetic soul and the Ghost's story suggest is nonfictional:

> What's Hecuba to him, or he to Hecuba,
> That he should weep for her? What would he do,
> Had he the motive and the cue for passion
> That I have? He would drown the stage with tears

And cleave the general ear with horrid speech,
Make mad the guilty and appall the free,
Confound the ignorant, and amaze indeed
The very faculty of eyes and ears.

                                                    (II.ii.585-92)

Hamlet casts himself in the role of spectator to "The Murder
of Gonzago," yet his performance at the play will overflow its
prescribed dimensions and partake of the very loss of control
his "Hecuba" soliloquy says *should* be his response. As the
Player's gradual involvement with Hecuba brings Polonius's
interruption, so Hamlet's growing emotion will interrupt
"The Murder of Gonzago." Not only does Hamlet not
glimpse the parallel between himself and Pyrrhus, but he
employs the equation between himself and the Player as a
pretext for his own excessive vehemence, rather than as a
warning that he himself must control his role more carefully
than does the Player his. Significantly, Hamlet's soliloquy
after the Player's speech refutes the advice he later gives to
the players: "use all gently; for in the very torrent, tempest,
and, as I may say, the whirlwind of passion, you must acquire
and beget a temperance that may give it smoothness"
((III.ii.6-9). If the Player's function suited "with forms" his
conceit of Hecuba, Hamlet should be warned by his own "cue
for passion," which will indeed drive him out of control during "The Murder of Gonzago." Hamlet might further have
equated the Player's response ("Could force his soul so to his
own conceit" [II.ii.579]) to that he attributes to "guilty creatures sitting at a play," who "Have by the very cunning of the
scene/ Been struck so to the soul. . . ." Not only might Hamlet have seen in his response to the Player a warning to himself, but, in the Player's response to Hecuba, a possible index
to Claudius's reaction to "The Murder of Gonzago." Tragically, Hamlet's play will induce in *him* the effect he had suggested it might produce in Claudius. In a sense, Hamlet
forces *his* soul to his own conceit.

Yet the Player's speech has a strangely therapeutic effect
on Hamlet in spite of its ominous content and ignored warnings. The "dream of passion" (II.ii.578) seems to relieve
Hamlet of a conscious burden, as dreams sometimes do; he
seems to release his problem vicariously through Pyrrhus.

After the speech comes Hamlet's most charitable moment, and the speech motivates that potential instrument of redemption, Hamlet's play. Had Hamlet drawn the parallel between Pyrrhus and himself and rejected the conception of revenger represented by Pyrrhus, he might have seen his own play's possibilities more clearly.

While Hamlet expresses but does not develop his play's potentiality, it is also true that the echo of a former Hamlet, patron of actors and the arts, amateur performer and playwright, is overwhelmed by the realities of Elsinore. Between his plans for the play and its presentation comes the scene with Ophelia with its scathing misogyny. "I say, we will have no more marriages," he tells her (III.i.154), denying matrimony to himself as well as to Ophelia. The line predicts his denial to Claudius of the sacramental possibilities of his play, and his later attempt to deny salvation to the apparently praying king. Underlying his inability to find meaning in sacrament is his continuing cynicism at the marriage of Claudius and Gertrude, displayed again as he embarks involuntarily for England:

> Ham. Farewell, dear mother.
> King. Thy loving father, Hamlet.
> Ham. My mother. Father and mother is man and wife, man and wife is one flesh, and so, my mother. (IV.iii.51-55)

Hamlet denies Claudius as father and emphasizes Gertrude as mother, thrusting at an incestuous marriage, and pointing through it at the "true" marriage that Claudius has violated and continues to violate. Hamlet denies Claudius by admitting that he *is* married to Gertrude, but has no status as "father" or husband *per se;* thus Hamlet obliterates the existence of Claudius with his irony and cancels the validity of the second marriage. Having been "one flesh" with King Hamlet, young Hamlet implies, Gertrude cannot be the same for any other man—thus is *she* denied Claudius, as Hamlet has insisted in the Closet scene. Hamlet's attitude toward Ophelia is obviously conditioned by his despair before his mother's marriage, but perhaps more attributable to Ophelia's willingness to be used in a game against him. She also represents the negative dynamic undermining the elements that must be joined in an harmonious world:

> Oph. Could beauty, my lord, have better commerce than with honesty?
> Ham. Ay, truly; for the power of beauty will sooner transform honesty from what it is to a bawd, than the force of honesty can translate beauty into his likeness. This was sometime a paradox, but now the time gives it proof. (III.i.109-15)

Ophelia's beauty conceals her dishonesty, her mission refutes the Prayer Book that colors her loneliness. The conflict between appearance and reality ("a paradox") is embodied in Ophelia ("proof"), who is prostituted by the plot of Polonius. Ophelia's defection, of course, is similar to that which the Ghost imputes to Gertrude in the "falling off" of his "most seeming-virtuous queen." The analogy between Gertrude and Ophelia allows Hamlet to assign only the most negative potentiality to the woman he had loved. "Conception is a blessing," he tells Polonius, "but not as your daughter may conceive" (II.ii.185-87). "Why wouldst thou be a breeder of sinners?" he demands of Ophelia:

> If thou dost marry, I'll give thee this plague for thy dowry: be thou as chaste as ice, as pure as snow, thou shalt not escape calumny. (III.i.123-41)

Ophelia's duplicity reminds him, apparently, of Gertrude's defection from her first marriage:

> Or, if thou wilt needs marry, marry a fool; for wise men know well enough what monsters you make of them. (III.i.143-45)

"Love," exclaims Claudius, "his affections do not that way tend!" (III.i.170). Hamlet himself has embarked on an anti-sacramental course even before his play; his lack of concord is not only described by Ophelia, but defined as her own loss of harmony as well:

> I, of ladies most deject and wretched,
> That suck'd the honey of his music vows,
> Now see that noble and most sovereign reason,

Like sweet bells jangled, out of tune and harsh;
That unmatch'd form and feature of blown youth
Blasted with ecstacy. O, woe is me,
T' have seen what I have seen, see what I see!

(III.i.163-69)

The charity that quickened in Hamlet, the "kind of joy" that penetrated his despair as the players arrived, deepens beyond the cynicism of the earlier Hamlet. His memory of his mother's marriage is renewed and sharpened by his confrontation with another symbol of false woman, Ophelia, and has intervened between his plans for the play and the moment of its performance. At the play, he is bitter, pursuing the theme of woman's frailty:

What should a man do but be merry? For, look you, how cheerfully my mother looks, and my father died within's two hours. (III.ii.132-35)

The memory of a king like Hamlet lingers no longer than does man's memory of a discarded whore, an ironic thrust at both Gertrude and Ophelia:

Then there's hope a great man's memory may outlive his life half a year; but, by'r lady, he must build churches then, or else shall he suffer not thinking on, with the hobby-horse, whose epitaph is, "For, O, for, O, the hobby-horse is forgot." (III.ii.139-45)

"Is this a prologue," Hamlet demands, "or the posy of a ring?" (III.ii.162).

Oph. 'Tis brief, my lord
Ham. As woman's love. (III.ii.163-64)

The point of Hamlet's "posy of a ring" becomes clear when we remember Gratiano's ring, "whose posy was. . . 'Love me, and leave me not.' " (*The Merchant of Venice*, V.i.148-50).

So obsessed is Hamlet with infidelity—his mother's and what he may consider to be Ophelia's—that he seems to forget that Claudius is his object. He turns to Gertrude:

Ham. Madam, how like you this play?
Queen, The lady protests too much, methinks.
Ham. O, but she'll keep her word. (III.ii.239-41)

Claudius interrupts the colloquy: "Have you heard the argument? Is there no offense in't?" (III.ii.242-43). Claudius perhaps thinks (or pretends to think, depending on his recognition of the dumb-show) that the play comments on his hasty marriage to Gertrude. Hamlet must demur, lest Claudius seize a pretext for halting the performance:

No, no, they do but jest, poison in jest. No offense i' th' world. (III.ii.244-45)

His response evokes a further question: "What do you call the play?" (III.ii.246). Hamlet calls it the mouse-trap, suggesting that he now conceives of it not as forcing a confession from Claudius or even as producing facial expressions discernible to two sets of informed eyes. The play becomes a rack:

'Tis a knavish piece of work, but what o' that? Your Majesty, and we that have free souls, it touches us not. Let the gall'd jade wince, our withers are unwrung. (III.ii.250-53)

Since Hamlet has reason to believe that Claudius's soul is *not* free, his words define, ironically, the potentiality of his play, which *must* touch Claudius, and his cynical rejection of its possibilities even as it develops. Hamlet's own soul is becoming less free as the performance continues. He identifies Lucianus as "nephew to the *king*" (III.ii.254; my italics), a slip containing a naked threat to Claudius and revealing Hamlet's increasing personal involvement in the drama being enacted before the court. As the play becomes more real for him, Hamlet abandons the role he has defined for himself, that of a spectator of a play and of careful observer of Claudius's face as the king's crime is reflected back at him from the stage. Hamlet becomes a participant, as Ophelia suggests: "You are a good chorus, my lord" (III.ii.255). But Hamlet's choric comment was about a *king*, not, as in "The Murder of Gonzago," a duke. Hamlet's movement into the play is a movement into personal bitterness, an abandonment of the calm objectivity in which he conceived the plan. Like the Player, he is losing his artistic detachment, merging with an *imitation* of an action. His play must pause while he vents more cynicism about love and marriage:

> Ham. I could interpret between you and your love if I could see
> the puppets dallying.
> Oph. You are keen my lord, you are keen.
> Ham. It would cost you a groaning to take off my edge.
> Oph. Still better, and worse.
> Ham. So you mistake husbands.
>
> (III.ii.254-62)

As Weston Babcock says of this colloquy: "He has spat out his bitterness on his mother and Claudius; now he flares at the girl who, he thinks, has betrayed him. The bait Hamlet had inserted in the trap for the King has caught himself."[15] As Madariaga says, "Shakespeare turns the tables of the experiment. It is the tester who is most tested of all."[16]

Having interrupted his play, Hamlet commands it to continue:

> Begin, murderer; pox, leave thy damnable faces and begin.
> Come, "the croaking raven doth bellow for revenge."
>
> (III.ii.262-65)

Since Lucianus's crime is not motivated by revenge, Hamlet reveals here that either he is anxious for the murder to be perpetrated so that revenge can follow, or, more probably, that he views the staging of the murder as a revenge on Claudius. The latter possibility is corroborated by the lines from *The True Tragedie of Richard the Third,* which Hamlet condenses, lines that point at Claudius's crime and at the emergence of King Hamlet's Ghost:

> Methinks their ghosts come gaping for revenge
> When I have slain in reaching for a crown;
> The screeking raven sits croking for revenge
> Whole herds of beasts comes bellowing for revenge.

Hamlet forgets in his rising excitement and deepening bitterness that his play was to represent "Something like the

murder of my father" (II.ii.624). It becomes instead, as his
"nephew . . . king" slip and his use of "revenge" suggest, the
murder of Claudius. Hamlet's inability to identify with Pyrrhus predicts his identification with Lucianus. Hamlet's
psychic participation in the smaller drama reveals what he
has become in the larger drama—a raven-hued man bellow-
ing for vengeance. Even Hamlet's lesser vision of his play
—that it might reveal to him and to Horatio Claudius's
guilt—surrenders for the moment before his inability to
separate art from life, sacrament from vengeance. Hamlet,
not Claudius, breaks down before the play. We approach the
play-within expecting to observe with Hamlet the guilt of
Claudius, hoping perhaps that Claudius will break down publicly, anticipating Hamlet's passive intensity. Instead, we find
the Prince, with whom we have been invited to associate so
strongly, writhing in the agony of his own hatred.

Alfred Harbage summarizes what follows: "As the act of
poisoning occurs, Claudius rises, crying for lights and rushing out, with all but Hamlet and Horatio following."[17] Sum-
maries must be simplified, but this omits the crucial fact that
Hamlet, not Claudius, interrupts the play for the final time.
At the moment of the poisoning, Hamlet leaps up and blurts
out the rest of the story:

> He poisons him i' th' garden for's estate. His name's Gonzago,
> the story is extant, and writ in choice Italian. You shall see anon
> how the murderer gets the love of Gonzago's wife. (III.ii.272-75)

The play is interrupted for the last time by what could be
construed as Hamlet's lunacy, or by what *is* construed as an
insult to Claudius (cf. III.ii.97-103 and III.iv.9), and then
"The King rises" (III.ii.276). Hamlet cries, "What, frighted
with false fire?" (III.ii.277). Gertrude asks Claudius how he
fares, and Polonius commands unnecessarily, "Give o'er the
play" (III.ii.279). Claudius flees, crying, "Give me some light.
Away!" (III.ii.280). That is all he says, no matter what agony
may have played across his countenance. The indelible impression both in the spectators of the larger play, who have
been privy to Hamlet's plan, and to the "spectators" on stage,
who have not, is that something in Hamlet—not Claudius

—forces the play's premature closing. Hamlet is unable to maintain his role as spectator—like the character in *Great Expectations*, who leaps onstage to rescue Desdemona from Mr. Wopsle, or like Partridge in *Tom Jones*, who cannot control his fear of the Ghost during a performance of *Hamlet*. There, however, the interruption is comic. Here, it is tragic.

Hamlet demonstrates in the play scene the lack of that control he advocated to the players and admires in Horatio: "Give me the man/ That is not passion's slave" (III.ii.77). Hamlet was not that man. He did precisely what he had instructed the clowns *not* to do:

> let those that play your clowns speak no more than is set down for them; for there be of them that will themselves laugh to set on some quantity of barren spectators to laugh too, though in the mean time some necessary question of the play be then to be considered. That's villainous. (III.ii.42-48)

By speaking more than was set down for him, Hamlet interrupts the consideration of the necessary question of both "The Murder of Gonzago" and *Hamlet*. Overcome by a compulsion born of excitement, bitterness, and hatred, the man betrays the artist, confirming in an ironic way his identification of himself with the Player, who also lost his artistic detachment before the emotional impact of his material. Just as Hamlet should step back and say, "Now, let it work," he leaps forward to mar what might have been his masterpiece. The desire to inflict pain overwhelms the possibilities of redemption, Hamlet's as well as Claudius's. As Goddard says, "In so far as he regards *The Murder of Gonzago* as [a work of dramatic art] and is willing to let it have its own way with the King, he is doing what his soul calls on him to do. But in so far as he regards it as a trap, an engine for torturing a victim, for catching not the King's conscience but the King himself, the play is nothing but a contrivance for murder on the mental plane."[18] The play reveals not the king's guilt— that is not shown explicitly in the text until his soliloquy— but Hamlet's desire to twist the wheel of the rack his play becomes. He has fallen from that moment when he could advocate charity even toward Polonius. And, as Hamlet falls,

his play diminishes, falling far short of the great possibilities
he had once ascribed to it.

The events immediately following the play suggest both
what it might have been and what it becomes. After it breaks
up, Hamlet excitedly compares Claudius and himself to animals: "let the strucken deer go weep,/ The hart ungalled
play" (III.ii.282-83). He has not caught a conscience, he has
wounded an animal. While he sees himself as a "hart ungalled," his performance at the play suggests that his heart was
hardly ungalled and that his words to Claudius then applied
to himself as well. The plural pronouns support the suggestion:

> Your Majesty and we that have free souls, it touches us not.
> Let the gall'd jade wince, our withers are unwrung.
> (III.ii.251-53)

Tillyard says that "Hamlet is painfully aware of the baffling
human predicament between the angels and the beasts, between the glory of having been made in God's image and the
incrimination of being descended from fallen Adam."[19] The
choice between man's alternatives is made, for Hamlet, in the
play scene. Hamlet translates the play's higher potential into
a bestial and fallen version, which wounds an animal and
traps himself as well.

Hamlet calls his play "false fire" (III.ii.277), which Kittredge defines as "the harmless discharge of a gun loaded
with powder only."[20] Thus Hamlet himself describes the inef-
fectuality of his play. "False fire" is part of what Roger L.
Cox calls "the dominant metaphor" of Hamlet—"the use of
weapons," particularly weapons that "miss the mark,"[21] as
Hamlet's play has done. It is no better, finally, than the plot
Polonius unfolds to his spy, Renaldo: "This bait of falsehood
takes the carp of truth" (II.i.63). In fact, Hamlet neglects the
purpose he had ascribed to his play, defined by Polonius relative to his petty intelligence-gathering: "By indirections [to]
find directions out" (III.ii.298). Says Hardison, "he has just
made an attempt to 'put Claudius to it,' and in spite of his
momentarily triumphant mood, he has failed. There has
been no confession, not even an unambiguous sign of

guilt."[22] Nor, one must add, does Horatio assent unambiguously to Hamlet's findings. Horatio had said, before the play, that if Claudius "steal aught the whilst this play is playing,/ And scape detecting, I will pay the theft" (III.ii.94-95). Afterwards, he merely agrees that he did "perceive" "Very well," and that he "did very well note him" (III.ii.299-301), hardly a clear corroboration of what Hamlet claims *he* saw. Horatio hints at the unnecessary destruction of an art form in responding to the "pajock" with which Hamlet closes a quatrain:

You might have rhym'd. (III.ii.296)

But Hamlet's harmony is gone. He can call his play a "comedy" (III.ii.304), but his interruption of it denies a comic ending to the tragedy for which he is now responsible.

For Claudius, however, the play has taken on the deepest of meanings. If Hamlet could not realize the fullest implications of his play, Claudius does clearly, if too late. The drama of his guilt enacted before him—the fragment of a play —drives him to his knees in an attempt at prayer. The question of what the full performance might have accomplished is answered by a confession that is private, hence mere self-torture. The "inward man," ruthlessly aware of his guilt, is helpless to free himself of it, trapped after the play in the lonely psyche Hardison describes, where "confession, the only way to relieve the pain, is prevented by ... fear of the consequences":

Pray can I not,
Though inclination be as sharp as will.
My stronger guilt defeats my strong intent,
And, like a man to double business bound,
I stand in pause where I shall first begin,
And both neglect. What if this cursed hand
Were thicker than itself with brother's blood,
Is there not rain enough in the sweet heavens
To wash it white as snow?

(III.iii.38-46)

The cleansing rain is called, in the Ministracion of Baptisme a "heavenly wasshing." But, like Richard, Claudius cannot embrace the principle that "whosoever does not receive the kingdom of Gode, as a lytle chylde: he shall not entre therin." Clearly, Claudius cannot rid himself of what the Baptism, following St. Paul, calls "the Olde Adam," "the old man"—that former self which must be discarded, along with "the vaine pompe and glorye of the world, with al covetous desires of the same, and the carnal desires of the flesh." Claudius's inclination is canceled by the equal power of his will and he commits a kind of blasphemy in being unable to pray, as defined by the Prayer Book's Commination Against Sinners:

> Lette us not abuse the goodnes of God, whyche calleth us mercyfully to amendment, and of hys endelesse pytye promysed us forgevenesse of that whyche is paste: If (wyth a whole mynde and true hearte) we return unto him. For though our synnes be red as scarlet, they shalbe as white as snow.

While Claudius can repeat the rhythm and imagery of the Admonition, he cannot achieve repentance.

Hamlet's play might have forced Claudius to do what he realizes is inevitable anyway, to confess, regardless of what protective façades he has erected between his guilt and this world:

> In the corrupted currents of this world,
> Offence's gilded hand may shove by justice,
> And oft 'tis seen the wicked prize itself
> Buys out the law. But 'tis not so above;
> There is no shuffling, there the action lies
> In his true nature, and we ourselves compell'd
> Even to the teeth and forehead of our faults
> To give in evidence.
>
> (III.iii.57-64)

Hamlet's play was conceived to produce precisely this effect—to strike so to the soul that the malefactor would be compelled to proclaim his crimes. G. R. Hibbard suggests that "the Prayer scene ... reveals unequivocally that repentance and the giving-up of the crown are actions of which the King is incapable."[23] But in the structure of *Hamlet,* the Prayer scene occurs *after* the play-within, and, by then, the question of the positive release of Claudius's guilt *is*

unequivocal. Its moment has passed. Claudius has been driv-
en back to a will that defeats his strong inclination toward
repentance. But this does not mean that his guilt, dumb to
him here in any effective sense, might not have spoken before the very different circumstances of its dramatic presentation. Why should Shakespeare make Claudius's troubled
conscience so manifest *before* the play-within, except to raise
the possibility of his confession? Otherwise, Claudius's guilt
leads to a soliloquy that is almost irrelevant to the dramatic
action, making its point only in the context of the character
of the king. True, the soliloquy provides a dimension of
irony to Hamlet's inability or unwillingness to kill a Claudius
apparently at prayer. It makes of Claudius a complicated
Machiavellian and allows us to watch him revert to cold-
blooded stratagem as the play moves on. But has Claudius's
conscience no real *dramatic* issue?

Clearly—Claudius speaks for Denmark here—he has
bought out the law, killing a king, marrying the queen, secur-
ing the election. Law is no longer a *principle* supporting a
rightful king, free of subversion by the chief magistrate, but
the corrupt creature of an unlawful king. As it did for
Richard, the law becomes the desperate improvisation of
Claudius—to bury Polonius in "hugger mugger" (IV.v.144),
to exile and attempt to execute Hamlet, to bury Ophelia in
sanctified ground, to divert the thrust of Laertes' threat into
a scheme to kill Hamlet. Laertes' rush toward Claudius suggests the results of crime compounded by further crime, the
nature of a world detached from history and tradition and
from the ceremonies celebrating them, the rituals of social
and political control and continuity:

> The rabble call him lord;
> And, as the world were now but to begin,
> Antiquity forgot, custom not known
> (The ratifiers and props of every word)
> They cry, "Choose we! Laertes shall be king!"
>
> (IV.v.102-6)

Polonius dies in Claudius's service. His murder encourages in
Laertes an action mirroring the political import of Claudius's
murder of King Hamlet. Claudius tried to behave as if the

world *were* new begun. We are reminded of Richard, who destroyed the premises of his own kingship, *and* of Boling-broke, who established the "best man" theory of kingship and found it returning to haunt him in Hotspur. But Laertes comes to revenge himself for Hamlet's crime—only that al-lows a once guilt-ridden Claudius to translate Laertes' vehe-mence into a dialogue remarkably in contrast to the re-strained and cautionary injunctions of the Ghost to Hamlet. Hamlet's killing of Polonius reverberates against Claudius's of King Hamlet. Hamlet has presented Claudius with another crime that must be concealed:

> this vile deed
> We must, with all our majesty and skill,
> Both countenance and excuse.
>
> (IV.i.30-32)

While Claudius never says directly that Hamlet has accused him of the murder of King Hamlet, he recognizes that Hamlet's murder of Polonius "may be laid to us" (IV.i.17) for not restraining "This mad young man" (IV.i.19). Indeed, Claudius's prediction proves accurate, and Laertes asks the very question Claudius anticipates (IV.vii.5-9). For all his shrewdness and considerable political skill, Claudius exem-plifies the plight of the guilty king, the Richard, Bolingbroke, or Macbeth, who "struggling to be free" is "more engag'd" (III.iv.68-69).

Claudius's recognition in his soliloquy of the distinction be-tween personal will and an order superior to will, and his in-ability to choose the latter, predicts the struggle of Macbeth, who has yet to lose his soul as he meditates his murder. Each can save his soul only at the expense of will, and the ele-ments of Claudius's will are identical to Macbeth's: "My crown, mine own ambition, and my queen" (III.iii.55). Like Macbeth after the murder, Claudius cannot say "Amen." Macbeth describes pity as "a naked new born babe" (I.vii.21); Claudius prays that his steel-stringed heart may "Be soft as sinews of the new born babe" (III.iv.71); each recognizes the condition toward which true repentance points, as defined by the end of the Second Part of The Homilie of Repentance:

"And from hence foorth let us endevour ourselves to walke in a new life, as new borne babes." The nature of each regicide suffers the division described by St. Bernard:

> False to its own nature, which is to be a divine analogue, [the soul] ceases at one and the same time to resemble God and to resemble itself. . . . Now, conscious of what it is in itself, it can ignore neither its own remaining and inherent capacity for greatness, nor the cruel loss of that greatness of which it is naturally capable. In other words it feels itself both like to God and faithful to itself inasmuch as its aptitude for divine things subsists, but at the same time false both to God and its own true nature; and hence it is rent in twain and feeling itself still like and seeing itself in part unlike, it conceives that horror of self which is the inner tragedy of the sinner's life.[24]

Claudius, like Macbeth, exhibits the trait that William Van Laan isolates in Everyman: "a felt need to pray . . . inhibited by an excessive worldliness."[26] "In short," says Hardison, "instead of cooperating with the tragic therapy like the townswoman of Lynn, Claudius resists it. The result is not catharsis—not a calming of the mind—but . . . an anti-catharsis, an intensification of the perturbations associated with guilt."[27] And, indeed, if we have an anti-catharsis, we also have an anti-prayer:

> My words fly up, my thoughts remain below.
> Words without thoughts never to heaven go.
>
> (III.iv.97-98)

Claudius, like his kingdom, is exiled from the only power that can save him, as he well knows. He is "rent in twain." Whether he would have had any choice but to cooperate with the tragic therapy of the play is a question that Hamlet's interruption has rendered forever unanswerable. But while Hibbard is correct to suggest that by this time Claudius is unequivocally committed to maintaining crown and queen, the question of Claudius's guilt is raised profoundly, to emphasize the opportunity Hamlet has missed—his only opportunity to fulfill the complicated requirements of the mission the Ghost has imposed upon him.

While the king attempts to pray, Hamlet accepts the Ghost's word "for a thousand pound" (III.ii.297). He never

questions it again. His reaction to the play is hardly that of
Claudius:

> 'Tis now the very witching time of night,
> When churchyards yawn and hell itself breathes out
> Contagion to this world. Now could I drink hot blood,
> And do such bitter business as the day
> Would quake to look on.
>
> (III.ii.406-10).

Even as the Ghost is accepted, one must wonder whether he
did bring "blasts from hell" (I.iv.41). The Eucharistic suggestion of "God's bodykins" has devolved to the vampiric overtones of "hot blood." We are reminded, perhaps, of Faustus's
"To him I'll build an altar and a church/ And offer luke
warm blood of newborn babes" (V.15-16). The hellish implications of Hamlet's speech link him with Pyrrhus:

> he whose sable arms,
> Black as his purpose, did the night resemble . . .
>
> (II.ii.474-75)

> Head to foot
> Now is he total gules, horribly trick'd
> With blood of fathers, mothers, daughters, sons . . .
>
> (II.ii.478-80)

The implications are underscored as Hamlet discovers the
kneeling king:

> Now might I do it pat, now he is praying;
> And now I'll do 't—and so he goes to heaven,
> And so am I reveng'd. That would be scann'd.
> A villain kills my father, and for that
> I, his sole son, do this same villain send
> To heaven.
> Oh, this is hire and salary, not revenge. . .
> Up, sword, and know thou a more horrid hent.
> When he is drunk asleep, or in his rage,
> Or in th' incestuous pleasure of his bed,
> At gaming, swearing, or about some act
> That has no relish of salvation in 't—
> Then trip him, that his heels may kick at heaven,
> And that his soul may be as damn'd and black
> As hell, whereto it goes.
>
> (III.iii.73-95)

Dr. Johnson calls these words "too horrible to be read or to be uttered."[27] They are so horrible, in fact, that critics from Coleridge on have viewed them as a rationalization of Hamlet's *real* reason for sparing Claudius. "The determination to allow the guilty King to escape at such a moment," says Coleridge, "is only part of the indecision and irresoluteness of the hero."[28] Battenhouse finds the speech not indicative of "a directly willed malice" in Hamlet. "There is enough humanity in him," says Battenhouse, "to balk at an act of open murder."[29] While the utter calculation of the speech suggests no mental conflict in Hamlet (as opposed, for example, to the fragmented first soliloquy), one might ask what soliloquy in all of Shakespeare does not represent what its speaker believes to be the truth? To argue otherwise is hopelessly to complicate Shakespeare's use of the convention. Hamlet believes what he says; his words are the logical conclusion of the desire to keep his vow of vengeance that overwhelmed him during the play scene. His deepest motivation, in fact, may be revealed as he puts up his sword. The full performance of "The Murder of Gonzago" might have cost Claudius his life, but it might have saved him his soul. He might have embraced the destiny of the "notoryus Synners" of the "Commination," "Putte to open penanunce in this world, that their soules might be saved in the daie of the lord." But revenge is *not* revenge, says Hamlet, unless the victim goes to hell. While Hamlet has been commissioned to "leave [Gertrude] to heaven," and must remind himself and be reminded by the Ghost of that injunction (III.iv.112-15), he has *not* been given a corollary command to send Claudius's soul to hell. The sacramental possibilities of his play unrealizable, Hamlet seems intent not on realigning Denmark with spiritual power, but on further divorcing outward sign and invisible grace. The Ghost had suggested an opposite process, so that Hamlet's acceptance of him as an "honest ghost" (I.v.138) comes ironically at the very moment that Hamlet has rejected his chance to be a minister. And, obviously, as he attempts to determine his foe's damnation, his mind has begun to absorb the "taint" the Ghost warned him to avoid.

Claudius himself defines accurately not only his own, but Hamlet's dilemma:

> My stronger guilt defeats my strong intent,
> And, like a man to double business bound,
> I stand in pause where I shall first begin,
> And both neglect.
>
> (III.iii.40-43)

Hamlet and Claudius are caught in the same trap. Hamlet too is bound to double business—to exact temporal vengeance *and* to ensure Claudius's eternal damnation. On the other side of his potentially redemptive drama, Hamlet reflects negatively the double task he might have performed with his play—to expose Claudius *and* to heal Denmark. Revenge has moved beyond "an eye for an eye" to "a soul for a soul." Hamlet extends the Old Testament code to its logical conclusion within a Christian world. He believes " 'Tis heavy" with his father (III.iii.84), although the Ghost has defined his fasting in fires as a temporary torture. Here, Hamlet's desire to send Claudius's soul to hell defeats his wish for revenge in this world—a strong guilt defeating a strong intent. Nothing could more clearly focus the failure of his great plan, and nothing could more clearly predict Hamlet's destiny, in this world, at least. The distinction made by Nicholas Trivet applies to Hamlet, once the play-within is over: "Although he recedes, with reference to the end, from the order of the divine will in one way, he nevertheless falls into the order of the divine will in another; for in leaving the order of mercy, he falls into the order of justice."[30]

After this pause, Hamlet arrives at Gertrude's closet and runs Polonius through. Hamlet indicts Gertrude for deepest sacrilege:

> Such an act
> That blurs the grace and blush of modesty,
> Calls virtue hypocrite, takes off the rose
> From the fair forehead of an innocent love
> And sets a blister there, makes marriage-vows
> As false as dicers' oaths; O, such a deed
> As from the body of contraction plucks
> The very soul, and sweet religion makes
> A rhapsody of words.
>
> (III.iv.40-48)

No matter how accurate Hamlet's indictment, it must ring hollow here, after his own destruction of his sacramental drama. Hamlet's farewell to Polonius contains reminders of his own behavior at the play:

> Thou wretched, rash, intruding fool, farewell!
> I took thee for thy better. Take thy fortune
> Thou find'st to be too busy is some danger.
>
> (III.iv.31-33)

Soon Hamlet demands of Gertrude, "What devil was't/ That thus hath cozen'd you at hoodman-blind?" (III.iv.76-77). What prompted Hamlet to thrust through the arras in a grisly version of blindman's buff? Hamlet's castigation of Gertrude throws back an image of his own loss of control:

> Rebellious hell
> If thou canst mutine in a matron's bones,
> To flaming youth let virtue be as wax
> And melt in her own fire. Proclaim no shame
> When the compulsive ardour gives the charge . . .
>
> (III.iv.82-86)

His play over, Hamlet is now the victim of that tragic irony wherein his own words "give the charge" against himself as well as those he may indict or accuse. As in the play scene, he moves beyond the limits of self-control he set on approaching Gertrude:

> I will speak daggers to her, but use none.
> My tongue and soul in this be hypocrites;
> How in my words soever she be shent
> To give them seals never, my soul, consent.
>
> (III.ii.414-17)

He has done more than speak daggers to Polonius, and exceeds the demands of his lecture to Gertrude. Her pleas of "No more!" (III.iv.101) are ineffectual. Only the Ghost interrupts Hamlet's bitter outpouring, showing more compassion for Gertrude in this melancholy family reunion than does Hamlet:

But, look, amazement on thy mother sits.
O, step between her and her fighting soul.
Conceit in weakest bodies strongest works.
Speak to her, Hamlet.

(III.iv.112-15)

While the Ghost comes "to whet [Hamlet's] almost blunted purpose" (III.iv.111), his effect on Hamlet is ambiguous:

Look you how pale he glares!
His form and cause conjoin'd, preaching to stones,
Would make them capable.—Do not look upon me,
Lest with this piteous action you convert
My stern effects; then what I have to do
Will want true colour, tears perchance for blood.

(III.iv.125-30)

A Hamlet who might substitute pity for vengeance, tears for blood—it is too late. As part of the fatal rhythm emanating from his interrupted drama, the body of Polonius grows cold at his feet. That the Ghost who demanded vengeance and who comes now to whet Hamlet's purpose should, in Hamlet's eyes, be an agent of its mitigation is perhaps the greatest irony in this intensely ironic scene. Hamlet's insight into that element of the Ghost which is piteous and which therefore evokes pity in Hamlet has been hinted from the first ("Alas, poor ghost"[I.v.4]) and was reiterated subtly in the Player's pity for Hecuba. But Hamlet's insight here reminds us merely that the opportunity for converting his own stern effects into a positive acting of the Ghost's dread command is past. The Ghost's twin injunctions—Hamlet's "purpose" against Claudius, and the destination of Gertrude's "fighting soul"—are repeated, but in a context that now makes them separate, if not contradictory (as they are for Gertrude), rather than as potentially twin halves of one august and creative event.

The Ghost departs. Hamlet reads Gertrude another of his lectures on self-control:

Refrain tonight,
And that shall lend a kind of easiness
To the next abstinence; the next more easy;

For use almost can change the stamp of nature,
And either master the devil or throw him out,
With wondrous potency.

                                                                III.iv.165-70)

It may be that Hamlet misreads the cumulative power of
sexual abstinence ("It would cost you a groaning to take off
my edge"). It would seem, however, that as he points Gertrude in one direction, he embarks on another. Use can almost change the stamp of nature. He closes the scene with a
curious mingling of harshness toward his victim and tender-
ness toward his mother, suggesting the division that has
begun to deepen in him. As in his response to the Ghost, his
"tongue and soul" seem to have become "hypocrites":

I'll lug the guts into the neighbor room.
Mother, good-night. Indeed this counsellor
Is now most still, most secret, and most grave,
Who was in life a foolish prating knave.—
Come, sir, to draw toward an end with you.—
Good-night, mother.

                                                                (III.iv.212-16)

Again, while Hamlet can instruct Gertrude to "confess
[herself] to heaven" (III.iv.149), he seems to be about the
devil's business. While he repents his murder of Polonius,
he is unsure whether he is scourge *or* minister, the former a
negative agent of God's intentions, whose own soul is lost in
his function, the latter an agent who remains uncontami-
nated by his actions as God's missionary. The balance is appropriate, since, while it seems clear that Hamlet is contaminated by Denmark's evil, and by his own after the play
breaks up, the question of his guilt is not easily answered.
Hamlet does, however, suffer the split between words and actions, between his piety and his murder, seemingly inevitable
in the tragic world. He reminds us that his actions at the play
refuted the words that conceived it.

At certain moments in Shakespeare's plays, his characters
are in control of the alternatives they face. As Auerbach says,
"the idea of destiny in Elizabethan drama is both more broadly
conceived and more closely linked to the individual character
than it is in antique tragedy."[31] Shakespeare makes it seem

that events are the products of a character's decision
—whether Brutus's to kill Caesar, Macbeth's to kill Duncan,
or Anthony's to return to Cleopatra after marrying
Octavia—even though we know that Holinshed or North has
already provided Shakespeare with a basically unalterable
framework of events. The imitation of decision turns the
framework into *drama*. After their decisions, the characters
become fragments in a flow of larger forces; Macbeth's murder of Duncan elicits the moral imperative of his damnation
and the political necessity of his temporal defeat. As Hamlet's
play begins, he controls the forces of appearance and reality
that have thus far been confusing him (in the persons of
Gertrude, Ophelia, the Ghost). When he limits his play to the
only realities he sees there, bitterness and hatred, he loses
control again. Immediately he is the victim of appearances
again—in believing the kneeling Claudius to be praying and
in blindly stabbing Polonius. To argue that the sparing of
Claudius or the killing of Polonius is the climax of *Hamlet* is
to deny that these events or events like them are inevitable
once Hamlet surrenders to hatred and once Claudius's guilt
achieves no effective release. It seems indisputable that
Claudius's prayer is not some random musing during a free
moment within his busy schedule, but a direct result of the
play-within. Hamlet discovers Claudius as Hamlet is going to
Gertrude's closet, his "present" summons directly attributable
to his insulting Claudius with the play. Hamlet's refusal to
kill Claudius can be read as the ultimate depth of the hatred
that clenched him during the performance of "Gonzago."
Polonius, of course, is behind the arras as Claudius's agent,
having reiterated Guildenstern's request that Hamlet meet
Gertrude "presently" (III.iii.391). Claudius's kneeling and
Polonius's eavesdropping are immediate products of the
play-within and its breakup, as are Hamlet's encounters with
them. Thus the two moments normally nominated for
"climax" are *results* of the play scene. After the great play
scene, with its centrality, its community, its sense of having
been carefully prepared for (not only by Hamlet but by
Shakespeare, who has been building toward it since
Rosencrantz's announcement in II.ii. of the coming of the

Players) only to be suddenly shattered, the play-without splinters off to a series of individual confrontations—as if a new and unknown dynamic must now be worked out, as, of course, it must.

Almost without exception, those who view the play-within-the-play as climax, call it "successful," a valid indictment of Claudius. Such a view accepts without examination Hamlet's interpretation of his production. The world of the play, however, views the production as a calculated insult of Claudius, and even Horatio is noncommittal. Such a "climax" can hardly be called a success. Even if it does indict Claudius, he evades any censure except that of Hamlet. And he has already had that in abundance. Regardless of the proof Hamlet feels he has received, his "political position" remains untenable. He must still go to England, and under guard, once he has killed Polonius. If the play-within is climax, it is that of a tragedy, a moral disaster that dooms Hamlet at the very moment he had begun to control the apparatus of appearance and reality. He could not wait to see whether reality would press outward from Claudius until the *king* broke up the play. Claudius seizes a pretext for escape, but thus seals his own doom as well.

Fredson Bowers suggests that heaven has placed Hamlet "in a position of a minister for whom public justice would be arranged at heaven's own pleasure."[32] Bowers does little with the Mousetrap scene, calling the Closet scene the climax of *Hamlet*. Yet the Mousetrap fits precisely the conditions he sets for Hamlet's ministerial function: "If Hamlet hopes to right the wrong done him and his father, he must contrive a public vengeance which will demonstrate him to be a minister of heaven's justice."[33] Bower's definition of a play's climax is "that scene in the play in which an action occurs which tips the scales for or against the fate of the protagonist in terms of the future action."[34] The play scene, then, becomes the climax of the play. By the time Hamlet is deceived into sparing Claudius or killing Polonius, his chance to be a minister has passed. He becomes again the victim of the very forces of appearance and reality he had so recently controlled. As Dover Wilson says, "The play scene is the central point of

Hamlet. It is the climax and crisis of the whole drama."[35]

In a later article, Bowers argues against the play-within as climax: "we may inquire what is the significant issue of this scene, what the fateful decision that thereupon makes the tragic catastrophe inevitable? Might not the identical scene serve as the climax for a denouement in which Hamlet succeeds in a well-planned revenge and ascends the throne of Denmark?"[36] Precisely.

Dame Helen Gardner would suggest that speculation about the possibility of Claudius's confession is irrelevant, since, as she skillfully shows, Shakespeare is committed to the pattern of revenge drama.[37] Again, however, Shakespeare does not make us feel that his character is subjected to a preconceived pattern. In fact, the drama *Hamlet* emerges from Hamlet's inability to subordinate the revenge thesis to a plan for restoring Denmark to spiritual health, and the play's central issues turn on Hamlet's ability to see that he *has* a solution, if he will only let it work.

It is easy to say, as Traversi does, that "There is . . . no question of the rightness or otherwise of revenge," that revenge is simply a "given" we must accept.[38] Shakespeare, however, often explores what for other dramatists would be initial premises. M. R. Ridley is correct when he says that "Shakespeare had not yet contrived a harmony between plot and character. Hamlet is not the right character for that particular plot."[39] Indeed, Hamlet is not fitted for the role of revenger, and the play depicts the struggle between the demands of the revenge code and Hamlet's nature. The struggle culminates at the central moment when the lives and souls of virtually all the characters balance on an artist's ability to understand what he has created. As Fiedler says of Hamlet's play, it has "an archetypal meaning quite independent of any individual's conscious exploitation of it."[40] The sacraments partake of a similar archetypal meaning. *Hamlet* follows the pattern of the revenge play, but Shakespeare makes Hamlet responsible for the imposition of that pattern on the other characters. To see *Hamlet* in relation to its *genre* is a useful corrective to studies that ignore generic considerations. Generic studies, however, tend to reduce

Hamlet to the level of *Antonio's Revenge.* One reason why
Hamlet will continue to fascinate us even after the many
parallels between it and the Marston play have blurred in our
minds is suggested by J. C. Maxwell: "in *Hamlet,* just because
the central moral question about revenge is not overtly
raised, and is, indeed, kept from the full recognition of the
hero, it can be built into the central fabric of the play. . . .
Yet that sense of incongruity between central figure and
background remains, and this is best attributed . . . to the decision to leave the framework of a revenge play standing,
while raising the moral problem of revenge only by implication and by that very fact giving it a more universal significance than it had had before on the English stage."[41] We
must be aware of *Hamlet's genre*—but we must be aware also
that *Hamlet* is an incomparable revenge play, emerging out
of the conflict between the nature of the task and the nature
of the man selected to fulfill it.

While Claudius's murder of old Hamlet is the source of
Denmark's disease, it tends to absolve Hamlet of any responsibility in the spreading of the contagion. He, after all, kills
Polonius, and sends Rosencrantz and Guildenstern to their
deaths, "not shriving time allow'd" (V.ii.47). It is difficult to
agree, however, with G. Wilson Knight and Derek Traversi[42]
that Hamlet is the *source* of the disease. This view, as John
Holloway says, claims "that Shakespeare meant his play to
depict the harm a society may incur from the disillusion of a
man suffering from the familiar Jacobean disease of melancholy; and threw in regicide, usurpation, and incest in the
royal line to enliven the middle distance."[43] Knight and
Traversi raise, however, the valid question of Hamlet's responsibility for the deadly events that engulf Denmark.
Granted that the contagion begins with Claudius's crime, to
what extent is Hamlet responsible for its spread? Granted the
way in which ritual is perverted in Denmark, could Hamlet's
play have been the great exception?

It is partly true that Hamlet's intervention in the play
shows that he is corrupted by the atmosphere surrounding
him. Suggestions of the lengths to which Hamlet's desire for
vengeance will drive him and of his latent anti-Christian bent

are conveyed in his strange simile on his mother's second
marriage: "Would I had met my dearest foe in heaven/ Ere I
had seen that day" (I.ii.182-83). Later, he *will* try to assure
his foes' damnation.

Hamlet's play, however, by seeming to be one thing to
Claudius, while being—potentially—another, represented a
benevolent paradox defeated in part by Hamlet's sense of
universal negation. He is infected with disgust and deep
doubts—"that the sun doth move" (II.ii.116), for example.[44]
Hamlet's interruption of his play can be termed symptomatic
of a malaise for which he is not wholly responsible. But Hamlet is the only one who has demonstrated the potential for
redeeming it—significantly in the scene with the players. And
in the soliloquy preceding his play, he uses the words "soul,"
"conscience," and, perhaps most significantly, "miraculous."
If he is a tragic hero, rather than a victim, he falls. His fall
results from his inability to retain his highest vision of his artistic creation—another way of saying that he fails to achieve
his own potential greatness. He is unable as the play develops
to surrender to forces larger than his own personality, forces
he himself has defined and set in motion. Instead, he becomes the victim of other forces, the negation that has begun
to work in Denmark before his play. His interruption of the
play makes the victory of these forces inevitable. Tragedy, of
course, involves the conflict of a hero *with* these forces, but it
is important to note that Hamlet had a chance to dispel them
with a redemptive drama, but actually promoted them by destroying that drama. Like any true tragic hero, Hamlet is
primarily responsible for what happens to him and to the lesser characters inhabiting his world. If his fall comes at the
moment he sees his play as a means of torturing Claudius,
and if he does identify himself with Lucianus, then his fall is
endowed with the mythic significance of Claudius's: "He
poisons him i' the garden for 's estate" (III.ii.272). Hamlet
becomes another poisoner, spitting his hatred into Claudius's
ear, when he might have restored the unweeded garden to
health.[45] At the moment his play breaks up, Hamlet descends
to the level of Claudius—as the ominous equation between
Pyrrhus and Hamlet predicted that he must—that is, unless

he could recognize his nonpyrrhic solution to his seeming dilemma. Hamlet's handling of his play translates it, indeed, into a "pyrrhic victory." In one sense Hamlet *does* restore Denmark to health, but at an appalling cost. He achieves Denmark's restoration only through its obliteration. That was sometime a paradox.

If Hamlet is not capable of restoring health to Denmark in a positive way, we should have to regard him as a passive spectator of his own destruction, no tragic hero, but a diminished being, who, as D. G. James says, "inhabits a middle region where philosophy and passion, judgment and honour, reason and blood, annul each other and leave him, for all essential purposes, helpless and angry, passive and violent."[46] This characterization is true of every Hamlet *except* the one who creates a play, a potential solution in art not available in life. The play, as Fiedler says, is "his only deliberately chosen act."[47] Arthur Sewell, however, suggests of Hamlet that "the puzzle and the explanation both lie in our common predicament, that action is imperative for man; but that all action whatsosver involves man in evil."[48] Dame Helen Gardner says something similar: "how can man secure justice except by committing injustice, and how can he act without outraging the very conscience which demands that he should act?"[49]* What they say is true, of course, of *individual* action, but not of Hamlet's play. Once it begins, it becomes a power independent of its creator. Hamlet releases forces that might relieve him of the necessity for further action, forces calculated to activate Claudius's guilt and his penitential imperative. Hamlet cancels what might have been a transcending of the dilemma defined by Sewell and Dame Helen. Had he allowed the charitable Hamlet of the Player's scene to remain alive, he might also have recognized the great responsibilities of his play. Negation intervenes, however, and he becomes a guilty creature sitting at a play, proclaiming his malefactions—either to torture Claudius, or worse, to send his soul to hell. After the play, the Knight-Traversi thesis pertains.

*Cf. Maynard Mack, who talks of "the unsatisfactory nature of the alternatives [Hamlet] faces. Any action involves him in a kind of guilt."

Hamlet, then, is as much a victim of himself as of the corrupt world of his play. This is as it must be if he is a tragic hero. The tragic hero is invariably his own worst enemy, no matter how much he and his apologists attempt to externalize his conflict. Perhaps modern criticism has pushed too far in the direction of Aristotle's "imitation of an action" and too far away from his "error in judgment." Are the two—one pointing to theme and design, the other to character and motivation—irreconcilable? Obviously not. Hamlet encompasses the themes of the larger play—of promise perverted and of appearance and reality—as he fails to recognize and thus destroys the promise of the play he presents for Claudius. The world of *Hamlet* is corrupted by a prior murder, but Hamlet creates the opportunity to achieve justice for the murder and to restore health to Denmark. He fails—and must become subject to the justice his failure demands.

Harold Rosenberg says that "the Central Intuition of Greek Tragedy . . . is, there is one unique fact that each individual anxiously struggles to conceal from himself, and this is the very fact that is the root of his identity."[50] This is also the central intuition of *Hamlet*. As Edith Sitwell says, "*Hamlet* is a hunting story—that of a man who is hunting his own soul, or the truth of his own soul, and who never finds it."[51] The failure of Hamlet's play suggests that the spiritual tragedy of Hamlet results from his inability to recognize that, for him, conventional revenge is unthinkable.

If *Hamlet* is a "tragedy" and if Hamlet is its hero, then at some point Hamlet makes a morally determinate action that presses him into the "tragic world." The process is more easily described in plays other than *Hamlet*—Macbeth's decision to murder Duncan, Othello's gradual descent into the obscene mind of Iago, Lear's concomitant decisions to divide his kingdom and reject Cordelia—one a political, the other a spiritual error. While the world of *Macbeth* is infected by Weird Sisters, that of *King Lear* infested with Edmund, Cornwall, Goneril, and Regan, and that of *Othello* inhabited by Iago, such elements are empowered only by the decisions of the central figure—decisions to embrace the suggestions of Weird Sisters or Iago, in Lear's case to pursue the thrust of

his obstinate will, and decisions to reject, knowingly or un-
knowingly, the value represented by a Duncan, a Desdemona, or a Cordelia. The problem is complicated in
Hamlet, first by the already fractured nature of his world,
and second by the typical "powerlessness" of the revenger.
Yet Hamlet's position is appreciably better than that of, for
example, Altofronto or Vendice, each of whom must disguise
himself even to enter the circle of the court, as, in another
way, must Hieronimo. Altofronto manipulates events toward
a bloodless coup that restores "right rule" to his dukedom.
Vendice sinks into delectation of his revenge and merits what
to some seems his gratuitous execution. Hieronimo dies amid
a bloodbath. Hamlet, like other revengers, must play roles
—his "antic disposition," for example. Ironically, however,
once he has finally assigned roles both to actors within "Gonzago" and to their alter-egos observing the play-within, he
cannot retain his own self-assigned role as spectator of
Claudius. Whether he listened to his own outline of the full
possibilities of his play-within or not, even his "testing thesis"
did not predicate his role as Claudius's *active* torturer. The
full potential of his play might *still* have been realized had
Hamlet merely retained his passive position as observer of his
uncle. But once he doffs an assumed passivity, Hamlet forces
the evil potentiality of the Ghost to become real and the
play-without to swing on the hinge of his error toward the
graveyard of the tragic world. Hamlet seizes a power, but
when he condenses it to the limits of his own will, he squan-
ders it almost immediately.

But Hamlet learns nothing from the disaster of his play.
On his way to England, he observes the march of Fortinbras
and his army against "a little patch of ground/ That hath in it
no profit but the name" (IV.iv.18-19). "Why then," says
Hamlet, "the Polack never will defend it" (IV.iv.23). "Yes,"
says the Norwegian captain, "it is already garrison'd"
(IV.iv.24). "This," Hamlet responds, "is th' imposthume of
much wealth and peace/ That inward breaks, and shows no
cause without/ Why the man dies" (IV.iv.27-29). Soon, however, he employs the example of Fortinbras's fighting for "an
egg-shell" (IV.iv.53), "for a fantasy and trick of fame"

(IV.iv.61) to justify his own revenge: "from this time forth/ My thoughts be bloody or be nothing worth" (IV.iv.65-66). While the example spurs Hamlet, perhaps comforts him as he moves *away* from Denmark, it clearly undermines his conclusion, suggests the futility of his *own* mission. Why is "this thing . . . to do" (IV.iv.44)—the killing of Claudius—if the example that exhorts him should *not* be done?

Many critics see Hamlet as a victim of irresolution. This claim, even if true, isolates a symptom rather than a cause. Behind any single explanation of Hamlet's character, whether it be procrastination or the rashness Grebanier proposes,[52] must lie a conflict. The conflict culminating in Hamlet's devising a play, then breaking it up, is seen often in Shakespeare: the struggle between a man's better nature and his worst, between self-control and savagery (as later in *Othello*), between insight and will (as later in *King Lear*), between conscience and ambition (as later in *Macbeth*). Among other things, *Hamlet*, like *Othello* and *Macbeth*, is a profound morality play, where good and evil angels struggle within a character, in a subtle way in which the identities of the angels become confused and confusing—like the identity of that good or evil angel, the Ghost.

Hamlet's play, like his own career (as recounted by Ophelia and as developed in the play itself), begins auspiciously but ends by refuting its potential. The careers of Ophelia and Laertes comment on Hamlet's, one by illustrating the ritual corruption from which Hamlet's play suffers, the other by providing the spectator with an education on revenge. The story of Ophelia, with its tension between piety and prostitution, and of the parallel revenger, Laertes, are variations in a minor key on Hamlet's spiritual tragedy.

Polonius early instructs Ophelia not to believe Hamlet's protestations of love, which she says have been accompanied "With almost all the holy vows of heaven" (I.iii.114). Her father's retort defines the force that will prevail over Ophelia. She will realize the fulfillment of no "holy vows," but will be figuratively prostituted by the corruption surrounding her:

Do not believe his vows; for they are brokers
Not of that dye which their investments show,
But mere implorators of unholy suits,
Breathing like sanctified and pious bawds,
The better to beguile.

(I.iii.127-31)

Polonius anticipates only seduction, and commands Ophelia
to reject the prince. Thus one of the world's promising beginnings is thwarted. Later, Ophelia becomes a pawn in
Polonius's plot to discover the source of Hamlet's madness.
The old man hands her a Prayer Book, "that show of such
an exercise may colour/ Your loneliness" (III.i.45-46). When
Hamlet sees her, however, appearance and reality seem to
have coalesced:

Soft you now!
The fair Ophelia! Nymph, in thy orisons
Be all my sins rememb'red.

(III.i.88-90)

The moment, like that of the coming of the Players, has risen
clear of Denmark's corruption. If only she is what she seems
to be, the promise of Hamlet's play as he *planned* it may be
fulfilled, if she is "honest" (III.i.103), the shape Hamlet has
seen may indeed become "an honest Ghost" (I.v.138). He requests her mediation for his sins—his most explicit reference
to the needs of his own soul. But the girl who would have
believed Hamlet's holy vows is now an actress playing piety;
her defection both predicts and promotes the failure of
Hamlet's play. She can only become "A breeder of sinners"
(III.i.123). Hamlet's plea for redemption descends to a cynical denunciation of men ("We are arrant knaves all; believe
none of us" [III.i.130-31]) and women ("God has given you
one face, and you make yourself another" [III.i.149-50]). He
offers her a choice between escape from this world to a con-
vent or contamination by this world, as in a brothel ("nun-
nery," as Dover Wilson points out, means both). Before
Hamlet's play, she is the target of his cynical view of marriage ("So you mistake husbands" [III.ii.262]). Ophelia's de-

ception contributes to Hamlet's cynicism in the Play scene
and thus to his failure to hold to or to consider more deeply
his original vision of his play.

Ophelia goes to *both* nunneries in her madness. She min-
les religious snatches with bawdy songs. The prayer "God be
at your table" (IV.v.44) is interrupted by the theme of lost
virtue:

> "Then up he rose and donned his clothes,
>   And dupp'd the chamber door;
> Let in the maid, that out a maid
>   Never departed more."
>
>   (IV.v.52-55)

"God 'a' mercy on his soul," she sings of her father, "And of
all Christian souls, I pray God" (IV.v.199-200). Ophelia's
prayers can only be ironic. She too is an emissary from
another world, the world of nature perverted, rendering
snatches of a remembered dispensation no longer possible
for her or for the world into which her madness emerges, of
a sacrament no more available to her than to the corrupted
world of which she is a model. But she reminds us of the
paradise lost that is the world of the tragedies, the paradise
once exemplified in Ophelia, plunging further and further
from sight as the murky atmosphere of the tragic world
chokes and deepens, obliterating positive value from sight
even as Ophelia's wits are shrouded in madness. In comedy,
characters move toward wholeness, toward integration of self
and fusion with a new society. In tragedy, as Ophelia shows,
the division of the self deepens until alienation from both
self and society becomes absolute.

Soon, her funeral train approaches. She ends up *between*
the two nunneries; while she is buried in sanctified ground
by order of the king, her death was dubious and she is interred
with "maimed rites" (V.i. 242) in spite of Laertes' objections:
"What ceremony else?" (V.i.245). Laertes has already com-
plained bitterly about the lack of "trophy, sword . . . hatch-
ment . . . noble rite . . . formal ostentation" (IV.v.214-15)
over the bones of Polonius, who was buried "In hugger-
mugger" (IV.v.84). Ophelia's truncated ceremony is further
disrupted by the brawl between Hamlet and Laertes, hardly a

proper conclusion for even a maimed sacrament. The marriage with which the play begins carried reminders of a recent funeral. Ophelia's funeral reminds a heartbroken Gertrude of a marriage that will never be:

> Sweets to the sweet; farewell!
> I hop'd thou shouldst have been my Hamlet's wife.
> I thought thy bride-bed to have deck'd, sweet maid,
> And not t' have strew'd thy grave.

(V.i.266-69)

We learn suddenly that the match *was* royally endorsed, regardless of Polonius's and Laertes' opinions to the contrary. It is the marriage Hamlet might have made had his father not been murdered. Ophelia would have been queen, but ends instead in an early and dubiously sanctified grave.

The Laertes story explores and rejects the revenge thesis. Ophelia's career is an adumbration of Hamlet's tragic conflict; her brother is a parallel revenger, as Hamlet admits: "by the image of my cause, I see/ The portraiture of his" (V.ii.77-78). It is the parallel he does not draw with Pyrrhus, when the exploration of such an insight might have helped him. But while Hamlet sees a similarity between himself and Laertes, he neither warns himself about Ophelia's brother, Polonius's son, nor questions his own motivation for revenge on the basis of Laertes' violence at Ophelia's grave. Dover Wilson is correct to assert that "all [Laertes] says and does is a reflection upon Hamlet,"[53] but it is the spectator who makes the inferences, not Hamlet.

Both Laertes and Hamlet are urged to waiting ships:

> Pol. Yet here, Laertes? Aboard, aboard, for shame!
>   The wind sits in the shoulder of your sail,
>   And you are stay'd for.

(I.iii.55-57)

> King. The bark is ready, and the wind at help.
>   Th' associates tend, and everything is bent
>   For England.

(IV.iv.46-48)

The lines enforce the Laertes-Hamlet equation, but, more important, remind us that between the first and second voy-

ages a seemingly safe world has grown dangerous for guilty
and innocent alike, that all relationships have pulled toward
their most negative possibilities, that Polonius is dead by
Hamlet's hand, and that the young revengers are set on a
course that must bring them into conflict. The characters of
Laertes and Hamlet are dissimilar, of course, in somewhat
the way those of Hotspur and Hal are. Hamlet's fits of resolve and recklessness alternate with other moods, while
calmness seldom visits the determined Laertes. The son of
Polonius, however, does express Hamlet's conflict, although
for Laertes it seems no conflict at all:

> How came he dead? I'll not be juggl'd with.
> To hell, allegiance! Vows, to the blackest devil!
> Conscience and grace to the profoundest pit!
> I dare damnation. To this point I stand,
> That both the worlds I give to negligence,
> Let come what comes; only I'll be reveng'd
> Most thoroughly for my father.
>
> (IV.v.130-36)

Conscience and grace against damnation and the devil—a
violent rephrasing of Hamlet's conflict, and the inevitable reduction of true ritual to "negligence." And again, revenge is
equated with damnation. If Hamlet wants Claudius's heels to
kick at heaven, Laertes is as extreme. "What would you un-
dertake," asks Claudius, "To show yourself and your father's
son in deed/ More than in words?" (IV.vii.125-27). "To cut
his throat i' th' church," snarls Laertes (IV.vii.128). But this
time the church offers no refuge from the sword, as
Claudius's reply suggests: "No place indeed, should murder
sanctuarize./   Revenge   should   have   no   bounds"
(IV.vii.129-30). Hamlet's desire for revenge is so boundless
that prayer forestalls murder only because the victim's soul
might be redeemed, hardly a revenge as Hamlet comes to
define revenge. When Hamlet appears at Ophelia's funeral,
Laertes shouts, "The devil take thy soul!" (V.i.282). Hamlet
tells him, "Thou pray'st not well" (V.i.283). What is Laertes'
prayer, however, but a concise version of Hamlet's wish for
Claudius's soul? The Laertes story demonstrates again, as
Hamlet does when he has the kneeling Claudius at his mercy

and as Pyrrhus does as he smites the fallen Priam, what revenge is, stripped of all rationalization. Even the unreflective
Laertes penetrates to an awareness of his sin: "And yet, 'tis
almost 'gainst my conscience" (V.ii.307), he says, before
thrusting the unbated and envenomed sword at Hamlet.
Hamlet expresses this insight but, like Laertes, does not explore it completely enough to save himself: "Thus conscience
does make cowards of us all" (III.i.83). The unfortunate
equation between conscience and cowardice suggests again
the basis of Hamlet's spiritual tragedy.

Act V is a pivot on which any interpretation of Hamlet or
Hamlet must turn. We have either the cleansing of a state or
its destruction, either the regeneration of Hamlet or his continued fall.

Many critics see a redeemed Hamlet in Act V. Karl Polanyi
says that "in the end our beloved hero retrieves some of life's
fulfillment."[54] Irving Ribner suggests that "by submission to
the will of God, Hamlet attains the victory."[55] "In Act I," says
S. F. Johnson, "he was a student prince; in Act V he is the
ordained minister of providence."[56] These views stem
primarily from Hamlet's philosophical statements to Horatio,
particularly this:

> Not a whit; we defy augury. There's a special providence in
> the fall of a sparrow. If it be now, 'tis not to come; if it be not to
> come, it will be now; if it be not now, yet it will come; the readi-
> ness is all. Since no man has aught of what he leaves, what is't to
> leave betimes? Let be. (V.ii.230-35)

C. S. Lewis calls this "The precise moment" at which Hamlet
finds his way again.[57] Others call it an awareness of "the
world's order,"[58] "a clear apprehension of the truth,"[59] and
"a glimpse of himself as a fragment of a mighty pattern."[60]
Hamlet has now ascended to "a willing compliance with the
workings of heaven."[61] In Act V, "his abnormally quick
sympathy has acquired some of the quiet of the vision inte-
grated and lived-up-to, some of the breadth of charity."[62]

Another group of critics demurs at Hamlet's redemption.
Granville-Barker says that Hamlet "never regains a natural
spiritual health, nor self-understanding."[63] Bradley, very

sympathetic toward Hamlet, says that the "readiness" speech expresses "that kind of religious resignation which, however beautiful in one aspect, really deserves the name of fatalism, rather than faith in Providence."[64] Schucking calls the speech "an admission that [Hamlet's] heart has grown old and that life holds nothing more of value for him."[65] Parrott calls it "a deadening fatalism,"[66] Stauffer a "desperate stoicism."[67] H. B. Charlton says that "the recognition of the will's impotence is accepted as . . . the calm attainment of a higher benignity, whereas it is nothing more than a fatalist's surrender of his personal responsibility. That is the nadir of Hamlet's fall."[68] And one might ask whether Hamlet's "If it be now, 'tis not to come . . ." is not merely an elaboration of Laertes' typically more trenchant "Let come what comes" (IV.v.135)?

We have, then, two Hamlets, one who ascends to become the agent of providence, another who surrenders to the relentless gravity of fate. And there *are* two Hamlets in Act V; it has been contrived so that much of what he says or does can be interpreted in opposite ways. His divided nature represents the radically divided world he might have united. His escape from the ship bearing him to execution in England can be called either a providential event proving (as it does to Hamlet) that "There's a divinity that shapes our ends,/ Rough-hew them how we will" (V.ii.10-11), or a mere accident. Many of his words in the graveyard can be termed a calm acceptance of the inevitability of death or cynicism about the meaning of life. His outburst at Ophelia's grave can be defined as genuine grief or as petulance that Laertes is playing the part of chief mourner ("Nay an thou'lt mouth,/ I'll rant as well as thou" [V.i.306-7]). Yet the Graveyard scene seems to confirm the pervasive cynicism that has gradually spread in Hamlet. The Hamlet whose "prophetic soul" pierced Claudius's "most painted word," who penetrated Ophelia's deception and condemned the "paintings" of women, seems to see through life itself—but only to the skull beneath the cosmetic of the flesh: "Now," he tells the skull of Yorick, "get you to my lady's chamber, and tell her, let her paint an inch thick, to this favour she must come. Make her laugh at that" (V.i.213-16).

Bradley calls Hamlet's apology to Laertes evidence of "all the nobility and sweetness of his nature":[69]

> What I have done
> That might your nature, honour, and exception
> Roughly awake, I here proclaim was madness.
> Was't Hamlet wrong'd Laertes? Never Hamlet!
> If Hamlet from himself to be ta'en away,
> And when he's not himself does wrong Laertes,
> Then Hamlet does it not, Hamlet denies it.
> Who does it, then? His madness. If't be so,
> Hamlet is of the faction that is wrong'd,
> His madness is poor Hamlet's enemy.
>
> (V.ii.241-50)

"It is only the rarest of men," says Grebanier, "who are equal to the honorableness of these words."[70] Hamlet's speech has a legalistic tone, however. It is, in fact, a prototype of a modern lawyer's defense of the psychopathic killer:

> They did not reason; they could not reason; they committed the most foolish, most unprovoked, most purposeless, most causeless act that any two boys ever committed . . . they killed him as they might kill a spider or a fly. . . . Are they to blame for it? . . . It is one of those things that happened . . . no human being could have done what these boys did, excepting through the operation of a diseased brain.

This paraphrase of Hamlet's apology to Laertes is, of course, a portion of Darrow's defense of Loeb and Leopold.[71] They killed him as they might kill a spider or a fly. "Why, man, they did make love to this employment," Hamlet says of his former school chums; "they are not near my conscience" (V.ii.57-58). Of Polonius—"a certain convocation of politic worms are e'en at him" (IV.iii.21). A spider or a fly. Which is the true Hamlet?—the sincerely repentant man or the clever defense attorney defending the psychopath who happens to be himself?

Hamlet, it seems, has been written to prove the truth of Hamlet's dictum that "there is nothing, either good or bad, but thinking makes it so" (II.ii.256). Hamlet may interrupt *his* play and limit it only to what he sees there; Shakespeare apparently does not. Shakespeare's play has the dual poten-

tial of the Mousetrap. *Hamlet* is designed to catch our con-
sciences in our providing the definitive comment that
Shakespeare avoids. As Harbage says, "only a seer can de-
duce Shakespeare's *intention* unless that intention is defined
as providing stimulus in order to get response."[72]

Clifford P. Lyons says that "the play obviously embodies
conflicting stresses; yet which emphasis does Shakespeare
make primary in Hamlet's story? Not both."[73] Are the stresses so evenly balanced in Act V that the spectator can emphasize either a redeemed or a fallen Hamlet and be at least
half right? There *are* two Hamlets in Act V, but one is
primarily an appearance, a continuing reminder of the potential we glimpsed in an earlier Hamlet who delighted in the
coming of the players and who devised a play himself. The
other is the negative reality emerging as the chaotic echoes
issuing from his disrupted drama circle malignantly through
himself and Denmark. That Shakespeare should build such a
dichotomy into his character is consistent with the play's constant contrast between the angelic and bestial possibilities in
man. The dichotomy expresses profoundly Shakespeare's
great theme—the discrepancy between appearance and reality. Certainly many of Hamlet's speeches remind us of the
Hamlet we have known. If we examine his actions, however,
he is a murderer, responsible for the deaths of Polonius,
Rosencrantz and Guildenstern (whose summary execution
shocks even the impassive Horatio), and Claudius. He causes
Ophelia's death indirectly and kills Laertes in self-defense.
The only death of which he can be absolved is Gertrude's,
although she dies by drinking a toast to his dueling skill.
Traces of a former Hamlet remain, but primarily to provide
a dimension against which his fall may be measured. (Milton
does something similar with Satan in Book I of *Paradise
Lost*.)

Dame Helen Gardner is right, of course, to insist that the
forces opposing the hero in tragedy often create or encourage the mechanisms of their downfall—as does Barabas in
The Jew of Malta, the Duke in *The Revenger's Tragedy*, and, for
an example even closer to *Hamlet*, Lorenzo in promoting
Hieronimo's play in *The Spanish Tragedy*.[74] Hamlet's play fits

this criterion as well as the duel scene. Not only does Claudius attend but he *encourages* the project.

> Pol. And he beseech'd me to entreat your Majesties
>   To hear and see the matter.
> King. With all my heart; and it doth much content me
>   To hear him so inclin'd.
>
>   Good gentlemen, give him a further edge,
>   And drive his purpose on to these delights.
>   (III.i.22-27)

Thus the denouement described by Dame Helen occurs *twice* in *Hamlet*. Hamlet's interruption of the first makes the second inevitable. The Duel scene is another great central celebration, but controlled by Claudius, not Hamlet. The Play scene became Claudius's way of turning the tables on Hamlet. Guildenstern, Polonius, and Gertrude interpret Hamlet's behavior as an offense against Claudius, not as a successful indictment of even his marriage, much less a proof of murder. And Hamlet loses the initiative he had only just gained. Claudius decides to send him to England *before* the death of Polonius (III.iii.1-6), although he later uses the murder as a pretext for the exile (IV.iii.42-48). The timing of the decision—after the play but before the murder—not only focuses on the play as climax, but strikes a telling blow to the murder of Polonius as "climax." The Play scene, a potential denouement, as Bowers suggests, becomes an inversion of the denouement Dame Helen describes, where control shifts from the villain to the person or forces opposing him. Immediately upon the interruption of Hamlet's play, control reverts to Claudius. His decision to send Hamlet to England also precedes his attempt to pray, and his order is absolute:

> Ham.   I must to England; you know that?
> Queen. Alack,
>   I had forgot. 'Tis so concluded on.
>   (III.iv.199-201)

Hamlet's behavior during the play allows Claudius to curb Hamlet's "madness" without challenge from any of the other "spectators," who apparently remember Hamlet's wild performance far more vividly than any details of his interrupted drama.

There are, of course, actual comparisons between the Play scene and the Duel scene. They are court functions, a vital consideration in performance, since they would be similarly modeled, with almost all of the characters on stage and all of the pomp attendant on the King's entrance:

> They are coming to the play; I must be idle.
>
> (III.ii.95)

> The King and Queen and all are coming down.
>
> (V.ii.212)

The architecture of each scene would require that space be reserved for the play and for the duel, also described as "play" (V.ii.295). Perhaps the deepest thematic comparison is found in the words of the Player King, describing the crucial difference between intention and result, touching not only the reversal of Hamlet's plans for his play but that of Claudius's for his duel:

> Our wills and fates do so contrary run
> That our devices still are overthrown;
> Our thoughts are ours, their ends none of our own.
>
> (III.ii.221-23)

The lines reach ahead to Laertes' "The foul practice/ Hath turn'd itself on me" (V.ii.328-29), and "He is justly serv'd;/ It is a poison temp'red by himself" (V.ii.338-39), and to Horatio's "purposes mistook/ Fall'n on the inventors' heads" (V.ii.395-96). Hamlet is able to reverse the flow of Claudius's stratagem toward his own revenge, but the process costs him his life. But the Duel scene reflects back across a gulf of irony to Hamlet's reversal of the movement of a potentially redemptive drama into the degradation of a torture device.

It is imperative to note, however, that Shakespeare allows us to retain our sympathy for Hamlet. Sympathy, however, should not substitute for pardon, any more than sympathy for Othello condones his strangling of Desdemona. To claim that "what is not near Hamlet's conscience is not near our own because he is our moral interpreter,"[75] is to evade complexity, to dismiss the discrepancy between word and action that is a prime source of irony. Some critics, overcome by sympathy, quote Hamlet's words and apologize for him. Others coldly list his actions and condemn him. Each group ignores the interaction between word and deed on which any interpretation of drama must be based. While we continue to respond to Hamlet's better nature, we must also deplore its subversion.

The fall of Hamlet and a glimpse of a former Hamlet are captured in his description of the deaths of Rosencrantz and Guildenstern. To illustrate the divinity that shapes our ends, he invokes the discovery of the plot on his life and the execution of his Wittenberg chums, "Not shriving time allow'd" (V.ii.47). No divinity shapes *their* ends. Is this the "breadth of charity" that Hamlet has supposedly attained? "In that was heaven ordinant," cries Hamlet (V.ii.48), having consigned his victims' souls to hell. "What a piece of work is a man!" he had exclaimed (II.ii.315). Now he says, with a snap of the fingers, "And a man's life's no more than to say 'One'" (V.ii.74). Is this "a willing compliance with the workings of heaven"? Hamlet claims that Rosencrantz and Guildenstern are not near his conscience and suggests that it is "perfect conscience" (V.ii.67) to kill Claudius. Yet something troubles him: "Thou wouldst not think how ill all's here about my heart" (V.ii.222).[76] Why? He does not fear death. He is confident that he will achieve his revenge. What could trouble him? "A kind of gain-giving," he says with some scorn, "as would perhaps trouble a woman" (V.ii.225)—a last unexamined prompting of conscience, perhaps, for the blood he has and is soon to shed, a final reminder of a Hamlet who might have allowed his play to proceed. Laertes, weeping for Ophelia, suggests that such gaingiving is linked to Hamlet's better self:

> It is our trick. Nature her custom holds,
> Let shame say what it will; when these are gone,
> The woman will be out.
>
> (IV.vii.188-90)

As conscience is cowardly, tears are womanly; neither Hamlet nor Laertes will substitute tears for blood. The rhythms of

Hamlet's earlier speech ("What a piece of work . . .") had imitated what Miss Mahood calls the "ebb and flow of exultant
individualism and deepening fatalism."[77] The Hamlet of Act
V seems to have surrendered humanism for fatalism, but the
play suggests that *each* alternative was superficial in comparison to the more comprehensive possibility he spurned.
Hamlet's weary heart feels the deeper alternative he has neglected, one he never expresses clearly himself, but which St.
Bernard defines:

> Now to recover charity is not only to become once more like
> God, and therefore like itself, but also, on account of the soul's
> intimate knowledge and sight of itself, it is to see God in His
> image at last restored by grace, and to rejoice in its own recover-
> ered splendour.

Neither humanism *nor* fatalism can be a medium toward this
recovery.

At Hamlet's most charitable moment, he had employed an
appropriate allusion to Communion. At his *least* charitable,
he repeats the suggestion, but with a difference. Before he
himself slumps toward death, he forces the contents of the
poisoned "chalice" (IV.vii.161) down the throat of Claudius:

> Here, thou incestuous, murderous, damned Dane,
> Drink off this potion! Is thy union here?
>
> (V.ii.336-37)

In this perverted ritual, Hamlet becomes the devil's priest,
conducting a macabre anti-Communion, forcing poisoned
wine down the throat of a dying man, hoping he will find his
"union" in Hell. The two mighty opposites come together for
a last instant, an anti-ritualistic confirmation of the spiritual
tragedy that has befallen both the anti-priest and the anti-
communicant. Such is the inevitable destiny and destination
of the two chief figures in a world they themselves have cut
off from the sacraments. Hamlet explicitly re-creates the
crime of Claudius by cutting him off through an anti-
sacrament that echoes back to the denial of last rites to King
Hamlet. Hamlet's anti-sacramental revenge fulfills the prediction made by the Pyrrhus-Hamlet equation and by the tor-

ture device his play became. That the word "union" need not be restricted merely to the pearl Claudius has dropped into the chalice is suggested by the ironic echo of Hamlet's words against the end of the First Homily on the Worthy Receiving of the Sacrament of the Body and Blood of Christ: "Whereas the faythful have their life, their abiding in him, their union, and as it were their incorporation with him." Since Hamlet assumes Claudius to be "damned," Hamlet's next line, "Follow my mother" (V.ii.338) suggests that he has not, as he sees it, followed the Ghost's injunction to leave Gertrude to heaven. "Union" would seem to refer, in one of Hamlet's final puns, to the marriage of Claudius and Gertrude in hell.

While Hamlet's action with the poisoned wine is profoundly anti-sacramental, a fulfillment of his earlier words over the kneeling Claudius (who would *then* have met the fate of the prostrate and defenseless king, had he not been "praying"), it is a fitting culmination to the Duel scene, a thrust of grim truth, like that of the envenomed point, through the deceptive tapestry Claudius has woven. Even as he arranges the wine, Claudius attempts to behave like a king, establishing an echo between his throne and the cosmic dimension with which that throne *should* have positive contact:

> The King shall drink to Hamlet's better breath
> And in the cup an union shall he throw . . .
> And let the kettle to the trumpets speak,
> The trumpet to the cannoneer without,
> The cannons to the heavens, the heaven to earth,
> "Now the King drinks to Hamlet."
>
> (V.ii.282-89)

Claudius masks his treachery by acting like the benevolent priest of a secular Communion. The emphasis on drinking wine *per se* has sacramental overtones, profoundly refuted by this final scene of *Hamlet,* as Charles Harris, D.D., explains in his "Excursus on 'the Grace of the Chalice' ":

> Not only are the religious associations of the Chalice of a most moving kind, but the common cup powerfully suggests human fellowship of an intimate, unselfish, generous and uplifting nature (cf. the institution of 'the loving-cup').[78]

We are reminded of Claudius's earlier "rouse" (I.iv.8):

> This gentle and unforc'd accord of Hamlet
> Sits smiling to my heart; in grace whereof,
> No jocund health that Denmark drinks to-day,
> But the great cannon to the clouds shall tell,
> And the King's rouse the heavens shall bruit
> Re-speaking earthly thunder.
>
> (I.ii.123-28)

When the sound of the king's celebration wafts to the parapets—an effect Keats effectively imitates in "The Eve of St. Agnes" (258-61)—Hamlet cynically undercuts the heavenly reverberations Claudius attributes to his drinking:

> The King doth wake to-night and takes his rouse,
> Keeps wassails, and the swagg'ring up-spring reels;
> And as he drains his draughts of Rhenish down,
> The kettle-drum and trumpet thus bray out
> The triumph of his pledge.
>
> (I.iv.8-12)

> This heavy-headed revel east and west
> Makes us traduc'd and tax'd of other nations.
> They clepe us drunkards, and with swinish phrase
> Soil our addition.
>
> (I.iv.17-20)

As in "The Eve of St. Agnes," sounds of the lower world briefly interrupt the mystery being enacted above.

Claudius's careful preparations turn on him when he realizes, in what must be a moment of personal agony balanced against the larger pattern of his stratagem, namely, his queen poised for an instant against his crown, that the potential "second tooth" of his plot has attacked in an unexpected direction: "Gertrude, do not drink. . . . It is the poison'd cup; it is too late" (V.ii.301-3). The play has already predicted this possibility in one of Shakespeare's ironic meshings of line with entrance:

> And that he calls for drink, I'll have prepar'd him
> A chalice for the nonce, whereon but sipping,
> If he by chance escape your venom'd stuck,
> Our purpose may hold there.
>   Enter Queen.
>   How, sweet Queen!
>
> (IV.vii.161-64)

"But 'tis not so above," Claudius had said in his effort to pray, "There is no shuffling, there the action lies/ In his true nature" (III.iii.60-62). Later he says to Laertes, "with a little shuffling, you may choose/ A sword unbated" (IV.vii.138-39). *That* shuffling once exposed in its true nature, Hamlet completes the play's anti-ritualistic pattern—perhaps a fitting end for Claudius, but saying something also of Hamlet's infection with Denmark's disease. For the fourth time, as in the Ghost's narrative, the player's speech, and Hamlet's play, a defenseless king is killed, this time by Hamlet. The administration of the poisoned chalice becomes the earlier moment where the action of Lucianus transformed itself before Hamlet's eyes into his own murder of Claudius.*

Seconds after his black mass, however, Hamlet magnanimously hopes that heaven will free Laertes of his sins (V.ii.343). Thus he only partially fulfills the requirement of the sick or dying man of the Visitacion of the Sicke: "to forgive from the botome of his hart, allpersons that have offended hym, and if he have offended other, to aske them forgevenesse." His contrasting treatment of Claudius and Laertes suggests again the "two Hamlets" of Act V, the great mission he abandoned, to revenge *and* to leave to heaven, functions he fulfills only by becoming two different persons simultaneously, and only through the tainting of his mind within the desperate improvisation he must pursue once he breaks up his play. His hope for Laertes is a reminder of the alternative he has rejected for Claudius in the Play scene, the Prayer scene, and in the king's last moment. The other alternative is represented by the corpses littering the throne-room floor. Immediately after Hamlet joins them, messengers from England add to their number with the news "that Rosencrantz and Guildenstern are dead" (V.ii.382).

While Hamlet the man quite obviously must embrace something other than "the Christian solution" within the bloody destiny of Act V, does that mean that *Hamlet* the

---

*Those who see "union" merely as "pearl," accepting only the literal meaning, ignore not only Hamlet's consistent wordplay, but the play's consistent treatment of ritual perversion. The word "union" keys verbally the visual metaphor of wine administered to a kneeling man. The moment of Hamlet's leaning over the dying Claudius not only fulfills the play's pattern of defenseless kings being killed, not only fulfills the hopes Hamlet expressed when he earlier *spared* the kneeling king, but fulfills the play's pattern of corrupted rituals.

play does? It may be that Hamlet becomes a subject for
tragedy because he neglects the alternative of a potentially
redemptive drama. While such a suggestion, according to
Hibbard, "comes very close to expressing the wish that
Shakespeare had made a different play,"[79] *Hamlet,*
preeminently among the tragedies, implies its potentially
"comic ending." It *was* there to be realized if it could be recognized by its instigator, who, however cynically, called his
play a "comedy" (III.ii.304). Unless we *feel* the possibility
that "things should or, at least, could have been different,"
unless we understand the profound meaning of the loss of
the comedy, we have lost the meaning of the tragedy.
Drama—and *Hamlet* preeminently—deals not merely with
what *does* happen, but also with what *might* happen. It is
perhaps too easy to say, as Jay Halio does, that "had Hamlet
observed the calling of a Christian to return ill not with ill,
but with good, he might not have plunged himself—and all
of the principal characters—into the course of tragic
catastrophe."[80] But the play *does* say that Hamlet expressed
the calling of a Christian in planning his own play, and the
dynamics of the play suggest strongly that at the moment
Hamlet makes the Christian approach irretrievable—on his
interruption of his play—he suffers his fall and becomes a
tragic figure. Laurence Michel is right, perhaps, to suggest
that "the Tragic Vision and Christianity are incompatible,"[81]
but to impute the rejection of the Christian alternative to
Shakespeare is not only to commit a negative "intentional fal-
lacy," but to forget that his character Hamlet makes the
choice within a play that may or may not be "Christian," but
that certainly frames Hamlet's tragic error within a Christian
context. The dichotomy between the alternatives and between the two Hamlets is summarized neatly by Horatio:

> Now cracks a noble heart. Good-night, sweet Prince,
> And flights of angels sing thee to thy rest!
> Why does the drum come hither?
>
> (V.ii.370-72)

While the last line could be termed a turning back to the
pressing rhythms of this world, it is difficult not to see irony

there. The first two lines are dear to the hearts of Hamlet's
apologists. The martial music of the next line, however, explicitly rebuffs the choir for which Horatio has called.

The spirit that I have seen may be the devil. It seems to
become the devil—"a guilty thing/ Upon a fearful summons"
(I.i.148-49)—as soon as Hamlet accepts it as a true ghost and
embraces without further qualification the revenge thesis.
Had he allowed his play to continue, the other potentiality of
the Ghost ("airs from heaven") might have emerged from the
murder of King Hamlet and from "The Murder of Gonzago." Hamlet, it would seem, made the Ghost the devil.
There is nothing, either good or bad, but thinking makes it
so. "Taint not thy mind," the Ghost had said. As the signet
ring of Hamlet's father sealed the deaths of Rosencrantz and
Guildenstern, so a lingering reminder of the Ghost is
brought to the final scene. Long before, Bernardo had
chided Horatio after the Ghost's appearance: "How now,
Horatio! You tremble and look pale" (I.i.53). Hamlet imputes
the same reaction to the witnesses of the final bloodletting:
"You that look pale and tremble at this chance. . ." (V.ii.345).
Hamlet identified the Ghost on the basis of his play, but in
allowing the play to become a torture device, he had already
made the Ghost the devil. Appropriately, in a play in which
all ritual is perverted, where prayer books are disguises for
duplicity, where the crown prince denies matrimony to himself and the woman he loves, where last rites are denied (to
King Hamlet, Rosencrantz, and Guildenstern), where a
crown prince wears mourning at his uncle's coronation,
where an audience rushes from a play leaving the actors
alone on stage, where funerals are obscene, where a toast to
a son is a poisoning of oneself, where damnation becomes an
imperative the hero forces down the throat of his dying antagonist, where duels are death traps, where even the changing of the guard reflects ritual malfunction, and where redemptive drama breaks up before guilt can be effectively released, the Ghost, an ambassador from another world sent to
enlist a minister to realign Denmark with the creative forces
of the cosmos, must become the devil. Fortinbras had been
dissuaded from revenge by his uncle (II.ii.61-71). Hamlet

had been born the day his father killed old Fortinbras
(V.i.163). Hamlet dies the day young Fortinbras takes over
the kingdom of Denmark without lifting a sword. The inner
revengers, Hamlet and Laertes, die. The third young man
who has lost his father decides against revenge and gains the
kingdom that might have been Hamlet's.

Hamlet could be a more Christian play than its "Christian"
commentators, invariably apologists for Hamlet, recognize.
It is not my wish to place it within that debatable *genre*
known perhaps oxymoronically as "Christian Tragedy," but
to suggest that if it *is* a Christian play, its full "Christian"
value does not, finally, reside in its central character, although he alone might have restored Denmark to spiritual
health. The play, as Battenhouse suggests, "shows tragedy
arising from various *un*-Christian responses in Hamlet and
others."[82] We discover not the season Marcellus mentions,
"Wherein our Saviour's birth is celebrated." Instead, a dying
man forces poisoned wine down the throat of another dying
man. What finer irony in a play treating so pervasively the
theme of appearance and reality than to have its most sensi-
tive character fail to recognize the alternatives struggling
within him. "I have that within which passeth show" (I.ii.85),
he had said. He had it within him to redeem the world and
reign as its king by so working Claudius's soul that justice
would have become the responsibility of an agency higher
than that of Hamlet's will. And he had it within him to destroy that world and die amid its wreckage. For all his intro-
spection, he never asks himself the question with which the
play opens: "Who's there?" (I.i.1). He is the victim of tragic
irony—the failure to recognize the central fact of his existence. He dies, as John F. Danby suggests, "a baffled . . .
young man."[83] He *may* end depraved as well, but that does
not mean that the play subscribes to the doctrine of man's
depravity, or fails to suggest the alternative to moral destruction that Hamlet might have embraced.

Fortinbras's equation of the throne-room to a battlefield
(V.ii.411-412) would seem to support Eliot's contention that
Hamlet "has made a pretty considerable mess of things."[84]
Dame Helen Gardner, however, objects to such censuring of
Hamlet:

Mr. Eliot might, however, have noticed that it is not merely
Hamlet who appears to feel at the close that if only the whole
truth were known. . . the name which he leaves behind him
would not be a "wounded name." Horatio's farewell to him and
Fortinbras' comment make no suggestion that what we have witnessed is a story of personal failure and inadequacy; and
Horatio's summary of what he will tell "the yet unknowing
world" does not include any hint that these things have come
about through the bungling of the dead Prince.[85]

But surely some of what Horatio says applies to Hamlet, as
well as Polonius, Laertes, and Claudius: "accidental judge-
ments, casual slaughters" (V.ii.393) can be assigned to the
murder of Polonius, "deaths put on by cunning and forc'd
cause" (V.ii.394) to the deaths of Rosencrantz and Guildenstern. "Purposes mistook/ Fall'n on the inventors' heads
(V.ii.395) can pertain to Hamlet's disastrous play as well as to
the deadly final scene. The only person Horatio explicitly ex-
culpates, in fact, is Claudius—for the killing of Rosencrantz
and Guildenstern (V.ii.383-85).

But those like Dame Helen who feel instinctively that the
final scene represents a victory for Hamlet are partially right.
The greatest Hamlet, the creative Hamlet, has been lost, but
a lesser Hamlet struggles through to a bloody victory. If
Hamlet's actions since the break-up of his play can be jus-
tified, they are so in terms of Fortinbras's command for
Hamlet's funeral:

> for his passage,
> The soldiers' music and the rites of war
> Speak loudly for him.
>
> (V.ii.409-11)

Hamlet's is a louder funeral, ironically, than that he described as his soldier-father's "quiet" inurnment (I.v.49).
While the funeral of a young soldier is invariably a ceremony
of wasted potential, it is also a celebration of heroism and
sacrifice. Hamlet becomes a soldier. If that role is diminished
compared to the creative one he had shown on the coming of
the players, it becomes necessary once the man betrays the
artist. Once he commits his tragic error, he does as well as he
can, as well as any one could do in the struggle against the
evil working *within* him as well as in the world around him.

The creative son who could see the Cross in the hilt of his sword (I.v.147) must finally, like his soldier-father, take the hilt in his hand. Hamlet's own life becomes necessary to the purgation of Denmark, but he gives it willingly, and can be said to have parted well and paid his score. Certainly, he retains to the end the sympathy we have granted him from the first. We continue to love him in spite of what he has done, in spite of what he may have become. "We love," as Robert Ornstein says, "the suggestion of Hamlet's former self."[86] Those traces of nobility which carry forward even to the end tend to dominate any catalogue of the evils to which Hamlet succumbs as Denmark and his own failure gradually poison his promise and destroy his embassy.

We experience at the end pity and terror in proportion to our celebration of Hamlet's greatness. We have witnessed the results of a potentially good man's struggle with evil. What might have been stays with us, even though Hamlet finds another ending. If he purges the state, it is at the appalling cost of that potential Hamlet we have glimpsed, the Hamlet many insist on seeing even at the end—because it **is** still there in brief flashes against the enclosing darkness, as in his exchanging forgiveness with his fellow revenger, Laertes. *Hamlet,* like many tragedies, explores the discrepancy between what a man might have been and what he must become, between what he might have done and what he finally must do. As for the destiny of his soul, his "rest" is, as far as the play tells us, a "silence" into which we cannot penetrate.

Richard II is not "tragic" in the full Shakespearean sense. While we see Richard making the decision that will precipitate his loss of his crown, we do not witness the decision that introduces division into his kingdom, his hand in Gloucester's murder. We witness the long denouement to the killing of a kinsman. Shakespeare, it would seem, planned a sequence of plays whose present is forever to be conditioned by what has gone before. He signals that intention by beginning the *Second Henriad* after the murder, but before the results can be truly measured. We sense then the *sequential nature* characteristic of the history plays, whatever else may be their generic premises. The "world" of *Richard II,* however, touching as it does upon the memory of England's deeper resonances, is "tragic." The plays that follow have lost that dimension of cosmic contact, are reduced to the stratagems of mere men, however endowed with prophecy, with the memory of things past, and with the teleological thrust of Shakespearean history.

In *Hamlet,* Shakespeare develops one of the basic designs of his tragedies, the intercourse between the hero and the invisible forces surrounding him. His hero may or may not recognize the nature of his connection with the supernature. Macbeth does, but defies it. Hamlet misinterprets it. Antony forces it to desert him. Coriolanus insists on his uniqueness, in defiance of the "nature of things"—that he is man of woman born. Othello and Lear wake up too late to an illumination that might have been saving had it been perceived earlier, had either recognized in time the merits of Desdemona or Cordelia. In *Hamlet* and in *Richard II,* a king is guilty of an unroyal and world-disrupting crime. In each a nemesis appears, a prince intent on setting the time right. But Bolingbroke cannot restore England to its sacramental unity. Not only is such a possibility not dreamed of in his pragmatism, but he is condemned to inherit a world drained by Richard of its larger potentiality. Bolingbroke is a sub-tragic figure destined to plod wearily through an enervated reign characterized by rebellion and inevitable reflections of illness eating away at the body politic. Hamlet, however, is not trapped by history. A character in a tragedy, he reaches a single moment where he might control the sequence of events. Before that moment, like Bolingbroke, he is the victim of a crime-before-the-play. After that moment, he is the victim of the very forces he might have dominated had he recognized the positive possibilities of his plan to encourage Claudius's "heavy burden" toward confession. In *Richard II* the "tragic world" erases itself toward the mundane plane of politics. In *Hamlet* it approaches its moments of decision, then, "after the fall," moves inexorably toward the death of almost all who inhabit it. In *Richard II* we observe a world

gradually drained of ritual, much as Arnold describes the re-
ceding of the "sea of faith... once at the full." In *Hamlet,*
ritual is out of joint at the outset, but we witness not its disappearance, rather its deepening perversion, a destruction
measured against the "miraculous organ" that Hamlet rendered dumb.

NOTES TO CHAPTER 2: *Hamlet*

1. West, *Shakespeare and the Outer Mystery,* p. 22. Battenhouse, in *Shakespearean
   Tragedy,* disagrees strongly. See pp. 243-44.
2. Battenhouse, *Shakespearean Tragedy,* p. 238.
3. David Daiches, "Shakespeare's Poetry," *The Living Shakespeare,* ed. Robert Gittings (New York, 1960), p. 124.
4. Battenhouse, *Shakespearean Tragedy,* p. 240.
5. Prince Hal provides the rationale behind his sojourn in Eastcheap, but Henry V
   does not impart to his audience or to his court his plan for manipulating England into foreign war. Henry V is appropriately distanced from us; as King he
   must be a more remote, withdrawn figure than he was as Hal. Vincentio offers
   conflicting reasons for his absenting himself from recognized authority, forcing
   us, I believe, to suspect his motives. See my "Henry V and the Nature of Kingship," *Discourse* (1970), and my forthcoming article on *Measure for Measure* in *SQ.*
6. O. B. Hardison, "Three Types of Renaissance Catharsis," *Renaissance Drama,*
   New Series 2 (Evanston, Ill., 1969), pp. 3-22. For a note on the word *presently,*
   see M. R. Ridley's New Arden Edition of *Othello,* p. 61, n213. For examples
   beyond the many that Ridley adduces, see *Hamlet,* II. ii. 170 (Polonius: "I'll
   board him presently"), and *The Tempest,* IV.i. 42-43. (Ariel: "Presently?" Prospero: "Ay, with a twink.")
7. Goddard, *The Meaning of Shakespeare,* p. 364.
8. Holland, *Psychoanalysis and Shakespeare,* p. 238.
9. Hardison, "Three Types of Renaissance Catharsis," pp. 4-5.
10. G. R. Hibbard, "The Year's Contributions to Shakespearian Studies," *Shakespeare
    Survey* 23 (1970): 149.
11. Cf. Battenhouse, *Shakespearean Tragedy,* p. 265: "Reminiscent bells, deep-down
    inklings of the higher order betrayed, haunt the career of tragic man."
12. Arthur Johnston, "The Player's Speech in *Hamlet,*" *SQ* 13 (1962): 24.
13. Johnston, "The Player's Speech," p. 27.
14. *Ibid.,* p. 28.
15. Weston Babcock, *Hamlet: A Tragedy of Errors* (Lafayette, Ind., 1961), p. 99. Since
    Hamlet does not carry his thinking to the point of asking what he would do
    were Claudius to confess publicly, conjecture on this point is irrelevant. Bab-
    cock, p. 101, has Hamlet "dash across the stage and run [Claudius] through
    with his rapier." It is idle to speculate what Hamlet might have done after the
    confession, but it is *not* idle to postulate the confession. Claudius, as regicide,
    would have paid a price beyond the heart's sorrow exacted from Alonso. Henry
    V, however, makes the distinction between temporal and eternal punishment in
    sentencing the traitors to death and at the same time hoping for their salvation
    (II.ii. 166-81).

16. Salvador de Madariaga, *On Hamlet* (London, 1948), pp. 89-90.
17. Alfred Harbage, *William Shakespeare: A Reader's Guide* (New York. 1963), p. 324.
18. Goddard, *Meaning of Shakespeare*, p. 369.
19. Quoted in Maynard Mack, "The World of *Hamlet*," *Yale Review* 41 (1952): 518.
20. G. L. Kittredge, *Hamlet* (Boston, 1939), p. 229.
21. Cox, *Between Earth and Heaven*, pp. 63-64.
22. Hardison, "Three Types of Renaissance Catharsis," p. 7.
23. Hibbard, "The Years Contributions," p. 149.
24. Gilson, *Spirit of Mediaeval Philosophy*, p. 296.
25. Thomas Van Laan, *"Everyman:* A Structural Analysis," *PMLA* 78, no. 5 (December, 1963): 467.
26. Hardison, "Three Types of Renaissance Catharsis," pp. 7-8.
27. *Johnson,* ed. Mona Wilson (Cambridge, Mass., 1951), p. 616.
28. *Coleridge's Writings on Shakespeare's Plays,* ed. Terrence Hawkes (New York, 1959), p. 163.
29. Battenhouse, *Shakespearean Tragedy*, p. 255.
30. Cf. St. Bernard: "The ills the soul now suffers do not replace the native goodness which is the original gift of the Creator, but they are superinduced on that goodness, and disturb it, deforming an order they can in no wise destroy." Gilson, *Spirit of Mediaeval Philosophy*, p. 295. Trivet is quoted in D. W. Robertson, *Preface to Chaucer* (Princeton, N.J., 1962), p. 26.
31. Erich Auerbach, *Mimesis* (Garden City, N.Y., 1957), p. 277.
32. Fredson Bowers, "Hamlet as Minister and Scourge," *PMLA* 70 (1955): 740-49.
33. *Ibid.,* p. 745.
34. *Ibid.,* p. 742.
35. Dover Wilson, *What Happens in Hamlet*, p. 138.
36. Fredson Bowers, "Dramatic Structure and Criticism: Plot in *Hamlet,*" *SQ* 15 (1964): 209.
37. Helen Gardner, *The Business of Criticism* (Oxford, 1959), pp. 25-51.
38. D. A. Traversi, *An Approach to Shakespeare* (New York, 1956), p. 100.
39. M. R. Ridley, "Plot and Character in the Plays," *The Living Shakespeare*, ed. Robert Gittings (New York, 1960), p. 82. Cf. Virgil Whitaker, *The Mirror Up to Nature* (Huntington Library, 1965), p. 201: "In *Hamlet* Shakespeare failed to make his borrowed plot and his moral interests coalesce."
40. Leslie Fiedler, "The Defense of the Illusion and the Creation of Myth," *English Institute Essays,* 1948 (New York, 1949), p. 76.
41. J. C. Maxwell, "Shakespeare: The Middle Plays," *The Age of Shakespeare*, ed. Boris Ford (Baltimore, Md., 1960), p. 210. For a discussion of *Hamlet's* superiority to other Elizabethan revenge plays, see J. J. Lawlor, "The Tragic Conflict in Hamlet," *Review of English Studies* 1 (1960), and Kenneth Muir, *Hamlet* (New York, 1963), pp. 55-61. For discussions relating *Hamlet* to Elizabethan ideas on revenge, see Eleanor Prosser *Hamlet and Revenge*, pp. 3-73; J. E. Hankins, *The Character of Hamlet and Other Essays* (Chapel Hill, N.C., 1941); Fredson Bowers, *Elizabethan Revenge Tragedy* (Princeton, 1940), pp. 3-61; Harold Jenkins, "The Tragedy of Revenge in Shakespeare and Webster," *Shakespeare Survey* 14 (1961); L. B. Campbell, "Theories of Revenge in Elizabethan England," *MP* 28 (1931); and Hiram Haydn, *The Counter-Renaissance* (New York, 1950), pp. 555-98.
42. G. Wilson Knight, *The Wheel of Fire* (London, 1949), p. 20. D. A. Traversi, *An Approach to Shakespeare*, p. 95.
43. John Holloway, *The Story of the Night* (Lincoln, Neb., 1961), p. 30.

44. For a discussion of *Hamlet's* relationship to the first years of the seventeenth century, see Paul Jorgensen, "Hamlet and the Restless Renaissance," *Shakespearian Essays,* ed. Alwin Thaler and Norman Saunders (Knoxville, Tenn., 1964), pp. 131-43.

45. On the matter of ritual, see Fergusson, *"Hamlet:* The Analogy of Action," and the interesting intertextual commentary by William W. Main in his edition of *Hamlet* (New York, 1963), particularly on p. 231. For an explicit equation of *Hamlet* with the archetype of the Fall, see Charles R. Woodard, "The Archetype of the Fall," *CE* 38 (1967): 576-80.

46. D. G. James, *The Dream of Learning* (Oxford, 1951), p. 49.

47. Leslie Fiedler, "The Defense of the Illusion," p. 90.

48. Arthur Sewell, *Character and Society in Shakespeare* (Oxford, 1951), p. 57.

49. Helen Gardner, *The Business of Criticism,* p. 50.

50. Quoted in Edith Sitwell, *A Notebook on William Shakespeare* (Boston, 1961), p. 82.

51. Sitwell, *A Notebook. . .,* p. 82.

52. Bernard Grebanier, *The Heart of Hamlet,* pp. 133ff.

53. Dover Wilson, *What Happens in Hamlet,* p. 263. See also Kenneth Muir, *Hamlet,* pp. 46-49.

54. Karl Polanyi, *"Hamlet,"* *Yale Review* 43 (1954): 350.

55. Irving Ribner, *Patterns of Shakespearian Tragedy,* p. 82.

56. S. F. Johnson, "The Regeneration of Hamlet," *SQ* 3 (1952): 206.

57. C. S. Lewis, "Hamlet: The Prince or the Poem," *British Academy Lecture* 28 (London, 1942): 148.

58. Theodore Spencer, *Shakespeare and the Nature of Man,* p. 108.

59. John Paterson, *"Hamlet,"* *SQ* 2 (1952): 54.

60. Bertram Joseph, *Conscience and the King* (London, 1948), p. 143.

61. Roy Walker, *The Time is Out of Joint* (London, 1948), p. 143.

62. Francis Fergusson, *"Hamlet:* The Analogy of Action," p. 142.

63. H. Granville-Barker, *Prefaces to Shakespeare* (Princeton, 1946), 1: 253.

64. A. C. Bradley, *Shakespearean Tragedy* (London, 1904), p. 143.

65. L. Schucking, *The Meaning of Hamlet* (Oxford, 1937), p. 167.

66. T. M. Parrott, *Shakespeare* (New York, 1931), 2: 403.

67. Donald Stauffer, *Shakespeare's World of Images* (New York, 1949), p. 126.

68. H. B. Charlton, *Shakespearian Tragedy* (Cambridge, 1948), p. 103.

69. A. C. Bradley, *Shakespearean Tragedy,* p. 122.

70. Bernard Grebanier, *The Heart of Hamlet,* p. 472.

71. Quoted in Maureen McKernan, *The Amazing Crime and Trial of Loeb and Leopold* (New York, 1957), pp. 176-79.

72. Alfred Harbage, *As They Liked It* (New York, 1961), p. 33.

73. Clifford P. Lyons, " 'It appears so by the story': Notes on a Narrative-Thematic Emphasis in Shakespeare," *SQ* 9 (1958): 294.

74. See Gardner, *Business of Criticism,* pp. 25-51.

75. Ornstein, *Moral Vision of Jacobean Tragedy,* p. 235.

76. Yet one critic can talk of the "confident heartwholeness of the new Hamlet" (i.e. the Hamlet of Act V): B. L. Reid, "The Last Act and the Action of *Hamlet,"* *Yale Review* 54 (1964): 78.

77. M. M. Manood, *Poetry and Humanism* (London, 1950), p. 64.

78. *Liturgy and Worship,* ed. Clarke, p. 375.

79. Hibbard, "The Year's Contributions," p. 149.

80. Jay L. Halio, "Hamlet's Alternatives," *Texas Studies in Literature and Language* 8 (1966): 179.

81. Laurence Michel, "Hamlet: Superman, Subchristian," *Centennial Review* 6 (1962): 242.

82. Battenhouse, *Shakespearean Tragedy*, p. 279.

83. John F. Danby, "The Tragedies," *The Living Shakespeare*, p. 123.

84. T. S. Eliot, "Shakespeare and the Stoicism of Seneca," *Selected Essays* (London, 1932), p. 23.

85. Gardner, *Business of Criticism*, p. 39. Cf. Patrick Cruttwell, "The Morality of Hamlet," in *Hamlet* (London, 1963), p. 128: "[Hamlet] has done things as we all do in wars, he would rather not have done; but he believes it to be a just war and, all in all, he has borne himself well."

86. Ornstein, *Moral Vision of Jacobean Tragedy*, p. 235.

3

Othello

Where love is great, the littlest doubts are fear.
—The Player King, *Hamlet* (III.ii.181)

    the more I see
Pleasures around me, so much more I feel
Torment within me, as from the hateful siege
Of contraries; all good to me becomes
Bane.
—Satan, *Paradise Lost* (IX.119-23)

And this is the condempnacioun, that lyghte is come into the
world, and men loved darckenesse more than lyghte.
—John iii, The Gospel for Monday in Wytson
weeke (*Book of Common Prayer,* 1559)

Of the "four great tragedies"—*Hamlet, Othello, King
Lear,* and *Macbeth*—*Othello* is the only one whose tragic action does not reach out to touch the ultimate confines of the
cosmos. Iago ascribes the sword fight between Cassio,
Roderigo, and Montano to solar influence: "As if some
planet had unwitted men" (II.iii.182). But we know who is
responsible. Othello repeats the cosmic suggestion after killing Desdemona:

> It is the very error of the moon;
> She comes more nearer earth than she was wont,
> And makes men mad.
>
> (V.ii.109-11)

Looking down at the strangled Desdemona, Othello solicits a response from the universe:

> Methinks it should be now a huge eclipse
> Of sun and moon, and that the affrighted globe
> Did yawn at alteration.
>
> (V.ii.99-101)

But there is *no* eclipse, there *is* no errant planet stroking men's minds to madness. It may be, as some critics suggest, that Othello's killing of Desdemona is analogous to the betrayal of Christ by Judas, but the response imputed to the cosmos at the moment of Christ's death simply does *not* occur in *Othello:*

> And there was a darckness over all the earth, untyll the ninth houre: and the Sonne was darkned. And the vayle of the temple did rente, even through the middest.

No Ghost returns to commission a Hamlet to revenge, no Weird Sisters echo the fearful impulses of a Macbeth's will, no stratospheric outrage shakes above Cyprus as above Scotland when Duncan is murdered, no storm rumbles through Othello's island, like that of Lear's kingdom, reflecting on the gigantic screen of the universe Lear's lightning-splintered mind, and reverberating with the anarchy he has engendered on earth. The great storm in *Othello* is, if anything, benevolent. It drowns the Turks sailing toward exposed and vulnerable Cyprus and grants safe passage to Venetians:

> Tempests themselves, high seas, and howling winds,
> The gutter'd rocks and congregated sands,
> Traitors ensteep'd to enclog the guiltless keel,
> As having sense of beauty, do omit
> Their mortal natures, letting go safely by
> The divine Desdemona.
>
> (II.i.68-73)

But the storm permits Iago to arrive as well, on the same

ship as Desdemona. Nature is there, but it does not interfere
with the actions of men nor seem to comment on them. It
lets them grope with flaring torches and unbated swords
through a night of error that is none of the doing of the
universe. The play does not expand outward from a central
crime—the murder of a King Hamlet or a King Duncan, the
combined crime of Lear in deposing himself and rejecting
Cordelia—to intersect the mystery in which the natural world
is wrapped. Instead, *Othello* closes in psychologically to a
single poisoned mind and narrows down physically, as Bradley says, to "a close-shut murderous room."[1] In the other
plays we pursue the concentric circles radiating outward
from the crashing of great crimes against the face of the
world. In *Othello,* we follow the sinking stone to its solitary
depth.

The early parts of *Othello* pursue a comic rhythm. Iago in-
flames Brabantio, who attempts to indict Othello before the
Duke and Venetian Council for marrying Desdemona.
Othello is accused of using "witchcraft" (I.iii.64) in wooing
the Senator's daughter, of employing "spells and charms
bought of montebanks" (I.iii.61):

> With some mixtures powerful o'er the blood
> Or with some dram conjur'd to this effect,
> He wrought upon her.
>
> (I.iii.104-6)

Desdemona has been "enchanted," bound "in chains of
magic" (I.ii.63-65). Egeus charges Lysander similarly before
the Duke of *A Midsummer-Night's Dream:* "This man hath
bewitch'd the bosom of my child" (I.i.27). The Venetian
Duke promises Brabantio that "the bloody book of law/ You
shall yourself read in the bitter letter/ After your own sense,
yea, though our proper son/ Stood in your action"
(I.iii.67-70). Egeus demands

> the ancient privilege of Athens,
> As she is mine, I may dispose of her;
> Which shall be either to this gentleman
> Or to her death, according to our law
> Immediately provided in that case.
>
> (I.i.41-45)

Hermia wishes that "my father look'd but with my eyes" (I.i.56), while Desdemona also sees with other than parental vision: "I saw Othello's visage in his mind" (I.iii.253). The Athenian problem is resolved by the complicated dream that scampers through "the palace wood, a mile without the town" (I.ii.104), the forest a metaphor for the unconscious mind. Egeus never brings sharp law against Hermia, and the play ends with the multiple marriages inevitable to the Shakespearean comedy. Shylock, too, has lost his daughter and, as part of his revenge against the Christian world which, he feels, has stolen Jessica, calls for law:

> "My daughter! O my ducats! O my daughter!
> Fled with a Christian! O my Christian ducats!
> Justice! the law! my ducats and my daughter!"
>
> (II.viii.15-17)

When he "crave[s] the law" (IV.i.206) against Antonio, Portia intervenes to preserve the comic ending. Othello's potent defense of his courtship combines with the Venetian need for his military prowess to free him of Brabantio's indictment. The lovers are united, as Romeo and Juliet might have been by their duke, had not the misplay of swords brought death to Mercutio and Tybalt, confirming in blood the family feud. The comic curve of *Othello* culminates in that moment after the storm, when the lovers meet in the perfection of their triumph over law and nature:

> It gives me wonder great as my content
> To see you here before me. O my soul's joy!
> If after every tempest come such calms,
> May the winds blow till they have waken'd death!
>
> (II.i.185-88)

But all is not well; while the play imitates superficially a comic rhythm at the outset, the deeper chords of tragedy have been struck. While the marriage of Othello and Desdemona can be placed within that comic pattern in which a father's will is overriden, the marriage raises problems. Obviously, it is a pretext for immediate discord, as Iago insists, typical of the "unusual" marriage of the plays of the period.[2] That Desdemona loves Othello is amply validated in the play,

but the couple have defied convention and hoodwinked the
eminent Senator Brabantio. Brabantio's is not merely the attitude of an outraged father. His accusation before the Senate is predicted by Roderigo:

> Your daughter . . . hath made a gross revolt,
> Tying her duty, beauty, wit, and fortunes
> In an extravagant and wheeling stranger
> Of here and everywhere.

                                                    (I.i.134-38)

His objection is that of the aristocrat, like Tom Buchanan's
anger over his wife's infatuation with Gatsby, "Mr. Nobody
from Nowhere." Even the loyal Emilia calls Desdemona's
marriage "her most filthy bargain" (V.ii.157). And although
she is incensed at the time at Othello for murdering Desdemona, her phrase seems to emerge from deep-seated conviction, seems to be the kind of latent ammunition that suddenly surfaces, for example, in a fight between a husband
and a wife. To certain elements of Venetian society, the
match is not good, and partakes of the destiny Hamlet ascribes to the marriage of Gertrude and Claudius: "It is not,
nor it cannot come to good" (I.ii.158).

The marriage, which included the deception of a Venetian
senator, one of Othello's commanders, suggests that Othello's
private life, his love for Desdemona, the call of his "body
natural," supersedes his public role, his Venetian generalship,
his "body politic." Thus the conflict between his two roles is
predicted before he assumes an independent body politic as,
not a functionary answerable to the Venetian command, but
supreme commander of Cyprus. The breach may seem small
at first, but it is enough to predict ruin's wasteful entrance.
The *difference* between Othello and Desdemona, between
the converted pagan and the fair Venetian, will be one of
Iago's chief weapons in his subtle war against the Moor.
Brabantio, a reasonable Venetian, can comprehend
Desdemona's love only in terms of witchcraft; it is simply un-
reasonable, unnatural:

> To fall in love with what she fear'd to look on!
> It is a judgement maim'd and most imperfect
> That will confess perfection so could err

Against all rules of nature, and must be driven
To find out practices of cunning hell,
Why this should be.

(I.iii.98-103)

He is attempting to define the indefinable—Desdemona's love, a quest as fruitless as a critic's trying to ascertain Iago's motivation. But the very transcendence of convention in Desdemona's love for Othello will be a trigger in Iago's manipulation of the Moor. Much later, Iago subtly reiterates Brabantio's charges:

She did deceive her father, marrying you;
And when she seem'd to shake and fear your looks,
She lov'd them most.

(III.iii.206-8)

Not to affect many proposed matches
Of her own clime, complexion, and degree,
Whereto we see in all things nature tends—
Foh! one may smell in such, a will most rank,
Foul disproportions, thoughts unnatural . . .
Her will, recoiling to her better judgement,
May fall to match you with her country forms,
And happily repent.

(III.iii.229-38)

This echo of Brabantio's accusation interprets "nature" for Othello from the narrow Venetian premises shared by Brabantio and Roderigo, making Othello a stranger to his *own* knowledge of Desdemona's love. There is, however, a flaw in Othello's love, as I will suggest. At that later moment in Cyprus, Othello embraces arguments he knew were false when lodged by Brabantio in Venice and accepts Desdemona's glimpse into the truth of his soul as a deviation from the social norm. The marriage points, as Alfred Harbage says, at a "certain obliviousness"[3] in Othello and Desdemona, a slighting of "proper forms." Desdemona proves she is "above Venice," above the racial restrictions a Brabantio or a Roderigo would assume. Othello proves he is not "of Venice," hence possibly a prey to a manipulator who can "interpret" Venetian custom for him:

Iago. I know our country disposition well;
  In Venice they do let Heaven see the pranks

> They dare not show their husbands. Their best conscience
>   Is not to leave 't undone, but keep 't unknown.
> Othello. Dost thou say so?
>
> (III.iii.201-5)

Othello is careful at the outset to place himself within the
context of Venetian hierarchy. He knows he is their mercenary. The senators are his "very noble and approved good
masters" (I.iii.77)—with the question of Senator Brabantio
begged. He feels that his own worth will override Brabantio's
outrage, that the "service [he has] done the signiory/ Shall
out-tongue [Brabantio's] complaint" (I.ii.18-19). The scene
shifts from Brabantio's personal grievance to affairs of state,
and Othello allows himself to be absorbed into the transition.
He accepts the defense of Cyprus in spite of his recent marriage, "Most humbly bending therefore to your state"
(I.iii.236), and promises that if Desdemona can accompany
him, he will not "your serious and great business scant"
(I.iii.268). He submits not just to the council's urgency, but to
the larger rhythms of nature with which the state must align
itself if its affairs are to prosper: "We must obey the time"
(I.iii.301).

Othello seems, then, in spite of certain scanting of Venetian custom, to be safely and consciously within the
framework that has made him such a trusted and effective
public servant. Iago, however, reveals a dangerous independence of such structure:

> Virtue! a fig! 'tis in ourselves that we are thus or thus. Our
> bodies are our gardens, to the which our wills are gardeners; so
> that if we will plant nettles or sow lettuce, set hyssop and weed
> up thyme, supply it with one gender of herbs or distract it with
> many, wither to have it sterile with idleness or manured with in-
> dustry, why, the power and corrigible authority of this lies in our
> wills. If the balance of our lives had not one scale of reason to
> poise another of sensuality, the blood and baseness of our na-
> tures would conduct us to most preposterous conclusions; but we
> have reason to cool our raging motions, our carnal stings, our
> unbitted lusts, whereof I take this that you call love to be a sect
> or scion. (I.iii.322-37)

Will, in his disquisition, is subordinate to no higher power, to
neither state nor heaven. Naked will—that of a Macbeth or

Edmund—is obviously not sanctioned by the political or theological dispensations that Shakespeare's plays display. Iago is capable of invoking *Heaven* as witness to his will:

> Heaven is my judge, not I for love and duty,
> But seeming so, for my peculiar end.

(I.i.59-60)

Iago pursues his plan to "plume up [his] will" (I.iii.399), to adorn it with badges of nobility and command normally conferred by a higher power, not evolved out of man's own motivation. Within the play's carefully defined hierarchy, Iago's is a debased and alien ethic. Mere will, unmotivated and uninformed by larger controlling realities, is a chief cause of tragedy, whether Richard II's, Macbeth's, or Coriolanus's, a destructive drive as demonstrated by the lustful and poisonous careers of Goneril and Regan and by Iago's reduction of "love" to a category under lust. Love becomes subordinated to one of the Seven Deadly Sins—as it must; for if individual will sits atop the hierarchy, love for another, an impulse *beyond* the mere self, must be rationalized into a subodinate drive, into the copulation of animals—rams tupping ewes (I.i.88-89), the beast with the two backs (I.i.117-18), the lascivious sport of goats and monkeys (III.iii.403). Ultimate love, in Iago's value system, can only be *self*-love and in this he is unique: "I never found a man that knew how to love himself" (I.iii.314-15), he tells Roderigo, neglecting to point out that he is that man. Any other love is bestial, and he sneers at Roderigo's version: "Ere I would say I would drown myself for the love of a guinea hen, I would change my humanity for a baboon" (I.iii.314-18). Lust is the only "love" that total self-love can admit, because its premises rest on gratification of the single will. Any other love *must* be bestial because it violates the basis of Iago's hierarchy, is thus a crime against "order." Love for Iago is "a lust of the blood and a permission of the will" (I.iii.338-40). While Iago's "order" is clearly contrary to the framework the play presents, epitomized by the Venetian duke, there is in Othello an element of self-love that will allow Iago to debase Othello's relationship to Desdemona to

self-love (or mere will) and, indeed, prompt Othello to exchange his humanity for bestiality.

Equally ominous is Iago's metaphor. The garden
—common medieval and Renaissance emblem, often implying Eden or, making the equation explicit, as in John of
Gaunt's description of England's paradise lost—must, if will is
its keeper, be a corrupt garden, not overseen by a benevolent
God, an unfallen Adam, or a rightful king like Duncan, who
tells Macbeth, "I have begun to plant thee and will labour/
To make thee full of growing" (I.iv.28-29). Iago's garden can
bring forth only deformed progeny:

> It is engend'red. Hell and night
> Must bring this monstrous birth to the world's light.
>
> (I.iii.409-10)

It is not that Eden sprung suddenly to sight by a cleft of initial light, but one conceived and nurtured in hellish murk.
Iago is an anti-creator, as his other metaphors of birth imply
(cf. I.iii.376-78, II.i.128-29). "For of our selves," says "The
second part of the Sermon of the Miserie of Man," "wee bee
crabtrees, that can bring foorth no apples. We be of our
selves of such earth, as can bring foorth but weedes, netles,
brambles, briers, cockle, and darnel." The fruits of such a
garden must be perverse, as they are in Iago's rationalization
of Roderigo's injuries:

> Cassio hath beaten thee,
> And thou, by that small hurt, hast cashier'd Cassio.
> Though other things grow fair against the sun,
> Yet fruits that blossom first will first be ripe.
>
> (II.iii.380-83)

Within his own metaphor, Iago has succeeded in "the dis-
planting of Cassio" (II.i.283).

Shakespeare begins his play with Iago, an obscene filter
through which we view Othello, even as we first see Macbeth
through the Weird Sisters who have mentioned his name. It
is doubtful that we credit for very long Iago's charge against
Othello in the preferment of Cassio, but certainly we fear for
Othello as we see Iago quickly fan the quiet, dark Venetian
streets to obscene shouts and the flicker of hurrying torches.

Iago effectively undercuts the play's "comic" opening, as, in a
more formal way, the Prologue of *Romeo and Juliet* warns
us against embracing that play's comic potentiality. The
world of *Othello* seems framed for the genius Iago displays
immediately. It is a world demanding sudden movement,
which must be roused from sleep "In this time of night"
(I.ii.94), must send messengers "post-post-haste" to Florence
(I.iii.46), must dispatch Othello to Cyprus. In such a world,
Iago is the master tactician, confirming the skill in battle he
imputes to himself. Much of the play occurs at night
—physical darkness through which Iago, alone, seems to see
clearly, and the darkness of doubt—about the truth of
Brabantio's charges, the size and direction of the Turkish
fleet, the identity of ships emerging from the storm to the
harbor of Cyprus, Cassio's birthplace (he is a Florentine, yet
described as a "Veronese" by one of the Gentlemen awaiting
his arrival in Cyprus [II.i.26]). In such a world, Iago is the
master creator of deceptive report and false evidence.

So superb is Iago, in fact, that some see him as the Devil.
He enlists the "tribe of hell" (I.iii.364) in his battle against the
"frail vow" (I.iii.361) between Desdemona and Othello. He
mentions "hell pains" (I.i.155), reminiscent perhaps of the
perpetual agony of Marlowe's Mephisto. He invokes "Hell
and night" as the womb out of which his plot emerges
(I.iii.409), and shouts "Diablo, ho!" (II.ii.160) as he exults in
the riot he is producing and directing. Othello, looking for
Iago's cloven foot, says, "but that's a fable" (V.ii.286), yet
tries to kill him: "If that thou be'st a devil, I cannot kill thee"
(V.ii.287). His faulty thrust could be evidence of the lost soldiership he has just recounted, very much as Lear does after
reporting his killing of the slave that was hanging Cordelia
("I have seen the day, with my good biting falchion/ I would
have made him skip" [V.iii.276-77]):

> Othello   I have seen the day
>   That, with this little arm and this good sword,
>   I have made my way through more impediments
>   Than twenty times your stop.
> (V.ii.261-64)

His effort against Iago, then, would be similar to Antony's

botched suicide—the once-great soldier who has lost his swordsmanship. Yet there seems to be something more than natural in Iago's sneering smile: "I bleed, sir, but not kill'd" (V.ii.288). And, a few lines later, Othello accepts Iago's devilish nature, if not the fable:

> Will you, I pray, demand that demi-devil
> Why he hath thus ensnar'd my soul and body?
>
> (V.ii.301-2)

Iago's reported confessions are necessary to bring matters to a swift conclusion and to focus at the end upon Othello. Yet they seem gratuitous from the standpoint of Iago's *character*. More convincing is his "From this time forth I never will speak word" (V.ii.304). We believe that he will not open his lips again, particularly "not to pray" (V.ii.305). We anticipate not his tortures beyond the play's end, but his silence. The case for Iago as Devil or a devil has been made far more convincingly than here,[4] and it holds a certain fascination, but if Iago is *not* human, there is no terror in his *choice* of evil. Mephistopheles is terrifying, but he *has* chosen. Iago chooses, and continues choosing before the momentum of his plot; that in itself is terrifying. The choice is real for Iago *and* for Othello. To make Iago a devil is to diminish Othello's role in his own fall.

While Iago is, in a sense, Othello's Mephistopheles, his mission is less clear. Mephisto is out for a soul. Furthermore, while Shakespeare leaves questions like what *is* the Ghost, who *are* the Weird Sisters deliciously ambiguous, he does not let us doubt that they are shapes from "another world," the undiscovered country from which travelers *do* return to the glimpses of the moon. Iago is not so identified, and, while we have no difficulty in attributing devilish motives to him, to make him *the* Devil or *a* devil is to give an "answer" to the mystery of iniquity even while Shakespeare is profoundly raising the question. And to make Iago a devil is to create an inconsistency in Shakespeare's characterization—to place an otherworldly character *within* the dramatic flow, rather than placing him at the edge of the central *human* drama, as he does the Ghost and Sisters. If Iago is a literal rather than a figurative devil, Desdemona must become a "Christ figure" and *Othello* becomes a morality play with an allegory of good and evil angels lurking at the right and left ears of a precariously balanced hero. Iago and Desdemona are abstractions in that they are characters in a play, imitations of the actions of "real people." If they participate in qualities —iniquity or virtue—then that participation does not *make* them those qualities, any more than it makes them a Satan or a Christ. They are not puppets pulled by the demands of an allegory.

Whatever Iago's motivation—whether merit spurned, sexual jealousy, the racial hatred implied by his slurs at Othello's bestiality—his motive hunting does seem to stem from the "motiveless malignity" Coleridge ascribes to him.[5] Obviously, Iago's lack of promotion is a rationalization, or, at most, only a fraction of the motive force for his hatred.* His early statement that Othello's "eyes had seen the proof" of his military merit (I.i.28) suggests that if Othello could be deceived *in* Iago, he can be deceived *by* Iago, through eyes opening on other "proofs" (III.iii.430). If Iago operates out of no premises other than the supremacy of his will, we have a character more terrifying than the assignment of a precise motive would make him. We have an evil man, who delights in disorder, revels in alarming the night with shouts and flames and swords, enjoys being both instigator and peacemaker, seems to perform his function superbly even after he has denied his office by fomenting fights and flustering superiors with wine or with the more virulent poison of jealousy. The riot he creates on the first night in Cyprus is a happy interlude to Iago, almost a "vacation":

> In troth, 'tis morning;
> Pleasure and action make the hours seem short.
>
> (II.iii.384-85)

Iago operates on the principle of alienation. Alienated himself from anything beyond the self, he will alienate Cassio from Othello, Othello from his self-control and Christianity,

---

*If merit spurned *were* his motive, his plot would need go no further once he has discredited Cassio, an event occurring before he begins to encourage Othello toward jealousy.

and from Desdemona. It is an already existing alienation—of
Desdemona from Brabantio—however, that gives him initial
scope in which to operate, just as Richard's original complicity gives Bolingbroke his opportunity to challenge Richard's
throne. While his plot against Othello could be read as
Venice's revenge against the man who has stolen a Venetian
"jewel" (I.iii.195), its origins clearly reside in his single will.
He has no fixed plan. Even its outlines cross his mind in
dark flashes:

> How, how?—Let's see:—
> After some time, to abuse Othello's ear
> That [Cassio] is too familiar with his wife . . .
>
> (I.iii.400-402)

Its execution is often brilliant improvisation, as in his stage
management of Othello's eavesdropping on Cassio's dispar-
agement of Bianca (Othello, of course, believes that Cassio is
discussing Desdemona). Iago is shown early for what he is:

> Make after him, poison his delight,
> Proclaim him in the streets. Incense her kinsmen,
> And, though he in a fertile climate dwell,
> Plague him with flies.
>
> (I.i.68-71)

He is a moral pyromaniac:

> Do, with like timorous accent and dire yell
> As when, by night and negligence, the fire
> Is spied in populous cities.
>
> (I.i.75-77)

Yet even he can perceive his moral ugliness; Cassio "hath a
daily beauty in his life/ That makes me ugly" (V.i.19-20).
Iago must transmogrify the world into his image, must make
the world as ugly as his anti-edenic garden, must translate
Othello's interior into the evil his face says he *should* be.
Like Milton's Satan, peering at Adam and Eve imparadised
in each other's arms, the sight of beauty becomes hateful to
him—"hell-pains" (I.i.155), he says, speaking of Othello.
Othello's belief in Desdemona must become "a cistern for
foul toads/ To knot and gender in" (IV.ii.61-62).

Iago would substitute "jealousy" for "judgement" (II.i.310-11), "madness" for "peace and quiet" (II.i.319-20), inverting the proper hierarchy of man's nature. Wine, in Iago's hierarchy, is incapable of sacramental elevation. It must be reduced to its lower, merely natural origins: "Bless'd fig's-end! The wine she drinks is made of grapes. If she had been bless'd, she would never have lov'd the Moor" (II.i.256-58). Although he has apprenticed himself in iniquity through the poisoning of Brabantio and the manipulation of Roderigo, and will soon produce in Cassio through wine a physical analogue to the psychic chaos he will encourage in Othello through his poisoned insinuations, he is hardly aware of all the details even as the Venetians reach Cyprus:

> 'Tis here, but yet confus'd;
> Knavery's plain face is never seen till us'd.
>
> (II.i.320-21)

He moves into his stratagem with *no* strategy, but with a basic premise and a superb command of tactics, with no mo-✳ tive other than sheer delectation in destruction. The details and dangers of his plot fascinate him—that alone is motivation. Iago has no goal other than Othello's destruction, and *that* makes him dangerous. He seems to care little about the consequences for himself, which he mentions only briefly and generally as his project careens toward its conclusion (V.i.20-21, 128-29).

The danger of Iago is suggested by the Venetian council, reasonable men attempting to place the movements of the Turkist fleet in the context of reason. The Turk *can't* be heading for Rhodes, argues the First Senator:

> We must not think the Turk is so unskilful
> To leave that latest which concerns him first,
> Neglecting an attempt of ease and gain
> To wake and wage a danger profitless.
>
> (I.iii.27-30)

Indeed, Iago *does* leave that latest which concerns him first. He moves through Roderigo, Brabantio, and Cassio—none of whom *really* concerns him—toward Othello, whose destruction is his sole concern. His maneuverings and deceptions are similar to those of the Turkish fleet. And Othello, toward whom he aims, is like Cyprus, once controlled by Egypt, "throughout its history subject to alien influences,"[6] and conquered by the Turk in Shakespeare's lifetime, as it is, figuratively, in his play. And there *is* no profit in Iago's maneuverings, other than the pluming up of his will, his sole arbiter. He is, as Alvin Kernan says, "an anti-life spirit which seeks the destruction of everything outside the self."[7] His "divinity of hell" perverts all positive value. The handkerchief, Othello's first gift to Desdemona, becomes in Iago's theology a "confirmation [as] strong/ As proofs of holy writ" (III.iii.323-24). Whatever he *is*, the drama shows him busily reconverting Othello to the pagan past from which the Moor emerged, *un*converting him from Christianity, often by the application of Christian precept—part of his consistently "double knavery" (I.iii.399). To Iago, Othello is an "erring barbarian" (I.iii.362), and Iago will risk everything to make him one. Iago is an agent of dark forces constantly encroaching on man's humane weal, forces to be propitiated only by the wisdom of authority. When that wisdom becomes corrupt, bright things come quickly to confusion and chaos is come again. But authority must be potentially corruptible to be prey to a Iago.

Othello's first moments as supreme commander seem, as I have suggested, to be the end of a comedy, the reunion of the lovers after the tempest. They stand in the clearing sky, cloud racks already below the Mediterranean curve, a few remnants of enemy mast and sail bobbing at Cypriot shores. We know, however, that Iago has come too. Still, has Othello shown himself susceptible to the potentiality of Iago's plot? A Iago can claim that his own jealousy of Emilia with the Moor, "Doth, like a poisonous mineral gnaw my inwards" (II.i.306), yet can also shrug his shoulders and say indifferently, "I know not if 't be true" (I.iii.394). It need not be true so long as it serves his purposes.

> But I, for mere suspicion in that kind,
> Will do as if for surety.

(I.iii.395-96)

When he decides to pursue Cassio, he gratuitously tosses him into the list of Emilia's lovers, an accusation simply not to be credited, any more than Roderigo can believe in a Cassio-Desdemona liaison. Jealousy serves Iago's purpose, as Othello's purpose will subordinate itself to jealousy. But why should it be so absolute to *him*? The only other jealous persons in the play are among the lesser personalities—Roderigo and Bianca, a victim of the very handkerchief that convinces Othello:

> What did you mean by that same handkerchief you gave me even now? I was a fine fool to take it. I must take out the work?—A likely piece of work, that you should find it in your chamber, and know not who left it there! This is some minx's token, and I must take out the work? There; give it your hobby horse. (IV.i.154-60)

The whore accuses Cassio of having a whore, as Iago claims Cassio "hath given [the handkerchief] his whore" (IV.i.187). Othello's jealousy would seem to place him in the play's meaner company.

We learn early that Othello is not only a great man but that he insists on that greatness. He utters his virtues with an expressed reluctance belying the words that follow:

> 'Tis yet to know,—
> Which, when I know that boasting is an honour,
> I shall promulgate—I fetch my life and being
> From men of royal siege, and to my demerits
> May speak unbonneted to as proud a fortune
> As this that I have reached.
>
> (I.ii.19-24)

> Rude am I in my speech,
> And little bless'd with the soft phrase of peace . . .
> I will a round unvarnish'd tale deliver
> Of my whole course of love.
>
> (I.iii.81-91)

The disclaimers conflict not only with the claim of royal blood, but with the very language in which Othello couches his story—the double epithets so necessary to the Othello rhetoric, as if the single word lacks power enough to permit his own power to escape to language, the sonorous phrases rolling like thunder across their latinate polysyllables.

Othello's tongue seems to savor his new language, not indeed "the soft phrase of peace," but certainly subdued to and re-created in his image. The words seem to emerge, to borrow a phrase of Fitzgerald's, from his platonic conception of himself. His disclaimers are not sustained against the superb language. Othello *is* royal, he *is* a great man from another world, a pagan converted to Christianity and Venetian service, but greater in his way than Venice, more absolute, more nearly perfect, and more vulnerable than Venice will ever be. And although Othello clears himself of the charges of witchcraft and poison, there *is* a magic in his words. He is a traveler from antique lands, recounting for an enthralled audience a fabulous career in which he was epic hero, not the functionary of a Venetian council evaluating intelligence reports in a war room filled with maps and staff officers, dominated by the reason of the duke. Othello casts himself as the solitary warrior, the Antony or Coriolanus, displaying a puissance that makes the actions of others who might have been there merely human, slight activities unworthy of mention in Othello's self-dictated dispatches:

> Wherein I spoke of most disastrous chances,
> Of moving accidents by flood and field,
> Of hair-breadth scapes i' th' imminent deadly breach,
> Of being taken by the insolent foe
> And sold to slavery, of my redemption thence
> And portance in my travel's history;
> Wherein of antres vast and deserts idle,
> Rough quarries, rocks and hills whose heads touch heaven,
> It was my hint to speak.
>
> (I.iii.134-42)

Desdemona learns from Othello's story to reject the "curled darlings of [her] nation" (I.iii.68), and to "consecrate" her "soul and fortunes" (I.iii.255) to "the visage of his mind" (I.iii.253).

Othello's control at the outset is absolute. Iago attempts to get at him through Roderigo:

> Nay, but he prated,
> And spoke such scurvy and provoking terms
> Against your honour

That, with the little godliness I have,
I did full hard forbear him.

                                                              (I.ii.6-10).

But Othello dismisses Roderigo with barely a word and claims that he is proof against the greater threat posed by Brabantio:

   Let him do his spite;
   My services which I have done the signiory,
   Shall out-tongue his complaints.

                                                              (I.ii.17-19)

He silences a threatened brawl with a majestic phrase that holds the hands of lesser men: "Keep up your bright swords, for the dew will rust them" (I.ii.60), and imputes to himself a knowledge requiring no external prompting: "Were it my cue to fight, I should have known it/ Without a prompter" (I.ii.83-84). He is superb, but perhaps the problem is that he knows it:

   My parts, my title, and my perfect soul
   Shall manifest me rightly.*

                                                              (I.ii.31-32)

It is perhaps dangerous that not only does Othello insist on his virtue, but he appears to recast Samson's sequence into an ascending order of values—parts (abilities), title (General), and *soul*. Should not the next step, if we accept Samson's placement of "myself" at the bottom of the hierarchy, be state or God? Instead, Othello comes back to *himself*, admittedly to his spiritual self, but with an ominous insistence on his soul's perfection. It is not *his* function to define the status of his soul. Ironically, *we* might make that assumption for him—but he assumes it for himself. The sequence of parts, title, soul circles back to Othello, and suggests not merely his egocentricity, but his *personal* susceptibility, a suggestion augmented by the fact that perfection in this

---

*Milton's Samson, on the contrary, integrates himself with the hierarchy he has defied, and achieves a definitive victory over the Philistines—hardly the one he had anticipated when he was muscle-bound into a Heraphic conception of strength: "expect to hear/ Nothing dishonorable, impure, unworthy/ Our God, our law, our nation, or myself" (1423-25).

world—a world where Iago can predict a corruption *beyond* the loss of Eden—is assailable. While the question of Desdemona's perfection is debatable in the context of a fallen world, and while she herself grants her "downright violence and storm of fortunes" (I.iii.250), her personal role, that of her will, in encouraging Othello to speak his love (an analogue of the Duchess's proposal to Antonio), she is clearly the most virtuous character in the play, making her also one of the most vulnerable. But *not* so vulnerable as Othello, because her virtue is a quality, not an *expressed premise* of personal worth. As Othello retells the story of his courtship for the Senate, he suggests that it was *not* his love for Desdemona that was the basis for his speaking, but her response to his story:

> I did consent,
> And often did beguile her of her tears
> When I did speak of some distressful stroke
> That my youth suffer'd. My story being done,
> She gave me for my pains a world of sighs . . .
> She lov'd me for the dangers I had pass'd,
> And I lov'd her that she did pity them.
>
> (I.iii.155-68)

Othello's *self*-conception, like that of Coriolanus and the later Antony, is a vital concomitant of his greatness. Let that *self* be shaken and all else falls apart—his occupation must go in a great flood of language that *un*creates as absolutely as it has created, couched in a predictably pagan context: "Th' immortal Jove's dread clamours counterfeit" (III.iii.356). In a more subtle way, and in spite of his allegiance to the Venetian cause, an element of will resides at the top of Othello's hierarchy as it dominates Iago's. Othello's premises, too, seem rooted in the self, not in the *deeper* knowledge Desdemona demonstrates. Othello, too, sees his *own* visage in his mind and celebrates it in his language, making of himself a counterfeit Jove. Were Othello's love like Desdemona's —the "unreflecting love" of Keats's phrase—it, too, would be unshakable. Clearly, Othello's is not the love of Sonnet 116:

Let me not to the marriage of true minds
Admit impediments. Love is not love
Which alters when it alteration finds,
Or bends with the remover to remove.
O, no! it is an ever-fixed mark
That looks on tempests and is never shaken;
It is the star to every wand'ring bark,
Whose worth's unknown, although his height be taken.

Desdemona loves the man who tells the story, but Othello loves her for loving his story.[8] Othello's conception of the *way* Desdemona loves is, typically, defective ("that she did pity them" [I.iii.168]). That is why *he* loved, in his self-reflecting way, but not why she loved. He loves Desdemona the admirer of Othello. Part of his tragedy, then, is that he wrongly forces Desdemona's love into his own very different, alien conception of love, into another category of his *self*-love.

Does the magnificence of Othello's language before the Senate hint at his enjoyment at retelling, generally but superbly, the story that won Desdemona? It would seem that Othello not only enjoys the greatness of his past exploits but must reiterate them at propitious moments. Clearly, the Duke is as impressed in his way as was Desdemona:

If virtue no delighted beauty lack,
Your son-in-law is far more fair than black.

(I.iii.290-91)

He, too, sees Othello's visage in his mind. But Othello seems content to have pleased *himself* with his rhetoric.

Such a reading of the Senate speech is amply validated by Othello's speech on landing in Cyprus. The scene is the terminus of the play's comic curve, and possibly the play's climax:

It gives me wonder great as my content
To see you here before me. O my soul's joy!
If after every tempest come such calms,
May the winds blow till they have waken'd death!
And let the labouring bark climb hills of seas
Olympus-high, and duck again as low

As hell's from heaven! If it were now to die,
'Twere now to be most happy; for, I fear,
My soul hath her content so absolute
That not another comfort like to this
Succeeds in unknown fate.

(II.i.185-95)

Wonder great as his content invites Othello to a language
that grows greater than content, denies content, or at least
makes it a concomitant of a perfection that must be doomed.
Othello compares the storm to death and the calm beyond to
paradise, and, in one sense, he is right. He has reached his
greatest moment and can only fall "as low/ As hell's from
heaven." But one reason why the pagan destiny adumbrated
at the end of his speech *will* come is that Othello creates an
absolute so defiant of the conditions of a fallen world, or of a
pagan human world, that the merest beginnings of the
demonstration of that impossibility must be the beginnings of
absolute destruction. Othello's own rhetoric tempts him toward the "Olympus" of his wave metaphor, reminiscent of
the mountains of his pagan past, "whose heads touch
heaven" (I.iii.141), and he places himself on the mountain of
his previous hyperbole. Perhaps more than a hint of *hubris*
pertains here; perhaps Othello is an Agamemnon treading
the fatal carpeting of his own rhetoric. His moment of absoluteness ignores his own inescapably human premises. Man
must bid such "absolute content" "Farewell" (III.iii.348). His
Olympian context denies a human future, indeed denies time
as an inevitable rhythm in the life of man.

Desdemona instructs Othello on the way to avoid Iago; she
asserts growth and development *beyond* this point:

The heavens forbid
But that our loves and comforts should increase,
Even as our days do grow!

(II.i.195-97)

But Othello is not listening:

Amen to that, sweet powers!
I cannot speak enough of this content;
It stops me here; it is too much of joy.

And this, and this, the greatest discords be
That e'er our hearts shall make!

(II.ii.197-200)

Indeed, his stop is here, this *is*, to use his appropriately nautical metaphor, the "very sea-mark of [his] utmost sail" (V.ii.268). He has opened himself up to a new dispensation, beyond Christian controls, and he might as well be Antony:

Let Rome in Tiber melt, and the wide arch
Of the rang'd empire fall! Here is my space.
Kingdoms are clay; our dungy earth alike
Feeds beast as man; the nobleness of life
Is to do thus, when such a mutual pair
And such a twain can do't, in which I bind,
On pain of punishment, the world to weet,
We stand up peerless.

(I.i.33-40)

Such a man must meet the pain of punishment; he ignores too much in his announcement of peerlessness. But the announcement is more ominous in Othello's case, for he allows a pagan vision to come between himself and his Christianity. Desdemona is his soul's joy in a Christian sense only if he pursues *her* conception of "increase," instead of stopping here in the perfection of a moment created by his rhetoric and by the conviction of absoluteness seemingly encouraged by *and* engendering that hyperbole. Indeed the heavens *do* forbid Othello's conception of marriage. The marriage service denies the absoluteness of mere human love, stresses "abid [ing] in [God's] love." Matrimony "instytuted of God in Paradise" is new-created by Othello in *his* metaphor of paradise, which ignores the sacramental significance of Christian marriage:

O God which haste consecrated the state of matrimonie to such an excellent misterie, that in it is signified and represented the spiritual marriage and unitie that is betwixte Christe and his Church: loke mercifully upon these thy servauntes, that . . . this man may love his wife, accordyng to thy worde (as Christe did love his spouse the Churche, who gave himself for it, lovyng and cherishing it, even as his owne fleshe).
For this cause shall a man leave father and mother, and shalbe

joined into his wife, and thei two shalbe one flesh. This mistery
is great, but I speake of Christe and of the congregation.

This is hardly to argue that Shakespeare's audience would
have recalled this portion of the marriage service at this
point, but that Othello ignores the basis of Christian
marriage—that two people enter into a sacramental relationship of *one* flesh through the agency of their mystical union
with Christ, which, in turn, is like that between Christ and his
Church, the moment of transmission of the elements being
the moment that fuses man with wife and both—now one
—with Christ. Clearly, Othello asserts a radically different
version of marriage, elevating himself to the role of creator,
ignoring any hierarchy, pagan or Christian, other than that
evolving from his metaphor. It is Othello, not Iago, who
makes of his marriage to Desdemona "a frail vow." A declaration of perfection is vulnerable to the least hint of imper-
fection. Othello includes Desdemona in his conception, in
spite of her demurral. She is part of that perfectness he announces. Iago must listen delightedly. Othello has told Iago
how he can win, how he can set the music down peg by peg.
    Cassio, too, has yielded to a pagan vision upon landing in
Cyprus, but he has done so *within* a system of values that do
not tempt him beyond his role as man or as lieutenant. His
praise of the "divine Desdemona" (II.i.73) might seem like
courtly excess:

> a maid
> That paragons description and wild fame;
> One that excels the quirks of blazoning pens,
> And in th' essential vesture of creation
> Does tire the ingener.
>
> (II.i.61-65)

While the words are consistent with Cassio's hyperbolic
mode, Desdemona's essential quality will stand the test of his
inability to find language adequate to it.
    Cassio's praise of Othello, however, moves into the pagan
world, preparing us for Othello's assumption of a godlike
role on his arrival:

> Great Jove, Othello guard,
> And swell his sail with thine own powerful breath,
> That he may bless this bay with his tall ship,
> Make love's quick pants in Desdemona's arms,
> Give renew'd fire to our extincted spirits,
> And bring all Cyprus comfort!

(II.i.77-82)

With Jove's assistance, Othello is propelled toward paradise. Cassio's language is almost a precondition for the coming of a god. And, indeed Cassio makes him one. For man, Prometheus was a benefactor, but to Zeus he was a traitor and was made to suffer for his defection. Cassio's speech, then, contains several levels of irony, each a prediction of Othello's tragedy. Othello is described in godlike terms, and, more ominously, as a competitor of the chiefest god, one who defied Olympus by arrogating to himself the role of mankind's benefactor. Othello will assume this role, but without any of the positive value of Prometheus's act—"else she'll betray more men" (V.ii.6). And the pagan usages conflict with Christianity, almost as if the pagan gods are alive in this play, and—as in the Old Testament, in Satan's temptation of Christ, in Sycorax, and in Milton's "Nativity Ode" and "Samson"—are competing with *the* God for control of man. Othello's is a *triple* tragedy—the fall of a great man, the downfall of a proud pagan, and the destruction of a soul in a Christian world (with the consequent enticement of the critic toward the disposition of Othello's soul in the afterlife). Othello will discard his conversion and become, in Shakespeare's transmutation of the myth, an anti-Prometheus, extinguishing fire and dousing the light and the warmth of the divine Desdemona. Cassio's words predict not only Othello's tragedy, but also his own more immediate, though less profound, discomfiting of Cyprus.

"The devil," says the "Homilie of the state of Matrimonie," "will assay to attempt all things to interrupt your hearts and godly purpose, if you will give him any entry." One could say that Iago is almost irrelevant to Othello's fall—if Othello *is* guilty of *hubris*, he *must* fall. But while he ignores mortality in his metaphoric enthusiasm, thus daring destruction, he also ignores Christianity, thus daring damnation. Iago *is*

there in the pattern Shakespeare creates, a nemesis in the
pagan sense, but, with his temptations and insinuations, more
of an evil angel in the morality sense. Listening to Othello,
Iago promises to reduce the Moor's Olympian aspirations to
something closer to the bad music that Othello is able to silence (III.i.):

> O, you are well tun'd now!
> But I'll set down the pegs that make this music,
> As honest as I am.
>
> (II.i.201-3)

The Clown's humor is really a prediction of Othello's ambivalence before the Iago music, which at once infuriates and
fascinates him: "the General so likes your music, that he desires you, for love's sake, to make no more noise with it"
(III.i.12-14). We know, on the basis of Othello's soaring
words, that Iago can orchestrate a different modulation, and
Othello predicts his own fall by invoking "unknown fate,"
which he applies to prove his happiness, but which we perceive in its more ominous sense. It is the fate of the pagan
world to whose magnificence Othello abdicates on landing in
Cyprus, whose highest mountain is, of course, Olympus.

A moment later, Othello, like Richard ("Mock not my
senseless conjuration, lords" [III.i.23]), claims to repent his
previous flight. His definition of what he has done, however,
does not eliminate the danger he does not recognize:

> O my sweet,
> I prattle out of fashion, and I dote
> In mine own comforts.
>
> (II.i.207-9)

He is doubly "out of fashion"—as man and as Christian
—and, as in his courtship of Desdemona, his "own comforts"
form the context of his words and, in that circularity which
inevitably returns to Othello, the *goal* of his words. Such a
rhythm—predicated on and returning to the self—cannot
explore any truth it might encompass.

Yet, within the context of the "negative capability," the
comprehensive understanding with which Shakespeare draws

his characters even as they commit their tragic errors, we must sympathize with Othello as he lands at Cyprus. He has survived the most hazardous of careers, one whose dangers he has some right to feel he has now escaped. His secret marriage was vehemently indicted by a powerful senator before the Venetian Senate, yet Othello's defense was so much more than adequate that it won the Duke, not to Othello's position but beyond it, to Desdemona's. The Turks lie beneath the very waves through which Othello and Desdemona have safely passed. Suddenly, his beloved stands before him in the clearing sky, and the man who has survived such danger can conceive only of consummation within the calm the heavens have granted. While Cassio's "hopes [are] not surfeited to death" (II.i.50), Othello's hyperbolic transcendence of the moment is explicable in the context of an overwhelming overabundance of good fortune and great joy. He has been delivered to this point in time. But as he tries to ride the wheel out of time, his fate becomes explicable as well.

The Homily on Matrimony suggests that one "folly is ever from our tender age growne up with us, to have a desire to rule, to think highly of ourselfe, so that none thinketh it meet to give place to another." The words point not merely at Iago, who has given place to Cassio, who thinks so highly of himself that his own will is supreme commander of his every act, but to Othello, commander of Cyprus, whose soul is as "perfect" as Iago's will is absolute. Their visions are radically contradictory, of course, Othello's expressing more than the truth and Iago's less. Even Iago's "victory" over Othello, while it exposes Othello's assumption of perfection, does not validate Iago's assumption of personal supremacy. For Othello, perfection depends on his awareness of it —every element must be in place in the static paradise he builds upon landing in Cyprus, a paradise whose only movement in this world must be downward, as both Desdemona and Iago imply in their different ways. Othello will be perfect in his jealousy, all elements fitted to it, his soldiership abandoned as his self-conception shatters (even as at first he relates Desdemona's infidelity to it: "Yet, 'tis the plague of great ones" [III.iii.273]), his paganism reconfirmed, his Christianity reborn in a grotesque perversion of the truth, overlaying his crime in Christian format, even as his original pagan heritage had been buried beneath his conversion, or, as "The Ministracion of Baptisme" suggests, "the olde Adam . . . maye be so buried . . . the newe man may be raised up." On first landing at Cyprus, Othello raises himself as a rival god to Iago's gardener of the will, and Iago cannot allow such self-creation to stand unchallenged. He is the most dangerous of the *Jacobean* "new men," not aiming at "success" like Edmund, incapable of a Bosala's conscience, not merely desperately world-weary as are Macbeth's two murderers (III.i.108-14). Othello would free himself of all limitations through language, even as his own words insist on an "unknown fate." Iago *is* free of any limitations except those imposed by his gardener will—his freedom is license—and, in a mirror of complete irony, he is as absolute as Othello. Othello's vision is *too* complete for this world—it must perish. Iago's vision is obviously incomplete, but his precise awareness of his premises and his undeviating devotion to them make him capable of defeating the other. The Othello vision lingers longer in the spectator's ear and aspiration, is more valid in its heroic excessiveness than is the malignant fertility of Iago's will. But like all imperfect visions in Shakespeare's tragedies, each must be destroyed. Othello's tendency toward *completeness*—absoluteness either of courage, love, or jealousy—coincides neatly with Iago's facility in splitting things in half and then encouraging the growth of the half to wholeness: "you have lost half your soul," he shouts to Brabantio (I.i.87). A soul is theoretically indivisible, yet Brabantio pursues Iago's fraction to his *total* disappointment before the Venetian council:

> If she confess that she was half the wooer,
> Destruction on my head if my bad blame
> Light on the man!
>
> (I.iii.176-78)

Iago tutors Brabantio into a mathematical definition of love—very much like the quantitative ethic Lear enunciates—which Othello also learns from Iago and which, like Brabantio's version, expands from a fraction ("keep a corner on the thing I love/ For other's uses" [III.iii.272-73]) to completeness. The Moor expresses his own debased definition of love with typical totality:

I had been happy, if the general camp,
Pioners and all, had tasted her sweet body,
So I had nothing known.

(III.iii.345-47)

The two antagonists are poised—Othello disarmed before the very potency of a language tempted beyond man's range, defying both pagan and Christian boundaries, and Iago, armed with a narrow but powerful view thah almost nonchalantly rules out concern for the very self it celebrates and that would seem to embrace almost consciously the damnation that must come to him—if an afterlife is an issue to Iago or the play.

A further factor, beyond Iago's iniquity and Othello's susceptibility, pressing the newly married couple toward disaster is the shift from Venice to Cyprus. In Venice, houses are not granges, are not isolated farms open to the incursions of thieves and wolves, are not far from the civic control asserted by the duke and his council. Cyprus, however, is a threatened outpost in the sea.[9] While the storm sinks the Turks, it also screens the island from the city and predicts, of course, the coming storm in Othello's mind. Cassio prays for Othello's safety in the storm:

O let the heavens
Give him defense against the elements,
For I have lost him on a dangerous sea.

(II.i.44-46)

Soon Cassio will lose Othello on the dangerous streets of Cyprus, coursing with drunken soldiers. And much later, Desdemona will kneel and tell Iago:

Good friend, go to him; for, by this light of heaven,
I know not how I lost him.

(IV.ii.150-51)

While she can still invoke the light of heaven, her kneeling to
Othello will remind us of the storm—the "wind [that] spoke
aloud" (II.i.5) in incomprehensible language, which, for her,
translates itself into Othello's voice:

> Upon my knee, what doth your speech import?
> I understand a fury in your words,
> But not the words.
>
> (IV.ii.31-33)

The Turk comes to Cyprus; Iago, playing courtly games
with Desdemona, says "Or else I am a Turk" (II.i.115). "I am
not what I am," he had said to Roderigo (I.i.65), appropriately recasting the words of Moses's God ("I am that I am")
to his own duplicity. We can assume that his denial of Turkish tendencies *points* at them for us. The tempest Iago per-
petrates with wine moves not toward the sure control of the
Venetian duke, but toward the potential anarchy of the
commander's mind:

> Perdition catch my soul,
> But I do love thee! and when I love thee not,
> Chaos is come again.
>
> (III.iii.90-92)

The absolutes sound again, but here in the negative corollary
to Othello's speech on landing; content and joy become possible chaos and perdition. Cyprus will become the "dark
world" of the tragedies—the midnights of Denmark, punc-
tuated by the passage of a Ghost; Scotland under Macbeth,
entombed in darkness; the violent realm of ex-King Lear; the
night of error through which Othello must wander until recognition comes, the tragic analogue to the "green world" of
the comedies, with their forests of Arden, Athenian woods,
and beautiful mountains, where complications work their way
out toward marriage rather than deepening toward death.
The monsters of the deep, the Turks, close in on man's il-
luminated clearings in the jungle, his Christian islands in the
sea, his bright but nervous mead halls surrounded by the
animals whose eyes reflect back from the outer darkness.
"Our wars are done; the Turks are drowned," Othello had

cried (II.i.204). Now the blackness of the enemy, seemingly
sunk beneath a benevolent ocean, will spread from Iago uncontrolled into the streets of Cyprus, where Roderigo dies in
a literal darkness emblematic of the deception of Othello:
"kill men i' th' dark!" cries honest Iago of himself (V.i.63).
Iago's quick movements through the streets and alleyways of
a strange city at night suggest that darkness is the element in
which he sees best. Iago is, in a way, the tragic counterpart of
Ariel, but Iago has no master.

Iago moves first against Cassio, making him the sacrificial
victim of an anti-sacrament, a parody of what Iago will accomplish later with Othello, but a vital prelude to his ensnar-
ing the Moor. The "celebration of [Othello's] nuptial"
(II.ii.7-8) becomes, for Cassio, a burlesque Communion. In
his drunkenness, Cassio reminds the celebrants that "god's
above all, and there be souls must be saved, and there be
souls must not be saved" (II.iii.105-7). He expresses his
"hope to be saved" (II.iii.110-11) and requests "God [to]
forgive us our sins" (II.iii.116), yet pulls rank on Iago in the
hierarchy of salvation: "the lieutenant is to be saved before
the ancient" (II.iii.113-14), thus suggesting that this anti-
ritual is serious only to a point; it represents the kind of
"error" or "excess" typical of comedy.

Cassio falls before the "devil drunkenness" (II.iii.297), and,
instead of achieving the purification promised in the Communion Service, is reduced to bestiality, to a shallower version of what Othello will become: "That we should, with joy,
pleasance, revel, and applause, transform ourselves into
beasts!" (II.iii.292-94). The "invisible spirit of wine"
(II.iii.283) does not confirm Cassio's soul to everlasting life.
In an "unbless'd cup" (II.iii.312) it costs him—in Cassio's
hyperbole—his immortality:

> Reputation, reputation, reputation! O, I have lost my reputation!
> I have lost the immortal part of myself, and what remains is bes-
> tial. My reputation, Iago, my reputation! (II.iii.262-65)

But surely an audience would agree with Iago that Cassio is
"too severe a moraler" (II.iii.301). And few spectators would
equate "reputation" with "immortality," particularly in the

context of the anti-mass they have just witnessed. The effect
of Iago's manipulation is within *Cassio,* and it is excessive.
We accept the fact that his lieutenancy is fairly lost, in spite
of Iago's part in it, but we reject Cassio's melodramatic over-
interpretation of what has happened to him.

We cannot, however, underestimate Iago's skill in producing this anti-sacrament. It spreads from its center chaotically
out into the body politic, a disjunctive analogy to Christ's Last
Supper, which appoints to His disciples "A kyngdom as my
father hath appoincted to me." Iago's celebration encourages
no peaceable kingdom on earth, but explodes into "a town of
war/ Yet wild, the people's breasts brimful of fear"
(II.iii.213-14). Appropriately, as a result of this anti-ritual,
Cyprus is frighted "From her propriety" (II.iii.176). The
anti-mass reduces the world to Iago's conception of it. Communion celebrates man's contact with God, permits him,
through his faith, to lift up his heart to Christ's residence in
heaven. The Communion is, first, a cleansing of the man,
then an elevation of the cleansed man to Christ. Iago's anti-
mass presses man downward: "To be now a sensible man, by
and by a fool, and presently a beast" (II.iii.310-12). If love is
a sect or scion of lust, it would seem that faith is subordinate
to sacrilege. Anything beyond Iago's will must be debased, its
qualities reduced to categories within a deadly sin. Iago is a
perverter not merely of people, but of the ceremonies with
which society celebrates its contact with powers which, if
properly recognized and encouraged, endow social actions
with spiritual validity.

Cassio's weakness before the wine predicts Othello's surrender to jealousy. As Othello will, Cassio surrenders his
command:

> What! in a town of war,
> Yet wild, the people's hearts brimful of fear,
> To manage private and domestic quarrel,
> In night, and on the court and guard of safety!*

(II.iii.213-16)

---

*Cf. Roy Battenhouse's comment on these lines: "The lines might equally apply
to Brabantio's situation in Act I. Note how, in the course of the play, Iago exploits,
first the father's love of reputation, then the friend's (Cassio's), then the husband's."

Cassio's was a "private and domestic quarrel,"* not a proper unsheathing of his sword against the enemies of Venice; it occurred at night, when civil control is difficult at best; and Cassio was chief guardian of order! The Turk, sunk in a "foul and violent tempest" (II.i.34) surfaces on the very streets of Cyprus in a "foul rout" (II.iii.210), a "vile brawl" (II.iii.256). The alarm bell designed to warn Cyprus of the Turk's approach summons the town to witness a fight between a noble Cypriot and one of his defenders. "Are we turned Turks," demands Othello, "and to ourselves do that/ Which Heaven hath forbid the Ottomites?" (II.iii.170-71). Othello's indictment is five-fold—the town is under martial law; it still trembles against the close brush of the Turk; Othello's conviction that Desdemona is "foul" (IV.i.212, V.ii.200), as "false as water" (V.ii.134), will bring against him the same charges he lodges against Cassio, and in his final speech Othello will read the indictment himself.

Clearly, the Cassio episode foreshadows what will happen to Othello, the play's *tragic* character. Cassio is, after all, part of a subdued comedy. He repents and, although wounded by Iago, takes command of Cyprus at play's end. We feel no fear that his temporary alienation from himself will be repeated. Indeed, Desdemona's pleas for Cassio could almost emerge from the comedies, proof of Shakespeare's ability to weave the lighter threads of one *genre* into the darker, deeper texture of tragedy:

> If I have any grace or power to move you,
> His present reconciliation take;
> For if he be not one that truly loves you,
> That errs in ignorance and not in cunning,
> I have no judgement in an honest face.

> (III.iii.46-50)

Desdemona appoints "three days" for the "reconciliation" of the "penitent" Cassio to Othello (III.iii.63). But the same term soon becomes Othello's sentence of Cassio:

*As was Brabantio's indictment of Othello before the Venetian Senate, which interrupted the plans for Cyprus's defense (I.iii.52-57).

Within these three days let me hear thee say
That Cassio's not alive.

(III.iii.472-73)

By the time those days are over, however, Desdemona and
Othello will be dead, and Cassio's accession in Cyprus will be
virtually irrelevant.

Earlier, in Venice, Othello knew his "cue to fight." In Cyprus his hand tightens around his sword-hilt:

If I once stir
Or do but lift this arm, the best of you
Shall sink in my rebuke.

(II.iii.207-9)

He makes a distinction between his body natural and his
body politic in dismissing Cassio, suggesting that the two
roles have begun to divide in him:

Cassio, I love thee;
But never more be officer of mine.

(II.iii.248-49)

Immediately, Desdemona appears, and Othello's rage builds,
directed at the very man he has just said he "loves":

Look, if my gentle love be not rais'd up!
I'll make thee an example.

(II.iii.250-51)

In his first intervention in a night brawl, Othello had silenced
swords with what might seem to be an echo of Christ: "Keep
up your bright swords, for the dew will rust them" (I.ii.59).*
His second intervention is belated, blood has been shed, and
he utters a precept: "For Christian shame, put by this bar-
barous brawl" (II.iii.172). The shift from the threat of a fight
to its actuality suggests that control of the streets of Cyprus,
now under Iago's direction, is less sure than it was in Venice.

*The "echo" calls for caution. One would hardly claim Hamlet's "Up, sword, and
know thou a more horrid hent" (III.iii.88) as an echo of Christ. Nor would Anne to
Richard ("well, well, put up your sword" [Richard III: I.ii.197]) nor Antonio to
Viola ("Put up your sword" [Twelfth Night: III.iv. 343]), nor, in a closer analogue to
Othello's lines, the Bastard's "Your sword is bright, sir; put it up again" and "Put up
thy sword betime" (IV.iii.79, 98) be so construed. The biblical versions read "Put up
thy sworde into his place" (Matthewe XXVI, 52) and "Put up thy sworde into the
sheathe" (John XVIII, 11).

Othello's shift from biblical quotation to Christian admonition suggests his transition from servant of Venice to Commander of Cyprus, thus hinting at the danger he and his command are in. His use of the word "monstrous" (II.iii.217) signals the danger, because we have watched Iago transform Cassio to bestiality. Othello's anger in the latter scene may stem from his leaving Desdemona's side in the night for a *second* time before the pull of an emergent occasion. The night in Cyprus is his "official" wedding night, while that in Venice had been his actual wedding night. Yet it would seem, in spite of Iago's several obscene observations to Brabantio, that the marriage had *not* been consummated in Venice.* Iago in Cyprus claims that Othello "hath not yet made wanton the night with" Desdemona (II.iii.16-17). The Herald's proclamation conveys a hint of Othello's anticipation, and perhaps a trace of the blame for the brawl in Cyprus, in that, again, he gives Iago scope to operate, inviting exceptions to martial law:

> every man put himself into triumph; some to dance, some to make bonfires, each man to what sport and revels his addiction leads him; for, beside these beneficial news, it is the celebration of his nuptial. So much was his pleasure should be proclaimed. All offices are open, and there is full liberty of feasting from this present hour of five till the bell have told eleven. (II.ii.4-11)

The fight, it would seem, occurs before eleven, and is partly the result of the opening of "offices" and the proclamation of "liberty," which when managed by Iago becomes license. That the proclamation has sexual overtones is suggested by Othello immediately afterwards, as he takes Desdemona to bed with him:

>   Come, my dear love,
> The purchase made, the fruits are to ensue;
> That profit's yet to come 'tween me and you.
>
> > (II.iii.9-11)

---

*Battenhouse comments: "It is a marriage eventually consummated in death—in a slaying of the beloved, which figuratively epitomizes the fate of any marriage marred by 'nighttime,' or clandestine motives. The progress of such a marriage is in terms of three nights, around which the play is structured. The first two nights are, so to speak, instances of coitus interruptus, the third of a perverse coitus that smothers."

It would seem, then, that Othello is summoned to the streets again from the very act he has been anticipating since the first night in Venice. If his anger has a sexual basis, we are prepared for the introduction of jealousy into his mind.

Othello himself begins to reflect the control of "judgement" by "madness," which Iago has told us he will induce in him:

> Now, by heaven,
> My blood begins my safer guides to rule;
> And passion, having my best judgement collied,
> Assays to lead the way.
>
> (II.iii.204-7)

To be led by passion, of course, is to allow a lower faculty to rule the higher. The inner light Desdemona had perceived has begun to darken ("collied" means "darkened"), as the blackness of the outer man impinges on the "perfect soul" within.* Othello himself predicts the loss of someone close to him, reminding us that the Duke had promised justice even though his "proper son/ Stood in the action" (I.iii.69-70):

> And he that is approv'd in this offence,
> Though he had twinn'd with me, both at a birth,
> Shall lose me.
>
> (II.iii.211-13)

Iago describes the brawl in terms that point at a further anti-sacramental action, an action against the "one flesh" of Desdemona and Othello. He will destroy their marriage just as he has made the night of its celebration loud with clangor and the cries of wounded men. His words would seem to aim at the activity he has contrived to interrupt—the consummation of the wedding of Desdemona and Othello:

> Friends all but now, even now,
> In quarter, and in terms like bride and groom
> Devesting them for bed; and then, but now—

---

*Battenhouse offers a qualification here: "There was a seed of blackness within the 'perfect soul' from the beginning, in the self-love that was concerned chiefly with reputation. Now this inner seed is flowering (under Iago's gardening) to make the inner man as black as his outer skin."

As if some planet had unwitted men—
Swords out, and tilting one at other's breast,
In opposition bloody.

(II.iii.179-84)

As Iago begins to poison Othello's mind, the Moor responds to one of Iago's typically inflammatory cautions, by saying: "Fear not my government" (III.iii.256), that is, my control of the situation. But "government" is used in the context of the private world of Othello and Desdemona and reiterates the split developing in Othello between his roles as commander and private man. Iago's anti-ritual with him will not have its effect "on stage," where it is expended by a hyperbolic Cassio, but will reach the audience with a horror that Othello, on stage, will not glimpse.

After his adroit management of Cassio's cashiering, Iago's plot embraces further definition. Because Desdemona is "of so free, so kind [that is, "humane," in the Jacobean dimension of the word], so apt, and so blessed a disposition" (II.iii.324-25), her goodness will intercede for Cassio and so contribute to the subtle dynamic that will infuriate Othello once he is infected with jealousy. Iago has previously denied Desdemona's "blessedness" to Roderigo (II.i.256-60), but one of his talents is to know the virtues of his antagonists and to use goodness against itself. Iago understands goodness even if he does not share it. He recognizes his opposite in Desdemona, who is "fram'd as fruitful/ As the free elements" (II.iii.347-48), who, then, participates, like Cordelia, in the creative and restorative forces of the universe that Iago opposes. Her power is such that, for her, Othello would turn away from the very religion to which he has been converted, would "renounce his baptism/ All seals and symbols of redeemed sin" (II.iii.349-50). Convinced of her infidelity, this is what he will do. The scene ends with Iago's enunciation of a psychic version of Cassio's drunkenness, which "put an enemy in [his] mouth ... to steal away [his] brain" (II.iii.291-92):

I'll pour this pestilence into his ear,
That she repeals [Cassio] for her body's lust;
And by how much she strives to do him good,

She shall undo her credit with the Moor.
So will I turn her virtue into pitch,
And out of her own goodness make the net
That shall enmesh them all.

(II.iii.362-68)

That the Turk was latent in Othello from the first was
suggested in Brabantio's charges of witchcraft, charges confirmed by Othello himself when he tells Desdemona that the
handkerchief *was* magic:

That handkerchief
Did an Egyptian to my mother give;
She was a charmer, and could almost read
The thoughts of people . . .
'Tis true; there's magic in the web of it.
A sybyl, that had numb'red in the world
The sun to course two hundred compasses,
In her prophetic fury sew'd the work;
The worms were hallowed that did breed the silk;
And it was dy'd in mummy which the skilful
Conserv'd of maiden's hearts.

(III.iv.55-75)

The handkerchief is an emblem of a magic that antedates
Othello's conversion, as Othello suggests when he talks of his
"fate" having him "wiv'd" (III.iv.64)—of a world irrelevant to
Desdemona's prayer for the "help [of] every spirit sanctified"
(III.iv.126). The handkerchief *had* been a form of "white
magic," its strawberries suggestive of purity and sweetness,
strawberries a symbol attributed to the Virgin Mary. But
strawberries could have grown in Iago's garden. They also
symbolize lechery, the negative "fruitfulness" (III.iv.38)
Othello discerns in Desdemona's hand: "hot, hot and
moist . . . a young and sweating devil there/ That commonly
rebels" (III.iv.39-43). As Othello's mind darkens, the handkerchief absorbs the characteristics of black magic, as does its
story, employed in so destructive a context.[10]
Othello's use of the handkerchief was an appropriate transition between his pagan background and the Christian beginning he makes with Desdemona. The handkerchief's
power to enforce fidelity was a pagan analogue to the invisible mysteries expressed in Christian matrimony. Othello's re-

telling of his pagan life to Desdemona was a precondition of his continuing that life with her in a Christian dispensation. His rendition provides a momentum to their relationship by making his strange past familiar to her, thus enclosing her within the vectors of his future. In fact, she falls in love with the man who has had such a history. Frost expresses the idea of a past leading to a future with beautiful simplicity in "Meeting and Passing":

> Afterward I went past what you had passed
> Before we met and you what I had passed.

Othello's use of the handkerchief *against* Desdemona, however, suggests that he does not fully understand or accept what Desdemona has passed—her Christian origins, clearly a deeper part of her character than is Othello's conversion for him. His use of the handkerchief as an agent of divorce not only undercuts its positive pagan qualities, but makes it anti-sacramental as well—"to the jealous confirmations strong/ As proofs of holy writ" (III.iii.323-24). "By reverting to this kind of magic," says David Kaula, "Othello is in a sense renouncing his baptism,"[11] rejecting that moment which brought him into the Christian dispensation. His repetition of the handkerchief's exotic history is a negative analogue to his previous description of his own past—that description which led *into* the Christian world—and signals his reversion to the remote pre-Christian time where charms, sybyls, and magic were competitors with Christian mystery, pagan means of contacting and releasing the invisible powers of the universe, practices opposed to and condemned by the new world Othello has entered. Othello validates Brabantio's charge:

> I . . . do attack thee
> For an abuser of the world, a practiser
> Of arts inhibited and out of warrant.
>
> (I.ii.72-79)

Time in Cyprus wheels backward to those moments when only Othello's wits, skill, and luck could help him, where no Christian deity stood near to guide him. The virtues of pa-

tience, humility, and forgiveness, never a profound concomitant of Othello's conversion, spin off into the sea, leaving the
ruling power shorn of his Christian veneer, reconfirmed in
the barbarism upon which Brabantio and Iago have insisted
from the first. Othello ignores the invisibility—the aspects of
spirit and faith—at the base of Christianity, and descends
with Iago's guidance to the level of tangible evidence. The
handkerchief seemed to have sacramental possibilities
—Desdemona treasured it as an emblem for her love for
Othello. Now it becomes a piece of proof in Iago's anti-
sacramental thrust:

> Iago.   Her honour is an essence that's not seen;
>   They have it very oft that have it not:
>   But for the handkerchief,—
> Othello. By heaven, I would most gladly have forgot it.
>   Thou said'st—O, it comes o'er my memory,
>   As doth the raven o'er the infectious house,
>   Boding to all—he had my handkerchief.
>
> (IV.i.16-22)

The Turk emerges from the sea within Othello—that
stormy sector overlaid by a Christian façade and translated
into precise service for the Venetian Command. "Another of
his fathom they have none," Iago had said (I.i.153), imputing
to Othello a depth like that of the sea. The Turkish fleet met
"mere [that is, "absolute"] perdition" (II.ii.3) in the tempest.
Later, Othello says "perdition catch my soul,/ But I do love
thee! And when I love thee not,/ Chaos is come again"
(III.iii.90-92). Later still, he frightens Desdemona about the
handkerchief: "To lose't or give't away were such perdition/
As nothing could match" (III.iv.67-68). By then, the irony of
the admonition has crept around Othello's soul—unseen to
him—because the Turk has not sunk beneath the sea but
boils within Othello, its hour returning in a grotesque second
coming, a reversion of Othello to the monstrous past he described for the Senate. Iago is the midwife: "As if there were
some monster in his thought," Othello says, "Too hideous to
be shown" (III.iii.107-8).

In describing his career for the Senate, Othello had told of "antres vast" (vast caves), of being "sold to slavery" by the "insolent foe" (I.iii.137-40). His previous history is a metaphor for his later control by Iago, who ensnares Othello with a psychic bondage more imprisoning than physical walls. In allowing Othello to eavesdrop on Cassio, Iago echoes the experience of Othello's otherworldly past: "Do but encave yourself . . . For I will make him tell the tale anew" (IV.i.82-85). The encaved Othello listens to a hideous parody of the story that had won Desdemona and the Duke to its truth. Trapped symbolically into his past experience ("antres vast"), Othello accepts Cassio's story as truth. The time Othello once obeyed in response to the emergent rhythms of Venetian danger, becomes the corrupted time ticking from Iago's will. "But yet keep time in all" (IV.i.93), he tells Othello, who obediently withdraws to hear Cassio. Iago maneuvers like the Turkish fleet, creating "a pageant/ To keep us in false gaze," as the First Senator had said (I.iii.18-19). The Duke's "judgement" (I.iii.9) was proof against that feint, but Iago engenders "jealousy so strong/ That judgement cannot cure" (I.iii.310-11).

Rather than employ direct accusation, Iago allows Othello to be the interrogator, enticing him into a macabre dance of question alternating rhythmically with Iago's caveats and cautionary homilies. Othello is fascinated even as he is driven to roaring:

> What dost thou say?
> Was not that Cassio parted from my wife?
> Who is 't you mean?
> Went he hence now?
> What dost thou say, Iago?
> Why dost thou ask?
> Why of thy thought, Iago?
> Discern'st thou aught in that?
> Is he not honest?
> What dost thou think?
> What didst not like?
> What dost thou mean?
> Why, why is this?
> Dost thou say so?

(III.iii.35-204)

The eager horror of Othello's questions proves Emilia's thesis on jealousy:

> But jealous souls will not be answer'd so;
> They are not ever jealous for the cause,
> But jealous for they're jealous. It is a monster
> Begot upon itself, born on itself.
>
> (III.iv.159-62)

Jealousy, like Iago's plot, once begun, develops its own momentum, providing more to feed upon the more it feeds upon Othello, permitting no return. Iago's metaphor is of a tenor similar to Emilia's:

> The Moor already changes with my poison.
> Dangerous conceits are, in their natures poisons,
> Which at the first are scarce found to distaste,
> But with a little act upon the blood
> Burn like the mines of sulphur.
>
> (III.iii.325-29)

Othello's flood of questions has allowed Iago to become Othello's tutor, to move the Moor from his desire "to be free and bounteous to her mind" (I.iii.266), from his willingness to wager his "life upon her faith" (I.iii.296), into the mind of Iago. Iago hesitates to allow Othello to "know [his] thoughts" (III.iii.154), but as part of Iago's suggestive tutoring in language and fascination, Othello demands a few lines later, "By heaven, I'll know thy thoughts" (III.iii.162). Othello insists on moving into Iago's mind, on knowing falsehood, and even provides Iago with a general pattern for him to complete in detail: "I'll see before I doubt, when I doubt prove" (III.iii.190). But doubt precedes the "ocular proof" (III.iii.360) Othello demands—the demand itself a proof of doubt. His movement is inevitably downward—as his speech on the quay at Cyprus suggests it must be—from knowledge, to doubt, to evidence which, however circumstantial, carries an instant indictment. Desdemona has already, jokingly, dismissed Iago's doctrine: "O most lame and impotent conclusion! Do not learn of him, Emilia, though he be thy husband. How say you, Cassio? Is he not a most profane and liberal counsellor?" (II.i.162-65). Othello is not there, nor can Desdemona hear her own ironies. But the spectator does.

Iago can even project Cassio's "dream" into the darkened theater of Othello's mind, forcing the Moor to interpret it. Iago utters his typical disclaimer, pulling Othello forward into the vacuum created by Iago's "unwillingness" to see anything in a mere dream:

> Iago. Nay, this was but his dream.
> Oth. But this denoted a foregone conclusion,
> 'Tis a shrewd doubt, though it be but a dream.
> (III.iii.427-29)

Having allowed Othello to make the point, Iago nudges him forward again, his alternation of cautions and conclusions making Othello almost literally a puppet:

> Iago. And this may help to thicken other proofs
> That do demonstrate thinly.
> Oth. I'll tear her all to pieces.
> Iago. Nay, but be wise; yet we see nothing done.
> She may be honest yet. Tell me but this,
> Have you not sometimes seen a handkerchief
> Spotted with strawberries in your wife's hand?
> (III.iii.430-35)

Since everything serves Iago in his stratagem, it may be that Cassio's "dream" had its genesis in Brabantio's, who dreamed of Desdemona's flight with Othello: "This accident is not unlike my dream" (I.i.143). Iago shouted a reality into Brabantio's ear. The fulfillment of *that* dream predicts the falsehood of Cassio's "dream" and its inevitable effect upon Othello. One could speculate that Brabantio's dream signaled his psychic *acceptance* of Othello, but that the impulse he had already demonstrated in so often inviting Othello to tell his story (I.iii.128-30) is translated into a perverted reality by Iago, rousing Brabantio from dream to nightmare. The duke's reinterpretation comes too late. Iago has infected Brabantio's mind with wit to believe only in witchcraft.

Othello's knowledge has never been so profound as Desdemona's, nor does he understand her: "she had eyes, and chose me" (III.iii.189). Not her eyes, however, but her

*in*sight "saw Othello's visage in his mind" (I.iii.253). Othello's
superficial understanding of her love, *not* the "soul to soul"
relationship predicated by the First Senator (I.iii.114),
Othello's inability to recognize that she saw through the exterior so abhorrent to Brabantio, sets the Moor up for the introduction of "ocular proof" (III.iii.360) and allows Iago the
most malicious pleasure in torturing him:

> Would you, the supervisor, grossly gape on—
> Behold her topp'd?
>
> > (III.iii.395-96)

Othello lacks Desdemona's penetration. Like Duncan, he
knows not how "to find the mind's construction in the face"
(I.iv.12); he "thinks men honest that but seem to be so"
(I.iii.406), imputes Iago's initial reluctance to speak to "close
dilations, working from the heart/ That passion cannot rule"
(III.iii.123-24). He forgets his own words on the previous
night: "Now, by heaven,/ My blood begins my safer guides to
rule;/ And passion, having my best judgement collied,/ Assays
to lead the way" (II.iii.204-7). Iago is not Horatio, however
(cf. *Hamlet* III.ii.68-79), and soon Othello is wagering his
soul on Iago's ability to produce visual evidence:

> Give me the ocular proof;
> Or, by the worth of mine eternal soul,
> Thou hadst been better have been born a dog,
> Than answer my wak'd wrath!
>
> > (III.iii.360-63)

Othello has done psychologically what he did physically when
he assigned Iago to escort Desdemona to Cyprus: "To his
conveyance I assign my wife" (I.iii.286). He could combat external monsters in his pagan past; once they are in his mind,
the combat must be suicidal. "Cannibals that did each other
eat" (I.iii.143) became jealousy "which doth mock/ The meat
it feeds on" (III.iii.166-67), and predicts Othello's action
against his "own flesh," Desdemona. Othello's reason has
been abandoned for his passion, his judgment has surrendered to a perverse appetite, and he has become like one of
the "men whose heads/ Do grow beneath their shoulders"
(I.iii.144-45). Yet, even as the "monster" enters his "mind"

(III.iv.163), even as Desdemona devolves to "a thing I love" (III.iii.272), his eyes transmit the truth to his soul:

> Look where she comes,
> If she be false, O, then heaven mocks itself!
> I'll not believe it.
>
> (III.iii.277-79)

Othello's proliferation of question upon question brings the hideous deformity of Iago's mind, "the green-ey'd monster" (III.iii.166), to birth in Othello's mind: "A horned man's a monster and a beast" (IV.i.63). Iago's question after Othello's fit taunts him with cuckoldry: "'How is it, General? Have you not hurt your head?" (IV.i.60). And we recognize the irony of Cassio, innocent of his role in Othello's fit, in his suggesting that Iago "Rub him about the temples" (IV.i.53), and the more terrible irony of innocent Desdemona's attempting to assuage the "pain upon [his] forehead" by binding it with her handkerchief (III.iii.284),* first gift of a Christian marriage now decaying, soon to be "proof" of her infidelity, its "magic" web becoming part of the unholy "web" (II.i.169) and "net" (II.iii.367) that Iago knits. "The divell," says the Homily on Matrimony, "whose temptation, if it be followed, must needs beginne and weave the web of all miseries, and sorrowes." Once Othello had been a doctor, "surgeon" for Montano's wounds (II.iii.253). He rejects the aid of Desdemona, and falls into a fit produced by Iago's perverted practice ("My medicine work!" [IV.i.46]), which allows Iago to pose as Othello's doctor—a typically dual action, to be the instigator and seem the healer:**

> The lethargy must have his quiet course;
> If not, he foams at mouth and by and by
> Breaks out to savage madness.
>
> (IV.i.54-56)

The spells of which Brabantio accused Othello are now used against him, but they are not magic: "Thou know'st," says

---

*Cf. Hiermione to Leontes: "You look/ As if you held a brow of much distraction" (*The Winter's Tale:* I.ii.147-48).

**He does the same for the very Cassio he has wounded: "I'll bind it with my shirt" (V.i.73).

Iago to Roderigo, "we work by wit, and not by witchcraft" (II.iii.378).

But Iago does more than assume the role of healer. He replaces not Cassio, but Desdemona. The early issue of the play, an "unnatural" marriage, emerges again in a macabre scene in which Othello and Iago participate in a parody marriage, another anti-ritual like the anti-mass Iago had celebrated for Cassio, but obviously more profound than its antecedent, pressing meanings upon the audience that reverberate back to Othello with deep dramatic, even tragic, irony—the discrepancy between what Othello does and what he *believes* he is doing.

Almost immediately upon Othello's fascinated reception of Iago's insinuations, the Moor tells Iago, "I am bound to thee forever" (III.iii.113). Soon that binding is consummated, the "frail vow" with Desdemona rent asunder. Othello exchanges the Christian controls imposed by his contract with Desdemona, for the pagan code of vengeance, for an ethic conceived in hell, hardly the "honorable state, instytuted of God in Paradise":

> Look here, Iago;
> All my fond love thus do I blow to heaven.
> 'Tis gone.
> Arise, black vengeance, from the hollow hell!
> Yield up, O love, thy crown and hearted throne
> To tyrannous hate! Swell, bosom, with thy fraught,
> For 'tis of aspics' tongues!
>
> (III.iii.444-50)

He kneels, invoking a cold and unbenevolent sky, analogue to a "heart . . . turn'd to stone" (IV.i.191-92):

> Now, by yond marble heaven,
> In the due reverence of a sacred vow
> I here engage my words.
>
> (III.iii.460-62)

Iago kneels, exchanging vows with Othello, again asking witness of a pagan cosmos:

> Do not rise yet.
> Witness, you ever-burning lights above,
> You elements that clip us round about,
> Witness that here Iago doth give up
> The execution of his wit, hands, heart,
> To wrong'd Othello's service! Let him command,
> And to obey shall be in me remorse,
> What bloody business ever.
>
> (III.iii.462-69)

They rise, fused in a bond that promises not life and "increase," with salvation beyond, but death and possible damnation. "All seals and symbols of redeemed sin" (II.iii.350) have been stripped away during the unholy ceremony:

> Othello.   I greet thy love
>   Not with vain thanks, but with acceptance bounteous,
>   And will upon the instant put thee to't:
>   Within these three days let me hear thee say
>   That Cassio's not alive
> Iago.   My friend is dead; 'tis done at your request.
>   But let her live.
> Othello.   Damn her, lewd minx! O, damn her! damn her!
>
> (III.iii.469-75)

Othello would have Cassio dead within three days, perhaps not an accidental reminder of the term Christ spent before He rose again, and Othello would damn his wife. But Desdemona is no longer his wife; the scene closes with Iago's echo of Othello's earlier expression of union ("I am bound to thee forever" [III.iii.213]): "I am your own forever" (III.iii.479). Iago has "ensnar'd [Othello's] soul and body" (V.ii.302), as we know but as Othello will learn too late. The reminders of the marriage service bubble up from a depth of rage and confusion in Othello, from the malignant satisfaction of Iago's profound egoism, creating a horrifying contrast to the marriage on which Iago has preyed from the beginning. Iago's "obey" reverberates against Desdemona's "whate'er you be, I am obedient" (III.iii.89), and will echo into the scene where Othello strikes her:

> Lodovico. Truly, an obedient lady . . .
> Othello.   And she's obedient, as you say, obedient,
>   Very obedient.
>
> (IV.i.259-67)

One of the reasons why the marriage of Iago and Othello occurs is that Desdemona has made a virtuous promise to Cassio that allows Iago to create a dark analogue in binding
Othello to him; "before Emilia here," Desdemona had said,
"I give thee warrant of thy place. Assure thee,/ If I do vow a
friendship, I'll perform it/ To the last article" (III.iii.19-22).
Desdemona's promise is consistent with her marriage vows to
Othello, yet before Iago's ability to "turn her virtue into
pitch" (II.iii.366), it becomes destructive of the bond it would
confirm.

Othello is now an ocean, uninformed by tidal controls,
pressing inevitably, as jealousy creates itself, one way. The
element in which the Turk was sunk is now Othello's deepest
fathom:

> Like to the Pontic Sea,
> Whose icy current and compulsive course
> Ne'er feels retiring ebb, but keeps due on
> To the Propontic and the Hellespont,
> Even so my bloody thoughts, with violent pace
> Shall ne'er look back, ne'er ebb to humble love,
> Till that a capable and wide revenge
> Swallow them up.
>
> (III.iii.453-60)

Desdemona recognizes almost immediately that the fair
visage she had glimpsed beneath Othello's dark exterior has
itself darkened. His "clear spirit" is "puddled" (III.iv.142):

> My lord is not my lord; nor should I know him
> Were he in favour as in humour alter'd.
>
> (III.iv.124-25)

And yet, although he seems not the man she married, although his "lordship," his sovereignty has been abdicated,
she rationalizes his behavior, echoing Iago, who had compared the sudden combatants, Cassio and Montano, to a
married couple:

> Nay, we must think men are not gods,
> Nor of them look for such observancy
> As fits the bridal. Beshrew me much, Emilia,
> I was, unhandsome warrior as I am,

Arraigning his unkindness with my soul
But now I find I had suborn'd the witness,
And he's indicted falsely.

(III.iv.148-54)

While her love continues, her marriage has been subverted. Othello, commencing on his agony of appearance versus reality, suggests that she does not partake of the inner reality, the sanctity, he thought he married. She is a "fair devil" (III.iii.478). He repeats Iago's suggestion of her fruitfulness, but reads there a negative lesson, beginning to embark upon his role as "priest":

This hand is moist . . .
This argues fruitfulness and liberal heart;
Hot, hot, and moist. This hand of yours requires
A sequester from liberty, fasting and prayer,
Much castigation, exercise devout;
For here's a young and sweating devil here
That commonly rebels.

(III.iv.36-43)

His sanctimony—not unlike Hamlet's in Gertrude's closet —suggests that the Iago "morality" now poisons his veins. Desdemona's fairness belies the blackness Othello imputes to her, even as the color of his own skin begins to tinge the inward man. He has lost contact with Desdemona's nature, once his "soul's joy"—although his contact with Desdemona's inward "visage" has been frail from the first. Now his metaphors for himself and Desdemona, once dangerously excessive in their grandeur, become grotesque progeny born in a mind pregnant with the obscene insemination of Iago:

I had rather be a toad
And live upon the vapour of a dungeon,
Than keep a corner of the thing I love for others' uses.
(III.iii.270-72)

a cistern for foul toads
To knot and gender in.
As summer flies are in the shambles.
(IV.ii.61-63)

Othello is driven down the chain of being to the monstrosity

Iago saw in his face from the beginning. Tapping against the
degrees of Othello's descent is Iago's ironic admonition to
"be a man," the advice he has previously pressed on
Roderigo (I.iii.340). But Othello applies his own inner blackness to Desdemona:

> Her name, that was as fresh
> As Dian's visage, is now begrim'd and black
> As mine own face.
>
> (III.iii.386-88)

Perhaps the most terrible aspect of Othello's deception,
however, is his assumption of the role as justicer for the
"crime" committed against him, in contrast with Heywood's
milder Mr. Frankford, no epic hero, who pursues a "kind"
approach with a wife who *has* betrayed him. Frankford marries her again in a way different from that of Othello, whom
Desdemona can still call "kind" (V.ii.125) with her final
breath.

"Do it not with poison," Iago urges, perhaps feeling that
his own subtle means of killing are inappropriate to the
animal-Moor, "strangle her in her bed, even the bed she hath
contaminated" (IV.i.220-21). "Good, good," Othello replies,
"the justice of it pleases; very good" (IV.i.222).

Opponents of the "reversion" theory will object that
Othello uses Christian formats in his "sacrifice" (V.ii.65) of
Desdemona.[12] And that is precisely the point. He has been
turned into a beast by Iago, but comes to Desdemona as a
"Christian." His reconversion is a disjunctive analogy, across
an almost infinite gulf of irony, to his original embrace of
Christianity. The "return" to Christianity is preceded by insis-
tences upon the damnation of his betrayers—of Desdemona:
"Damn her, lewd minx! O, damn her! damn her!"
(III.iii.475), "Ay, let her rot and perish, and be damn'd tonight" (IV.i.191-92); and of Cassio: "To confess, and be
hang'd for his labour;—first to be hang'd, and then to
confess.—I tremble at it" (IV.i.38-39). The latter sequence
—first to be hang'd and then to confess—is better contrived
to work damnation on the soul of the dead man, to send him
to confession after death, where there "is no shuffling," like

the souls of Rosencrantz and Guildenstern, who "go to 't" not "shriving time allow'd" (V.ii.47-48). Othello repeats the rhythm as he looks at sleeping Desdemona: "I will kill thee/ And love thee after" (V.ii.18-19). And his words are true.

Unlike Hero in *Much Ado About Nothing* or Hermione in the more somber *A Winter's Tale*—two other falsely accused women, seemingly killed by the slanders of the men they love—Desdemona returns to life only to profess her innocence and to absolve Othello:

Desdemona. A guiltless death I die.
Emilia.　　O, who hath done this deed?
Desdemona. Nobody; I myself. Farewell!

(V.ii.122-24)

Then, like the Cordelia of whom Lear begs a word, Desdemona merges with silence. Some see in Desdemona an analogue to Christ. Her dying fusion of innocence and forgiveness, they say, must remind us of Christ on the Cross. Cassio has called her "divine" (II.i.73), Roderigo finds her "full of the most bless'd condition" (II.i.254-55), even Iago recognizes her goodness. Cassio's words as she arrives at Cyprus enshrine her as a Seraph, surrounded by adoring light—but we must remember Cassio's tendency toward hyperbole:

You men of Cyprus, let her have your knees.
Hail to thee, lady! and the grace of heaven,
Before, behind thee, and on every hand,
Enwheel thee round!

(II.i.84-87)

Desdemona's statement to Emilia that she would not betray her husband "For the whole world" might remind us of Christ's similar rejection of Satan's offer of "all the kingdomes of the worlde" (Luke IIII, 5). Emilia is of this world and would "venture purgatory" to make her husband "a monarch" (IV.iii.76-77). She echoes Iago's insinuations to Othello on women's infidelity:

Let husbands know
Their wives have sense like them; they see and smell

> And have their palates both for sweet and sour
> As husbands have.
>
>   (IV.iii.94-97)

But Desdemona refuses to descend to Emilia's doctrine of "a wrong for a wrong":

> Heaven me such uses send,
> Not to pick bad from bad, but by bad mend.
>
>   (IV.iii.105-6)

She maintains the consistency she displayed earlier when she saw Othello's "visage in his mind" (I.iii.98-101), penetrating the surface abhorrent to Brabantio:

> And to his honours and his valiant parts
> Did I my soul and fortunes consecrate.
>
>   (I.iii.254-55)

She enunciates a concept radically different from that of Brabantio and Iago, in which the senses are subordinate to *in*sight, the ability to look through the surface to "the very quality of my lord" (I.iii.252). G. K. Hunter likens Desdemona to Beauty in the fairy tale. Desdemona, like Beauty with the Beast, "denies the beastly (or devilish) appearance to proclaim her allegiance to the invisible reality."[13] Such allegiance is demonstrated when Desdemona herself places the façade of appearance before reality, as she awaits word of Othello's ship:

> I am not merry; but I do beguile
> The thing I am by seeming otherwise.
>
>   (II.i.123-24)

She maintains a cheerful exterior for the other anxious people on the quay. It is her role as the commander's wife, a giving up of personal feelings to larger obligations.[14]

Othello's words after the murder have some symbolic value beyond their failure to elicit a cosmic response:

> It is the very error of the moon;
> She comes more nearer earth than she was wont,
> And makes men mad.
>
>   (V.ii.109-11)

If Desdemona is to be equated with the moon as a symbol of Diana's chastity and, possibly, with the moon as an emblem of the Virgin Queen, Elizabeth, as in Spenser, Shakespeare, Jonson, *et al.*, her coming "nearer earth," to Othello, would be a metaphor for her infidelity, which has indeed produced a form of "lunacy" in him. The dual possibilities of "moon"—chastity and inconstancy (cf. *Romeo and Juliet* [II.ii. 109-11])—capture both Desdemona's honesty *and* Othello's misconception of her. Indeed, Othello's doubts about the meaning of the moon focus his doubts about Desdemona. The moon is mutable:

> Think'st thou I'd make a life of jealousy,
> To follow still the changes of the moon
> With fresh suspicions?

> (III.iii.177-79)

Yet, Desdemona's "name . . . was a fresh/ As Dian's visage" (III.iii.386-87). He repeats the suggestion, gazing at her as she sleeps: "That whiter skin of hers than snow,/ And smooth as monumental alabaster" (V.ii.4-5). Desdemona's "commonness" is, for Othello, an offense against the universe, including the moon as symbol of purity, which must shut its eyes before her "deeds" (IV.ii.76):

> What committed!
> Heaven stops the nose at it, and the moon winks.

> (IV.ii.76-77)

Immediately before his imputation of "error" to the moon, Othello has talked of "a huge eclipse/ Of sun and moon" (V.ii.99-100). The medieval equivalent of "sun," of course, would be Christ, as in the Anglo-Saxon "Phoenix," Chaucer's Prologue, and the Bible's "the Sonne was darkned." The late sixteenth-century equation would suggest Elizabeth: "The mortal moon hath her eclipse endur'd" (Sonnet 107). But Desdemona, innocent like Christ, "chaste and fair" like Elizabeth, endures her eclipse only long enough to utter her dying words.

Tragically, Othello reduces Desdemona to a world where lack of faith makes women beasts, not realizing that in the world the play depicts she is the precious jewel his own heart turns to stone:

> If Heaven would make me such another world,
> Of one entire and perfect chrysolite,
> I'd not have sold her for it.

(V.ii.144-46)

Othello has done precisely what Desdemona, in her deeper knowledge, rejects in her discussion with Emilia. Othello gives the world away—a pearl richer than all his tribe—like an ignorant "Indian" discarding something whose value he does not comprehend, or like Judas casting Christ away, "sold" for the mere silver of the lesser world of mere men. While the "Indian" reading suggests Othello's reversion to "erring" barbarism (I.iii.362), the "Judean" reading is perhaps preferable, because it imputes to Othello a knowledge of Christ and Christian practice, which makes him more culpable than merely an ignorant savage. Ignorance alone does not constitute tragedy. Othello should have known better. But the thrust of the analogy does not make Desdemona Christ nor Othello Judas. To press the suggestions would remove from the murder of Desdemona by a radically deluded man its *own* terror. The analogy is there —if it is at all—to underline the horror of *this* deed, the murder of this innocent.

It is also clear, however, as West suggests, that the play "may be read as concerned with Christian choices."[15] Othello's descent from a "soul [whose] content [is] absolute" (II.i.193) to a raging "Would I were be satisfied!" (III.iii.390) graphs the fall he suffers. His soul seemed linked to Desdemona's in a Donnian sense ("Thy firmnes drawes my circle just,/ And makes me end, where I begunne"). But the unity was based on self-esteem, Othello's rhetoric ending where it had begun—with himself. His own words predict, even predicate, his fall, but while he retains his oneness with Desdemona—or his sense of it—he is impregnable: "My life upon her faith!" (I.iii.295). When he begins to doubt Desdemona, he must doubt himself as well, and begins to commit the moral suicide typical of the Shakespearean betrayer.

When Macbeth murders Duncan, or Lear denies Cordelia, each betrays himself, because each violates the world order within and surrounding the tragic hero, the inner and outer mystery, microcosm and macrocosm. In rejecting Desdemona, in destroying his solemnly vowed contract, Othello casts off his allegiance to a power more comprehensive than his will; as Cassio says, Desdemona is "our great captain's captain" (II.i.74), his wife, the agency through which Othello achieves that something outside of himself which confirms his own being. In his betrayal, however, Othello begins to obey a time more distant than that of the emergency that dispatched him to Cyprus, one prior to his "baptism" one more narrowly centered than the world of Christian rhythms, which reach out from the individual to modulate with the mystery of the supernature: that time he described for the Venetian Senate when his own will was arbiter of his fortune.

Contrasting with Othello's movement toward bestiality, toward the destiny Brabantio had warned against ("For if such actions may have passage free,/ Bond-slaves and pagans shall our statesmen be" [I.ii.98-99]) is Desdemona's increasing demonstration of virtue. One descends; the other, in affliction, grows. Shakespeare employs another ironic movement in the careers of Lady Macbeth and Macbeth, one beginning in firm control and ending in murky madness, the other commencing in fear and hallucination and dying in valorous bestiality. But the terms in *Othello,* obviously, are different. Desdemona follows the precepts of the "Homilie of the state of Matrimonie": "if thou can'st suffer an extreme husband, thou shalt have a great reward therefore: But if thou lov'st him only because he is gentle and courteous, what reward will God give thee therefore? But I exhort . . . women that they would patiently beare the sharpnesse of their husbands." Desdemona does *not* make the excuse that the Homily suggests Sara also did not make to Abraham: "for thy love [I] have forsaken my kindred and my countrey, and have the want of both my friends and kinsefolkes, and am thus come into so farre countreys with thee." Emilia—so vividly contrasted with Desdemona in their discussion of the world and its worth—makes this protest *for* her:

Hath she not forsook so many noble matches,
Her father and her country and her friends. . . ?

(IV.ii.125-26)

Desdemona, however, has embraced Sara's role and now accepts Othello's "whore" as her "wretched fortune" (IV.ii.128):

Unkindness may do much:
And his unkindness may defeat my life,
But never taint my love.

(IV.ii.159-61)

"Unkindness," of course, reflects not merely Othello's harshness but the loss of that quality, that humaneness, Desdemona saw in his mind. Othello has lost his kindness—his link with humankind. He has become, like Macbeth, another species, subhuman, inhuman, nonhuman.

The Homily's advice on the husband who beats his wife relates directly to Othello's striking of Desdemona before Lodovico and the Venetian emissaries:

But yet I meane not that a man should beat his wife, God forbid that, for it is the greatest shame that can be, not so much to her that is beaten, as to him that does the deed. But if by such fortune thou chancest upon such an husband, take it not too heavily, but suppose thou, that thereby is laid up no small reward hereafter; and in this lifetime no small commendation to thee, if thou canst be quiet. . . . For it is an extreme point, thus so vilely to entreat her like a slave, that is a fellow to thee of thy life, and so joyned unto thee before time in the necessary matters of thy living. And therefore a man may well liken such a man (if he be called a man, rather than a wild beast) to a killer of his father or his mother.

The Homily provides an exegesis on Lodovico's horror at Othello's striking Desdemona. Iago had predicted the scene in his earlier "excuse" of Cassio: "As men in rage strike those that wish them best" (II.iii.243). Lodovico censures Othello's passion much as Montano had Cassio's drunkenness—each with the expert encouragement of Iago.*

---

*Iago's skill in encouraging a "new" consciousness within Othello and the analogy between the duped Cassio and the radically wronged Desdemona emerges in parallel passages, of which the former is Iago's and the latter, significantly, Othello's:

Is this the noble Moor whom our full Senate
Call all in all sufficient? Is this the nature
Whom passion could not shake? whose solid virtue
The shot of accident nor dart of chance
Could neither graze nor pierce? . . .
What, strike his wife!

(IV.i.275-83)

The Homily makes clear the equation between command
and marriage, both of which Othello violates:

> For even as the King appeareth so much the more noble, the
> more excellent and noble he maketh his officers and lieueten-
> ants, whom if he should dishonour, and despise the authority of
> their dignitie, he should deprive himselfe of a great part of his
> owne honour: Even so, if thou doest despise her that is set in the
> next roome beside thee, thou does much derogate and decay the
> excelencie and virtue of thine own authoritie.

By striking Desdemona, Othello commits a more than personal sin. "This would not be believ'd in Venice" (IV.ii.252),
Lodovico exclaims. And Othello's action predicts his greater
crime, where he "Beat a Venetian" (V.ii.354). "Beat" would
seem to apply as much to the homielitic context of the scene
before Lodovico as to Othello's actual strangling of Desdemona.

The precise nature of Othello's *self*-betrayal is made explicit in the priest's admonition to the husband in the marriage
service:

> Ye housbandes love your wives, even as Christ loved the
> Churche, and hath geven hymselfe for it, to sanctifie it, pur-
> gying it in the fountaine of water, throughe the worde, that he
> might make it unto hym selfe a glorious congregacion, not hav-
> ing spot, or wrincle, or any suche thyng, but that it should be
> holy and blameless. So men are bound to love their owne wyves,
> as their own bodies. He that loveth his owne wife loveth hym
> selfe. For never did any man hate his own fleshe, but nourisheth

You see this fellow that is gone before:
He is a soldier fit to stand by Caesar
And give direction.

(II.iii.126-28)

O, the world hath not a sweeter creature!
She might lie by an emperor's side
And command him tasks.

(IV.i.194-96)

& cherisheth it, even as the Lorde doeth the congregacion, for
we are members of his body: of his flesh, & of hys bones.

"The fountain from the which [Othello's] current runs"
(IV.ii.59) neither dries up nor is "discarded" (IV.ii.60) as
Othello suggests; rather, it is exchanged for the compulsive
course of the Pontic Sea, the black tide whose direction is irreversible. Tempests may, as Cassio has said, omit their mortal natures for Desdemona's passage, but the Turk approaches her:

Desdemona.   Hark! Who is't that knocks?
Emilia.   It's the wind.

(IV.iii.53-54)

The storm moves toward Desdemona's room, where her
wedding sheets are laid in her own pathetic effort at white
magic,* toward a smaller island of sadness and loss and continued light.[16] "Methinks," Montano had said of the storm,
"the wind hath spoke aloud at land" (II.i.5). The Second
Gentleman had remarked "The wind-shaked surge, with high
and monstrous main" (II.i.13). Wind, storm, Turk,
monster—these forces, concentrated now in Othello, knock at
Desdemona's door.

The "frail vow" that joined them, the mystical incorporation of man with wife and of their oneness with Christ, devolves in the words of the marriage exhortation to the satisfaction of "mennes carnall lustes and appetytes, lyke brute
beastes that have no understandyng." The "holy misteries"
are perverted to the ribald rituals of the brothel as Othello
orders Emilia to display

Some of your function, mistress:
Leave procreants alone and shut the door;
Cough or cry "hem" if anybody come,
Your mystery, your mystery; nay, dispatch!

(IV.ii.27-30)

Desdemona pleads her innocence:

---

*We may wonder whether the marriage *has* been consummated.

> No, as I am a Christian!
> If to preserve this vessel for my lord
> From any other foul unlawful touch
> Be not a strumpet, I am none.
>
> (IV.ii.82-85)

The allusion to her purity carries overtones of the Communion Cup, as Macbeth makes clear when he talks of putting "rancours in the vessel of my peace" (III.i.67). The dynamics of the world have been so carefully dictated by Iago that the motives of one (Desdemona for Cassio, Othello for the handkerchief) conflict with *and* augment the motives of the other.[17] Truth (Desdemona, even now a "rose-lipped Cherubin" [IV.ii.63]) becomes falsehood ("whore" [IV.ii.89], "commoner" [IV.ii.73], "strumpet" [IV.ii.81]). Proof that Iago has caught a greater fly than Cassio in his web (II.i.169-70) is Othello's equation of Desdemona to "summer flies" (IV.ii.66). Iago has managed not merely to render Othello a beast but to make a beast of Desdemona before the willful eyes of Othello.

Rancors infect his once "perfect soul" and he completes his ritual with Emilia, showing that he knows not what he does:

> You, mistress,
> That have the office opposite to Saint Peter
> And keep the gate of hell! You, you, ay, you!
> We have done our course; there's money for your pains.
>
> (IV.ii.90-93)

Coming to an embodiment of the "perfect wife" of the Homily, and capable even of expressing that perfection, he sees himself in hell—which is where he has put himself. The reference to the devil's gatekeeper predicts the fuller treatment of damnation and the gates of hell in *Macbeth,* and points at the similarities between Othello's crime and Macbeth's—the killing of a good and trusting person, on whose life the murderer's health and soul depends, in a close-shut murderous room. But Macbeth is not deluded as to Duncan's quality. Here, Desdemona is cast as devil. A further irony is that the one person (besides Iago) who might clear her stands just beyond earshot at the whorehouse hell-gate. Emilia's vindication of Desdemona will come in the same room—but too late.

The irony would be profound were Othello merely venting his indignation at a defenseless innocent. The Christian emphasis he so wildly misapplies sharpens the irony and, of course, raises issues more comprehensive than mere temporal questions. Othello had told Iago that he "had been happy . . . So [he] had nothing known" (III.iii.345-47), thus revealing the thin surface of his conversion to a Christianity whose emphasis is on inward spiritual reality. Married to a Desdemona he should know the truth, and, in fact, he continues to express it even after he has been convinced of the falsehood. But—as with the damned—the continued assertion of truth is torture to him. He ironically fails the test of faith, the central test of all Christians after Thomas, by believing that Desdemona has failed the same test. The irony is deepened by the fact that there *is* nothing to know, except the truth. Mere innocence, however, is seldom its own best defense. Perhaps the most terrifying dimension of the Othello-Desdemona confrontation is that innocence is all she has, and her very ignorance of the web that has been woven around her leaves her defenseless.

Othello kills her not for himself, but for mankind ("else she'll betray more men" [V.ii.6]), for the "cause" he proclaims to his "soul," but with which he will not sully the "chaste stars" (V.ii.2), perhaps an admission that the stars, visible elements of the outer mystery, might repudiate his "cause." Othello has risen from his fit to grand generalizations, but his universals are falsely predicated, like the homilies of Iago, which would be sound doctrine if not refuted by their hidden premises of hatred dictated by absolute will. Othello becomes the prey of platitude, a tendency he demonstrated from the first. But as Iago's goal refutes his own good advice, even as that advice furthers his goal, so Othello continues to receive the imagery of truth, even as he moves closer to the murder. "If she be false, O, then heaven mocks itself!" he had said, "I'll not believe it" (III.iii.271-78). And even at the end, Desdemona's perfection sways him. Beauty tortured Iago, who has translated that torture to Othello, now alienated like Milton's Satan from the ground of his own being and hence from positive response to nature and the supernature beyond it:

Oh, balmy breath, that dost almost persuade
Justice to break her sword!

(V.ii.16-17)

But he is abstract justice; the assumed political role rebuffs the specific communication directed through his senses to the deepest element of his nature, his soul. He is judge who coerces testimony to an already-decided verdict. He is priest as well as magistrate, clerk as well as priest. Othello's mind, infected with the Iago vision rather than filled with metaphors for his own grandeur, continues to create its world, first of monstrosities more hideous than he had seen in his past. Now, as a version of his self-conception returns, Othello, a son of "royal seige" (I.ii.22), reassumes a solitary role not as epic hero single-handedly battling a world of foes, but as judge, priest, and executioner, striking a final blow for the world against its chief betrayer. Calvin's distinction applies profoundly to Othello: "[Man] is able to understand God's mysteries only in so far as he is illumined by God's grace. He who attributes any more understanding to himself is all the more blind because he does not recognize his own blindness."[18]

He puts out a light, reversing the opening of a religious service, suggesting that the ceremonies that follow will be a sacrilege, but appropriate symbolically to a play full of false rite and imagistically consistent with a play whose medium is darkness—of night, of ignorance, and of soul, echoing the admonitions of the Homily on the Resurrection: "yea, how dare wee be so bold to renounce the presence of the Father, the Sonne and the holy Ghost? . . . and fear not I say the danger and perill of so traiterous a defiance and departure? . . . let no folly loose the thing that grace hath so preciously offered and purchased, let not willfulnesse and blindnesse put out so great light that is now shewed to you." From a pagan standpoint, Othello has become anti-creator, his role opposite to that of the god who brought fire to man:

once put out thy light,
Thou cunning'st pattern of excelling nature,
I know not where is that Promethean heat
That can thy light relume.

(V.ii.10-13)

Iago's malignant garden of the will dictates that Othello can kill but not create:

> When I have pluck'd the rose
> I cannot give it vital growth again,
> It needs must wither.
>
> (V.ii.13-15)

It is perhaps not accidental, particularly within the context of the positive attributes attached to strawberries, that the rose is preeminently a symbol of the Virgin Mary. Although he has talked of killing souls, Othello attempts to follow precise Christian formats in his "sacrifice" of Desdemona. As in Iago's sermons, Christian precept is subverted to opposite goals, but Othello does not know this:

> Have you pray'd to-night, Desdemon? . . .
> If you bethink yourself of any crime
> Unreconcil'd as yet to Heaven and grace,
> Solicit for it straight. . .
> I would not kill thy unprepared spirit;
> No; heavens forfend! I would not kill thy soul.
>
> (V.ii.25-32)

The scruples—such as Hamlet does not demonstrate when he comes upon the kneeling Claudius or sends Rosencrantz and Guildenstern, the commission for their deaths in hand, to England—merely emphasize the horror of the deed by enclosing it in a superficially correct pattern whose rhythms and forms are profoundly in conflict with the action they assist, and whose admonitions point back with tragic irony at the admonisher. Othello's language now condemns him, an ironically inevitable condition of its circularity:

> Desdemona. Then Heaven
>   Have mercy on me!
> Othello   Amen, with all my heart!
>
> (V.ii.33-34)

> Desdemona. O, Heaven, have mercy on me!
> Othello.   I say, amen.
>
> (V.ii.57)

Othello's "heart" is deceived by false assumptions, as his "Christianity" had covered the potential pagan beneath. His black face had not concealed from Desdemona his inner quality, however. Nor here can his external observance hide his inner tumult, the monster in his thought:

> Alas, why gnaw you so your nether lip?
> Some bloody passion shakes your very frame.
>
> (V.ii.43-44)

"My lord is not my lord," Desdemona had said (III.iv.124)—indeed, Othello has been turned inside out, in the manner of Emilia's metaphor for Iago's apparently also—though not equally—foolish jealousy of Emilia:

> Some such squire he was
> That turn'd your wit the seamy side without,
> And made you to suspect me with the Moor.
>
> (IV.ii.145-47)

Roderigo has also been "turn'd almost the wrong side out" (II.iii.54), an inevitable consequence of the will's uninhibited operation on the outward actions of man.

Othello warns Desdemona about lying, employing the Iago rhythm: "Take heed of perjury" (V.ii.51), and when she cannot confess that she gave the handkerchief to Cassio, calls her "perjur'd woman" (V.ii.63). But clearly his own perjury is at issue. He has wagered "the worth of [his] eternal soul" (III.iii.361) on Iago's version of her infidelity. And when he discovers his error, he damns himself:

> when we shall meet at compt,
> This look of thine will hurl my soul from heaven,
> And fiends will snatch at it . . .
> Whip me, ye devils,
> From the possession of this heavenly sight!
> Blow me about in winds! roast me in sulphur!
> Wash me in steep-down gulfs of liquid fire!
>
> (V.ii.273-80)

While Desdemona's final words predict no such look, Othello cannot judge himself in the context of eternity—his sentence is not his province, indeed is as presumptuous as his judgment of Desdemona or of a critic's assignment of his soul to hell. The final imagery of his speech, however, suggests that

he begins to see himself as a Turk deserving "mere perdition" beneath a sea of fire.

Lodovico assumes a control that Othello silences with a
sharp "Soft you" (V.ii.338). I am still in charge here, he
seems to say. He reverts to his original mission in Cyprus,
aligning his sword with the Venetian thrust against the Turk:

> Set you down this;
> And say besides, that in Aleppo once
> Where a malignant and a turban'd Turk
> Beat a Venetian and traduc'd the state,
> I took by th' throat the circumcised dog,
> And smote him thus.
>
> (V.ii.351-56)

He had threatened Iago: "Thou hadst been better have been
born a dog/ Than answer my waked wrath!" (III.iii.362-63).
Iago transformed Cassio into a beast "as full of quarrel and
offense/ As my young mistress's dog" (II.iii.52-53). Now
Othello takes action not against the "Spartan dog" (V.ii.361),
Iago, but against the pagan beast he has himself become.

The "Othello Music"[19] recurs in his final speech. Although
his only double epithet is "malignant and . . . turban'd," the
speech is set against a pagan background of "base Indians"
(if we accept Quarto's reading) and "Arabian Trees" dripping
"medicinal gum," not framed within a recognizable Christian
context unless we accept Folio's "Judean." Thus one could
claim that Othello does not recognize the full depths of his
crime—but that is to ignore his own ominous predictions for
his soul at judgment, and his acceptance of Emilia's sentence
of anyone who would wrong Desdemona:

> Othello. Whip me ye devils!
>
> (V.ii.277)

> Emilia. O heavens, that such companions thou'dst unfold,
>   And put in every honest hand a whip
>   To lash the rascals naked through the world
>   Even from the east to th' west.
>
> (IV.ii.141-44)

The pagan cast of his final speech presses toward Othello's
indictment of himself as Turk. He is telling his story

again—his voice seems to dwell inevitably on what has happened to *him* (as opposed, for example, to Lear at the end, gazing for Cordelia's breath)—but is this the full-blown confidence of the undefeated general or the absolute rhetoric of the perfect man who, as his doubts were activated, made "a life of jealousy" (III.iii.177), the words of a man "cheering himself up"?[20] He indicts himself within his dictation of Lodovico's report to Venice, and thus some vindication accrues, particularly since the indictment itself is qualified and his sorrow is imaged in an exotic simile. Yet sorrow is there, as is a full expression of Desdemona's worth, whether she was discarded by Iscariot or an Indian. Above all, the indictment leads to the self-execution. The shifting mosaic of the language allows for varying interpretations, but it is Othello's definition that counts. Shakespeare, as usual, leaves further commentary to his spectator, expressing implicitly his profound confidence that *he* will understand, or recognizing, perhaps, that these things are to be understood in different ways by each auditor of his play.

In his own eyes, Othello is an enemy of the state. Here, in contrast to his murder of Desdemona, his roles as judge and executioner are properly fused; "he that was Othello" (V.ii.284) returns. He does not use the poison he had proposed to Iago for Desdemona—the subtle agency of the Iago world in which Othello became entangled—but the weapon he understands, the sword; and with it he does the state a final service, executing the enemy, who happens to be himself. Sacramentally, he destroys his own flesh *for* destroying his own flesh, that of his wife. His act places him back within the system that he had discarded for the will Iago had encouraged to monstrosity. Whether he enters some valley of epic heroes to be greeted by Antony and Aeneas, or into hell's flames, purgatorial fire, or the bliss of a forgiving Desdemona's gaze is not at issue, except insofar as Othello accepts whatever fate lies beyond the final successful thrust of his sword.

Evil is self-destructive in *Othello*. The futility of Iago's "success" says as much, as does the necessity of Othello's executing himself. He dies kissing Desdemona, and while his final kiss may be a reminder of Judas, certainly it is a recognition of fatal error and, combined with his "I kiss'd thee ere I kill'd thee" (V.ii.358), an acceptance by Othello of its consequences—his own death. Desdemona and Othello lie together in death on the very bed he had thought "lust stain'd" (V.i.36) and had promised to splatter with "lust's blood" (V.i.36). They lie on the wedding sheets Emilia had spread at Desdemona's request, married in death on the stainless bed Othello's mind translated into a "cistern for foul toads/ To knot and gender in" (IV.ii.61-62), and finally into an anti-shrine for profound sacrilege. He glimpses his error during his terrifying moments on the far side of tragedy; he stands forgiven by Desdemona, at least, and he regains control of himself and his commission at the end. The play says nothing more; as Iago suggests, "What you know, you know."

NOTES TO CHAPTER 3: *Othello*

1. A. C. Bradley, *Shakespearean Tragedy*, p. 177.
2. When the Duchess of Malfi marries her steward, Antonio, she must propose to him and must conceal her subsequent pregnancy. Her love, an emanation of her womanhood, conflicts with her position as duchess. Another second marriage, Gertrude's in *Hamlet*, poses problems not just for young Hamlet, but for a throne stained by incest.
3. Alfred Harbage, *William Shakespeare*, p. 348. In addition to Portia's abhorrence of Morocco ("Let all of his complexion choose me so": II. vii. 79), which Harbage notes, one should mention Claribel's "loathness" at marrying "an African" (II.i. 125 and 129). On the fault of Desdemona's secret marriage to Othello, see Margaret L. Ranald, "The Indiscretion of Desdemona," *SQ* 14 (Spring 1963): 127-39. Clifford Leech offers a concise and informative discussion of secret marriages in *The Duchess of Malfi* (New York, 1963), pp. 53-55. Thomas McFarland's chapter on *Othello* offers the most incisive treatment of the subject I have seen: *Tragic Meanings in Shakespeare* (New York, 1966), pp. 60-91.
4. The play, of course, offers evidence linking Iago to the Devil. Typical of the myriad commentators who ascribe diabolic motives to Iago's malignity are Robert H. West, *Shakespeare and the Outer Mystery* (Lexington, Ky., 1968), p. 99: "Iago is mysterious in his origins and purposes, and like hell's, his mystery is that of iniquity"; Daniel Stempel, "The Silence of Iago," *PMLA* 84, no. 2 (March 1969): 204: "Iago has been mastered by a radically evil will for which he has supplied both motive and opportunity"; E. K. Chambers, *Shakespeare: A Survey* (New York, n.d.), pp. 220-21: "his dramatic function is that of the incarnation of the forces of evil, of the devil himself"; and Harry Morris, "No Amount of Prayer Can Possibly Matter," *Sewanee Review* 77 no. 1 (Winter 1969): 20: Iago is "a devil." Marvin Rosenberg, "In Defense of Iago," *SQ* 6 (1955): 145-58, sees Iago as merely a "thwarted human being," no devil, who

takes his problems—possibly his ulcers—out on others. Rosenberg provides an excellent summary of opinions regarding Iago. For a reexamination of Iago from the Coleridgean point of view, see Elinor S. Shaffer, "Iago's Malignity Motivated," *SQ* 19 (Winter 1968): 195-204. For Iago psychoanalyzed, see Norman N. Holland, *Psychoanalysis and Shakespeare* (New York, 1964), pp. 248-55, and Robert Rogers, "Endopsychic Drama in *Othello*," *SQ* 20, no. 2 (Spring 1969): 205-15. For a judicious summary of the Iago question, see Leah Scragg, "Iago—Vice or Devil?" *Shakespeare Survey* 21 (1968): 53-65. On the villain in Shakespeare who cites Scripture, see Ernest A. Strathmann, "The Devil Can Cite Scripture," *SQ* 15, no. 2 (Spring 1964): 17-23.

5. As I suggested in the section on *Hamlet,* it is possible for a character's deepest motivation to remain unperceived even by the most perceptive character in the play—Hamlet, for example. If Iago *is* a devil, his motives are clear. If not, and I do not subscribe to the simplicity of the devil theory, his motive-hunting (including his patently ridiculous suspicion of Cassio *re* Emilia) may conceal a deep racial hatred which, though it is precisely a motive for which the rationalist **could find no words, could be expressed in performance (as it was, for example, in Olivier's version).** While some performances have made Othello an Arab, the play emphasizes that he is as black as Aaron, the Moor of *Titus Andronicus,* as Morocco, whose complexion offends Portia, or as the "black pagans" against whom the elder Mowbray fought (*Richard II:* IV.i.94). The black man has the white woman and Iago can't stand it, as his gross references to Brabantio imply. That such hatred can lead to wild and irrational action is suggested by the theory I have heard advanced regarding events at Oxford, Mississippi, on the night that James Meredith enrolled. The violence that seethed over the campus surprised even those who had "expected trouble." But the reason why **red necks turned purple** that night is that—*whether they realized it or not*—Meredith's entrance upon the soil of "Ole Miss" represented the deepest fear of the white southerner—miscengenation. "Ole Miss," after all, means not "Old Mississippi" but was the name the slaves gave to the wife of the plantation owner. Therefore, when Meredith set foot on the campus—so goes the theory. I suggest that a similar deep racial fear and hatred works within Iago. Since the point is in no way integral to the argument of my chapter and since it is speculation, I offer it here in a note. It should be further noted, however, that Cinthio's version of the story makes the racial question much more overt than does Shakespeare. But just as the question of the rightness or wrongness of revenge becomes implicit, hence more profound and powerful in *Hamlet,* so the matter of race works beneath the surface in *Othello.* As Charlton says, "This hint of Cinthio's ['Not to marry a man divided from us by Nature, Heaven, and mode of life'] is seized by Shakespeare and becomes a main motive in the thematic structure of Othello." *Shakespearian Tragedy,* p. 116. That Shakespeare understood the nature of irrational hatred is not a product of Freudian critics, as Shylock proves:

> Some men there are love not a gaping pig;
> Some, that are mad if they behold a cat;
> And others, when the bagpipe sings i'th' nose,
> Cannot contain their urine: for affection,
> Master of passion, sways it to the mood
> Of what it likes or loathes. Now, for your answer:

As there is no firm reason to be rend'red
Why he cannot abide a gaping pig;
Why he, a harmless necessary cat;
Why he, a woollen bagpipe; but of force
Must yield to such inevitable shame
As to offend, himself being offended;
So can I give no reason, nor I will not,
More than a lodg'd hate and a certain loathing
I bear Antonio, that I follow thus
A losing suit against him. Are you answer'd?

(IV.i.47-62)

This "explanation" of Iago's "motive" places Iago within the human range. One of the satisfying results of such a placement is that it makes Othello *more* responsible than had he been ensnared by a devil. Seeing Iago as human also helps us to feel the impact his brief interview with Desdemona has upon him (IV.ii.110-72). Goddard suggests that Iago's ineffectual response to Roderigo's demands (IV.ii.173-252) results from his having been shaken "to the foundation" by his encounter with Desdemona. "For the first time in [Iago's] life," says Goddard, "he has encountered a force more powerful than his own diabolic nature." *The Meaning of Shakespeare,* pp. 96-99. The impact is greater, I suggest, if we see Iago as *human,* as we must, I believe, in performance. The reaction Goddard imputes to Iago, however, resembles that of Satan upon encountering Eve: "That space the Evil one abstracted stood/ From his own evil, and for the time remain'd/ Stupidly good, of enmity disarm'd" (*Paradise Lost,* IX.463-65). Othello is also temporarily dissuaded from his "cause": "Oh balmy breath, that dost almost persuade/ Justice to break her sword!" (V.ii.16-17). Cf. *Twelfth Night.* V.i.112-115.

6. *Columbia Encyclopedia* (New York, 1947), p. 459. Historically, Cyprus was captured by the Turks (1571) and its Venetian commander brutally murdered. Shakespeare could have known this through Richard Knolles's *The Generall Historie of the Turkes,* published in London in 1603. Cinthio's version of the Othello story appeared in 1565. Assuming that Shakespeare read the original version and not a translation, which would have incorporated the events of 1571, *Othello* represents a dramatic analogue to the murder of the Christian governor of Cyprus, Marco Antonio Bragadino. On the relationship between the play and history, see Emrys Jones, "Othello, Lepanto, and the Cyprus Wars," *Shakespeare Survey* 21 (Cambridge, 1968): 47-52.

7. Alvin Kernan, "Introduction" to *Othello* (New York, 1963), p. xxx.

8. Battenhouse's phrase "the self-pleasing love. . .central to every tragic hero," may seem too inclusive. But certainly it applies to Othello, as to Agamemnon and Oedipus, the Antony of *Antony and Cleopatra,* King Lear, Coriolanus and, crucially, *not* to Prospero. *Shakespearean Tragedy,* p. 226.

9. On the "geographic element" in *Othello,* see Kernan's fine "Introduction," pp. xxiii-xxxv.

10. On the question of witchcraft, see David Kaula's effective refutation of the witchcraft-love equation proposed by R. B. Heilman in *Magic in the Web* (Lexington, Ky., 1956): "Witchcraft is a metaphor for love" (p. 225). As Kaula suggests, magic and love are differentiated throughout the play: "Othello Possessed: Notes on Shakespeare's Use of Magic and Witchcraft," *Shakespeare Studies* 2 (1966): 112-32.

11. Kaula, "Othello Possessed," p. 125.
12. H. B. Charlton, in his excellent discussion of *Othello*, suggests that when Othello's "innermost being is stirred to its depths, he breaks out into utterances of a remoter and more mystically articulated religion." *Shakespearian Tragedy,* p. 120. See also Bradley's explicit rejection of the theory in *Shakespearean Tragedy,* pp. 152-62.
13. G. K. Hunter, "*Othello* and Colour Prejudice," *British Academy Lecture* 53 (1967): 152.
14. Desdemona's use of a fair appearance to hide her personal concern contrasts directly with the external concern of Iago for Othello, which conceals the ancient's malevolent purpose. Shakespeare does something similar with Malcolm in IV.iii of *Macbeth;* Malcolm is the spiritual antithesis of Macbeth as Desdemona is of Iago. As Bernard Spivack shows in *Shakespeare and the Allegory of Evil* (New York, 1958), pp. 155-76, the medieval vice employed deceit, particularly a virtuous façade, in tempting his victims to damnation. Typical is Satan in Bale's *Temptation* (1538):

> A Godly pretence, outwardly, must I bear,
> Seeming religious, devout and sad in any gear.

Marlowe, of course, includes such figures (Mephistophilis and the Evil Angel) in *Dr. Faustus,* but makes one crucial transition from the world of the morality play to tragedy in *internalizing* Faustus's debate, thereby lending a psychological dimension to the spiritual contest and compounding the *human* issue involved (see particulary V.1-16). This is not an Everyman moving in the world described by Willard Farnum: "So long as the moral dramatist and his audience conceive that a universal law of justice, under which a man lives and engages himself with his destiny, is dominated by the force of mercy, then recognition of tragedy must necessarily be small." (*The Medieval Heritage of Elizabethan Tragedy,* p. 193.) The issue becomes tragic when the issues moves inward, when the will of the tragic hero may become so infected by its increasing insistence upon itself that damnation becomes a *real* dramatic possibility, not merely a premise to be discarded as an Everyman begins to merge with sacramental rhythms. The will of the early Everyman is a superficial manifestation of this world. It is erased as Everyman aligns himself with that deeper level of will which coincides with God's will. Everyman imitates Christ in Gethsemane, as every Christian must be to be saved. For the tragic hero, however, the superficial level of will—pride, ambition, whatever keeps the character from being "preeminently virtuous"—becomes dominant as it is insisted upon, thrusting the character into the insoluble paradox of tragedy, where his will and the order of the world collide. Regardless of what these great dramatists believed, they achieve a coalescence of medieval philosophy (Aquinas and St. Bernard particularly) and dramatic form. Medieval drama represented the imposition of the inevitably victorious doctrine *upon* the "hero." Renaissance drama allows the hero real choice, and at times his choice—like Lear's—annihilates any doctrine or ethic that man might embrace. It is worth noting, furthermore, that medieval tragedy, represented by such works as Chaucer's "Monk's Tale," Lydgate's "Falles of Princes," Baldwin's *Treatise of Morall Philosophy,* and the many editions of *A Mirror for Magistrates,* places its characters on fortune's wheel, with its eventual downward dynamic. Regardless of cautionary moral decorations, in such works the moral is the fall. Lydgate's moral is tagged on to his title almost as an afterthought: "A Treatiese excellent and compendious, shewing and declaring in manner of tragedye, the falles of sondry most notable Princes and Princesses with other Nobles, through ye Mutabilitie and change of unstedfast Fortune together with their most detestable & wicked vices." Once man has submitted to the rule of Fortuna, the wheel *must* turn—as it does for Edmund at the end of *King Lear* ("The wheel is come full circle". V.iii.174), regardless of the merits or demerits of the characters. Lear's wheel is one of "fire" (IV.vii.47), a perceived damnation from which he escapes, as I will suggest, by embracing a spiritual dimension beyond that of the pagan Goddess Fortuna. It is true, however, that even the *De Casibus* literature becomes more emphatic on moral failings as it approaches the great dramatic moment of the later stages of Elizabeth's reign. John Higgins's introduction to his 1574 *Mirrour for Magistrates* stresses virtue and its rewards, vice and its punishments, so as to realign man's destiny with a comprehensible moral philosophy. Indeed, Higgins adumbrates one of the central themes of Elizabethan Drama, particularly of the revenge play, by fitting punishment with crime, making each punishment represent the criminal's retribution upon himself for his defection from virtue and, of course, making each punishment the revenge of the world order as well. For a good summary of the transition from medieval forms of tragedy to renaissance drama see, in addition to Spivack and Farnum, Lily Bess Campbell, *Shakespeare's Tragic Heroes: Slaves of Passion* (Cambridge, 1930). For an equally valuable discussion of the transition from the miracle play to Shakespearean comedy; see R. G. Hunter, *Shakespeare and the Comedy of Forgiveness* (New York, 1965). For an illuminating discussion of the development from the morality play to Elizabethan tragedy, see David M. Bevington, *From Mankind to Marlowe* (Cambridge, Mass., 1962).

15. West, *Shakespeare and the Outer Mystery*, p. 139. The most complete case for Othello's damnation is Paul N. Siegel's "The Damnation of Othello," *PMLA* 68 (1953): 1068-78, and his *Shakespearean Tragedy and the Elizabethan Compromise* (New York, 1957), pp. 119-41. See also Seigel's "The Damnation of Othello: an Addendum," *PMLA* 71 (1956): 279-80, and his letter to the editor, *SQ* 9 (1958), answering Edward Hubler's article, "The Damnation of Othello: Some Limitations of the Christian View of the Play," same issue, pp. 295-300. See also S. L. Bethel, "Shakespeare's Imagery: The Diabolic Images in *Othello*," *Shakespeare Survey* 5 (1952): 62-80.

16. Kaula sees her wedding sheets as "the symbol of her chastity and the original condition of her marriage," a counter-magic against the fatal handkerchief. "Othello Possessed," p. 131, n 44.

17. An analogous situation occurs in *Middlemarch,* where Dorothea's efforts to assist Causabon in his "great work" exacerbate his sense of failure, increasing his efforts at self-protection and thus, in turn, pressing Dorothea to further efforts.

18. John Calvin, *Institutes of the Christian Religion*, ed. John T. McNeill, trans. F. L. Battles (Philadelphia, Pa., 1960), 2:20-21.

19. To borrow G. W. Knights's phrase from *The Wheel of Fire.*

20. Eliot, "Shakespeare and the Stoicism of Seneca," p. 8. Eliot's statement has a certain validity if we accept Othello's enjoyment of his own oratory. It is difficult to believe, however, that "cheering himself up" is his primary motive. He is, in a sense, giving the speech that silence cuts from Hamlet's throat.

4

King Lear

Rich gifts wax poor when givers prove unkind.
                                        —*Hamlet,* III.i.101.

In nature there's no blemish but the mind,
None can be call'd deform'd but the unkind.
                                        —*Twelfth Night,* III.iv.402-2.

King Lear is a comedy swallowed up in tragedy. The mistake the man makes, the error of the king's body natural, leads to spiritual atonement, to reconciliation with nature, and to recognition of the supernature, which Lear realizes within himself as he experiences its residence within Cordelia. The error of the king as body politic, however, destroys what the man has achieved, forcing his transcendent insights toward deepest pain, obstructing their possible flow into his kingdom. No "new society," redeemed by the expulsion of sin and error, emerges from the experience of Lear the man. Lear the king has insured that the ending of his personal history and that of his kingdom will be "cheerless, dark, and deadly" (V.iii.290).

The play is a history of the world. Elton demonstrates the king's (and the play's) development from "pagan belief to disbelief," from a syncretic beginning, in which many pagan and some Christian elements inhere, to a "fifth act [which]

237

shatters . . . the foundations of faith itself."[1] Elton is right;
King Lear is a dynamic play, hardly the static doctrine its
"Christian," or "pagan," or "existentialist" critics would make
it. But part of its dynamic, which Elton explains away uncon-
vincingly, is Lear's journey toward the insight represented by
Cordelia. It is not so much that *King Lear* is "a Christian
play about a pagan world," as J. C. Maxwell suggests;[2] that is
to render it static, however inherently ironic would be the
structure Maxwell imputes to the play. Muir is more accurate
to suggest that "Shakespeare remains in the background; but
he shows us his pagan characters groping their way towards a
recognition of the values traditional in his society."[3] Lear, at
least, makes such a pilgrimage. Elton would deny that "traditional" (i.e., "Christian") values are embodied in the play and
suggests that any evidence of Christianity in *King Lear*
results from "the multiple vision of the Elizabethan age . . . its
illogical syncretism, and . . . its mingling of disparate and divided worlds."[4] Lear's awakening to Cordelia, however, is as
deeply (if not explicitly) "Christian" as any scene in Shakespeare. It is not the play's last scene, of course. The play
moves on, as it must, granted the momentum of Lear's political error, into the pervasive darkness of the ending, into a
world wholly inhospitable to man's brighter visions and, indeed, to man himself (V.iii.289-90). But this movement
makes *King Lear* the world's history—from its pagan beginnings, in which whatever gods there be are called by pre-
Christian names (although they seem not to notice men
crawling between earth and sky), to a Christian moment of
repentance and forgiveness, and on into a world where invo-
cations of deity reverberate against an emphatically empty
sky, where all possibilities for man in this world are "dead as
earth" (V.iii.261), and where the Last Judgment delivers only
a negative sentence.

The play's comic curve shows Lear the man making an
error in judgment—an avoidable error, since his instincts fa-
vored Cordelia—in rejecting her. He sinks beneath the burden of an error compounded by his preferment of Goneril
and Regan into madness, a psychic death, a descent into an
underworld inhabited by the obscene images that his sud-

denly thwarted will releases into his mind. He rises to the
sight of Cordelia, born again into a new life that is the antithesis of the old. Lear may have rejected the insight represented by Cordelia and awaiting recognition within Lear in
the first scene, but until the reconciliation scene the world
has been neither Christian nor totally pagan. It has mingled
pagan usages and Christian suggestions not merely in a
syncretic medley, but has balanced the competing elements
precariously in suspension within a context that Lear must
finally define. Recognition comes, but too late to sustain a
state "gor'd" by the savagery Lear himself has released. Insofar as the "outer mystery" exists in the play, it emerges
from within Lear, as at last he recognizes *Cordelia* as his
"child" (IV.vii.70), someone not controlled by the bestial appetite and animal lust that Lear, in his downward movement
toward madness, has considered to be the operative principle
in the world. Lear embraces, however briefly, the *real* meaning, the spiritual innerness of the "kindness" and "nature"
explored in so many variations by Lear and the other characters of the play. But the tragic movement, Lear's error in dividing his kingdom, empowering Goneril, Regan, and Cornwall, granting an Edmund opportunity to "make it" within
the shattered realm, overrides comedy, destroys Cordelia,
and quite explicitly denies her any "resurrection." She does
not "come back to life" like Hero or Hermione, is denied
even the final forgiving words of a Desdemona. Cordelia has
forgiven already, of course, but her silence in death breaks
Lear's heart, and no new dispensation issues outward once
the queen who has been compassionate and the king who
has learned compassion are dead.

  King Lear is a cosmic tragedy not because it reverberates,
like *Macbeth,* against the furthest reaches of the universe,
nor, as in *Othello,* because a deceived man kills an embodiment of virtue, but because the earth is denied Lear's insight
into what he has learned. In this respect, *King Lear*
resembles *Hamlet,* since Hamlet also denies his world the efficacy of the healing and creative potentiality he expresses
but does not explore. In *King Lear,* "All blest secrets,/ All . . .
unpublish'd virtues of the earth" (IV.iv.15-16) lie finally

"dead as earth" (V.iii.261) beneath "the weight" of a "sad time" (V.iii.323) as bereft at the end of positive possibility as were Richard's England, Claudius's Denmark, and Macbeth's Scotland at their darkest. Lear discovers the "blest secret," but it is snuffed out, becoming only a lost elevation against which his great final pain may be graphed. As in *Hamlet,* the potential comedy—the possible emergence into a violent and dishonest world of a new society based on fusion with positive supernature—is the dimension against which the tragedy must be measured.

It is difficult to determine "the order of the world" at the beginning of *King Lear.* We infer order primarily by its violation and by the gradual results of the opening scene, the first three acts being a kind of denouement for initial error. We infer that the well-ordered political entity is like a well-governed family, with a controlling father in charge. We do not enter the explicitly "fallen world" of *Hamlet* and *Macbeth,* the world mentioned at the beginning of so many of the Homilies—the world to be transcended by the individual who can faithfully receive the Eucharist or to be further alienated by the Hamlet, Claudius, or Macbeth who cannot embrace the principles he expresses. In *King Lear,* "The mysteries of Hecate and the night," (I.i.112), "Apollo" (I.i.161), and "high-judging Jove" (II.iv.231) balance against suggestions of a Christian world, where Edgar is Lear's "god-son" (II.ii.93), where Kent "eat[s] no fish" (I.iv.18), where the sun suggests the Christlike principle attributed to it in the Anglo-Saxon Phoenix and Chaucer's Prologue—is a "sacred radiance" (I.i.111); in the Homily on the Nativity, unfallen man is compared to "the Sunne in brightness and light [which] exceedeth every small and little star in the firmament"—and where the rejected Cordelia is endowed by France with the positive attributes of the New Testament paradox:

> Fairest Cordelia, that art most rich being poor,
> Most choice forsaken, and most lov'd despis'd.
>
> (I.i.253-54)

Like *Everyman* and *Dr. Faustus,* the opening of *King Lear* echoes with pagan usages. But in the case of the former plays, paganism is misapplied within a Christian world to which Everyman wakes up in time and Faustus too late. No Christian universe surrounds the action of *King Lear.* Yet the experience of Lear evolves toward the Christian insight latent in his strangely undefined kingdom, awaiting recognition that only experience can bring. Lear has never had any experience other than that attendant on the flexing of his omnipotent will. He discovers that he is *not* "everything," as he has been told, is not "ague-proof" (IV.vi.107), nor proof against the deeper pain that cuts him to the very brains (IV.vi.197). But the pain, the gradual removal from Lear of the "additions" of kingship and will, is precisely the stripping away of the negative qualities that lie between the "inward man" and his full achievement of the sacraments. Before such a moment can come, however, he must defy his own instinct—his instinct for Cordelia—as the Mariner must shoot the albatross. But if that were all Lear had done, his play would be a comedy—grace, as Delora Cunningham suggests in her useful distinction between comedy and tragedy, would have been applied in time.[5]

Time at the outset—and throughout the play—seems deliberately vague, compared to the great majority of Shakespeare's plays, which can be "placed" in time or within a coherently drawn historical period. In *King Lear,* we seem to hear voices emerging from the deeps of an unfathomed prehistory, from what Maynard Mack calls a world "bare, stark, faintly pagan." Yet we also sense the Jacobean world, "whose typical figures," Mack continues, "are the mighty King, the household Fool, the Machiavel or 'new man' Edmund, the supple Oswald, the Bedlam beggar. And with this we must establish a keen sense of sumptuousness and opulence just the reverse of what is bare, stark, and primitive."[6] Assuming that Shakespeare wrote the Fool's lines on Merlin, whose "prophecy" will be made at some later time in history, it would seem that Shakespeare intentionally confuses time and is more concerned with what can be shaped out of a world whose frame of natural rhythms—the controlling reflections of supernature—is tenuous, a world whose definition will reside in human decision rather than within a precisely defined Christian *or* pagan dispensation. Like *A*

Midsummer-Night's Dream, King Lear has the "detached" quality of fantasy, however savage and dark compared to the spangled brightness of the comedy. *King Lear* partakes of the "dream-like" attributes William H. Chaplin ascribes to it.[7] As it enters our senses, it *feels* like dream, projecting an irrational world at us, combining elements that in "reality" would not be linked, but that in dream are often bewilderingly fused, creating a world of partial recognitions, involuntary movement, suspended volition, of experiences indigenous to the world of dream. The great exception to the "bad dream" is the reconciliation scene, although it begins, for Lear at least, in nightmare.

As our hold on time and, indeed, on reality is uncertain at the outset, our moral bearings must be ambiguous. King Lear has been the ordering agent, but plans to divide his kingdom, ignoring in that action his inclination toward Albany, an intuition time will justify. The slow and finally futile development of Albany suggests the process Lear imposes on his once united kingdom; virtue is driven into hiding and emerges only to face the more powerful force Lear has willfully, if unwittingly, released. In giving power to Cornwall, Lear encourages an aspect of his own worser self, unredeemed by any of the quality suggested in Lear's inclination toward Albany and Cordelia:

> You know the fiery quality of the Duke;
> How unremovable and fix'd he is
> In his own course.
>
> (II.iv.93-95)

The opening scene generates unseen vectors whose meaning, as Albany later says, can be ascertained only in "th' event"' (I.iv.370). Although most commentators describe Lear's disinheritance of Cordelia as his primary blunder at the outset, the division of his kingdom is of equal importance, a "political" decision preceding his "moral" decision.[8] Lear's surrender of power is, by extension, the abdication of God, the removal of the ruling principle from a world that requires it, the principle that gives all relationships within the kingdom their own relevance, as Cordelia attempts to suggest to Lear

(I.i.97-106). Lear's surrender is particularly crucial since he has so obviously been so powerful. While we sense that Gloucester and Kent have been his loyal subordinates, we find little evidence in Lear's Britain of a defined hierarchy, a developed *system* of authority, the structured government that even Claudius's Denmark displays. Even had there been such a government in Britain, Lear's decision to dismember the kingdom destroys whatever may have been its previous political structure. But Lear's is the basic removal, and as with the political entity, so with the family: "The father," as La Primadauye says in *The French Academy,* "is the true image of the great and soveraign God, the universal father of all things." And the moral decision has immediate political consequences—the kingdom is redivided and, significantly for the later action, Cordelia marries France, not Burgundy.

Having released in its beneficiaries a lust for power, the political decision ramifies beyond politics, toward the blinding of Gloucester and the hanging of Cordelia. But the two strains can be distinguished at the outset. As Derek Traversi says, "Lear is at once father and King, head of a family and ruler of a state, and his tragedy is developed throughout in relation to both these aspects of his person."[9] The consequences of Lear's actions in the opening scene *seem* political, as if the play must explore a superficial aspect of his decisions before it can probe the human issues lying deeper than politics. One reason why *King Lear* is a tragedy and not the tragi-comedy of Nahum Tate is that the initial political mistake continues to develop, even after Lear discovers what he half-knew in scene one—who Cordelia is. He engenders a jungle of calculation, lust, and ambition not to be propitiated by his own imitation of the Christian experience.

In his anger at Cordelia's "rebuff," Lear unwittingly defines what he is doing to his kingdom:

> The barbarous Scythian,
> Or he that makes his generations messes
> To gorge his appetite shall to my bosom
> Be as well neighbour'd, piti'd, and reliev'd
> As thou my sometime daughter.

(I.i.118-22)

Lear has already encouraged a version of reciprocal cannibalism, gorging the appetite of his will with the words of
his daughters and rewarding them with huge chunks of himself as body politic. Immediately, his metaphor fulfills itself,
as he tells Albany and Cornwall to "digest" (I.i.130)* the third
denied Cordelia for being unable to "heave/ [her] heart into
[her] mouth" (I.i.93-94), unwilling to subordinate truth to
appetite, heart to mouth. Lear's staging of the scene, as
Cordelia's refusal implies, with its willful gorging on flattery
and the rewards of flattery, refutes true ritual, where
"spiritual fode" is consumed in the "heart by faith, with
thankesgeuynge."

Lear discovers that the words of Goneril and Regan evaporate as they are spoken. What becomes real is what he has
given away, digested between his daughters:

> Fool. Nuncle, give me an egg, and I'll give thee two crowns.
> Lear. What two crowns shall they be?
> Fool. Why, after I have cut the egg i' th' middle and eat up the meat,
> the two crowns of the egg. When thou clovest thy crown i' th'
> middle and gav'st away both parts, thou bor'st thine ass on thy
> back o'er the dirt.(I.iv.170-77)

> thou hast pared thy wit o' both sides, and left nothing i' th' mid-
> dle. (I.iv.204-5).

> "He that keeps nor crust nor crumb,
> Weary of all, shall want some."
>
> (I.iv.217-18)

Lear has denied himself "creatures of breade," visible signs
of invisible grace, by promoting the cannibalism of his
daughters. But it was he who insisted upon becoming a
wrathful "dragon" (I.i.124), a beast to be slain only by a
Beowulf, St. George, or Red Cross Knight, by a *defender* of
the realm, a beast associated with Satan in Revelation:

> the great dragon, that olde serpent, called the devil and Satan
> (12:9)

*Although the first scene seems to invest power in the two dukes. Lear has given
the land to Goneril and Regan, thus encouraging a rivalry between husband and
wife that culminates in the dissension between Goneril and Albany, and in the debate over Edmund after the battle of Act V.

the dragon, that olde serpent, which is the devil and Satan (20:2)

The "great rage in him" will be "kill'd" (IV.vii.78-79), but not before the dragon-king has divested himself of his own nourishing qualities, has become "a sheal'd peascod" (I.iv.219) and has transmitted only venom to his offspring. Goneril, predictably, becomes a cannibal:

"The hedge-sparrow fed the cuckoo so long,
That it had it head bit off by it young."

(I.iv.235-36)

A predatory "sea-monster" (I.iv.282), a "kite" (I.iv.284), a "wolf" (I.iv.330), a "fox" (I.v.340), a "boar" (III.vii.58), a "tiger" (IV.iii.40), her ingratitude "sharper than a serpent's tooth" (IV.iv.310), she becomes the dragon's daughter, in Albany's metaphor an unkind feeder on its own kind:

Humanity must perforce prey on itself
Like monsters of the deep.

(IV.iii.49-50)

Goneril eats Lear's heart, in a dim analogy to Prometheus,[10] who also gave to man, but was punished by the gods not the beneficiaries: "She hath tied/ Sharp tooth'd unkindness, like a vulture, here" (II.iv.137-38). She has "struck [Lear] with her tongue,/ Most serpent-like, upon the very heart" (II.iv.162-63).

The Fool, however, suggests that it is Lear who has killed his heart by placing it in a context that must destroy it:

Lear.   O me, my heart, my rising heart! But, down!
Fool.   Cry to it, nuncle, as the cockney did to the eels when she put
        'em i' th' paste alive; she knapp'd 'em o' th' coxcombs with a
        stick, and cried, "Down, wantons, down!" (II.iv.122-27)

The Fool has previously offered his "coxcomb" to Lear (I.iv.108), and here predicts not merely the struggle between Lear's mind and his rising heart, but also his approaching obsession with concupiscence and obscene appetite. If Lear's heart is rising, the Fool suggests, it is an ironic counter-movement to his descent from the throne. The eel metaphor suggests the emergence of Lear's body natural, whose promptings he suppressed in equating Albany and Cornwall and in banishing Kent and Cordelia. Lear admits that *he* has created these cannibals: "'Twas this flesh begot/ Those pelican daughters" (III.iv.76-77)—young pelicans supposedly fed on their mother's blood. Lear, in fact, predicts a savage response in Regan when she learns of Goneril's defection:

> When she shall hear this of thee, with her nails
> She'll flay thy wolfish visage.

> (I.iv.329-30)

This imputation, however, is the wish of Lear's will, the will that has set a family against itself in bestial competition by feeding other wills, by making wills independent of the ordering principle asserted by the father. Within the "feeding" metaphor, Goneril expresses a truth when she suggests that Lear "must needs taste his folly" (II.iv.294). The internecine family strife he has encouraged reaches back in the family history to an anti-sacramental threat against Lear's dead wife, the only mention of his queen in the play:

> Regan . . . If thou shouldst not be glad,
> I would divorce me from thy mother's tomb,
> Sepulchring an adulteress.

> (II.iv.131-34)

The lines accuse Lear's queen of having borne Goneril by some other man—he, not Lear, must be the sire of such monstrosity. But Lear's terrible curses are curses against himself—*he* is the cause in nature that has made these hard hearts, both as father and by denying his *role* as father:

> Hear, Nature! hear, dear goddess, hear!
> Suspend thy purpose, if thou didst intend
> To make this creature fruitful!
> Into her womb convey sterility!
> Dry up in her the organs of increase,
> And from her derogate body never spring
> A babe to honour her!

> (I.iv.297-303)

> Blasts and fogs upon thee!
> Th' untented woundings of a father's curse
> Pierce every sense about thee!
>
> (I.iv.321-23)

> You nimble lightnings, dart your blinding flames
> Into her scornful eyes! Infect her beauty,
> You fen suck'd fogs, drawn by the powerful sun,
> To fall and blast her pride!
>
> (II.iv.167-70)

> But yet thou art my flesh, my blood, my daughter;
> Or rather a disease that's in my flesh,
> Which I must needs call mine; thou art a boil,
> A plague-sore, an embossed carbuncle,
> In my corrupted blood.
>
> (II.iv.224-28)

The curses progress from the summoning of an ironically addressed "dear goddess," to a "father's curse," invoking the fouler and more destructive elements of nature and the local landscape, to an awareness that the disease is *within* him as well as in his daughters. The potentiality within Lear for such curses confirms his ability to produce a Goneril and a Regan. Again, he admits as much in his image of *self*-cannibalism:

> Is it not as this mouth should tear this hand
> For lifting food to 't?
>
> (III.iv.15-16)

His own disordered nature is most at issue, as his attribution of corruption to *his* blood attests. And if the pelican daughters *are* feeding on this blood, as they are in each digesting half of Lear's body politic, they must become increasingly corrupt.

Lear's will, now thwarted, has been elevated in Goneril and Regan, who will die by preying on themselves in lustful competition for Edmund, who himself preys on his brother and leaves his father defenseless before the "boarish fangs" that would rend the "anointed flesh" of Lear (III.vii.58). Gloucester, like Lear's kingdom, is left defenseless, "tied to th' stake" (III.vii.54) and baited by the dogs Lear has released. Yet Gloucester, too, is victimized by a self-engendered disgust with his own creation:

Our flesh and blood, my lord, is grown so vile
That it doth hate what gets it.

(III.iv.150-51)

Lear has set mere appetite loose on Britain, the rich seemingly eating sumptuously, but participating in a gorging that will expand beyond control and bring death instead of fulfillment; the "unfed sides" (III.iv.30) of the poor sustained by the foul food Edgar describes:

Poor Tom, that eats the swimming frog, the toad, the tadpole, the wall-newt, and the water; that in the fury of his heart, when the foul fiend rages, eats cow-dung for salads; swallows the old rat and the ditch-dog; drinks the green mantle of the standing pool. (III.iv.134-39)

This diet, reminiscent of the unhallowed witches' brew in *Macbeth*, predicts the poisoned appetite of Goneril and Regan. "Filths," as Albany says, "savour but themselves" (IV.iii.39). "Weeds," as Cordelia says, "grow/ In our sustaining corn" (IV.iv.6), but the corn is threatened by more than weeds, and Lear, the neglectful shepherd, can do nothing to stem the incursion:

"Sleepest or wakest thou, jolly shepherd?
    Thy sheep be in the corn;
And for one blast of thy minikin mouth,
    Thy sheep shall take no harm."

(III.vi.43-46)

Lear cannot recall the hungry "sheep" who grow to ravenous beasts of prey, nor can he arrest the despoilment of the realm he has given away. A commentary on Lear's defection from responsibility is that of "The Sermon for Whitsunday": "Now to discern who are truely his, and who not, we have this rule given us, that his sheepe doe alwayes heare his voice." Lear, the potential good shepherd of his kingdom, is now powerless, having let his sheep lose to eat Britain's corn, and to grow monsterlike to eat each other.

The opening scene reveals the bastardy of Edmund, introduced with self-serving amusement by Gloucester, once precisely the "wanton boy" he will accuse the gods of being (IV.i.38). The emphasis is on the violation of order, the yield-

ing to the base instinct of the will and flesh, the combination
that becomes appetite. Edmund is another of the long line of
alienated or disinherited Jacobeans (Hamlet, Lodovico,
Bosala, Altofronto, Vendice, Wendoll, Bussy D'Ambois, De
Flores, *et al.*). The play opens on the further edge of order,
about to step out from under the controlling frame that
Lear, however willfully, held together and into what the un-
folding drama will reveal. And we know that Edmund, introduced in the context of the breaking of kingdoms, will devolve toward the ambition that operates most effectively
within an unsettled political context. Conceived outside of
orderly sanctions, Edmund encourages the tiny chaotic center
of his origin outward to push away whatever order there had
been, until the moment of his conception becomes another
metaphor for the world of the play. His rejection of his
father's superstition is unexceptional (I.ii.128-45), but he replaces egocentric astrology with neither sound pagan nor
sound Christian doctrine.

Edmund shows all the manipulative mastery of Iago. He
engineers a parody of the opening scene for Gloucester,
reiterating the words and themes of the scene for a mind already unsettled by it, therefore susceptible to the insinuation
of the scene into his personal world. Edmund hides his letter
with Cordelia's phrase: "Nothing, my lord" (I.ii.31), forcing
curious Gloucester into the vacuum of Edmund's reticence
and drawing him further into condemnation of the child who
loves him most. "But goes thy heart with this?" Lear asked
Cordelia (I.i.107). Gloucester asks, "Had he . . . a heart or
brain to breed it in?" (I.ii.60-61). Like Othello, Gloucester
betrays an eagerness to be betrayed: "Let's see, let's see"
(I.ii.45). When Edmund counsels caution—the Iago incite-
ment to deeper suspicion—Gloucester asks Othello's question: "Think you so?" (I.ii.96) and rushes toward Othello's
answer: "He cannot be such a monster" (I.ii.102). As Othello
will be "satisfied" with "ocular proof," so Edmund arranges
"auricular assurance" for Gloucester's "satisfaction" (I.ii.99).

While Edmund displays the rationalist's contempt for
superstition, he admirably translates Gloucester's thesis into
an ominous prelude to his "warning" to Edgar, like Iago
shifting premises to meet occasion, making what Edmund has

learned from Gloucester his overture to his brother, as he
had used the opening scene to ensnare his father:

> I promise you, the effects he writes of succeed unhappily; as
> of unnaturalness between the child and the parent; death,
> dearth, dissolutions of ancient amities; divisions in state, menaces
> and maledictions against king and nobles; needless diffidences,
> banishment of friends, dissipation of cohorts, nuptial breaches,
> and I know not what. (I.ii.156-63)

Edgar can smile at the "sectary astronomical" (I.ii.164), but
Edmund's predictions of "unnaturalness," combined with
further obvious echoes of the content of scene one, create
the context within which he can introduce the "heat of
[Gloucester's] displeasure" (II.ii.176) against Edgar. Edmund,
like Iago with Cassio, promises his aid: "I'll serve you in this
business" (I.ii.194). Thus Edmund gains control of both
halves of his dynamic scheme, "a credulous father and a
brother noble" (I.ii.195). Othello and Edgar share the quality
by which manipulators thrive:

> The Moor is of a free and open nature,
> That thinks men honest that but seem to be so.
>
> (I.iii.405-6)

> a brother noble,
> Whose nature is so far from doing harms
> That he suspects none.
>
> (I.ii.195-97)

And it is, of course, one of the qualities of Hamlet that
Claudius uses against him:

> He, being remiss,
> Most generous and free from all contriving,
> Will not peruse the foils.
>
> (IV.vii.135-37)

The net Edmund "weaves" (II.i.17), like that of Iago, is con-
structed not only of the virtue of his victim, but of the several roles Edmund skillfully interthreads simultaneously
—friend to his brother, loyal son to Gloucester, and follower
of his own will:

I hear my father coming. Pardon me,
In cunning I must draw my sword upon you.
Draw; seem to defend yourself; now quit you well.
Yield! Come before my father. Light, ho, here!—
Fly, brother.—Torches, torches!—So, farewell.
Some blood drawn on me would beget opinion
Of my more fierce endeavour. I have seen drunkards
Do more than this in sport.—Father, father!—
Stop, stop!—No help?

(II.i.30-38)

And Edmund, like Iago, is elevated: "Loyal and natural boy,
I'll work the means/ To make thee capable" (II.i.86-87). As
Iago transforms Othello to monstrosity, Gloucester becomes,
metaphorically, what Edmund would make him, a sinful man
treading a chaos, carrying an emblem of Edmund's nativity:

Now a fire in a wild field were like an old lecher's heart; a small
spark, all the rest on 's body cold. Look, here comes a walking
fire. (III.iv.116-19)

The differences between Iago and Edmund—for all of
their similar skills in manipulating the credulous and
unsuspecting—are basic, however. Iago is the god created in
the image of his own will. He exists solely for the gratification of that will within which he would encompass the world,
as, for a time, he does, with no goal other than his sadistic
delight in device and destruction. Edmund sees himself as
unsanctified energy:

Why brand they us
With base? with baseness? bastardy? base, base?
Who in the lusty stealth of nature, take
More composition and fierce quality
Than doth, within a dull, stale, tired bed,
Go to the creating a whole tribe of fops,
Got 'tween asleep and wake?

(I.ii.9-15)

He was created in the full excited heat of a dark rendezvous,
not drowsily conceived in half-slumber. The illicit energy
poured into his conception partakes of a "nature" unalloyed
by anything except the "rough and lecherous" (I.ii.143) instant that transmitted those qualities from Gloucester to the

womb of Edmund's mother, and it has nothing to do with
other sanctions: "Fut, I should have been that I am, had the
maidenliest star in the firmament twinkled on my bastardizing" (I.ii.143-45). I am that I am, he claims. His nature is the
"lusty stealth" of his bastardizing, which evolves into the lusty
stealth of Edmund himself. As Iago would reduce the world
to the deformed confines of his will, Edmund would translate
the world into his concept of nature, free of any controls. As-
tronomy is an easy target, but religion, we suspect, could also
be dismissed by Edmund as mere superstition or rationalization, a laughable "divine thrusting on" (I.ii.136-37). Edmund
would make the world the world of his "making," a world of
fierce stealth, lusty practive, secret energy, and energetic sec-
recy, within which he will rise, at the expense of the "natural
order" against which his "nature" is pitted:

> Well, my legitimate, if this letter speed
> And my invention thrive, Edmund the base
> Shall top th' legitimate. I grow; I prosper.
> Now, gods, stand up for bastards!
>
> (I.ii.19-22)

One basic difference between Edmund and Iago is that the
former subscribes to a version of "Social Darwinism," with
Nature as presiding deity. Edmund's motivation is clear
—advancement within the "new order" Lear engenders. Edmund, unlike Iago, has a goal within the world, not merely
within his will, and when the wheel to which he binds himself
turns downward, he accepts the revolution cheerfully
enough (V.iii.174).

But Edmund's instincts could be controlled, however uncontrolled were his auspices. He will go abroad again to try
his fortunes (I.i.33-34) as a soldier—even bastards can serve
in the well-ordered state. But he stays to try his luck upon
Lear's dismembered state. Lear not only releases such forces
from the strict categories of control within which they can
serve, but encourages and empowers them. Were it not for
the opening Lear provides, Edmund's attack on legitimacy
would hardly be a threat. As it is, Edmund brilliantly employs Lear's thesis by ascribing it to Edgar: "I have heard him

oft maintain it to be fit that, sons at perfect age, and fathers declin'd, the father should be as ward to the son, and the son manage his revenue" (I.ii.76-79). Lear's opening speech becomes Edmund's opening wedge. Lear's ideas reflect from "Edgar's letter" with their willful reality; Edgar promises Edmund that "If our Father would sleep till I wak'd him, you should enjoy half his revenue for ever" (I.ii.54-56). The scheme is "Unnatural" (I.ii.81) and "monstrous" (I.ii.102), of course, to Gloucester, who guesses that Lear's division of his kingdom, and his alienation from the play's other king, France, is part of a deeper complex of ominous beginnings:

> Kent banish'd thus! and France in choler parted!
> And the King gone tonight! subscrib'd his power!
> Confin'd to exhibition! All this done
> Upon the gad!
>
> (I.ii.23-26).

But he does *not* see that these unsettling doubts have made him susceptible to Edmund's machinations. And however unscrupulous Edmund is, Lear has given him the rhetoric and rubric of Edmund's plan and has created for it its context of success by making the atmosphere murky with Lear's own impetuous misjudgments.

While some critics applaud Lear's division as a politic move designed "that future strife/ May be prevented now" (I.i.45-46),[11] that the natural succession may be clarified before his death, and while Lear does not, like Gorboduc, destroy the line of succession, his own words suggest that his action is primarily a matter of personal convenience:

> To shake all cares and business from our age,
> Conferring them on younger strengths, while we
> Unburden'd crawl toward death.
>
> (I.ii.40-42)

One of his "darker purpose[s]" (I.i.37), furthermore, would seem to be, as Roy W. Battenhouse suggests, to feed "his unacknowledged love of self-esteem."[12] While he gives up "power" (I.i.132) and "sway" (I.i.139) in return for a solicited flattery, he does not abdicate. He retains "The name and all th' addition to a king" (I.i.138). He would seem to desire what Battenhouse calls "a superworldly status . . . the freedom of a demigod, accountable to no one outside himself."[13]

Lear's map is a map of his mind, rigidly defined, clearly charted ("even from this line to this" [I.i.64]), evidence of the "mind-forged manacles" encumbering him, who even in his documented rashness (I.i.153, 299) always imposed the explicit directives of his "headier will" (II.iv.105)—as he does in the first scene. His is a physical kingdom reducible to a chart, unendowed by any invisible presences, pagan or Christian. His opening ritual is a parody of God's giving the earth to unfallen man. Lear gives it to those his inclinations favor *less* than her from whom he denies it; he allows his "frame of nature" to be "wrench'd" "from the fix'd place" (I.iv.290-91). The earth is Lear's, he claims, and the fullness therein. In *his* hands, he believes, "are all the corners of the earth." Lear's map and his disposition of it abrogate God's ownership of "the whole circuit of the world, and all the plenty that is in it." He has believed that he as body politic was "everything" (IV.vi.106), has "but slenderly known himself" (I.i.297), that is, has slender knowledge of the king's second body, an aspect of the king's person which even that unintrospective monarch, Henry V, has considered at length (*Henry V,* IV.i.247-301). Lear and his kingly robes have been as one as he acts with what Coleridge calls "the inveterate habits of sovereignty,"[14] habits that press him into the role of God, or Apollo. He can insist that others observe their "allegiance" to him (I.i.170), but he enunciates no concept of reciprocity from *him*. He ignores the reciprocal basis of relationships defined by Cordelia:

> You have begot me, bred me, lov'd me: I
> Return those duties back as are right fit.

> (I.i.98-99)

Cordelia defines true allegiance, not that demanded by Lear in his wrath from Kent.

Insight into what Lear is really doing in the opening scene is provided by comparing his actions to those attributed to a king by Thomas Dekker in this prayer from *Foure Birds of Noahs Arke:*

> Thou hast called mee (O Lord) being but a worme of the earth, and raised to riches, as it were, even out of dust, to be a Ruler over others: bestow on mee therefore the spirit of Wisedome, that I may first learne how to governe my selfe: for the perfect knowledge of a mans self, brings him (O God) to the true knowledge of thee. Humble mee (O my Maker) in this toppe of my height: that my head being lifted up to honor, my heart may not swell up with pride: give mee a mind not to execute my owne will but thine: give me an eye that may not lust after my owne profit, but the advancement of thy glorie, and the good of the Commonwealth. As thou hast placed mee, to bee a Pillar to uphold others, so grant that I may not proove a weake Pillar, to throw my selfe downe; and with my fall to bruise others that stand under me.

Admittedly, Lear is not bounded by the Christian universe of Dekker's prayer, but his actions impinge on *whatever* God or gods there be—unless Lear *is* the god of the play, in which case the opening represents the suicide of the ruling principle.

The question of an ex-king has been explored by Shakespeare in *Richard II,* and, as Bolingbroke discovered, there is no valid answer. The abdication of Richard, who placed his hand on one side of the crown and forced Bolingbroke's to the other, finds its ominous analogue in *King Lear:*

> The sway, revenue, execution of the rest,
> Beloved sons, be yours; which to confirm
> This coronet part between you.
>
> (I.i.139-41)

Rumors of civil war reach Lear's kingdom as quickly as they do Bolingbroke's. An invasion from France forestalls domestic war in Britain, but Bolingbroke's projected Crusade crumbles before rebellion, and it will be his son's invasion *of* France that brings peace, temporarily, to England. The history plays yield a precise analogue to Lear's decision. In *Henry IV,* Part I, the rebels, Hotspur, Worcester, Mortimer, and Glendower, confident before the fact, begin to "divide our right/ According to our threefold order ta'en"

(III.i.70-71). Mortimer describes the various sectors of the map in language anticipating Lear's division:

> All westward, Wales beyond the Severn shore,
> And all the fertile land within that bound,
> To Owen Glendower.

(III.i.76-78)

> Of all these bounds, even from this line to this,
> With shadowy forests and with champains rich'd,
> With plenteous rivers and wide-skirted meads,
> We make thee lady.

(I.i.64-67)

While Lear's geographical definition is predictably less precise, his echo of the rebels sundering the kingdom plays negatively against his own division. The ominous comment in *Henry IV* is augmented by Hotspur's peevish objection to the way the Trent cuts into his territory, a prediction that, *had* the "indentures tripartite" (III.i.80) become operative after Shrewsbury, England would have been subject to a new civil war. It would seem that Hotspur would not long have endured his neighbor, Glendower. *King Lear* implies the development of a similar antipathy between Albany and Cornwall.

Scene one shows Lear disregarding the basic premises of kingship. It is not just that he ignores his instinct toward Albany, and not just that he divides his kingdom. His actions emerge from a willful confusion between king as body politic and king as body natural. The theological aspect Kantorowitz ascribes to the concept of the king's two bodies applies profoundly in scene one, regardless of its "pagan" setting. The conflict within Lear is predicted by Gloucester, who has a son "by order of law" and "a knave [who] came something saucily to the world before he was sent for" (I.i.19-22). Yet Edmund "must be acknowledg'd" (I.i.24). Gloucester makes no distinction between legitimacy and license, between "law" and the "good sport" of Edmund's "making" (I.i.23). Nor does Lear distinguish between the prerogatives of a king in office and the cravings of the man beneath the robes. He covers the latter, illegitimately, in the plurality of the former:

> Know that we have divided
> In three our kingdom; and 'tis our fast intent
> To shake all cares and business from our age,
> Conferring them on younger strengths, while we
> Unburden'd crawl toward death.
>
> (I.i.38-42)

> now we will divest us both of rule,
> Interest of territory, cares of state.
>
> (I.i.50-51)

However intentionally ironic was Richard's dramatization of his deposition, he "undid himself" with an "I"—aware that the man was undecking the king's pompous body. Lear's plural *could* be valid until the moment at which he completes the ceremony, at which time "I" would be necessary, since he would have surrendered the elements of his plurality. Lear, however, has no intention of doing so—he has given up responsibility but wishes to "retain" prerogative—"the name, and all th' addition to a king" (I.i.138). His body natural may wish to crawl unburdened towards death, but "*we/* Unburden'd crawl" is oxymoronic. "We" must include the burdens of kingship or it is inapplicable. But Lear as body politic has apparently never been challenged; he has equated the king's two bodies into one willful totality ("They told me *I* was everything" [IV.vi.106]) so that his use of the royal plural even after it is no longer appropriate is consistent with the willful character described by Goneril and Regan and exhibited at the outset by Lear. His royal plurality is like the cartoon character who takes several steps into thin air before he looks down and discovers that he stands in contravention of the natural law of gravity, even as Lear does of the premises of kingship. His words to Gloucester in Cornwall's castle are a litany of the roles he has himself destroyed:

> The King would speak with Cornwall; the dear father
> Would with his daughter speak, commands her service.
>
> (II.iv.102-3)

But Lear has placed himself in a position where he must sue, not command, and his use of the word "King" is only his second since the opening scene, an index of its irrelevance within the two dukedoms he has carved from his map.

As Lear violates the law of the body politic, he reveals the body natural of a willful child. He has known himself only as king, "he hath ever but slenderly known" any other self (I.i.296-97). But as his royal plurality would maintain itself *ex post facto,* the body natural insists on the gratification for which Lear has invented the opening scene, body politic being used to color the needs of body natural. Cordelia's sudden "Nothing, my lord" (I.i.89), jars Lear loose from his façade. Suddenly he is not king but father, and an unnatural father at that, denying the very "bond" (I.i.95) Cordelia has just emphasized, the true reciprocity based on premises deeper than mere will, deeper than the self-interested reciprocity of the bartering ritual Lear has formulated. Lear rejects his own role in Cordelia's creation and, thus, presses himself further toward the willfulness inherited from him by Goneril and Regan, whose wills he has just empowered. His reaction, the natural man breaking through the royal pose, suggests not so much the offended father as the spoiled child suddenly rebuffed, perhaps even the jilted lover summoning up his most devastating rhetoric:

> Here I disclaim all my paternal care,
> Propinquity and property of blood
> And as a stranger to my heart and me
> Hold thee from this forever.
>
> (I.i.115-18)

Lear *claims* that he can deny "property of blood," with the desperation of a Coriolanus denying Volumnia, the certainty of an Othello declaring his content "absolute," or the ferocity of a Lady Macbeth praying to be unsexed. But the verbal assertion of independence does not make it so "in the nature of things"—if anything, it signals that it will *not* be so. Lear is *worse* than Gloucester here, denying creativity *per se,* rather than admitting it, no matter how unsanctified its origins. The rejection of Cordelia, of course, predicts those further emanations of his will, his curses of Goneril and Regan culminating in his raging demand for the destruction of the world

(II.i.1-9). Lear cannot both swear "by the power that made [him]" (I.i.210) *and* deny his relationship to Cordelia, but the contradiction underlines the one-sidedness of Lear's conception of his relationship to the world. Ultimately, in the storm, he suggests that if the world will not conform to his will, he will destroy it. He becomes the reverse of the bestowing god of scene one. He becomes a god who would revenge himself against the world—for his own folly.

Lear refutes his disclaimer of "parental care" almost immediately, when he admits that he wanted Cordelia to care for *him:*

> I lov'd her most, and thought to set my rest
> On her kind nursery. Hence, and avoid my sight!—
> So be my grave my peace, as here I give
> Her father's heart from her.
>
> (I.i.122-25)

His words echo the anti-marriage of Richard II and his queen, and, indeed, the first scene has been an anti-ritual, not a ceremony celebrating contact with deeper mysteries, but a set piece dictated by the needs of Lear the man for further furbishing his self-esteem. Lear seems to give away, but does so only to supply his own wants, like an insecure child buying friendship, or, as the Fool later suggests, like a father purchasing affection:

> "Fathers that wear rags
> Do make their children blind;
> But fathers that bear bags
> Shall see their children kind."
>
> (II.iv.48-51)

Lear promises his "largest bounty" to the daughter who can say she loves "us most" (I.i.52-53). Loving "us," of course, is equivalent to loving not Lear as man or father, but Lear as a king who will distribute his body politic. Yet Lear has not really set up a contest. He has erected a format into which words of affection can emerge. He has already determined who gets what—as Gloucester says (I.i.3-7) and as Lear makes clear in reserving "A third more opulent" (I.i.88) for Cordelia. The entire scene is predicated on precisely the falseness with which Lear has structured it, and it finds its truth in Lear's

admission that he looks upon all things as created to please
him:

> Better thou
> Hadst not been born than not t' have pleas'd me better.
>
> (I.i.236-37)

France is correct to call Cordelia Lear's "best object" (I.i.217).
While Lear claims to have loved her most, and while that
claim suggests a valid instinct, which Lear's experience will
nurture toward insight, the part he sets for Cordelia in the
opening scene suggests that she has been an object to Lear,
valuable only as it reflected pleasing facets to the kingly eye,
something like Browning's collector-duke's "next duchess":
"Though I repeat, his fair daughter's self, as I avowed at
starting, is my object."

Kent attempts to suggest to Lear that his "wrath" (I.i.124)
is the product of his "body natural": "What wouldst thou do,
old man?" (I.i.148). The king, he implies, is with the body,
but the body is not with the king. He further implores Lear
as king to "reserve thy state" (I.i.151), that is, retain your
power over your state (since Lear does reserve "state" in its
sense of formal observances) until your anger has cooled and
your folly is still capable of rectification. But Lear in his rage
tosses his kingdom away, defying "our nature and our place"
(I.i.176), that is, the premises of his kingship, and, as we
know but Lear cannot "See" (I.i.159), his individual nature in
overriding his preference for Cordelia. "Thou swear'st thy
gods in vain," says Kent (I.i.163), implying that Lear is in
conflict with the "order of things." However inactive the
gods may be in this world, Lear is employing them as ad-
juncts to his will—only one of the *hubristic* tendencies in his
ritual of self-gratification. Yet, typically, he accuses those who
would recall him to the personal limitations that are interfer-
ing with his discharge of his kingly duties (Kent), and to the
proper nature of all relationships, individual and political
(Cordelia), of pride: "Let pride, which she calls plainness,
marry her" (I.i.131), he says of his "sometime daughter"
(I.i.122) while branding his friend a victim of "strain'd pride"
(I.i.172). Lear's is the exaggerated pride, an appearance of

kingship serving the man beneath the robes, who when challenged grows more tyrannical, displaying natural pride, the *hubris* of the man, not a proper emanation of temperate kingship. Lear, not Cordelia, destroys the opening ritual, by prohibiting it from opening into the truth Cordelia represents but cannot utter within a restrictive format, clenched tighter by the further imposition of his will upon an already willful production. "Fare thee well, king!" Kent sneers, "Sith thus thou wilt appear,/ Freedom lives hence, and banishment is here" (I.i.183). The Fool repeats Kent's version of Lear's world: "Why, this fellow has banish'd two on's daughters, and did the third a blessing against his will" (I.i.114-15).

In banishing Cordelia, Lear reveals himself as a willful old man, or, in that concomitant of his early actions, a petulant child:

> Old fools are babes again and must be us'd
> With checks as flatteries, when they be abus'd.
>
> (I.iii.19-20)

Goneril is right—another example of that subtle technique whereby Shakespeare allows a character to speak a truth and at the same time to imply that the truth emerges from the character's own self-interest. By surrendering to flattery, as he did in scene one, Lear suffers checks. By behaving childishly, he becomes a child again—not a child in the New Testament sense, but a spoiled brat who does nothing and demands everything: "Let me not stay a jot for dinner; go get it ready," he commands in the Duke of Albany's palace (I.iv.8-9). But the movement *through* the willful child is a precondition for the rebirth that Lear, unlike Richard, Claudius, or Macbeth, *will* experience. That experience lies far beyond the first scene, however, from which Lear exits with a reversion to the royal plural, an implicit denial that it is the man who has acted to destroy both king *and* man:

> we
> Have no such daughter, nor shall ever see
> That face of hers again.—Therefore be gone
> Without our grace, our love, our benison.
>
> (I.i.265-67)

Another Lear, stripped of his plurality, his "lendings" (III.iv.114), his sanity itself, of the layers of will that separate him from the rejected truth of scene one, will see that face of hers again, for the first time.

Since Lear does not reserve his state, the split between the king *qua* king and Lear as old man-spoiled child, between the body politic that has been "everything" to Lear and the body natural he has neglected, will widen intolerably, with results Goneril predicts: "If our father carry authority with such disposition as he bears, this last surrender of his will but offend us" (I.i.309-10). As she later protests:

> I had thought, by making this well known unto you,
> To have found a safe redress; but now grow fearful,
> By what yourself, too, late have spoke and done,
> That you protect this course and put it on
> By your allowance; which if you should, the fault
> Would not scape censure, nor the redresses sleep,
> Which, in the tender of a wholesome weal,
> Might in their working do you that offence
> Which else were shame, that then necessity
> Will call discreet proceeding.
>
> (I.iv.224-33)

By this time, Lear's authority is gone—Goneril can wrap her protest within a threat of chastisement. As Lear's "body natural" recognizes what it has done, its insights are rendered impotent by what the "body politic" has also done. The problem is compounded, of course, by Goneril's assumption of the power Lear had explicitly delegated to Albany (I.i.132-34): "be then desir'd/ By her, that else will take the thing she begs,/ A little to disquantity your train" (I.iv.268-70), and later, in a disjunctive analogy to the command of Goneril, by the necessity of Cordelia's becoming commander in name, at least, of the army France has been forced to abandon before political necessity (IV.iii.3-7). But it takes no Peter Brook to tell us that one hundred knights riding to the whim of a rash old ex-king constitute a threat:

>   A hundred knights!
> 'Tis politic and safe to let him keep
> At point a hundred knights; yes, that on every dream,

Each buzz, each fancy, each complaint, dislike,
He may enguard his dotage with their powers,
And hold our lives in mercy.

(I.iv.345-50)

      both charge and danger
Speak 'gainst so great a number. . . . How, in one house,
Should many people, under two commands,
Hold amity? 'Tis hard; almost impossible.

(II.iv.242-45)

While the two sisters work from their wills outward, and thus
lead some critics to discredit their assessment of the threat
Lear poses, and although they have inflamed the very wrath
they claim to fear, they have a point. His presence becomes,
inevitably, a problem in the kingdom he has sundered. Lear
has already threatened Goneril:

   Thou shalt find
That I'll resume the shape thou dost think
I have cast off forever.

(I.iv.330-32)

He reiterates the theme on leaving Goneril: "To take 't again
perforce" (I.v.43). One meaning of these lines, as Dr. Johnson suggests, is that Lear is "meditating on his resumption of
royalty."[15] And, of course, the threat of Lear's reaccession is
compounded by rumors of civil war (II.i.7-15; III.i.19-29;
III.iii.8-21)—a war forestalled only by Cordelia's invasion
from France, motivated by Lear's "right" (IV.iv.28) in his
now "scattered kingdom" (III.i.31).

Lear's ambiguous resignation creates a world in which
proper relationships are warped and "the bond crack'd," as
Gloucester says (I.ii.118). Lear has, as the Fool reminds him,
"mad'st thy daughters thy mothers" (I.iv.188). Lear has become, to Oswald, "My lady's father" (I.iv.87). He must learn,
in reversal of the normal family hierarchy, to become "an
obedient father" (I.iv.256), to "put down [his] own breeches"
and accept the chastisement of "the rod" he has given his
daughters (I.iv.189-90). He had refused Cordelia his "benison" (I.i.268), but by removing himself from his proper role
as father, he has sinned more deeply, in the Fool's analysis of

his folly, against Goneril and Regan: "Why this fellow has banish'd two on's daughters, and did the third a blessing against his will" (I.iv.114-16). The Fool's indictment of Lear as father points clearly at his political folly. It is bad enough that he has divided his kingdom—that leads to almost immediate rumors of civil war (II.i.11-15)—but he has abdicated his authority as king. It is grimly appropriate that having retained "all th' addition to a king" (I.i.138), he is soon housed in a barren out-building, whose "comfort" Gloucester "will piece out . . . with what addition [he] can" (III.vi.2-3). Lear, himself, expresses what has happened in his mock kneeling:

> Do you but mark how this becomes the house:
> "Dear daughter, I confess that I am old;
> Age is unnecessary. On my knees I beg
> That you'll vouchsafe me raiment, bed, and food."
>
> (II.iv.155-58)

> Why the hot-blooded France, that dowerless took
> Our youngest born, I could as well be brought
> To knee his throne, and squire-like, pension beg
> To keep base life afoot.
>
> (II.iv.215-18)

Lear *will*, symbolically, "knee his throne," by kneeling to France's queen. His acts of will have encouraged the latency of other wills, with which his now clashes. He has created an impossible world, and no matter how responsible Goneril and Regan are for the spread of its evil, Lear's first decision allows potential malevolence to escape. As John Lawlor says, "the author of 'the time' is Lear himself. What 'the time' does to man is in reality what some men do to others; and of all men the King must bear responsibility for the time . . . it is no accident that men are as the time is. The world is as Lear made it: he opened the gate that let this folly in."[16] One could agree, perhaps, with Harold Wilson that "if we find Lear's culpability at the centre of the tragedy, we surely miss the full compass of the tragedy itself";[17] events grow out from the central follies and finally are greater in their monstrous insanity than Lear's early mistakes might have led us—and certainly Lear—to expect. But it is hard to agree with Alfred Harbage that the " 'immeasurable evil' is not traceable to measurable faults, or misunderstandings."[18] This thesis holds that Lear had no control at the outset over the malevolent potentialities within his kingdom. The preponderance of evidence suggests that he did control, but that his "misunderstanding" of the grounds of his own being—as king *and* man—led to "measurable faults," thence to admittedly "immeasurable evil." To deny this sequence is to deny Lear's stature as tragic hero. Lear's terrible curse of Goneril (I.iv.297-311) is a product of his earlier mistake. He set in motion the forces that have made Goneril "a thankless child" (I.iv.311), and when he curses her, he curses himself, cutting himself off from creativity just as he hopes the gods will deny Goneril, driving himself deeper into the posture of an old man whose will has been thwarted by a will he set up in power. The curse emerges, as St. Clare Byrne says, from "the bitter, vindictive anger of old age, so hurt that it would destroy its own parenthood by invoking sterility upon its child."[19] To locate the evil outside Lear—as he tries to do—is, as in his curse of Goneril, to ignore its source, or, at very least, to ignore the blunders of King Lear that have nurtured to maturity the very monstrosity he now curses. While the world of *King Lear* cannot be termed explicitly "fallen" as can the worlds of *Richard II* and *Hamlet,* Lear's decision encourages into his world precisely the qualities ascribed to the world "before Christes comming" in the Sermon of The Nativity: "all men universally in Adam, corrupt trees, stony ground, full of brambles and bryers, lost sheepe, prodigall sonnes, naughty unprofitable servantes, unrighteous stewardes, workers of iniquity, the broode of Adders, blinde guides, sitting in darknesse and in the shadow of death: to bee short nothing else but children of perdition, and inheritours of hell fire."

The split between prerogative and authority creates ripples of doubt throughout the kingdom—is man to be loyal to powerless virtue or to empowered evil? In a disjunctive analogue to the rejection of Lear by his daughters, Cornwall's servant, "A servant that he bred" (IV.iii.73), who has served the duke since the servant was a "child" (III.vii.73), rises up

and slays his master. Symbolically, a son kills a father, but in
this instance, unlike the example of Goneril, Regan, and
Edmund, the offspring stands up for the good against an evil
father (and thus reminds us of Cordelia and, particularly, of
Kent). The servant is stabbed in the back by Regan (a double
violation of order, in the treachery of the attack and the fact
that the sword is wielded by a woman) and his body thrown
"Upon the dunghill" (III.vii.97).[20] Virtue exists. A positive
ethic emerges as the play develops, in spite of or perhaps in
inevitable response to the evil shadow that spreads across the
former kingdom. But the servant saves neither Gloucester's
eyes nor himself. The other servants rush after blinded
Gloucester, but, typical of the "new society" emerging from
Lear's first decision, they are, however virtuous, mere servants. Kent, though a messenger of "the King" (II.ii.135), is
stocked, despite the "small respects" and "too bold malice"
the action shows "Against the grace and person" of Lear
(II.ii.137-38). Although the stocking of his messenger is,
symbolically, an attack upon the king, Regan knows that the
power lies elsewhere:

> My sister may receive it much worse
> To have her gentleman abus'd, assaulted,
> For following her affairs. Put in his legs.
>
> (II.ii.155-57)

Kent and Oswald—each a loyal servant of a very different
commander—represent the factions Lear has posed so uneas-
ily against each other. Gloucester can commiserate with Kent
in the stocks (II.ii.159-61) and with Lear as the storm approaches (II.iv.303-5), but must obey the commands of
Cornwall: "Come, my Lord, away" (II.ii.158:F.), "come out o'
th' storm" (II.iv.312). Gloucester's impotence, like that of
Kent in the stocks, symbolizes what Lear has done to potential virtue—disarmed it, or, at best, pitted it against a more
powerful adversary. The plight of Kent and Gloucester
foreshadows the final destruction of virtue. Kent in the
stocks is the precursor of Cordelia hanged. Still, however,
Regan is right:

O, sir, to wilful men,
The injuries that they themselves procure
Must be their schoolmasters.

(II.iv.305-7)

While her words emanate from a will that rationalizes her driving of Lear into the storm, and while Lear's will dictates the partial truth of his being "more sinned against than sinning" (III.iii.60), he is responsible for the political turmoil that now boils across Britain. At the same time, however, as Regan's aphorism suggests, his extreme willfulness is a prelude to his abandonment of will, his embrace of a more comprehensive and satisfactory set of values.

Lear rushes out of politics into the storm and out of his mind as well. Whatever the storm is *per se,* it is, like that in *Othello,* a separation between two worlds, in this case between the kingship Lear has surrendered and the humanity to which he will awaken. The storm is a series of metaphors applied to it by those observing it. Regan is right to call the elements "schoolmasters . . . to willful men" (II.iv.305-7). Kent, like the Old Man in *Macbeth* (II.iv.1-4), cannot recall its equal, and sees the storm, also rightly, as a death to man, as it will be for "the Old Man" in Lear:

the wrathful skies
Gallow the very wanderers of the dark,
And make them keep their caves. Since I was man,
Such sheets of fire, such bursts of horrid thunder,
Such groans of roaring wind and rain, I never
Remember to have heard. Man's nature cannot carry
Th' affliction nor the fear.

(III.ii.43-50)

"Thou were better in a grave," Lear says to Edgar, "than to answer with thy uncover'd body the extremity of the skies" (III.iv.105-7), and it is out of this tempestuous "grave" (IV.vii.45) that Lear will emerge.

The storm is, possibly, symbolic of the dissolution of the weal, of the chaos Lear has released in Britain; Kent and Gloucester point at its political connotations by calling it "the tyranny of the open night" (III.iv.2), and "this tyrannous

night" (III.iv.156). It also suggests the clash of wills within
the ruling group, Lear's nightmare of insanity, "the tempest
in [his] mind" (III.iv.12) stronger than storm, and, since it is
so powerfully personified, some malign deity:

> the impetuous blasts, with eyeless rage,
> Catch in their fury, and make nothing of.

> (III.i.8-9)

But the lines point back to the King Lear of scene one, as
much as to the storm. Lear may allegorize the storm into a
furious god ("Blow, winds, and crack your cheeks! . . . Rum-
ble thy bellyful!"[III.ii.1, 14]), but he also feels it as a cold
and driving *storm*. Whatever else it may be, it is *nature*—not
outraged supernature, as is the storm in *Macbeth*, nor elements wrapped within a benign purpose, as is Prospero's
tempest. The storm may be nature out of control, an echo in
the sky of the dark violence of Edmund's nativity, but it is
not a product of Lear, merely a vehicle for his fleeting
metaphors, as various interpretations of his experience flash
and thunder through his mind. It is doubtful that the storm
has anything to do with the gods, as Elton suggests it does:
"the gods are indifferent to weakness and oppression;
perhaps even further, such appeals [as Lear's in II.iv.191-94]
serve only to exasperate them and summon their cruelty."
Writing of his pagan world, Elton emphasizes the response of
the heavens: "And divine cruelty has no limits."[21] More to
the point than the malign "sport" (IV.i.39) imputed to the
gods is the storm's reflection of the impotence of *man's* will.
Lear's curses of his daughters, his plea to the gods to "send
down and take my part" (II.iv.191-194), his indictment
of the "servile ministers" who have joined "with two pernici-
ous daughters" (III.ii.21-22), are clearly products of his
thwarted will, which becomes more thwarted the more insisted upon, and of Lear's vehement resistance to knowledge.
Goneril, Regan, and Cornwall bask before the fires of
Gloucester's castle. Lear has put himself out into the storm,
into a nature that can be as violent, uncontrolled, and arbi-
trary as any king. For Lear's will, the storm is also an agent of
justice, specifically a "summoner," hailing sinful man to the
heaven's revenge:

> Close pent-up guilts,
> Rive your concealing continents, and cry
> These dreadful summoners grace.
>
> (III.ii.57-59)

The storm picks up fragments of Lear's mind, and is better seen as a reflector of his veering and wheeling imagination than as an emanation of some superhuman agency. The cause in nature, after all, that makes these hard hearts is, as Lear has yet to learn, the will that cancels the heart's impulse, as Lear's has done. Lear admits as much in brief instants of rational awareness, when he echoes France's words to Cordelia: "The art of our necessities is strange/ And can make vile things precious" (III.iii.70-71), and when he finds in his heart "one part . . . that's sorry" for his Fool (II.ii.72-75). These are stages in his movement toward Cordelia, who waits beyond the storm, beyond his madness. Against his imperious demand for dinner (I.iv.8-9) he places his insistence that the Fool enter the hovel "first" (III.iv.26). But his partial admissions and the dawning of charity within him alternate with wild schemes for revenge—and even his charity emanates from kingship:

> Take physic, pomp;
> Expose thyself to feel what wretches feel,
> That thou mayst shake the superflux to them,
> And show the heavens more just.
>
> (III.iv.33-36)

He claimed in scene one "To shake all cares and business from our age" (I.i.40), but has not yet, like Richard, shaken "off the regal thoughts/ Wherewith [he] reigned" (*Richard II*, IV.i.163-64); he has yet to coalesce his fleeting admissions into a sustained vision of his humanity. While Lear can hardly be called a patient sufferer, it is helpful to see his story, as Maynard Mack, Robert Ornstein, John Holloway, and Jan Kott do, as cast in the Joban pattern, which emphasizes man's finitude, rather than to define the storm as the interpenetration of any God or gods into man's insignificant world.

Elton is also right. *King Lear*'s beginnings, like those of *Everyman* and *Doctor Faustus*, convey undeniably pagan colora-

tions. Yet for all its Jupiters and Apollos, the gods are remarkably *in*active in *King Lear.* "Thou swearest thy Gods in
vain," says Kent to Lear (I.i.163), and the taunt could be applied to *any* reference to the gods in the play—whether they
are defined as gentle deities, personally guarding the well-
being of man, revenging agents, accomplices of human evil,
or flexings of a benevolent cosmos. They simply aren't there,
as they are in *Julius Caesar* in the storm before the murder,
which, however Cassius rationalizes it, coincides with
Calpurnia's foreboding, or as they are in *Cymbeline*, where
Jupiter appears personally and throws a thunderbolt, or as
they are in *Antony and Cleopatra,* where the God Hercules,
whom Antony loved, leaves the general amid the rumblings
of subterranean music. Further proof of the gods' absence is
provided by Edgar's contrivance with Gloucester on the fic-
titious cliffs of Dover, which proves to Gloucester "that the
clearest Gods, who make them honours/ Of men's impossibilities, have preserv'd thee" (IV.vi.73-74), but which we
know proves only that Edgar is a clever manipulator and that
Gloucester remains credulous and superstitious. Edgar
merely tricks Gloucester out of the pattern into which Edmund had similarly tricked him.[22]

Regardless of the references to the gods and regardless of
a politics gone mad, like Hitler's "Jewish policy" or America's
"Vietnamese intervention," the meanings of the early parts of
Lear develop on the human plane, involving, as Lawlor says,
"what some men do to others."[23] Never does the action rise
beyond humanity (except in Cordelia's countering of Lear's
ritual of appetite and in France's acceptance of Cordelia,
which will be discussed below), although certainly it sinks
below the human level toward an imitation of bestiality (and
it takes no "Elizabethan World Picture" to remind us of that
possibility). Edgar's "foul fiend" is a fictional and, typically
for Edgar, allegorical version of what men do to each other.
Lear's defection is a model for that of the world of the play,
a defection from "kindness." David Horowitz reminds us of
the multiple sixteenth-century meanings of kindness, a word
vitiated by that aspect of semantic change known as speciali-
zation:

"Kind" for the Elizabethans and for preceding periods referred first of all to nature. It means "native," "implanted by nature," "Innate," "naturally fitting," "belonging to this particular
natural kind or species," hence also "related by kinship," something held "by right of birth," "lawful," "rightful," "kindly."
...In its Elizabethan form therefore, the word "kind" possesses
both an ontological and an ethical dimension... *to be kind
(human) is to be kind:* to possess the generic human qualities of
love, compassion, generosity, gratefulness, gentleness, benevolence, etc. To be human is to be humane.[24]

As Stella Brook suggests "The noun *kynde* 'kind' can be used
in Middle English where we would now use 'nature,' and
there is good reason to suggest that the original sense survived into the Sixteenth and early Seventeenth Centuries."[25]
That it did is suggested twice by Hamlet: "A little more than
kin, and less than kind" (I.ii.65), "kindless villain!" (II.ii.609).
He does not say "unkindly villain"—that would be a tautology
then as now—but emphasizes that Claudius's unkindness has
exiled him from any natural relationship. *Lear* and Lear emphasize "kindness" constantly, in the sense of likeness and
naturalness: Lear exiles himself from his own best intuition:

I lov'd her most, and thought to set my rest
On her kind nursery.

(I.i.125-26)

One of Lear's knights, whose "duty," like Kent's, "cannot be
silent" (I.iv.70), reports the inevitable progress of Lear's decision:

There's a great abatement of kindness appears as well in the
general dependants as in the Duke himself also and your daughter. (I.iv.65-67)

Lear translates Regan's "kindness"—her feeling for
him—into unkindness, showing that while he understands
the latter, he has yet to learn the truth of the former:

I have another daughter,
Who, I am sure, is kind and comfortable.
When she shall hear this of thee, with her nails
She'll flay thy wolvish visage.

(I.iv.327-30)

The Fool, however, predicts Regan's similarity to Goneril:

> Shalt see thy other daughter will use thee
> kindly; for though she's as like this as a crab's
> like an apple, yet I can tell what I can tell.
>
> (I.v.14-16)

And Lear excuses himself with self-serving recollections of his initial "kindness":

> I will forget my nature. So kind a father!
>
> (I.v.35)

> O Regan, Goneril!
> Your old kind father, whose frank heart gave all,—
> O! that way madness lies; let me shun that;
> No more of that.
>
> (III.iv.19-22)

Yet he admits, indirectly and perversely, his own unkindness:

> Death, traitor! nothing could have subdu'd nature
> To such a lowness but his unkind daughters.
> Is it the fashion, that discarded fathers
> Should have thus little mercy on their flesh?
> Judicious punishment! 'Twas this flesh begot
> Those pelican daughters.
>
> (III.iv.72-77)

Not only would kindness have recognized Albany, Cordelia, and Kent, but Goneril, Regan, and Cornwall, each faction representing a potentiality *within* Lear, hence within his kingdom. Lear might have advanced the one, controlled the other, instead of doing the opposite. Lear's encouragement of "unkindness" is perhaps best expressed in Albany's scornful metaphor about Goneril:

> She that herself will sliver and disbranch
> From her material sap, perforce must wither
> And come to deadly use.
>
> (IV.ii.34-36)

By this time, of course, Goneril has developed into an independent strain of poisonous growth, but it was Lear who did the initial disbranching. While Goneril finds Albany's "text. . .foolish" (IV.ii.37), it echoes her own fate *and* Lear's mistake. The original text would have been familiar to the Jacobean:

> Abide in me, and I in you: as the branche cannot bear fruit of it selfe, except it abide in the vine, no more can ye except ye abide in me.

> If a man abide not in me, he is cast forth as a branche, and withereth: and men gather them and cast *them* into the fire, and they burne. (John 15:4, 6)

The Geneva gloss to these admonitions reads "We must be rooted in Iesus Christ by faith which commeth of the word of God." While Goneril's end, if it be fire (her self-destructive lust would seem to make flames superfluous), would be deserved, one must recall Lear's original dismembering. The tree metaphor captures intimately his unkindness because it relates not just to the branches of the tree but to its root and trunk—the King. The true role of king is captured by Duncan, who plants men and labors to make them full of growing. Another biblical reference linking Lear and Goneril is that in Mark II: 13-14, 20-21:

> And seeing a figge tre afarre of, that had leaves, he went *to se* if he might finde any thing there on: but when he came unto it, he founde nothing but leaves: for the time of figges was not yet.

> Then Iesus answered, and said to it, Never man eat fruite of thee hereafter while the worlde standeth: and his disciples heard it.

> And in the morning as they passed by, they sawe the figge tre dryed up from the rootes.

> Then Peter remembered, and said unto him, Master, beholde, the figge tree which thou cursed it, is withered.

The Geneva gloss tells us that "This was to declare howe much they displease God which have but an outward shew & appearance without fruit."[26] Lear's curse of Goneril parodies Christ's withering of the fig tree, suggesting the negative concomitant of Lear's godlike pose of largess in scene one:

> Hear, Nature! hear, dear goddess, hear!
> Suspend thy purpose, if thou didst intend
> To make this creature fruitful!
> Into her womb convey sterility!
> Dry up her organs of increase,
> And from her derogate body never spring
> A babe to honour her!
>
> (I.iv.297-303)

Lear's curse is superfluous *per se,* but profoundly ironic. Edmund's adjuration of his "goddess" "Nature" was at least a plea on behalf of his "natural" status, unratified by social or religious legitimacy. However willful and destructive the results of Edmund's binding himself to a nature defined as "dark and vicious" (V.iii.172), his vow is *not* a demand that nature destroy itself. Edmund, at least, celebrates his nativity, however unimmaculate it was. Lear enjoins nature against itself. His curse is an emanation of the death of his own self, which he is experiencing and resisting. Both, however, demonstrate what Miss Parker calls "the paradox of Christian doctrine, that nature without grace *is* unnatural."[27] Still, Lear showed in his preference for Albany and Cordelia and his preference for Kent, which had been in force before the play (as I.i.142-45 tells us) and which is confirmed in Caius, the beginnings of an ability that could have penetrated false façades. His will betrays him to appearances. But that hint of "something else" in Lear, the dim and unrecognized set of values that perceives the merits of Albany and Cordelia, the quality that evokes the devotion of Kent, the Fool, Gloucester, and Cordelia, prepares us to accept its profound emergence.

Lear's inability to trace the impulses of his heart upward into kingly action was "unkind," however. His protestations of kindness are, like much of what he says before his storm is over, extensions of his willful demand that he be right, even though all the world be leveled:

> And thou, all-shaking thunder,
> Strike flat the thick rotundity o' the' world!
> Crack Nature's moulds, all germens spill at once
> That makes ingrateful man!
>
> (III.ii.6-9)

While Lear claims to "tax you not, you elements, with un-kindness" (III.ii.16), he demands that they destroy all kind-ness, the earth itself, and the seeds therein. Having given the world away, he would now destroy it. His cry to the storm is an extension of his curse of Goneril. Much as we sympathize with the old man, beard blown parallel to the earth he curses level, his cosmic outrage conveys a Hitlerian ring. His words suggest a motivation even deeper than revenge; universal de-struction would destroy his *own* guilt. *He,* after all, has been "ungrateful man," and his ingratitude antedates that of Goneril and Regan. There is something in his words of the desire for annihilation for which Faustus cries at the end. Lear's preoccupation with his daughters' reciprocal unkind-ness also emerges from the insanity of insisting upon will: "Didst thou give all to thy daughters? And art thou come to this?" (III.iv.49-50), "Has his daughters brought him to this pass?" (III.iv.65). His insistence on self-rightness perpetuates his blindness:

> Fool. Come hither, mistress. Is your name Goneril?
> Lear. She cannot deny it.
> Fool. Cry you mercy, I took you for a joint-stool. (III.vi.51-55)

He has lost all contact with his "kind," but that loss is evi-dence of a detaching from him of will, that version of non-sanity which must be discarded before he can achieve sanity. The sanity of kings is seldom questioned, as Shelley suggests in "England, 1819," and as Shakespeare shows in *Macbeth,* where the king also raves at "a stool" (III.iv.68). Macbeth's inability to differentiate between a stool and the image of his guilt staring back at him, of course, represents a more direct reflection of his own evil.

It is hard to agree with William Rosen that the "Poor naked wretches" speech represents the "complete transforma-tion" of "Lear's whole personality."[28]* Set as it is between violent

---

* An even earlier index of potential charity in Lear is his refusal to indict Cornwall's feigned indisposition:

> No, but not yet; may be he is not well.
> Infirmity doth still neglect all office
> Whereto our health is bound; we are not ourselves
> When nature, being oppress'd, commands the mind

expressions of Lear's will, the speech can be defined as only the
beginning of charity, the repressed kindness boiling up from
deep beneath the surface of kingship and mingling with the wild
seethings of his will. While Lear identifies with Edgar, it is on the
basis of a bestial "kindness," a frantic desire to become the mere
mad animal, the "thing itself" that (III.iv.110-11) Edgar represents. It is a debased impulse: "unaccommodated man is no more
but such a poor, bare, forked animal as thou art. Off, off, you
lendings! Come; unbutton here" (III.iv.110-14). It is true, however, that Lear's fascination with the "philosopher" Edgar
(III.iv.159) represents his sudden interest in the "body natural"
that Edgar represents and that Lear is now experiencing for the
first time. Edgar is a prelude to Cordelia, but when Lear meets
her again, his nature will be *elevated* to the level she truly represents, not degraded to the obscene level Edgar feigns. But Lear's
words will echo profoundly at the play's ending, when he will
repeat the request of the button, when he *will* see "the thing
itself," Cordelia dead. More layers must be stripped away before
we can remark the "complete transformation" of Lear. Here he
is deceived, insisting that Edgar's daughters have reduced him
thus. Actually, as Horowitz points out, he is looking at an image
of his own error: "Poor Tom is Edgar, driven out by his father,
and hence not Lear's image but Cordelia's. If Lear saw truly, he
would see in Edgar his own crime, not a sympathetic
suffering."[29]

Robert Heilman's rhapsody on this scene resonates effort-
lessly beyond what the play permits a critic to say: "the poor
naked wretches of the play, the victims of the world, will sur-
vive in spirit. The gorgeous are doomed. In proud array,
Lear failed; uncrowned, half-naked, he is saved."[30] While one
can sympathize with these sentiments, they equate salvation
with a raging insanity. They do not account for the profoundly egocentric and negative cast of Lear's moments of

To suffer with the body. I'll forbear;
And am fallen out with my more headier will,
To take the indispos'd and sickly fit
For the sound man.

                                                              (II.iv.106-13)

This temporary pardon defines a process in contrast to that which Lear will undergo, where the "tempest in [his] mind" (III.iv.12) is dominant over the "oppressed
nature" Kent ascribes to him (III.vi.104-5).

"charity" during the storm. While Lear grants pardon *before* knowing the "cause" (IV.vi.111), "none does offend" (IV.vi.172) because *all* offend. This is hardly a charitable insight. Lear's quest for justice must be viewed within the context of his own injustice, as Granville-Barker notes: "Where Lear, such a short while since, sat in his majesty, there sit the fool and the outcast, with Kent whom he banished beside them; and he, witless, musters his failing strength to beg justice upon a joint stool. Was better justice done, the picture ironically asks, when he presided in majesty and sanity and power?"[31]

The trial scene (III.vi) is, in fact, a parody of the initial love test, the "justice" of the second reflecting the "justice" of the first in an ironic mirror, delivering indictment rather than reward. In each, Lear gives directions, dictating the order of the ritual ("Now, our joy. . ." [I.i.84]; "Now, you she foxes!" [III.vi.24]), as imperious in his madness as he was in his "sanity." Lear arraigns Goneril first and swears an oath against her: "before this honourable assembly, she kick'd the poor king her father" (III.vi.50), as she had sworn her fulsome oath earlier within another public ritual dictated by Lear. He insists that Regan be anatomized to "see what breeds about her heart" (III.vi.81). He, of course, as parent, has bred that heart in her and as king has encouraged its corruption. Implicit in the trial scene is the silent Cordelia. Lear is too obsessed with vengeance to introduce Cordelia to himself or to the trial. Were he sane, his trial would devolve into an indictment of himself. His will, even in madness, cannot relax to allow that much knowledge through. Lear's madness is a kind of death, the death he must experience before he can be born again to a concept not of universal depravity but of transcendent love. Stripped of all authority —even that of the mind's ability to discern man from thing—he is almost ready for his long repressed "body natural" to emerge and to find it reflected back to him without irony in Cordelia's charity. His initial impulse toward Cordelia survives the destruction of his will, indeed is what remains after the imperious "old man" is obliterated. A reminder of that old man reflects from Edgar, who throws "his head" at the dogs, who leap "the hatch" (III.vi.67-76) and flee, set loose on the kingdom, as Lear had released them by throwing *his* head—giving up his crown. In the next scene, Edgar's ficticious dogs materialize in Gloucester's metaphor: "I am tied to th' stake, and I must stand the course" (III.vii.53).

Cordelia herself undergoes a change during the play —from "truth" to "love." In neither role, however, is she the mere embodiment of some allegorical meaning. In the first scene she represents that part of the outer mystery which expresses truth but which, like Christ, must be recognized, must resonate against the "inner mystery" of man. Her muteness before Lear is similar to Christ's before Pilate—the inability of the person who sees beyond the finite to express anything that temporal power, absorbed in finitude, can comprehend, the inability of a value system that sees beyond the material to be encompassed within a worldly format. All Cordelia can do is "Love and be silent" (I.i.63). Yet she expresses the *true* relationship between daughter and father:

> Good, my Lord,
> You have begot me, bred me, lov'd me: I
> Return those duties back as are right fit;
> Obey you, love you, and most honour you.
> Why have my sisters husbands, if they say
> They love you all? Haply, when I shall wed,
> That lord whose hand must take my plight shall carry
> Half my love with him, half my care and duty.
> Sure I shall never marry like my sisters,
> To love my father all.
>
> (I.i.97-106)

As Traversi suggests, "her insistence upon the 'bond' rests on a proper understanding of the nature of things and no rhetorical profession can strengthen it because it lies as a condition of health at the foundation of human normality."[32] Cordelia says no more than what Desdemona said to Brabantio in a similar ritualistic setting:

> But here's my husband;
> And so much duty as my mother show'd
> To you, preferring you before her father,

So much I challenge that I may profess
Due to the Moor, my lord.

(I.iii.185-89)

Cordelia echoes the familiar words of the Marriage Service
(another "Christian" thread amid this "pagan" fabric): "Then
shall the Priest saye to the woman. 'Wilt thou have this man
to thy wedded housband, to lyve together after Gods or-
dynaunce, in the holy estate of matrimony: wilt thou obey
hym, & serve him, love, honour & kepe him, in sycknes & in
health: And forsakynge al other, kepe the only to him so
long as you both shal live?" And again: "For this cause shall a
man leave father and mother and shalbe ionined unto his
wife, and thei two shalbe one flesh." But here no Venetian
council mediates between the dragon and his wrath. Lear's
will is unimpeded.

Cordelia's emphasis on "half" and "all" underlines her
scorn of the "auction," as Harbage calls it,[33] in which words
are given for "bounty" (I.i.53), protestations for "A third
more opulent" (I.i.88), the calculus of self-interest upon
which Lear insists, the discrepancy between mouth and heart
that he demands and that Cordelia alone of the sisters resists.
It is difficult to agree to Cordelia's embrace of the commercial ethic. According to Battenhouse, she "views love as a
commodity to be measured and apportioned. . . . This
mathematical formula for a dividing of love in halves according to merit is strangely like Lear's proposal to divide his
lands in thirds according to merit. Both cases imply a substitution of calculation for the spirit of free giving." With
Lear, Cordelia is guilty, says Battenhouse, of "a boastful
self-righteousness."[34] Such a view, of course, overlooks the
possibility of Cordelia's irony—her parody of the equations
of self-interest (which, like parody, *will* bear a "strange" likeness to Lear's test)—overlooks Kent's defense of her speaking
"justly" (I.i.186) and "most rightly" (I.i.186), France's sense of
her intrinsic value (and his acting upon that sense, as opposed to Lear's stifling of it), Cordelia's straightforward rejection of Burgundy's mercenary motives (I.i.250-52), her admonition to her sisters that their deeds parallel their words,
and the fact that her thrusts at Lear's folly anticipate as we

soon learn, those of her *alter ego,* the Fool. Battenhouse suggests that Cordelia "fails [her initial test] principally because she is interpreting filial love without brotherly love. She is viewing her father only as a demanding creditor, not as a fellow man, who, having fallen among thieves, needs compassion."[35] But Lear has put *himself* among thieves. Cordelia can only *become* a thief within the format prescribed for her. She must revert to her bond and attempt to reassert a proper definition of relationships, the definition Lear disregards but which emerges again and again through negative analogies in the scenes that follow his willful abdication of kingly, familial, and human responsibility. Indeed, Lear himself will explicitly vindicate Cordelia's injunction of her bond when he arrives at Regan's: "Thou better know'st/The offices of nature, bond of childhood. . ." (II.iv.180-81). If Cordelia's "half" and "all" convict her of mere calculation, Desdemona's reiterated "so much" (I.iii.186, 188) is equally culpable. What Horowitz says of *The Merchant of Venice* applies with slight alteration to Lear's opening pageant of the will:

> the law in this world-commercial context has been transformed out of its role as an instrument of natural moral order to become, instead, the instrument of my lord commodity, and gain. . . . The commercial law of commodity stands above the moral law of kind.[36]

Cordelia's refusal to "heave [her] heart into her mouth" (I.i.93-94) makes the stiff set piece of scene one *dramatic*—it forces choice upon Lear. Unless he chooses Cordelia, releasing her kind of energy into his kingdom, she cannot speak. The rest of the play is the working out of Lear's decisions here. Time alone will tell him what choice he had—and one of his choices will cancel the other he finally makes. As in the other "Christian" tragedies, the truth is smothered; in *Hamlet,* it is expressed but not recognized, then gradually stifled as Hamlet shatters his play and struggles on into the darkness; Othello literally strangles it, yet Desdemona absolves him almost posthumously with her last words; Macbeth kills Duncan in his sleep, "shut up/ In measureless content" (II.i.16-167) for eternity as it turns out. Here, Lear silences the truth—not just of Cordelia, but of himself, since it is potentially a shared truth, a truth of the self as well as of the universe. Lear careens off on his imperious tangent (the process of "commodity" described by Faulconbridge in *King John* II.i.561-98) to discover a different and intangible definition of commodity, which Gloucester suggests: "our mere defects/ Prove our commodities" (IV.i.22-23), and which Lear has already outlined: "I am cold myself. Where is this straw, my fellow?/ The art of our necessities is strange/ And can make vile things precious" (III.iii.69-71).

Burgundy, like Bassanio, has come to wive it wealthily. When he learns that Cordelia is no longer "dear" (I.i.199)—loved *and* valued—that "her price is fall'n" (I.i.200), he backs awkwardly away. Lear falls into Brabantio's error by describing Cordelia to France as "a wretch whom Nature is asham'd/ Almost t'acknowledge hers" (I.i.215-16). Lear sees *himself* as nature, a god who can create and uncreate through the motion of his mighty will. But France, during his brief and memorable moment in this play, suggests that it would require a *new* religion, a striking reversal of any previous doctrine, to convince him of Cordelia's alleged unnaturalness (I.i.222) or monstrosity (I.i.223):

> which to believe of her
> Must be a faith that reason without miracle
> Should never plant in me.
>
> (I.i.224-26)

His disbelief reverberates not only against Cordelia's "taint" (I.i.224) but against Lear's assumption of nature's role. Nature still exists, France suggests ("Should never *plant* in me"), regardless of the expanded will of any king, and we remember that this is a king speaking. France reverses the previous ritual, where piety was employed by Goneril and Regan to fulfill appetite. He recognizes in Cordelia true value—"the thing itself"—the essential quality untrammeled by the materialistic equation that Burgundy made of her. Burgundy, like Goneril and Regan, would have been happy to phrase a speech of "love" as long as the words were transmuted to wealth. The speeches of Goneril and Regan represent a kind of "reverse alchemy" where words become gold

but where intangible value is debased. France bases his action
on an ethic that embraces invisible value as *real,* thus allowing
a small comedy to emerge from the wreckage of the opening
scene and predicting Lear's own journey toward the same
ethic. France's experience is an immediate version of the
slower, agonizing, but "comic" progress of the play's other
king. But the early Lear merely reiterates the premises of his
balked will: "Better thou/ Hadst not been born than not t'
have pleas'd me better" (I.i.236-37). This prediction of his
curse of Goneril suggests clearly the conflict that is developing within Lear's body natural between his will ("t' have
pleas'd *me*") and his undiscovered self—that nature which he
gave his daughter Cordelia and that supernature in which
each shares and must participate, positively or negatively, in
this play a potentially *inward* awareness, not a "given" of the
cosmic context. Lear's experience, at first, would seem profoundly negative, as his will drives him through the storm
and finally destroys the old Lear, the mind that pursued only
will and which banished truth. Once the eyeless arrogance
has been erased in madness and once insanity has been
soothed away in sleep, Lear is ready to awaken to the Cordelia he here says should not have been born. It is hard to
agree with Harold Wilson that Cordelia displays "inflexible
pride in the opening of the play."[37] The pride and the inflex-
ibility are Lear's. The contrast between the two—one bound
up in the uses of this world, the other able to enunciate, before being silenced by a god-king who knows only his own
absoluteness, the deeper bond that is the real basis of a
society—is summarized by the Homily on Rogation Week:

> If the merchaunt and worldly occupier knew that God is the giver
> of riches, hee would be content himself with so much as by just
> meanes approved of God. . . . Besides to beleeve certainely God to
> bee the authour of all the giftes that we have, shall make us to bee in
> silence and patience when they bee taken againe. . .if by any adver-
> sitie his goodes bee taken from him, how fumeth and fretteth he?
> How murmureth hee and dispayreth?. . .wee shoulde rather submit
> our selfe in patience, than to have indignation at Gods rodde, which
> peradventure when hee hath corrected us to nurture, he will cast it
> into the fire.

That Cordelia represents far more than the "little-seeming substance" Lear imputes to her (I.i.201) is emphasized by France, who echoes the famous sonnet in saying, "Love's not love/ When it is mingled with regards that stands/ Aloof from the entire point" (I.i.241-43). Lear sees her as "substance," however insignificant. France discerns in her an *essential* quality, untrammeled by commercial considerations, a sacramental depth of which her "substance" is but the outward manifestation. "She is herself a dowry" (I.i.244). And reminders of Christ accrue to Cordelia:

> Fairest Cordelia, that art most rich being poor,
> Most choice forsaken, and most lov'd despis'd!
>
> (I.i.253-54)

According to the Homily of the Nativity, Christ "became obedient to the Law, to deliver us from the curse of the Law, who became poore to make us rich; vile to make us pretious. . . ." Cordelia resists the "old law"—the will of Lear that has dominated the dispensation now ending—by enunciating a principle embraced by France. Her "law" is an internal condition, a "bond" based on the *essential* relationship between father and daughter, partaking indeed of an external social aspect, but not imposed from without by external power. Cordelia, not Lear, represents something that alters not when it alteration finds. That Lear has "begot. . .bred. . .[and] lov'd" Cordelia (I.i.49) elicits from her a response sanctioned by both nature and society: "I/ Return those duties [i.e., of nature, love, and obligation] back as are right fit" (I.i.99). *Hers* is the love Goneril claims for herself, "A love that makes breath poor and speech unable" (I.i.61), because Cordelia's love emerges from the deep premises of a world order that *must* be felt inwardly to be understood. To attempt to express it to those who *don't* understand is indeed to reduce it to inexpressibility and to *be* reduced to silence. Cordelia's will is aligned with deeper sanctions. Lear's will is reflected back to him by empty ritual of words whose goal is wealth. When the external props of will—the map of his world and the knights provided as his guard of honor on his progress to the grave—disappear, that will must suffer in its nakedness until it too is destroyed. Then the "Cordelia ethic" will emerge from within Lear, as his speech on going to prison will demonstrate. Lear will finally come to where Cordelia was in the first scene, and will express her meaning as France does, placing a proper valuation on "packs and sects of great ones" (V.iii.18), exchanging his greatness for the profound "mystery of things" (V.iii.16). Cordelia's ethic is that of the New Testament, based on spiritual value, on the inner meaning of the law, on the "fulfillment" of the law that Christ states is his mission (Matthew 5:17). To apply such a reading to the first scene might be to urge it too insistently toward a "Christian" reading, were Cordelia not there, but particularly were France not there to accept the fulfillment Cordelia represents, which Lear tries to obliterate but merely defers, obliterating his old will in the process.

Lear denies her "our grace, our love, our benison" (I.i.268). His royal plurality does not yet understand that what the king has done to the political man is not so profound as what the king has done to the essential man. In denying Cordelia his blessing, he alienates himself from the ground of his own being, stands aloof from the entire point. He has been, as France says, "unkind" (I.i.263), has broken the bond between himself and nature. One king recognizes Cordelia in a sudden revelation:

> Gods, gods! 'tis strange that from their cold'st neglect
> My love should kindle to inflam'd respect.
>
> (I.i.257-58)

She awaits recognition by the other, who strides out with an obviously ironic exit line, "Come, noble Burgundy" (I.i.270). Lear will repeat his initial error, equating love to quantity, in facing Goneril and Regan:

> [To Gon.]   I'll go with thee.
> Thy fifty yet doth double five and twenty,
> And thou art twice her love.
>
> (II.iv.261-63)

Regan is right. Lear "hath ever but slenderly known himself" (I.i.297). Such ignorance in a man hampers him and his relationships; in a king, who is two men, political and natural, lack of self-knowledge involves much more. The political ramifications of Lear's decision have been partially traced. The other thread of the play, Lear's struggle back to Cordelia, is the more profound. It is a journey to a truth that has its analogue, among others (Job, Jonah, the Prodigal Son, the Wandering Jew) in the journey of the Magi, the movement of temporal power from another country to a new dispensation, to the embracing of a new principle. And Lear, like Eliot's Magi, has "A cold coming. . ./ Just the worst time of the year/ For a journey, and such a long journey:/ The ways deep and the weather sharp. . . ." Finally Lear, like Eliot's unillusioned Magi, is "glad of another death":

> he hates him
> That would upon the rack of this tough world
> Stretch him out longer.
>
> (V.iii.313-15)

Cordelia's identification with transcendent principle is made even more explicit than Desdemona's. Shakespeare's emphasis on this point would seem suspicious, almost ironic, were there any evidence to undercut Cordelia. There are differences between Cordelia and Desdemona, of course. The latter is a patient sufferer and forgiver. She never emerges from a passive role. Cordelia is a patient sufferer at first, then a forgiving and healing force whose military effort fails, in a strange analogue to her worldly "failure" of scene one. Cordelia's *grace* has a power far beyond Desdemona's, and it succeeds completely with Lear and those of his party, if only temporarily. What Shakespeare seems to be doing is setting up not the reconciliation scene, which needs no overt "Christian" keying beyond itself, but the ending, Cordelia dead. Suffice it that her tears, "holy water from her heavenly eyes" (IV.iii.32), contrast with the "court holy water" (III.11.10) of flattery. Like Christ, she goes about her father's business (IV.iv.23-24), not her own:

    All bless'd secrets,
All you unpublish'd virtues of the earth,
Spring with my tears! be aidant and remediate
In the good man's distress.

(IV.iv.15-18)

O my dear father! Restoration hang
Thy medicine on my lips, and let this kiss
Repair those violent harms that my two sisters
Have in thy reverence made!

(IV.vii.26-29)

Her tears represent the compassion which, as *The Tempest* shows, is a precondition for grace, and Lear accepts them as something very different from the "woman's weapons" he had scorned (II.iv.280). She appeals here not to the gods, but to the healing supernature with which she is in contact. It is Christ, says the "Sermon on Rogation weeke," "that gave mee the true instruction of. . .the vertue of rootes, and whatsoever is hid and secret in nature." Cordelia stands in the tradition of Christ, Edward the Confessor, who "solicits Heaven" to empower his "healing benediction" (IV.iii.149, 156) and about whom sacramental associations cluster, and Prospero, who summons "heavenly music," "the best comforter" to "cure. . .brains/ Now useless boil'd within [the] skull" (V.i.52-60). She who has so recently been disowned promises to him "that helps [Lear] all [her] outward worth" (IV.iv.10), a pledge reflecting back on the negotiations of the opening scene, and an analogy to Desdemona's refusal to break her faith "For the whole world" (IV.iii.79). She is further associated with the role of Christ, who redeems the world from the Fall of Adam and Eve:

    Thou hast one daughter
Who redeems Nature from the general curse
Which twain have brought her to.

(Iv.vi.209-11)

Muir disagrees with Danby on this point, saying, "Not Adam and Eve, as Danby fancifully suggests, but Goneril and Regan."[38] It may be that the first meaning a spectator might glimpse would be Goneril and Regan, who have indeed helped to translate the kingdom into a violent jungle, but—*"redeems Nature from the general curse"*? The comprehensiveness of the phrase, combined with an unspecified "twain" and the other suggestions linking Cordelia to the *agape* most completely embodied in Christ, plus Shakespeare's extensive use of the Fall of Man in these plays (particularly in *Macbeth,* written so close in time to *King Lear*)—these considerations insist on the archetypal interpretation.

Even if the persistent linkage of Cordelia with aspects of Christ's mission were somehow "accidental" or "unintentional," and even if we agree with most of Elton's *prisca theologia* argument, relating Cordelia to various Renaissance conceptions of the virtuous pagan but ignoring the Christian analogues that are more obvious and more fundamental to Renaissance thought (*and* theology), even if we maintain that Lear's "sovereign shame" (IV.iii.44) is *not* evidence of the man's repentance for the king's "unkindness/ That stripp'd her from his benediction" (IV.iii.44-45),* and even if we reject what seem to be clear tendencies in the play thus far, the reconciliation scene alone would convince us that Lear's journey has been toward a Christian revelation, that the great storm has been, as Holloway suggests, analogous to the final storm of the world, beyond which lies judgment—and redemption for some.[39]

The scene re-creates as nearly as any other in Shakespeare the experience of the Christian revelation, particularly when contrasted with Edgar's awkward and rhetorical contrivance with the blinded Gloucester on the cliffs of Dover, which does not move Gloucester into a new awareness but which, by manipulating his credulity and superstition, merely reconfirms his former self ("I do remember now" [IV.vi.75]), a parody of the fall of Lear into madness and from thence into a *new* set of values. As Nicholas Brooke says of the reconciliation scene: "a radically different sense of regeneration is de-

---

* Compare, for example, Kent's lines, "these things sting/ His mind so venomously, that burning shame/ Detains him from Cordelia" (IV.iii.47-49), and the Homily on Repentance: "when they committed any heinous offence, or some filthy or abominable sinne, if it once come to light, or if they chance to have a thorough feeling of it, they bee so ashamed (their owne conscience putting before their eyes the filthinesse of their acte) that they dare looke no man in the face, much lesse that they should be able to stand in the sight of God."

veloped, one whose bearings are so much more natural than
moral than it rather contradicts than supplements Edgar's
sententiae."[40] Here, no character calls a nonevent a "miracle,"
as Edgar does of Gloucester's short tumble (IV.vi.55). Here,
unlike Edgar's manipulation, the words coincide with what
we *see;* Kent *is* "good Kent" (IV.vii.1), Cordelia *is* "good
madam" (IV.vii.23). The scene is almost wordless compared
to Edgar's manipulation. His meanings are *in* the words, not
implicit in *experience*. The reconciliation scene is
sacramental—words and actions are merely emanations of its
profound depth of feeling and meaning. It tosses out no
grand generalizations about man and the clearest gods, but is
endowed with images of serenity and metaphors of spiritual
transition—music, the "fresh garments" (IV.vii.22) placed on
Lear, the saving sleep denied him previously (III.vi.105-7),
medicine (IV.vii.27), the "fair daylight" (IV.vii.52) into which
he wakes. Its meaning is expressed at one of its deepest levels
by The Homily Against The Fear of Death: "holy Scripture
calleth the bodily death a sleepe, wherein mans senses be (as
it were) taken from him for a season, and yet when he
awaketh, he is more fresh than he was when he went to bed."
The scene is an oasis of light between the savagery of storm
preceding it and the butchery of battle that deepens toward
the "cheerless, dark, and deadly" ending (V.iii.290). The images and metaphors of IV.vii, however, merely underline the
human experience—Cordelia's self-effacing concern, Lear's
bewilderment on waking, his shame before his daughter. In a
line that at once captures the still frail bearings of Lear's
mind *and* the truth of the scene, Lear insists that it is his
birthday: "Fourscore and upward, not an hour more nor
less" (IV.vii.61).[41]

Lear comes "out o' the' grave" (IV.vii.45), born again to
witness the miracle of Cordelia's forgiveness, a divine love
because it transcends the ruthless spirit of calculation Lear
himself has engendered:

> I know you do not love me; for your sisters
> Have, as I do remember, done me wrong:
> You have some cause, they have not.
>
> (IV.vii.73-75)

Traces of the old love-commodity equation linger in Lear's mind, but are erased by Cordelia's "No cause, no cause" (IV.vii.76). Cordelia was "right" in scene one. Now her love consumes mere truth, mere "cause," the mere justice of man. Unlike Gloucester, Lear is not reconfirmed in weakness. Lear admits that he is mere man—he has learned of mere man in the storm—and "a very foolish fond old man" (IV.vii.60), an "old and foolish" man (IV.vii.85) at that, afraid he will be mocked.

Most commentators agree with Muir that when Lear awakens to the sight of Cordelia, "he thinks he is in hell":[42]

> You do me wrong to take me out o' the' grave.
> Thou art a soul in bliss; but I am bound
> Upon a wheel of fire, that mine own tears
> Do scald like molten lead.

(IV.vii.45-48)

The lines recall the story of Lazarus (Luke 16:19-26, Geneva Version):

> There was a certain rich man, which was clothed in purple and fine linnen, & fared well and delicately every day.
> Also there was a certeine begger named Lazarus, which was laied at his gate full of sores,
> And desired to be refreshed with the crommes that fel from the rich mans table: yea & the dogs came & licked his sores.
> And it was so that the beger dyed, and was caryed by the Angels into Abrahams bosome. The riche man also dyed and was buried.
> And being in hell in torments, he lift up his eyes and saw Abraham afarre off, & Lazarus in his bosome.
> Then he cried & said, Father Abraham have mercie on me, & send Lazarus that he may dippe the tip of finger in water, and coole my tongue: for I am tormented in this flame.
> But Abraham said, sonne, remember that thou in thy life receivedst thy pleasures, and likewise Lazarus paines; now therefore is he comforted and thou art tormented.
> Besides all this, between you and us there is a great gulfe set, so that they which would go from hence to you, can not, neither can they come from hence to us.

The rich man had turned Lazarus away as Lear rejected Cordelia, rendering her "poor" (I.i.253) and "forsaken" (I.i.254). Lear now sees himself as the rich man, viewing a soul in bliss across the impassable gulf of eternity. The Bible story reinforces the agony of Lear's awakening by suggesting the sense of absolute separation from salvation. (And it is worth emphasizing that Lear's words express unmistakably the concept of an afterlife: "soul in bliss," "You are a spirit, I know; where did you die" [IV.vii.46, 49]).[43] The overwhelming power of the scene derives not only from the emotional momentum of the scenes that precede it, but from its Christian analogues. The kneeling of Lear to his "child, Cordelia" (IV.vii.69), for example, is a version of the archetypal kneeling of the Magi before Christ, as depicted by the masters, showing almost invariably the oldest, white-bearded king actually kneeling beside the manger, temporal power acknowledging the transcendency of divine love. The Lazarus analogue lends deeper emotional impact to the bridging of the gulf between Lear and Cordelia than would pertain had Shakespeare not reminded us of the rich man forever on the wrong side of bliss. (And anyone who has ever emerged from the terror of a nightmare into the concerned gaze of a loved one can share Lear's moment of incomplete transition.) A suggestion, perhaps, of the saving moisture craved by the rich man, is the "tears" (IV.iv.17-18), which prove "aidant and remediate/ In the good man's distress" (IV.iv.17-18), helping Lear to realize that both he and Cordelia live: "Be your tears wet?" (IV.vi.71). Lear is able to disengage himself from his nightmare of damnation—to cross the great gulf —not only because of Cordelia's love, but because he has been transformed from rich man to Lazarus in the storm, has learned "to feel what wretches feel" (III.iv.34), has learned, as the Geneva gloss to the Lazarus story says, "how little glorious titles availe."

While Maynard Mack suggests a Lear-Nebuchadnezzar parallel, his illustrative parable seems to come closer to the Lear-Lazarus equation:

In one common form of this archetype, the king comes from swimming or his bath to find his clothes and retainers gone. His role has been usurped by an angel sent from heaven to teach him, in the words of the Magnificat, that God humbles the proud and exalts the humble. In his nakedness, he finds that the evidence of his kingliness, indeed his whole identity, is gone. Assertions that he is in fact the king and efforts to regain his throne lead those around him to mock him as a madman. Standing at last among the beggars outside his own palace, wind torn, tormented by hunger and thirst, he acknowledges his true position, repents his former arrogance. . . . In the finest of all the retellings of the archetype, the repudiated king is not driven out but made the court fool and compelled to take his food with the palace dogs.[44]

Lear's progress, then, encompasses the career of the rich man *and* Lazarus. The contradictory quality of his experience is captured when he interprets his waking to Cordelia's love as a vision of his own damnation. He does not realize at that moment that the transition from rich man to Lazarus has been completed within him.

Another version of the abased king occurs in the Sermon for Whitsunday in a bitter attack on the Pope. "What greater pride can there bee," demands the Homilist, "then that one should preferre his own judgement before the whole congregation, as though he onely had the spirit of God?" The castigation of the papacy points at Lear's original pride. But what Hildebrand does to "Henry the Emperour" seems analogous to what Lear's pride has done to himself: "to stand at the gates of the citie in the rough winter, bare footed and bare legged, onely clothed in Lincie wolcie, eating nothing from morning to night, and that for the space of three dayes." Henry's plight is reminiscent of Lazarus's, neglected outside the rich man's gate, and of Lear's, reduced to the state of Lazarus.

Lear's kneeling to Cordelia reminds us of his mocking knee to the absent Goneril:

> Ask her forgiveness?
> Do you but mark how this becomes the house:
> "Dear daughter, I confess that I am old;
> Age is unnecessary: on my knees I beg
> That you'll vouchsafe me raiment, bed, and food."
>
> (II.iv.154-58)

As Heilman says, Lear, in kneeling to Goneril, is "the ironic critic of a violation of nature which is symbolized by the father's being a suppliant to his child."[45] While Cordelia *has*

provided the elements for which Lear cynically asked
Goneril, his kneeling here is not that of a king (representative of "the house") kneeling to a subordinate, but an old
man kneeling to the representative of a superior power. The
scene is almost wordless, compared to the rhetorical, ritualistic, imprecatory opening. The words that reach the surface
here are the bare suggestions of the deeper experience the
scene conveys largely without words—that of the human
will's shaping itself to patterns of the comprehensive order
that includes mere human will within it and that assists the
will that recognizes it. Lear finally feels the body natural
more completely than the body politic, the "old man" Kent
saw from the beginning. No words are adequate to Lear's
recognition, or to the kneeling that imitates it. Its significance
must be felt or remain unperceived. Certainly, inflated language would insult (and diminish) our perception of the
scene's experience. Lear emerges, as Kent says, into his "own
kingdom" (IV.vii.77), and we cannot be certain at this point
that he speaks of Britain. He seems instead to have awakened
into a kingdom beyond this world, that suggested by the
"Sermon against the Feare of Death": "the life in this world,
is [like] a Pilgrimage in a strange countrey, farre from God,
and that death, delivering us from our bodies, doth send us
straight home into our owne countrey."

The reconciliation scene resonates with overtones of the
Sacrament of Baptism, requiring, as the Homily on Whitsunday suggests, "no other element. . .but onely water whereunto
the word is joyned, it is made [then] a full and perfect sacrament." The "great rage" in Lear is "kill'd" (IV.vii.78-79), the
"old man" or "old Adam," as the Baptism Service terms the
former life, is dead. All elements inhibiting his participation
in sacrament have been stripped away.* It is his birthday, the
day close to that appointed in the Elizabethan rubrics for
Baptism:

* Cf. *Henry V:*
   Consideration like an angel came
   And whipp'd th' offending Adam out of him.

                                                              (I.i.28-29)

The pastours and curates shal oft admonish the people, that they deferre not the Baptisme of enfantes any longer than the Sonday, or other holy day, next after the childe be borne.

Stella Brook suggests that "the Prayer Book phrase *the old Adam* has passed into spoken folk-lore in the superstition that a baby ought to cry at his Christening in order to 'cry the old Adam out of him.' "[46] The baptismal suggestions of the reconciliation scene are strengthened by Lear's emphasis, just before he is found by Cordelia's scouts, on the sound of "old Adam" emerging into this fallen world:

> we came crying hither.
> Thou know'st, the first time that we smell the air,
> We wawl and cry. . .
> When we are born, we cry that we are come
> To this great stage of fools.
>
> (IV.vi.182-87)

Lear touches Cordelia's tears, "holy water from her heavenly eyes" (IV.iii.32), to confirm his awakening. The tears become, then, the medium whereby "the newe man" is "raysed up," whereby "all carnal affections. . .dye" in him, "and that all things belonginge to the spirite. . .live and growe" in him. The washing away of carnal affections would seem to be unnecessary in an old men, yet Lear's obsession and disgust with lust and bestial appetite suggest the necessity of their cleansing by the presence of his third daughter. Invited to violate nature in scene one, Cordelia redeems it here. Since Lear comes "out o' th' grave," the scene is also a resurrection. Baptism partakes of the resurrection archetype, as the Homily on the Resurrection makes clear: "the olde man with his workes be put off and the newe bee put on."*

Clearly, a new spirit enters Lear in this scene, and it can be explained theologically by recalling the function of the Holy Ghost: "Such is the power of the holy Ghost, to regenerate man, and as it were to bring foorth a new, so that they shall be nothing like the men that they were before." The

---

* The fresh garments placed on Lear as he slept emblematize an inward transition, of course, and also suggest the clothes an infant would wear at his baptism.

Sermon for Whitsunday goes on to cite Christ, who "sayd to
Nicodemus, unlesse a man be borne anew, of water and the
spirit, he can not enter into the kingdome of God: he was
greatly amazed in his mind, and began to reason with Christ,
demanding how a man might bee borne which was olde?"
Christ's answer is "the holy Ghost. . .inwardly worketh the
regeneration and new birth of mankinde." The spiritual quality Lear attributes to Cordelia (IV.vii.46, 49) comes alive in
him. That he asks the "spirit" Cordelia "where did you die?"
reverberates strangely, as if Lear is groping for the details of
a story he cannot know. Cordelia's "death" combined with
suggestions of the function of the Holy Ghost ("to sanctifie
and regenerate") reminds us that the Holy Ghost, according
to John (15:39), is a product of a post-Calvary extension of
Christian mystery: "This spake [Christ] of the Spirit which
they that beleved in him, shulde receive: for the holie Gost
was not yet *given* because that Jesus was not yet glorified."
Cordelia would seem to have introduced to Lear the concept
of "the Comforter, which is the holie Gost" (John 14:26).
The irony of the suggestion, however, is that it is Cordelia
alive who releases this new spirit. With her death it too will
die, not be released to the faithful of this world as it was
after Christ's death and ascension. Lear's recognition of Cordelia finds its meaning only in him as human, and great as
his transformation is, his insight is not permitted to intersect
and inform the history of Lear's kingdom.

While Elton interprets Lear's speech to Cordelia as they go
off to prison as "stoic," as "Boethian. . .contemptus
mundi. . .and syncretic,"[47] it is difficult not to find a reiteration in Christian terms of the insights of Lear's awakening:

> When thou dost ask me blessing, I'll kneel down,
> And ask of thee forgiveness: so we'll live,
> And pray, and sing. . .
>
> (V.iii.10-12)

It suffices, perhaps, that Lear, like Christ *or* the stoic, places
a true valuation upon greatness and authority:

> Who loses and who wins; who's in, who's out;
> And take upon 's the mystery of things
> As if we were God's spies; and we'll wear out,

In a wall'd prison, packs and sects of great ones,
That ebb and flow by th' moon.

(V.iii.5-19)

The seeming great ones move like tides to the whim of the
inconstant moon, dull sublunary lovers, like the acquisitive
characters in the early *Lear,* whose soul was sense, whose
world, like Burgundy's was inhabited only by things, like
those with no feeling for the *mystery* of things, for the forces
lying behind and beyond the tangible. The beginnings of the
play demonstrated Lear's potential for insight—his preference for Albany and his love for Cordelia. Had he explored
these promptings of his own nature *about* his own nature and
about "kindness" in its extended sense, he would have chosen
Cordelia as France did.

Evidence that Lear has achieved a specifically *Christian*
revelation is provided by comparing his speech on going to
prison to the Homily on Rogation Week:

> I might with many words move some of this audience to
> search for this wisedome ["universall and absolute knowledge"],
> to sequester their reason, to followe Gods commaundment, to
> cast from them the witts of their braines, to favour this
> wisedome, to renounce the wisedom and policie of this fond
> world, to tast and savoure that whereunto the favour and will of
> God hath called them, and willeth us finally to enjoy by his
> favour.... They which have this wisedome of God, can gather
> by the diligent and earnest studie of the worldlings of this pres-
> ent life, how they waite their times, and applie themselves to
> every occasion of time and to get riches, to encrease their lands
> and patrimonie. They see the time passe away, and therefore
> take hold on it, in such wise, that other whiles they will with losse
> of their sleepe and ease, with suffering many paines, catch the
> offer of their time, knowing that that which is past cannot bee
> returned againe, repentance may follow, but remedy is none.
> Why should not they then be spiritual wise in their generation,
> waite their time to increase as fast in their state, to winne and
> gayne everylastingly? They reason what a bruite forgetfulnesse it
> were in man indued with reason, to be ignorant of their times
> and tides.... Let the miserie and short transitorie joyes spied in
> the casualtie of our dayes, move us while we have them in our
> handes.... Let us bee found watchers.... If we do our en-
> deavour, we shall not neede to feare. We shall bee able to over-
> come all our enemies that fight against us.

Lear's speech is in response to Cordelia's dejection on her
behalf: "For thee, oppressed king, I am cast down;/ Myself

could else out-frown false Fortune's frown" (V.iii.5-6). Lear is
comforting *her*, reading *her* the text on their imprisonment.
Obvious similarities exist between Lear's speech and the
Homily, but the latter's importance is not as a possible
"source" for the speech (the Homily cites no biblical sources
for the section I have quoted), but as an index to Lear's attainment of a "superworldly" status quite different from that
he insisted upon at the opening, when he wished to ride to
the whim of his own will. The speech demonstrates that, like
France, he has learned the true value of "the world," and is
not merely contemptuous of it, as Elton claims, but aware of
the value of higher knowledge, the value of the ability to observe "the mystery of things." The role Lear assigns to himself and Cordelia as "God's spies," combined with a rebirth
confirmed by Cordelia's tears, would seem to undercut West's
suggestion that "whatever benefits of his love for Cordelia
Lear may achieve, the play says nothing explicit about his
love of God. Cordelia's love may draw Lear to heights, but it
would seem to do it by human decency, not by sacramental
power."[48] Lear's obliviousness of the consequences of going
to prison after losing a battle—as politically naive as was his
initial division of his kingdom—reflects the "otherworldli-
ness" he has achieved, another contrast to the "superworld"
he insisted upon at first.

He had the chance at the beginning to nurture his kingdom toward Cordelia, toward her "kind nursery" (I.i.126)
and the "unpublish'd virtues" (IV.iv.15) represented by her
in the world of the play. While he finds them as body
natural, he had denied them as body politic and thus their
efficacy has been denied the kingdom. Time reveals his
human error to him—time and his own obstinate, perverse,
and heroic search for the fusion of "justice" and "nature."
But time has moved on in the political world, now a jungle of
conflicting lusts and ambitions. He has discovered a guiding
premise for the validity of his initial insights into the quality
of Albany and Cordelia, but has no format through which to
enunciate that premise, a fact endowing his rigid ritual of
scene one with profound *ex post facto* irony and lending irony
as well to his movement to a prison in a kingdom whose

prisons he once controlled. Lear and Cordelia are captives of those advanced by Lear's political error, and his words come as they move to the prison where she will die. Having paused for Lear's awakening, the greatest comic scene in Shakespeare, the play moves on. Albany's prediction links these two last parts of the play—the transcendent reunion and bleak ending:

> If that the heavens do not their visible spirits
> Send quickly down to tame these vile offences,
> It will come,
> Humanity must perforce prey on itself
> Like monsters of the deep.
>
> (IV.ii.46-50)

Cordelia—to Lear a "spirit"—finds "the great rage. . .in him" more than tamed (IV.vii. 78-79), but she arrives on a personal plane only. Lear has called for a revenging deity to descend and take his part. If a savior comes, however, it is as Christ comes, a nonmilitary, unavenging, New Testament personality. Her army is defeated by that led by the representative of "this world," Edmund, and once it is defeated, the latter half of Albany's prophecy eventuates.

The monsters Lear has released do not crawl docilely back to their cages merely because he has experienced a conversion. Mere anarchy has been loosed upon the world and while, as in *Macbeth*, a Crusade is launched from another land, here the Crusade fails. In the world of *King Lear,* virtue is finally irrelevant; it has no more efficacy than words to a hungry tiger about the moral life one has led, than the child's cry to his mother as they enter the gas chamber that he has been a good boy. As Brooke says, "a revelation of forces opposite to the monsters of the deep. . .does not make the latter unreal; nor does it make the forces equal."[49] As D. G. James says, "In the world which Shakespeare is now rendering, merit is made as powerless as possible and is then destroyed."[50] If the play exhibits an oasis of light, it also moves on to a final darkness. If Lear achieves a Christian insight, he is unable to perpetuate it. His atonement for the mistake of the man does not absolve him of the king's error.

The final scene explicitly denies the providence Edgar arranged for Gloucester and cancels forever Lear's awakening to a new dispensation. Justice *seems* fulfilled in the defeat of Edmund ("The gods are just": [V.iii.110]) and in the deaths of Goneril and Regan ("This judgment of the heavens" [V.iii.231]). But the trumpets bringing Edmund to justice signal a further Judgment defying a neat allegorical interpretation. Albany's plea for Cordelia ("The gods defend her" [V.iii.256]) is followed by Lear's entrance with his dead child. The gods either have not heard, are not there, or do not respond to man's requests of them. Battenhouse claims for Edgar's triumph, "the subplot's. . .mitigating [of] the tragedy by revealing a token or earnest of future betterment."[51] Edgar's triumph is rather the reverse, a false hope, and, typical of Edgar, a melodramatic mimicry of cosmic justice. The ending of *Richard II* with its "false codas," its illusory encouragement of Bolingbroke, is the analogue here.

Yet some insist on salvaging solace from this final scene. G. Wilson Knight finds love to be the theme of the ending and employs the dying Edmund as his example:

> The primary persons, good and bad, die into love. Goneril and Regan, flint-hearted, bend before that universal principle. They die by passion for their Edmund, beautiful as a panther, and as deadly. They, like he, are below humanity: yet they know love. So, too, in the ravenous slaughter of wood or ocean, love rules creation. That universal pulse is strong within the naturalism of *King Lear*, beats equally in the hearts of Goneril and Cordelia. And what of Edmund? He has loved only himself, with a curious consciousness of his fascination. May that be counted love? Edmund does not disclose his order for Cordelia's death which would, according to his cunning device, never otherwise have been laid to his charge till, seeing the bodies of Goneril and Regan brought in, his heart is flamed by the tragic pathos of their passionate sacrifice: "Yet Edmund was beloved." He recognizes love at last, its mystery, its power, its divinity. He knows himself to die aureoled in its unresisted splendour. Now he speaks quickly: "I pant for life. Some good I mean to do. . ./ Nay, send in time." Again, the *Lear* universe travails and brings forth its miracle.[52]

What Lear brings forth is a *dead* child, no miracle. The play closes with the deaths of Cordelia and Lear, not the aureoled passage of Edmund. Edmund's change of heart, like Lear's, comes too late. The action he has set in motion—the captain and his sword—cannot be forestalled. Edmund's effort is a final ironic analogue to Lear's initial decision and of his later repentance, which, however profound, arrives too late. As Lawlor says, "Repentance and Forgiveness are the greatest goods; but it is act and consequence that play the decisive part."[53]

The value of this "love" of Knight's is debatable; it seems closer to lust, and results, in the case of Regan, in the poisoning with which unbridled appetite is so often punished in Jacobean tragedy. This "love" produces murder and suicide: "The one the other poisoned for my sake,/ And after slew herself" (V.iii.240-41). While love for Edmund kills, his curiously deferred repentance cannot save. Had it saved Cordelia, it would have had a value we could applaud. To impose the word "miracle" upon it is to do precisely what Edgar did with Gloucester's nonfall. Finally, if Edmund's repentance is so significant, why is his death "but a trifle" (V.iii.295) to Albany and those looking at Lear and the dead Cordelia? Beyond the storm, as Holloway suggests, Cordelia waited, as beyond the last day wait redemption and man's initiation into the framework of eternity.[54] But *King Lear* would suggest that beyond redemption, beyond the greatest benefits of the Christian orientation, waits only the deepest pain man can know.

To make Cordelia a "Christ-figure" would be to suggest that Shakespeare is oriented toward "truth," as Auerbach suggests the Bible is.[55] Since Shakespeare is oriented toward "response," he creates a character representing "truth"—not a figure in an allegory, but one whose "truth-bearing" qualities dominate the imitation Shakespeare presents—a character to whom a spectator would respond *most* profoundly if, like Desdemona and Cordelia, she were to suffer an unjust death. The murders of Cordelia and Desdemona participate in the archetypal killing of Christ. They are *not* that, but they are to be felt within that context—the death of *agape* as well as of a dramatic character. The dangers of their being allegorized are minimized on stage, as opposed to the closet,

because, as Auerbach suggests, when "what is perceived. . .by
the spectator is weak in a sensory impression. . .all one's interest is directed towards the context of meanings."[56] The
importance of Cordelia and Desdemona, in either case, is not
what they mean in any abstract formulation outside of the
dramatic context, but what they mean within the play and
within the developing ironic distance between us and Othello,
as *he* doubts Desdemona, us and Lear as *he* rejects Cordelia.
Our response to them within the play dictates their "second
meaning"—how we respond to the murder of something
good by a deluded man or by a world run amuck. This latter
meaning, the "final cause" of Cordelia and Desdemona, is
defined by Auerbach: "the goal of the tragic poet [is] to rob
us of our emotional freedom, to turn our intellectual and
spiritual powers. . .in one direction, to concentrate them
there."[57]

The most persuasive effort to redeem the ending is, of
course, Bradley's:

> it seems almost beyond question that any actor is false to the
> text who does not attempt to express, in Lear's last accents and
> gestures and look, an unbearable *joy*.[58]

Seconding Bradley, Theodore Spencer says, "In his own
mind she lives; and it is the discovery that Cordelia is alive,
that life is the reality under the apperance, that the reality is
good—it is this that breaks his heart at last."[59]

Lear dies deluded, then, like Gloucester, prey to what he
wants to believe, like Gloucester, blind to the truth, his "look
there, look there!" (V.iii.311) mere wish-fulfillment; he dies
in the blindness of the insanity that allowed him to see
Goneril in a joint stool. This reading makes Gloucester's experience normative and is an affront to the depth of Lear's
experience, which drives through to a bleakness as profound
as the miracle of his reunion with Cordelia, an affront to a
play that does not, finally, lie to us. Edgar, after all, *is* alive;
Cordelia, dead. This reading represents the critics' wish-
fulfillment. *King Lear* shows us, finally, a world bounded by
no comforting justice, as Dr. Johnson tells us:

> A play in which the wicked prosper and the virtuous miscarry may doubtless be good, because it is a just representation of the common events of human life.[60]

King Lear's ending is, simply, an extreme and heightened but "*just* representation of the common events of human life," as Johnson, who so often transcended his own critical tenets, recognized. *King Lear* is not the reflection of a theory of art-as-instruction, or the sober exemplification of some orthodox "world picture." *King Lear* presents the world that the twentieth century has brought through more complacent theories, and while that world may include transcendent reconciliations, it also includes despair that cannot be rationalized. In the sources, Cordelia dies *after* Lear. Does Shakespeare alter his inherited text merely to have Lear die deluded?

Lear's "Pray you, undo this button" (V.iii.309) reminds us of his effort to strip off his "lendings" (III.iv.114), to "unbutton here" (III.iv.114) upon seeing what he took to be the "thing itself," Edgar. Now at the end, he sees the thing itself, not the alive and feigning Edgar but the dead and real Cordelia. While her death can hardly be called a "common event of human life," it repeats the Crucifixion, which Eliot in *Murder in the Cathedral* and Shaw in *Saint Joan* suggest is hardly uncommon: "Must then a Christ perish in torment in every age to save those that have no imagination?" In *King Lear,* everything, as France says, is "dismantle[d]" (I.i.220); even revelation and redemption are stripped, in ill-timed fulfillment of Lear's demand, from the thick rotundity of the earth. Cordelia, who once summoned the "unpublish'd virtues of the earth" (IV.iv.16), now lies "dead as earth" (V.iii.261), her rich potentiality as barren for this world as Chaucer's "droghte of March" would have been if uninspired by "Aprill with his shoures soote." As Elton says, "The Fifth Act shatters. . .the foundations of faith itself."[61]

But what of Lear? "Let us be sure," says Lawlor, "that [Lear] escapes punishment"; he achieves "no *final* realization of the waste he has wrought."[62] To deny Lear his final recognition of the *death* of Cordelia is to deny him tragic stature. Her death results from his initial error in surrendering his power. While that surrender led to the education of the man beneath the king, it led with equal inevitability to the destruction of what he had learned—of the truth that might have flowed into his kingdom. That Cordelia's death is *not* to be construed in any context of redemption or of hope is suggested by Lear's echo of the Homily Against the Fear of Death:

> If it be so,
> It is a chance which does redeem all sorrows
> That ever I have felt.

(V.iii.265-67)

> For death shall bee to him no death at all, but a very deliverance from death, from all paines, cares, and sorrowes, miseries, and wretchedness of this world, and the very entry into rest, and a beginning of everlasting joy.

It would be tempting to believe, even on the basis of the Homily, that Lear *does* see Cordelia alive, that his vision validates her continued life for his heart even if not for the world of the play. But such a reading makes the play "Christian" at precisely the moment where it presses a very different emphasis. There is so little evidence at play's end of *anyone's* entry into "everlasting joy" that critics seem compelled to read such an entry into Lear's final moment, into a world the text calls "cheerless, dark, and deadly" (V.iii.290). It is *that* pain, which Lear faces unblinkingly, that we must face as well. Having rejected Cordelia at the outset, Lear achieved an "entry into rest" in spite of himself, setting his "rest" finally on Cordelia's "kind nursery" (I.i.125-26). But that moment occurs *before* her death and becomes a dimension against which to measure Lear's sorrow. "Lear's anguish," Battenhouse suggests, "is much like that of a disciple assisting at the burial of all his earthly hopes." This insight strikes precisely the right note, but he continues: "are not the darkest hours just before dawn, and is not the Dark Night of the Soul the traditional preface to mystic vision?"[63] Perhaps, but analogy is not proof. And where *is* the analogue? What validates the assumption that Shakespeare is writing within the frame of the allegory Battenhouse ascribes to him? That the Good Friday analogy might apply, however, is suggested by

Lear's "O, you are men of stones,/ Had I your tongues and eyes, I'd use them so/ That heaven's vault should crack" (V.iii.257-59). Lear's rage at the apparent lack of response of the onlookers and his suggestion of a universal sundering is reminiscent of the Sermon of the Death and Passion of Christ, which recasts Matthew's account of the Crucifixion: "While Christ was yet hanging on the Crosse, and yealding up the Ghost, the Scripture witnesseth that the vayle of the Temple did rent in twaine and the earth did quake, that the stones clave asunder. . . . Shall man shew himselfe to bee more hardharted than stones. . .?" A Good Friday without a Resurrection becomes a Doomsday—"the promis'd end" (V.iii.263), or at least, in Edgar's typical filtering of reality, "an image of that horror" (V.iii.264).

Battenhouse complains that "Nicholas Brooke [infers] that the play at its ending *invalidates* the Christian hope of redemption. Only a blind or dogmatic skepticism would so infer."[64] The play invalidates the possibility of the Cordelia ethic's emerging through Lear into his kingdom, blocks the translation of Lear's original insight in preferring Cordelia into a "new society," ruled by the compassionate principle of Cordelia, not by the rigid will of Lear, which was capable only of becoming dragonlike when challenged. The Christian hope of redemption is hardly invalidated *per se*—it is not the function of Shakespeare's drama to approve or to refute doctrine—but that hope is snuffed out in and for the world of the play. The lips of the play's final speakers shape no redemption, neither a hope for a long earthly life nor for the world's realization of the meaning of Lear's positive experience. The final words accept the death Lear has accepted.

Lear should be permitted the dignity of seeing the ultimate ramification of his first error. That he *does* see is suggested by an odd reminder of the opening scene, where Cordelia quoted the words of the Marriage Service to him. At the end, Lear repeats the rhythms of the Service:

> Her voice was ever soft
> Gentle and low; an excellent thing in woman.
>
> (V.iii.272-73)

> So that the spirite be mild & quiete, whiche is a precious thing
> in the sighte of God.

His words can be interpreted as evidence of his failing mind,
of his belief that at this instant Cordelia lives, of his disorien-
tation at this terrible moment, but they convey his sense of
who Cordelia *was*—that perfect woman described in the Marriage Service and already personified by Shakespeare in Desdemona. Those psychiatric interpreters who see Lear as
merely another latent Mr. Warren (in Fitzgerald's *Tender is
the Night)* might reflect on the fact that the father who has
never responded to his daughters *as* women can not have
been much of a father. The pathos here (and by extension,
the tragedy) is that Lear responds to Cordelia the woman
after she is dead, remembers the quality of the voice he
couldn't hear in scene one. An implicit marriage *does*
occur—their spirits are wed. Lear goes off to prison not like
the "smug bridegroom" he said he would be as he met death
(IV.vi.202), but with a new-found joy of discovery and of anticipation of the further discoveries he and Cordelia will
achieve about "the mystery of things." "We two alone will
sing like birds i' the' cage" (V.iii.9), he says, predicting for
himself and Cordelia one of the aspects of matrimony mentioned in the Priest's opening exhortation: "the mutual
societie, helpe, and comfort, that the one ought to have of
the other, bothe in prosperity and adversitye." Lear defines
this purely spiritual marriage in describing the nature of
their kneeling to each other: "When thou dost ask me blessing, I'll kneel down/ And ask of thee forgiveness"
(V.iii.10-11). Cordelia seems to have come, finally, "to love
[her] father all." France seems almost irrelevant to her concern for Lear—almost, because France supplied the army she
importuned in "her ag'd father's right" (IV.iv.28). But death
follows hard upon Lear's reunion with Cordelia, his union
with himself.

Shakespeare takes pains to enforce the final bleakness, to
deny any comfort. No Malcolm steps in to wave all clouds
away, no angel echelons sing anyone to rest. No one *on stage*
remarks Lear's paroxysm of joy. Edgar, typically, believes
that Lear "faints" (V.iii.311) and tries to revive him with

words similar to those he used with his father: "Look up, my lord" (V.iii.313); (cf. "Do but look up," to blind Gloucester [IV.vi.59]). Kent rebuffs Edgar's effort with words suggesting that Lear's life has been torture, with Cordelia's death the final unbearable twist of the wheel:

Vex not his ghost; O, let him pass! He hates him
That would upon the rack of this tough world
Stretch him out longer.

(V.iii.314-16)

To make Lear the victim of deluded joy, to force one of Edgar's aphorisms on his final words, to deny that Lear is facing the fact of Cordelia's *death*, is to deny the validity of his experience, the reality of his pain, the relationship between his first mistake and the dead child he now holds in his arms, and the meaning of the play that bears his name. While Walter Kaufmann is wrong to label Shakespeare a modern existentialist, his words are consonant with the ending of *King Lear:*

Even with the word "nothing" Shakespeare had his sport; the confrontation with death is there no less than resolution, man's abandoned state, and above all the sheer absurdity of life. And what remains to man? The liberating feeling of pervasive disillusionment; the joy of honesty, integrity, and courage; and the grace of humor, love, and comprehensive tolerance: in one word, nobility.[65]

The ending achieves a final alienation from any order external to human experience; yet by doing so, it places a final stamp on Lear's hard-earned nobility. The last lines of the play convey confusion as to who will *reign* (V.iii.319-22), as if Lear's experience has worn out the possibilities for this world, and a marvelously appropriate textual uncertainty exists as to who has the final four lines, usually definitive in Shakespeare, not for what is said, but for who speaks. Whoever has them, they offer no solace:

The weight of this sad time we must obey;
Speak what we feel, not what we ought to say.*

* The line reminds us of Cordelia's speaking of truth in scene one.

The oldest hath borne most; we that are young
Shall never see so much, nor live so long.

(V.iii.323-26)

Whoever has them, their speaker has learned something. If
the lines are Albany's (as the Quarto assigns them), he shows
that his belief in "This judgement of the heavens" (V.iii.231)
was illusory. If they are Edgar's (as in the Folio), he sees
through his own efforts to coerce experience into an allegory
of benevolence. The final lines provide a negative context for
both Albany's "justicers" that "are above" (IV.ii.78-79) and
Edgar's "clearest gods, who make them honours/ Of men's
impossibilities" (IV.vi.73-74). "Christian tragedy," if the *genre*
exists within Shakespeare's canon, involves the destruction of
the Christian hope, whether in a character's rejection of it, as
in Hamlet, Othello, Macbeth, or Lear in his initial decision in
banishing Cordelia, or, in the case of the ending of *King
Lear,* in the snuffing out of Cordelia, just as her profound
comedy struggles to be born. The final words of the Folio
are the stage direction "Exeunt with a dead March."

As Maynard Mack says of the ending of *King Lear,* "only a
profound sense remains that an epoch, in fact a whole dispensation has closed."[66] Yet the play is tragic because it suggested the possibility of a new dispensation opening up.
Whatever the play's pagan bearings, virtue has emerged only
to be quickly extinguished. The hanging of Cordelia has no
positive results, no rising again (regardless of the hope ascribed to Lear by almost a century of critics), no broadcast of
disciples from out of the central insight, no flowing of new
wine into the ancient veins of the world. Albany had said,
"the King has come to his daughter" (V.i.21), suggesting
more than just "the King has come to his senses," suggesting
that Lear has come to his better self, to all that Cordelia, his
other daughter, represents. Lear says, in seeming refutation
of Christian hope, "Thou'lt come no more" (V.iii.307). And
his reiterated "never" (V.iii.308) seems to seal the Cordelia
ethic in its tomb. *King Lear* may be, as Maxwell says, "a Christian play about a pagan world,"[67] but at the end a world that
might, through its king, have embraced a Christian ethic, lies
dead as earth. *King Lear* is a history of the world because it

depicts in the ignorance of its willful king, the world's rejection of the Christian vision, and in his waking again, its *ex post facto* discovery of the truth. The end of the play is reminiscent of the exhausted world of Hemingway's Great War, the war that seemed to go on forever, of the parched and rainless expanse of Eliot's Wasteland, and of the post-human world described by Camus:

The years we have just gone through have killed something in us. And that something is simply the old confidence man had in himself, which led him to believe he could always elicit human reactions from another man if he spoke to him in the language of common humanity.

What is affirmed at the end of *King Lear* is not order or justice, but *experience:* "we that are young/ Shall never see so much," and the inevitability of death: "nor live so long" (V.iii.325-26). What lies beyond this the play does not tell us. It focuses on this world, on the human error and the sub-human monstrousness that insist that in *King Lear,* at least, the Divine Comedy must *precede* the Last Judgment.

Notes to Chapter 4: *King Lear*

1. William R. Elton, *King Lear and the Gods* (San Marino, Calif., 1966), pp. 336-37.
2. J. C. Maxwell, "The Technique of Invocation in *King Lear*," *MLR* 45 (1950): 142. Edmund Chambers, however, claims that "the plot, which deliberately rejects the Christian interpretation of the universe, is set in a pagan environment. The heavens are invoked in a pagan termonology, as Nature, or under the names of the classic deities. Pains are taken, contrary to the usual disregard of anachronisms in the plays, to avoid the introduction of Christian language or Christian sentiments." *Shakespeare: A Survey* (New York, n.d.), pp. 245-46. A partial list of Christian echoes and allusions (some, admittedly, as Elton suggests, products of "the play's peculiarly multiple syncretic vision," p. 237) would include Cordelia's "Oh dear father,/ It is thy business that I go about" (IV.iv.23-24); the possible echo in France's "Fairest Cordelia that art most rich being poor" (I.i.253) of 2 Corinthians 6: 10: "as poore, and yet making many rich: as having nothing, and yet possessing all thinges"; Lear's evocation of "hell...darkness...the sulphurous pit" (IV.vi.130); Gloucester's "hell-black night" (III.vii.59), and his use of the word *heaven* (IV.vi.229)—perhaps a necessary substitution if *King Lear* were written after the passage of the Profanity Statutes); and the Third Servant's "Now, heaven help him!" (III.viii.106) (the singular "heaven" suggests that the punctuation of "Gods spies" [V.iii.17]—unpunctuated in both Q and F.—should be "God's," not as Muir renders it, "Gods' "; see his n17, p. 200 of the New Arden Edition); Edgar's re-

hearsal of the Ten Commandments (III.iv.80-83, 95-99) and of the Seven
Deadly Sins (III.iv.85-95); the Gentleman's reference to Cordelia's tears as
"holy water from her heavenly eyes" (IV.iii.32); Albany's "devil" (IV.ii.59);
Lear's " 'Ay' and 'No' too was no good divinity" (IV.vi.101-102), which has two
possible biblical sources: 2 Corinthians 1: 18-19: "Yea God is faithfull, for our
word to you was not yea, and nay, For God's sonne Iesus Christ. . .was not yea
and nay, but in him it was yea," and James 5:12: "but let your yea be yea, and
your naye, naye, lest ye fall into condemnation," Lear's "drench'd our steeples"
(III.ii.3), Edgar's "Prince of Darkness" (III.iv.147), and his "Childe Rowland"
(III.iv.185; Roland being Charlemagne's nephew and the hero of *Chason de
Roland*); and the Fool's references to "priests," "heretics," and "churches"
(III.ii.81-90), although admittedly in "a prophecy Merlin shall make" (III.ii.95).
3. Kenneth Muir, "Introduction," *King Lear* (New Arden Edition, Cambridge,
   Mass., 1964), p. lvii.
4. Elton, *King Lear and the Gods*, p. 334. For a summary of the pagan-Christian debate relative to *King Lear*, see Elton, *King Lear and the Gods*, pp. 3-8. Elton, of
   course, develops the pagan view and is unfair, I believe, to characterize "Christian" critics as espousing the "view that *Lear* is an optimistically Christian
   drama." The translation of Christian themes into dramatic form need not be
   optimistic. On this question, see Kenneth Myrick, "Christian Pessimism in *King
   Lear*," *Shakespeare 1564-1964*, ed. Edward A. Bloom (Providence, R.I.,) pp.
   56-70. In addition to Elton's concise review of the debate, see Hiram Haydn,
   The Counter-Renaissance, pp. 636-51 (Haydn sees the play as a "fight for supremacy" between "the protagonists of Nature and Stoicism" [p. 638]), and Sears
   Jayne, "Charity in *King Lear*," *SQ* 15, no. 2 (Spring 1964): 277-88 (Jayne sees
   the play as "harshly pagan" [p. 287]). A further Christian interpretation, not
   mentioned by Elton, is Irving Ribner, " 'The Gods are just': A Reading of *King
   Lear*," *Tulane Drama Review* 2 (1958): 34-54 (Ribner emphasizes *King Lear's*
   kinship to the morality tradition). O. J. Campbell, "The Salvation of Lear,"
   ELH 14 (1947): 93-109, sees *King Lear* as a morality play and an expression of
   Elizabethan stoicism, but sees Lear as an unstoical man. Paul N. Siegel, "Adversity and the Miracle of Love in *King Lear*," *SQ* 6 (1955): 325-36, sees the play as
   an expression of "Christian Stoicism." Maynard Mack, *King Lear in Our Time*
   (Berkeley, Calif., 1965), pp. 61-62, equates Edgar with the Morality hero:

   > Edgar is attended by "fiends" who have misled him through a partly
   > moralized landscape of "fire and flame," "bog and quagmire," and has
   > been tempted to suicide with knife and halter, as happens often to the
   > Morality hero. Recollections of the Seven Deadly Sins, which he has prac-
   > ticed (III,iv,85-90) and of the Ten Commandments, which he now bids his
   > hearers keep (III,iv,80-83, 95-99), run through his wild chatter, in which
   > we recognize at some moments the morality theme of Pride and Corrupt
   > Sensuality turned out of doors.

   Edgar becomes, then, an *allegory* of Lear's experience, and comments upon it
   only insofar as allegory highlights the simpler outlines of more complex modes.
   Lear will reiterate the suicide theme ("If you have poison for me, I will drink
   it": IV.vii.72). Both Elton and H. B. Charlton (*Shakespearian Tragedy*, pp.
   189-229) stress the overt Christianity of *The True Chronicle History of King Lear*.
   But that Shakespeare has not imported the Christian machinery intact from the
   older play does not exclude a "Christian" interpretation of *King Lear*.
   Shakespeare's plays often question the premises from which other dramatists
   begin. In the case of King Lear, the question of Christianity is not answered
   but asked, and the result is that it is more powerfully operative on the mind

and imagination of the spectator. As Maxwell says of *Hamlet,* "just because the central moral question about revenge is not overtly raised, and is, indeed, kept from the full recognition of the hero, it can be built into the central fabric of the play." Shakespeare: The Middle Plays," *The Age of Shakespeare,* p. 10.

5. Dolora Cunningham, *"Macbeth:* The Tragedy of the Hardened Heart," *SQ* 14 (1963): 46.

6. Maynard Mack, *King Lear in Our Time,* p. 77.

7. William H. Chaplin, "Form and Psychology in *King Lear,*" *Literature and Psychology* 19 (Fall-Winter 1969): 31-45.

8. The distinction between "moral" and "political" aspects of the play and the King will probably be clear to most readers. It is essentially the Aristotelian distinction between "ethics" and "politics," but "moral" has more spiritual connotation than "ethics." To use "spiritual" would be misleading, for at this point in the play Lear's spiritual self is still latent beneath the layers of his will. "Political" can be taken to suggest that which affects the king *qua* king—his relationship to his realm. "Moral" suggests the man and his relationships to other men. Ernst H. Kantorowitz's definition of "the king's two bodies" applies generally here.

9. D. A. Traversi, *"King Lear,"* *Stratford Papers on Shakespeare,* 1964, ed. B. W. Jackson (Toronto, 1965), p. 183. See also Traversi's useful discussion of Cordelia's "bond" in *An Approach to Shakespeare,* pp. 181-87. Other informative discussions of Lear's relationship to his daughters are Theodore Spencer, *Shakespeare and the Nature of Man,* pp. 135-52, particularly pp. 142-45, and William Rosen, *Shakespeare and the Craft of Tragedy* (Cambridge, Mass., 1960), pp. 1-51, particularly pp. 1-9.

10. Cf. *Othello,* II.i.81 and V.ii.10-13.

11. Robert Ornstein, *The Moral Vision of Jacobean Tragedy,* p. 264: "His division of the kingdom among three daughters to 'prevent future strife' seems eminently sensible and has disastrous consequences only because two of his daughters are Goneril and Regan." One might reply by saying that two of his daughters *are* Goneril and Regan, a "given" Lear could have examined. Sigurd Burckhardt calls "the error" (the division of the kingdom) "a noble one." *Shakespearean Meanings* (Princeton, N.J., 1958), p. 240. Francis G. Schoff claims that "For this point. . .that Lear is derelict in duty and shows lack of political wisdom in his resignation of rule. . .evidence is in effect non-existent. The play, in short, fails completely to support any such thesis." "King Lear: Moral Example or Tragic Protagonist?" *SQ* 13 (Spring 1962): 159-60. The current chapter could be considered a rebuttal to Professor Schoff's assertion. In addition, one could cite *Gorboduc,* and King James's vehement stand against the division of his kingdom. Elton states that "James hoped even that the names England and Scotland should vanish in the name of Britain." *King Lear and the Gods,* p. 244, n175. On the question of sixteenth- and early-seventeenth-century opinion regarding the division of a kingdom, see David S. Willson, "King James I and Anglo-Scottish Unity," *Conflict in Stuart England,* ed. William A. Aiken and Basil D. Henning (New York, 1960), pp. 41-55. On *King Lear* and *Gorboduc,* see Barbara H. C. De Mendonca, "The Influence of *Gorboduc* on *King Lear,*" *Shakespeare Survey* 13 (Cambridge, 1960): 41-48. Sears Jayne suggests that "what matters most in the first scene is not the dissolution of the kingdom, but. . .that he is alienated from the person he most loves, and whose love he most needs. . . ." "Charity in *King Lear,*" p. 278. While this emphasis is probably valid, it tends to emphasize one action to the exclusion of another. Lear's two acts in the first scene cohere in

the death of the person he most loves. For an analysis of the political disorder *per se* in *King Lear,* see Edwin Muir, "The Politics of *King Lear,*" *Essays in Literature and Society* (London, 1949), pp. 31-48. For other negative views of Lear's division of his kingdom, see Harold S. Wilson, *On the Design of Shakespearian Tragedy* (Toronto, 1957), p. 191; John W. Draper, "Political Themes in Shakespeare's Later Plays," *JEGP* 35 (1936): 61-93; and Clifford Leech, *Shakespeare's Tragedies and Other Studies in Seventeenth Century Drama* (New York, 1950), p. 77. For suggestions that Lear violates natural law in the first scene, see Hardin Craig, *An Interpretation of Shakespeare* (New York, 1949), pp. 207-8; Irving Ribner, *The English History Play in the Age of Shakespeare* (Princeton, 1957), p. 249; James L. Rosier, "The Lex Aeterna and *King Lear,*" *JEGP* 53 (1954): 578; Theodore Spencer, *Shakespeare and the Nature of Man,* p. 142; and Virgil Whitaker, *Shakespeare's Use of Learning* (San Marino, Calif., 1953), pp. 303-4. All but Whitaker emphasize Lear's division of his kingdom. Whitaker concentrates upon the rejection of Cordelia.

12. Roy W. Battenhouse, "Shakespeare's Moral Vision," p. 163.
13. *Ibid.,* p. 163.
14. *Coleridge's Shakespearean Criticism,* ed. Thomas M. Raysor, 1:55.
15. Quoted by Kenneth Muir in the New Arden *King Lear,* p. 58, n40. Muir applies the statement to Lear's "To take't again perforce!" (I.v.43) and compares I.iv.330-32. I am unable to find Johnson's statement in a primary source. In his madness, Lear not only reiterates the threat, but multiplies his army by ten: "To have a thousand with red burning spits/ Come hissing in upon 'em." (III.vi.15-16).
16. John Lawlor, *The Tragic Sense in Shakespeare* (London, 1960), pp. 166-68. On time in *King Lear,* see Elton, *King Lear and the Gods,* p. 106, n71.
17. Harold Wilson, *On the Design of Shakespearian Tragedy,* p. 193.
18. Alfred Harbage, *William Shakespeare: A Reader's Guide,* p. 414.
19. M. St. Clare Byrne, "*King Lear* at Stratford-on-Avon," *SQ* 11 (1960): 205.
20. A connection between this "disloyal" servant and the "loyal" Oswald is established when Oswald shouts "Out, dunghill!" to Edgar (IV.vi.249). Cornwall denies burial to the servant who has slain him by ordering, "throw this slave/ Upon the dunghill" (III.vii.96-97). Oswald begs his slayer, Edgar, to bury him ("If ever thou wilt thrive, bury my body" [IV.vi.253]). Shakespeare would seem to be employing pagan conventions regarding burial (cf. *Antigone,* as opposed to Act V, scene 1 of *Hamlet*). Whether the "pagan/Christian" question can be resolved is debatable, as shown by the following lines:

Unto a dunghill, which shall be thy grave,
And there cut off thy most ungracious head. . .
Leaving thy trunk for crows to feed upon.
                          —Iden to the corpse of Cade, *II Henry VI,* IV.x.76-81.

Some loving friends convey the Emperor hence
And give him burial in his father's grave.
My father and Lavinia shall forthwith
Be closed in our household's monument.
As for that ravenous tiger, Tamora,

No funeral rite, nor man in mourning weed,
No mournful bell shall ring her burial;
But throw her forth to beasts and birds to prey.
Her life was beastly and devoid of pity,
And being dead, let birds on her take pity!

Lucius in *Titus Andronicus*, V.iii.191-200

21. William Elton, *King Lear and the Gods,* pp. 330-31. Elton seconds Gloucester's
formulation comparing men to flies killed for sport (p. 332).

22. It is hard to agree with Traversi that Edgar becomes "increasingly the mouth-
piece for the play's deeper meanings" ("King Lear," p. 195), or with R. A.
Foakes that Edgar represents "the norm" from which the "aberration" of evil
deviates ("Shakespeare's Later Tragedies," *Shakespeare: 1564-1964,* p. 100). If
Edgar mouths the play's deeper meanings—if the work can be reduced to
aphorisms—then it doesn't mean very deeply. For dissenting opinions on
Edgar's role, see Nicholas Brooke, *King Lear* (New York, 1963), particularly pp.
36-47, and my "Malcolm and Edgar," *Discourse* 11, no. 4 (Autumn 1968):
430-38. For a defense of Edgar "as the wise and active pattern for man in a
tough world," see Hugh Maclean, "Disguise in *King Lear:* Kent and Edgar," *SQ*
11 (1960): 49-54.

23. John Lawlor, *The Tragic Sense in Shakespeare,* p. 166.

24. David Horowitz, *Shakespeare: An Existential View* (New York, 1965), pp. 117-18.
On "kindness" see also Charlton, *Shakespearian Tragedy,* pp. 226-27.

25. Stella Brook, *The Language of the Book of Common Prayer* (New York, 1965), p.
145.

26. Cf. Albany to Goneril:
She that herself will sliver and disbranch
From her material sap, perforce must wither
And come to deadly use.

(IV.iii.34-36)

And the Anglican Commination against Sinners:
So that every tree which bringeth not forth good fruict, is hewen downe, and
cast into the fire.

Also, Albany to Goneril:
You are not worth the dust which the rude wind
Blows in your face.

(IV.iii.30-31)

And Psalms 1:4:
The wicked are not so, but as the chaffe, which the wind driveth away.

27. Parker, *Slave of Life,* p. 132.

28. Rosen, *Shakespeare and the Craft of Tragedy,* p. 41.

29. David Horowitz, *Shakespeare: An Existential View,* p. 83.

30. Robert Heilman, *This Great Stage: Image and Structure in King Lear* (Baton Rouge,
La., 1948), p. 86. See also W. R. Keast's ruthless rebuttal of Heilman's thesis:
"Imagery and Meaning in the Interpretation of *King Lear,*" *MP* 57 (1949):
45-64.

31. H. Granville-Barker, *Prefaces to Shakespeare,* 1: 294. For an excellent discussion
of justice in *King Lear,* see Lawlor, *The Tragic Sense in Shakespeare,* pp. 153-83.

32. D. A. Traversi, "King Lear," p. 185. For a concise summary of "Cordelia criticism," see John F. Danby, *Shakespeare's Doctrine of Nature* (London, 1961), pp. 114-25. On Cordelia as Christ-figure, see S. L. Bethel, *Shakespeare and the Popular Dramatic Tradition* (Durham, N.C., 1944), pp. 66-68; Paul N. Siegel "Adversity and the Miracle of Love in King Lear," pp. 325-36; and William W. Main, *King Lear* (New York, 1962), pp. 173-83.

33. Alfred Harbage, *William Shakespeare*, p. 401.

34. Roy W. Battenhouse, "Shakespeare's Moral Vision," p. 165.

35. Battenhouse, *Shakespearean Tragedy*, p. 284.

36. David Horowitz, *Shakespeare: An Existential View*, p. 122.

37. Harold Wilson, *On the Design of Shakespearian Tragedy*, p. 184.

38. Danby's suggestion occurs in *Shakespeare's Doctrine of Nature*, p. 125. Muir's objection is in the Arden *King Lear*, p. 183, n208. Battenhouse, in "Shakespeare's Moral Vision," p. 158, supports Danby.

39. On the meaning of the storm, see John Holloway, *The Story of the Night*, pp. 76-77 ("For the Elizabethans, the End of the World was a living conviction and even something of a current fear") and H. B. Charlton, *Shakespearian Tragedy*, pp. 207-12 ("The storm becomes the dynamic symbol of the energy which vitalizes the play's universe").

40. Nicholas Brooke, *King Lear*, p. 45.

41. Cf. a similar use of the birthday motif:

> Cleopatra: It is my birthday.
> I had thought t'have held it poor; but, since my lord
> Is Antony again, I will be Cleopatra.
>
> (III.xiii.185-87)

42. Kenneth Muir, *King Lear* (New Arden ed.), p. 190, n47.

43. Elton must, of course, fit these lines into his pagan theory as if the play emerged from a static set of doctrinal premises. He writes the lines off as an example "of the play's peculiarly multiple syncretic vision" (p. 237), suggesting that while the lines "may well indicate. . .the happy state of the virtuous soul," it could be "pagan as well as Christian" (*King Lear and the Gods*, p. 258). The point, I believe, is that this is a scene in a play—the first of *King Lear's* "two endings"—one whose effect is the result of a dynamic development. To see Cordelia as patterned rigidly upon a theory is to smother drama in doctrine.

44. Maynard Mack, *King Lear in Our Time*, p. 50. Cf. Dr. Faustus, also pleading from the far side of salvation: "See, see, where Christ's blood streams in the firmament!/ One drop would save my soul—half a drop!" (XIV. 86-87), and Donne in sonnets 5 and 6 of the La Carona sequence: "Moyst with one drop of thy blood, my dry soule." Shakespeare alludes directly at least twice to the Lazarus story: Falstaff refers to his platoon as "slaves as ragged as Lazarus in the painted cloth where the glutton's dogs licked his sores" (*I Henry IV*, IV.ii.27-29), and where the Hostess refers to Falstaff as "in Arthur's bosom, if ever man went to Arthur's bosom" (*Henry V*, II.iii.9-11), and at least once to Nebuchadnezzar: "I am no great Nebuchadnezzar, sir; I have not much skill in grass" (*All's Well that Ends Well*, IV.v.21-22).

45. Robert Heilman, *This Great Stage*, p. 142.

46. Brook, *Language of the Book of Common Prayer*, p. 200.

47. William Elton, *King Lear and the Gods*, p. 239.

48. West, *Shakespeare and the Outer Mystery*, p. 159.

49. Nicholas Brooke, *King Lear*, p. 47.
50. D. G. James, *The Dream of Learning*, p. 111.
51. Battenhouse, *Shakespearean Tragedy*, p. 275.
52. G. Wilson Knight, *The Wheel of Fire*, p. 206. For a qualification of Knight's view, see John Holloway, *The Story of the Night*, pp. 91-95, and Sears Jayne, "Charity in *King Lear*," pp. 277-88.
53. John Lawlor, *The Tragic Sense in Shakespeare*, p. 174.
54. John Holloway, *The Story of the Night*, pp. 76-77.
55. Auerbach, *Mimesis*, p. 13.
56. *Ibid.*, p. 49.
57. *Ibid.*, p. 11.
58. A. C. Bradley, *Shakespearean Tragedy*, p. 234.
59. Theodore Spencer, *Shakespeare and the Nature of Man*, p. 152.
60. *Samuel Johnson on Shakespeare*, ed. W. K. Wimsatt, Jr. (New York, 1960), p. 97. I will not attempt to list the many critics who have absorbed Bradley's thesis uncritically. Several who qualify Bradley or disagree with him are John Peter, *Complaint and Satire in Early English Literature* (Oxford, 1956), pp. 211-12; J. Stampfer, "The Catharsis of *King Lear*," *Shakespeare Survey* 13 (Cambridge, 1960), pp. 1-19; Robert Ornstein, *The Moral Vision of Jacobean Tragedy*, pp. 273-76; Nicholas Brooke, "The Ending of *King Lear*," *Shakespeare: 1564-1964*, pp. 71-87, and *King Lear*, pp. 47-60; and D. G. James, *The Dream of Learning*, p. 104. For views that do not commit themselves either to the Bradleyan or the "existential" ending, see Maynard Mack, *King Lear in Our Time*, pp. 110-17, and Helen Gardner, *"King Lear,"* The John Coffin Memorial Lecture, 1966 (London, 1967), pp. 26-28.
61. William Elton, *King Lear and the Gods*, p. 337.
62. John Lawlor, *The Tragic Sense in Shakespeare*, p. 168.
63. Battenhouse, *Shakespearean Tragedy*, p. 288.
64. *Ibid.*, p. 290.
65. Walter Kaufmann, *From Shakespeare to Existentialism* (New York, 1960), pp. 18-19.
66. Mack, *King Lear in Our Time*, p. 86.
67. Maxwell, "The Technique of Invocation in *King Lear*," p. 142.

5
Macbeth

The just cause of the bad angels' misery is their departure
from that High Essence to turn back upon themselves...what
can cause the will's evil, the will being sole cause of all evil?

St. Augustine, *The City
of God* (XII, vi)

Ah, Jesus! is all come hereto?
Lo, fair words maketh fools fain;
They promise and nothing will do certain.

Everyman, 378-80

What, is great Mephistophilis so passionate
For being deprived of the joys of heaven?
Learn thou of Faustus manly fortitude.

*The Tragical History of
Dr. Faustus* (III, 98-100)

In medieval art, according to Erich Auerbach, "everything
tragic was but a figure or reflection of a single complex of
events, into which it necessarily flowed at last—the complex
of the Fall, of Christ's birth and passion, and the Last
Judgement."[1] If these great tragedies reflect the outlines of
some profound allegory, if they imitate the rhythms of Christian myth, the allegory is hardly the same for each of them.
King Lear would seem to emerge from a movement encompassing the Fall, the birth of Christ, and a Last Judgment in

314

which good and evil are equally condemned, in which no mediator intercedes for humanity with whatever ruling power there may be. Part of the play's power to disturb emanates from its *not* following a "usual" allegorical pattern. Indeed, *King Lear* refutes the comedy it educates its audience to anticipate. In *Macbeth* Shakespeare selects a different sector, or arrangement, of myth for its dramatic shaping—the Fall, a further fall, which imitates that of both Adam and the Angels, into a damnation-on-earth (and, in Scotland, *of* earth), and the coming of a Messiah who *does* redeem the world.

At the end of *King Lear,* Albany's effort to behave as spokesman for some ruling principle is drowned by the final sorrow:

> you, to your rights,
> With boot, and such addition as your honours
> Have more than merited. All friends shall taste
> The wages of their virtue, and all foes
> The cup of their deservings.
>
> (V.iii.300-304)

The words are noble enough, but are not rooted in any reality of the "justice" they attempt to imitate. "O, see, see!" Albany must cry (V.iii.304), gazing upon Lear and his dead child. Malcolm's words resonate with his conviction—and ours—of his positive alliance with "the grace of Grace" (V.viii.72). He is the son of Duncan, who embodied the God-like principle in Scotland and who was murdered in a sacrilege that, like the murders of Desdemona and Cordelia, draws upon the Crucifixion to underline its horror. Assisted by the product of a "miracle birth," Macduff, and the sacrifice of the son of Old Siward, Malcolm restores Scotland to the rhythms and propriety of "measure, time and place" (V.viii.73), to that order splendidly expressed in "An Exhortation concerning good order, and obedience to Rulers and Magistrates":

> Almighty God hath created and appointed all things in heaven, earth, and waters, in a most excellent and perfect order. In Heaven, hee hath appointed distinct and severall orders and

states or Archangels and Angels. In earth hee hath assigned and appointed kings, princes, with other governours under them, in all good and necessary order. The water above is kept, and rayneth downe in due time and season. The Sun, Moone, Starres, Rainebow, Thunder, Lightning, Clouds, and all Birdes of the ayre, doe keepe their order. The Earth, Trees, Seedes, Plants, Hearbes, Corne, Grasse, and all manner of Beasts keepe themselves in order: all the part of the whole yeare, as Winter, Summer, Moneths, Nights and Dayes, continue in their order: all kindes of fishes in the Sea, Rivers and Waters, with all fountaines. Springs, yea, the Seas themselves keepe their comely course and order: and man himselfe also hath all his parts both within and without, as soule, heart, minde, memory, understanding, reason, speech, with all and singular corporall members of his body in a profitable, necessarie, and pleasant order: every degree of people in their vocation, calling and office, hath appointed to them their duty and order: some are in high degree, some in low, some kings and princes, some inferiours and subjects, priests, and laymen, masters and servants, fathers and children, husbands and wives, rich and poore, and every one have neede of other, so that in all things is to bee lauded and praised the goodly order of God, without the which no house, no Citie, no Commonwealth can continue and endure, or last, for where there is no right order, there reigneth all abuse, carnall liberty, enormitie, sinne, and Babylonicall confusion. Take away Kings, Princes, Rulers, Magistrates, Judges, and such estates of Gods order, no man shall ride or goe by the high way unrobbed, no man shall sleepe in his owne house or bedde unkilled, no man shall keepe his wife, children, and possession in quietnesse, all things shall bee common, and there must needes follow all mischiefe, and utter destruction both of soules, bodies, goodes, and common wealthes.

This is the order Macbeth violates virtually point by point, from its cosmic dimensions to the inmost recesses of his humanity, and the results for Scotland are as the Homily says they are. This is the order Malcolm definitively restores, promising in his last lines a version of the ceremony with which comedies end—his coronation. The vivid contrast between what Macbeth has meant and what Malcolm will mean to Scotland is summarized neatly by the Homily on Rogation Week: "If [God's] especiall goodness were not everywhere present, every creature should be out of order, and no creature should have his propertie wherein hee was first created."

The opening scenes of *Macbeth* project a fallen world, one

that seems to have eaten of the fruit of the tree of good and evil and cannot tell the two apart. Ambiguity—"Fair is foul, and foul is fair" (I.i.11), "fair and foul" (I.iii.38)—resounds ominously through the early portions of the play, as two of Banquo's utterances testify:

> Good sir, why do you start, and seem to fear
> Things that do sound so fair?
>
> (I.iii.51-52)

And more negatively:

> Thou hast it now: King, Cawdor, Glamis, all,
> As the weird women promis'd, and, I fear,
> Thou play'dst most foully for't.
>
> (III.i.1-3)

Moral confusion is concentrated, of course, in Macbeth:

> This supernatural soliciting
> Cannot be ill, cannot be good.
>
> (I.iii.130-31)

>   function
> Is smother'd in surmise, and nothing is
> But what is not.
>
> (I.iii.140-42)

The words of the opening scenes, like those two spent swimmers of whom the wounded Captain speaks, "cling together/ And choke their art" (I.ii.8-9). Often the lines say two things about Macbeth—they praise him as a hero and, prophetlike, predict his coming treason:

>   Norway himself,
> With terrible numbers,
> Assisted by that most disloyal traitor,
> The Thane of Cawdor, began a dismal conflict;
> Till that Bellona's bridegroom, lapp'd in proof,
> Confronted him with self-comparisons,
> Point against point, rebellious arm 'gainst arm.
>
> (I.ii.5-56)

The lines suggest that Macbeth confronted Cawdor as well as Sweno—a self-comparison that becomes an ominous mirror reflecting treason present and future. The hint is reinforced by the adjective "rebellious," which points across the sentence to modify the second arm—Macbeth's. This subversion of a line's primary meaning recurs in Ross's greeting to Macbeth:

> The King hath happily receiv'd, Macbeth,
> The news of thy success; and when he reads
> Thy personal venture in the rebels' fight
> His wonders and his praises do contend,
> Which should be thine or his.
>
> (I.iii.89-93)

"Personal venture in the rebels' fight"—his heroic effort against rebellion *and* his personal role in the ultimate treason. The contradictory lines continue, the poetry itself committing treason against its ostensible meaning:

> He finds thee in the stout Norweyan ranks,
> Nothing afeard of what thyself didst make,
> Strange images of death.
>
> (I.iii.95-97)

The word "strange" reminds us, perhaps, of the earlier startling contrast between Lennox's description of Ross's approach and Ross's first words:

> Lennox.   What a haste looks through his eyes! So should he look
>   That seems to speak things strange.
> Ross.   God save the King!
>
> (I.ii.46-47)

Ross's mention of Macbeth "in the stout Norweyan ranks" predicts that Macbeth will soon be among the enemies of the king, making a stranger image of death, "The great doom's image" (II.iii.83). That "horrid image" (I.iii.135) has already frightened him.

In that Macbeth is a man in a fallen world, the play concerns the further fall of man—the loss of his soul. But in that Macbeth stands closest to royal favor (with the exception of Malcolm) in a potentially redeemable world, his fall parallels that of Lucifer, who stood closest to God (with the exception of the Son). That the falls of Lucifer and Adam are equatable is suggested by the Homily on the Passion: "Adam. . .in eating the apple forbidden him, at the motion and suggestion of his wife. . .was cast out of Paradise. . .no longer a citizen of heaven: but a fire brand of hell, and a bond slave of the Divell." "Christian philosophy," says Walter C. Curry, "recognizes two tragedies of cosmic importance: 1) the fall of Lucifer and a third part of the angelic hosts, who rebelled against God and were cast out, and 2) the fall of Adam, who was originally endowed with perfection and freedom but who set his will against God's will and so brought sin and limited freedom upon mankind."[2] Macbeth's fall draws on the combined archetypes of the falls of Lucifer and Adam—and on more, of course, since it is also his own.

The play abounds in allusions to fallen angels. The Porter mentions "Belzebub" (II.iii.4) even as Macbeth's soul is absorbing the dimensions of its fall. Suspicious of Macduff, Malcolm says that "Angels are bright still, though the brightest fell" (IV.iii.22). Thinking perhaps of Macbeth, Malcolm recasts what his father once said about finding the mind's construction in the face:

> Though all things foul would wear the brows of grace
> Yet grace must still look so.
>
> (IV.iii.23-24)

Malcolm is paraphrasing the Geneva gloss on Genesis iii; here, the bright deceitful angel is linked to the myth of Eden:

> As Satan can change himselfe into an Angel of light, so did he abuse the wisdome of the serpent to deceive man.

The play is full of direct references to "Devilish Macbeth" (IV.iii.117). He is a "hell-kite" (IV.iii.217) and a "hell-hound" (V.viii.3). Hell can produce neither a "devil more damn'd/ In evils" (IV.iii.56-57) nor a "hotter name" (V.vii.6). Recognizing that Macbeth is doomed, Macduff taunts him as a subordinate fiend:

> Despair thy charm!
> And let the angel whom thou still hast serv'd

Tell thee, Macduff was from his mother's womb
Untimely ripp'd.

(V.viii.13-16)

As Nevill Coghill suggests, it is "as if the war in Heaven were still going on and Macbeth had allowed himself to be dragged in on the wrong side."[3]

One of the metaphors underlying and underlining the dramatic shaping of the play is that of winged things—guilt and innocence, darkness and light, order and disorder, nature and supernature, are consistently imaged as things that fly. The effect of the imagery is to *contrast* the "two worlds" of the play, the sub-nature of damnation, to which Macbeth plunges Scotland and himself, and the supernature, which returns to restore harmony to a kingdom echoing to the beat of dark wings.

Most of the birds and creatures winging through the world of the play are negative elements emerging from order perverted. The Witches "Hover through the fog and filthy air" (I.i.11), producing from each quarter of the compass winds that starve their enemies and leave them sleepless (I.iii.19-23). The Witches disappear into their own element:

Banquo.   Wither are they vanish'd?
Macbeth.   Into the air; and what seem'd corporal melted
             As breath into the wind.

(I.iii.80-82)

Later, after they have translated Macbeth's demand into the imagery of Banquo's issue, Macbeth will curse them: "Infected be the air whereon they ride" (IV.ii.138). Scotland's atmosphere is infected by "Lamentings heard i' th' air; strange screams of death,/ And prophesying with accents terrible/ Of dire combustion and confus'd events/ New hatch'd to th' woeful time" (II.ii.61-64). The hatching of winged things brings strange sounds and unnatural events to Scotland's filthy air:

The raven himself is hoarse
That croaks the fatal entrance of Duncan
Under my battlements.

(I.v.39-41)

At the moment of the murder, Lady Macbeth hears the "owl. . .shriek. . .the fatal bellman/ Which gives the stern'st goodnight" (II.ii.3-4)—the owl, "The obscure bird/ Clamour'd the livelong night" (II.iii.64-65), in contrast to the "bird of dawning" Marcellus mentions, genius of "wholesome" nights (*Hamlet,* I.i.160-62). A "mousing owl," violating the hierarchy within which it has been placed, rises up and becomes a hawk, downing a kingly "falcon, tow'ring in her pride of place" (II.iv.12-13). "Wool of bat. . .and howlet's wing" are among the ingredients of the Witches' horrible broth (IV.i.15-17). Lady Macduff, left like a "Poor bird" (IV.ii.34) by her husband's flight, condemns it as contrary to the instincts of nature:

> He loves us not,
> He wants the natural touch; for the poor wren,
> The most diminutive of birds, will fight,
> Her young ones in her nest against the owl.
>
> (IV.ii.8-11)

She is, however, "in this earthly world, where to do harm/ Is often laudable, to do good sometime/ Accounted dangerous folly" (IV.ii.75-77); she is trapped in Macbeth's world, where even the wren flees its offspring, leaving them no escape: "Whither should I fly?" (IV.ii.73). Malcolm pretends to be a "vulture" (IV.iii.74) to test Macduff, but after Macduff is reconciled to Malcolm's virtue, Macduff must employ Malcolm's metaphor to express the reality of Macbeth's slaughter of his family:

> All my pretty ones?
> Did you say all? O hell-kite! All?
> What, all my pretty chickens and their dam
> At one fell swoop?
>
> (IV.iii.216-19)

As they did to the "merciless Macdonwald" (I.ii.9), "The multiplying villainies of nature. . .swarm upon" (I.ii.11-12) Macbeth, who invokes the instruments of darkness in the shrouded forests near his castle, before his murder of Banquo:

> ere the bat hath flown
> His cloister'd flight, ere to black Hecate's summons
> The shard-borne beetle with his drowsy hums
> Hath rung night's yawning peal, there shall be done
> A deed of dreadful note. . .
> Light thickens, and the crow
> Makes wing to the rooky wood;
> Good things of day begin to droop and drowse,
> Whiles night's black agents to their preys do rouse.
>
> (III.ii.40-53)

But the "other world" of the play, of light, innocence, natural order, and the positive supernature is also represented by things that fly. Even the entrails of birds inform upon Macbeth:

> Augures and understood relations have
> By maggot-pies and choughs and rooks brought forth
> The secret'st man of blood.
>
> (III.iv.124-26)

The swarming villainies of nature become, for Lady Macbeth, "thick-coming fancies/ That keep her from her rest" (V.iii.38-39). Their own natures turn against them, their own inner reflection of the great creative universe that circumscribes the action condemns them. When Macbeth's will was aligned with order, he was as an "eagle" to a "sparrow," the former obviously superior to the latter in the battle against Scotland's enemies (I.ii.35), as opposed to the perverted triumph of the "mousing owl" over the "falcon" (II.iv.12-13). Duncan apologized to a victorious Macbeth because the "swiftest wing of recompense is slow/ To overtake thee" (I.v.17-18). In Duncan's world, the "temple-haunting martlet" was symbolic of "procreant" nature (I.vi.4-8), while "angels trumpet tongu'd" were agents of an outraged supernature, which would greet his murder by mounting "heaven's cherubin. . . Upon the sightless couriers of the air" (I.vii.19-23). Even knee-deep in murder, Macbeth expresses the order he would destroy:

> Banquo, thy soul's flight
> If it find heaven, must find it out to-night.
>
> (III.i.141-42)

And, as Fleance escapes, Macduff also flees, moving ahead of the time Macbeth would subdue to his will:

> Time, thou anticipat'st my dread exploits:
> The flighty purpose never is o'er took
> Unless the deed go with it.
>
> (IV.i.144-46)

The wings of positive recompense now fly faster than Macbeth's will and the revenge he himself has predicted marshals beyond Scotland's borders, soon to be lined with the thanes who "fly" (V.iii.7) from Macbeth:

> Some holy angel
> Fly to the court of England and unfold
> His message ere he come, that a swift blessing
> May soon return to this our suffering country
> Under a hand accurs'd.
>
> (III.vi.45-49)

The "powers above/ Put on their instruments," enlisting in Malcolm's crusade (IV.iii.238-39). "Angels are bright still" (IV.iii.22) and, in the world of *Macbeth* more than in any of the other tragedies, represent an order superior to that of the fallen angel, Macbeth, and his winged world of ravens, bats, beetles, rooks, usurping mousing owls, and unnameable agents of night, rousing to their defenseless preys.*

Duncan's actions during the opening scenes, however, share their quality of ambiguity. He attempts to engender Eden on earth, yet helps to promote his murder. As Macbeth returns from battle, Duncan assumes the role of Creator, his rightful role within the Kingdom of Scotland:

> I have begun to plant thee, and will labour
> To make thee full of growing.
>
> (I.iv.28-29)

Macbeth is in a state of grace. If he remains under this beneficent aegis, "signs of nobleness, like stars shall shine/ On all deservers" (I.iv.41-42). One such sign is the diamond, noblest

---

* Many of the birds of the play—ravens and crows, for example—are "talking birds" and thus reflect the play's focus on "strange voices." I am indebted to an unpublished essay on *Macbeth* by Jef D. Bocke for this insight.

of gems and like a star, with which Duncan greets Lady Macbeth "By the name of most kind hostess" (I.i.15-16). As Derek Traversi says, "Duncan's brief appearances before his murder are invariably invested with images of light and fertility to which are joined at moments of deepest feeling the religious associations of worship in a magnificent comprehensive impression of overflowing *grace*."[4] But while encouraging Eden, Duncan promotes treason. In language that through an ominous rhyme reverberates again with Delphic tones, the king invests Macbeth with the traitor's title, thus moving Macbeth closer to the traitor's reality:

> No more that thane of Cawdor shall deceive
> Our bosom interest. Go pronounce his present death,
> And with his former title greet Macbeth.
>
> (I.ii.63-65)

No more shall *that* Cawdor deceive us, but what of the new one? The "careless trifle" (I.iv.11) that Cawdor discards becomes the "honest trifle" (I.iii.125) that wins Macbeth. The pervasive confusion of the opening scenes is suggested best when even Duncan echoes the Weird Sisters (I.i.4), as Macbeth had done earlier (I.iii.38): "What he hath lost, noble Macbeth hath won" (I.ii.67). Duncan incites treason further by establishing his estate on Malcolm, just as Milton's God exalts his Son and activates Satan's dormant disobedience.[5] Macbeth adjures the stars to hide their fires (I.iv.50), instructing his own signs of nobleness to extinguish themselves and so facilitate the attainment of his "black and deep desires" (I.iv.51).

Macbeth's maskings of illumination are not merely attempts to hide his crime from the view of a heavenly power, but deliberate efforts at self-deception. He would divorce will and knowledge:

> The eye wink at the hand; yet let that be
> Which the eye fears, when it is done, to see.
>
> (I.iv.50-53)

> I am afraid to think what I have done;
> Look on't again I dare not.
>
> (II.ii.51-52)

Later, turning to "outrun the pauser, reason" (II.iii.117),[6] he hopes to act so quickly that knowledge cannot catch up with deed—perhaps the most profound implication of his race with time:

> Strange things I have in head, that will to hand,
> Which must be acted ere they may be scann'd.
>
> (III.iv.139-40)

This insistence that his will achieve itself in isolation from knowledge results not only in the defeat of the angelic potentiality but in the man's descent to bestiality.[7] In addition to being a "hell-kite" (IV.iii.217) and a "hell-hound" (V.viii.3), he has lost that "human kindness" (I.v.18) his wife had feared. His senses become virtually inert, his compassion dead, his head like the hide of an animal:

> I have almost forgot the taste of fears.
> The time has been, my senses would have cool'd
> To hear a night-shriek, and my fell of hair
> Would at a dismal treatise rouse and stir
> As life were in 't.
>
> (V.v.9-13)

The vivid imagination that had projected warning visions before the murder of Duncan and guilty images after the murder of Banquo is gone. When Macbeth dons his armor he is not a man but a horse:

> Blow, wind! come, wrack!
> At least we'll die with harness on our back.
>
> (V.v.51-52)

He is an isolated bear surrounded by many enemies:

> They have tied me to a stake; I cannot fly,
> But, bear-like, I must fight the course.
>
> (V.viii.1-2)

Macduff repeats the metaphor as he hears the "brute" Macbeth under attack: "By this great clatter one of greatest note/ Seems bruited" (V.vii.21-22). If Macbeth yields, Macduff promises to exhibit him as genus "tyrant" (V.viii.27), as "our

rarer monsters are" (V.viii.25). Macbeth scorns this verbal
version of bear-baiting:

> I will not yield
> To kiss the ground before young Malcolm's feet,
> And to be baited with the rabble's curse.
>
> (V.viii.27-29)

He has "done the deed" (II.ii.15), "a deed without a name"
(IV.i.49), as Macduff tells us: "Tongue nor heart/ Cannot
conceive nor name thee" (II.iii.69-70). "To know my deed,"
he had said, " 'twere best not know myself" (II.ii.73). This divorce between deed and knowledge, will and nature, makes
Macbeth, like Beatrice-Joanna, "the deed's creature."[8] His
kingdom will suffer, as it must, from its monarch's divorce
from nature, developing that identity which to admit is only
agony and self-revulsion:

> cruel are the times when we are traitors
> And do not know ourselves.
>
> (IV.ii.18-19)

> Alas poor country!
> Almost afraid to know itself.
>
> (IV.iii.164-65)

Macbeth is not merely a fallen angel, nor merely a man
whose will drives him down the chain of being to bestiality,
but a fallen hero as well. Our introduction to Macbeth—aside
from the ominous reference by the Third Witch (I.i.8)—is
the bleeding Captain's epic description of Macbeth's prowess:

> For brave Macbeth—well he deserves that name—
> Disdaining Fortune, with his brandish'd steel,
> Which smok'd with bloody execution,
> Like Valour's minion carv'd out his passage
> Till he fac'd the slave;
> Which ne'er shook hands, nor bade farewell to him,
> Till he unseam'd him from the nave to th' chaps,
> And fix'd his head upon our battlements.
>
> (I.ii.16-23)

Drama, as Aristotle tells us, consists in "action not narrative."
What, then, is the point of a narrative that aligns the hero

with large abstractions ("Valour's minion"), and with the gods ("Bellona's bridegroom": I.ii.54), shows him daring super-natural odds ("Disdaining Fortune": I.ii.17), and provides him with the typical epic hero's role of fighting through to confront the chief antagonist and achieve some great feat of the sword? Shakespeare sets up a contrast *between* narrative and action, between the report of Macbeth's heroism in bat-tle, where the blood he sheds brings him honor, and our vir-tual witness of his murder of Duncan, a "deed" that comes far closer to "memoriz[ing] another Golgotha" (I.ii.40) than his unseaming of Macdonwald. The epic rendition is one of the play's several variations of the contrast between the ex-ternal and the internal man.[9]

One event is rendered through an externally observed and artificial narrative, the other is felt with its perpetrator. The Captain's narrative helps the play's auditor to grasp the di-mension of grandeur that so recently pertained to Macbeth, and, by contrast, to feel the terrible reality of the murder of Duncan and the concomitant fall of Macbeth. Not the least of the ironies developing from scene two is that Macbeth *was* worthy of the epic stature the Captain grants him. Like an epic hero, his actions expressed not *his* nature but a larger reality; he personified valour and Scotland, he was "justice" "arm'd" with "valour" (I.ii.29). The ensuing tragedy will im-itate the action of *his* will—which the epic hero does not ex-hibit *for himself*, unless, like Achilles, he becomes virtually a tragic hero—as it battles with his nature and with the more comprehensive entity he embodies in Scotland's battle. As tragic hero—as king—Macbeth will also represent Scotland, but, as in tragedy, the positive order will *resist* the hero, in-stead of shining through its heroic embodiment, as it does in the epic, as it had in Macbeth. Macbeth becomes the embod-iment of a different set of abstractions, of "wither'd murder," moving " 'Gainst nature still" (II.iv.27), "a death to nature" (III.iv.28), not an epic preserver of the natural order. Ulti-mately, it is Macbeth's head that sits on the battlements.

Lady Macbeth, her husband's "partner in greatness" (I.v.11-12), shares his fall. She, too, tries to mask her deed from God, to divorce knowledge from will within herself:

Come, thick night,
And pall thee in the dunnest smoke of hell,
That my keen knife see not the wound it makes,
Nor heaven peep through the blanket of the dark
To cry, "Hold, hold!"

(I.v.51-55)

Lady Macbeth is an "Eve-figure," the "spur" to intention of
which Macbeth speaks (I.vii.25): "look like the innocent
flower,/ But be the serpent under 't" (I.v.66-67). Some will
argue that the Weird Sisters are the spur to Macbeth,[10] and
because this is partially true, Shakespeare is careful to create
many links between them and Lady Macbeth. Twice, she
echoes their words and rhythms:

1. Witch. All hail, Macbeth! Hail, to thee, Thane of Glamis!
2. Witch. All hail, Macbeth! Hail to thee, Thane of Cawdor!
3. Witch. All hail, Macbeth! that shalt be King hereafter!

(I.iii.48-50)

Lady Macbeth.   Glamis thou art, and Cawdor, and shalt be—
                 What thou art promis'd.

(I.v.16-17)

Lady Macbeth.   Great Glamis! worthy Cawdor!
                 Greater than both, by the all-hail hereafter!

(I.v.55-56)[11]

She would denature herself like the Sisters, whom Banquo
would have called women had their beards not forbidden the
interpretation (I.111.45-47):

Come, you spirits
That tend on mortal thoughts, unsex me here,
And fill me from the crown to the toe top-full
Of direst cruelty! Make thick my blood;
Stop up th' access and passage to remorse,
That no compunctious visitings of nature
Shake my fell purpose, nor keep peace between
Th' effect and it! Come to my woman's breasts
And take my milk for gall. . .

(I.v.41-49)

One of the ingredients tossed into the caldron by the Third
Witch is "Gall of goat" (IV.i.27). Like the Sisters, Lady Mac-

beth would be an "instrument. . .of darkness" (I.iii.125), creator of a hellish atmosphere of "filthy air" (I.i.12):

> Come, thick night,
> And pall thee in the dunnest smoke of hell.
>
> (I.vi.51-52)

She would make permanent the prediction of sunset made by the Third Witch (I.i.5):

> O never
> Shall sun that morrow see!
>
> (I.vi.61-62)

Lady Macbeth seems to be attempting to become Lilith, Adam's shadowy first wife, whose name means "of the night," a demon or vampire, or, in medieval folklore, a witch believed to be a menace to little children, as Lady Macbeth claims to be (I.vii.54-59). According to the modern witch, Alex Sanders, "the witches of the Renaissance indulged in infanticide."[12] Lilith is associated with a screech owl, as are Lady Macbeth (II.11.3-4,16) and the Third Witch. Thus Lady Macbeth, who feels "the future in the instant" (I.v.59), is linked with the Third Witch, the Witch of the future. Lady Macbeth's intrinsic association with witchcraft is suggested by Donald Nugent, who isolates two "common denominators found rather universally in witchcraft. . .sexuality (in symbol or in fact) and power. . . . Witchcraft is a means of artificially heightening the will in ages when men feel flattened by misfortune. It is hubris-enhancing, and it can tempt men to be 'as gods.' "[13]

In a play full of metaphors of fulness, Lady Macbeth explicitly contradicts not only the "milk of human kindness," which fills Macbeth (I.v.18), but the capacity of Duncan, who wishes that Macbeth had "less deserv'd,/ That the proportion both of thanks and payment/ Might have been" his (I.iv.18-20), who would "labour/ To make [Macbeth] full of growing" (I.iv.28-29), whose "plenteous joys" are "wanton in fulness" (I.iv.33-34), who sends "great largess to [Macbeth's] offices" (II.i.13-14), and is "shut up/ In measureless content" (II.i.16-17), who is, like King Edward of England, a bestower

of "sundry blessings" (IV.iii.158) and "full of grace"
(IV.iii.159). Lady Macbeth demands that the "spirits/ That
tend on mortal thoughts. . .fill [her] from the crown to the
toe top-full/ Of direst cruelty" (I.v.51-44). Duncan's plen-
titude, overflowingly full, yet in his recognition of Macbeth's
merit incapable of rewarding him completely, is translated by
Lady Macbeth into a calculus of duplicity:

> All our service
> In every point twice done and then done double
> Were poor and single business to contend
> Against those honours deep and broad wherewith
> Your majesty loads our house. For those of old,
> And the late dignities heap'd up to them,
> We rest your hermits.
>
> (I.vi.14-20)

But while Lady Macbeth has attempted to make herself a
Lilith, she has been forced to employ the feminine qualities
of Eve to tempt Macbeth. She has not been unsexed. Her
share in the qualities of the Sisters is only verbal, a rhetorical
equation that will prove disastrous if she bases her actions
upon it—as she does, of course:

> Give me the daggers. The sleeping and the dead
> Are but as pictures. 'Tis the eye of childhood
> That fears a painted devil.
>
> (II.ii.53-54)

She forgets that she herself has seen with the eyes of
childhood—with the vision of her own intrinsic
"kindness"—only moments before:

> Had he not resembled
> My father as he slept, I had done't.
>
> (II.ii.13-14)

We learn suddenly that she, like Shakespeare's heroines, had
been a child, that her attempt to subvert her nature has been
unsuccessful.[14] The blood-covered body of Duncan will become a picture that will pursue her into the hellish murk of
her madness: "Yet who would have thought the old man to
have had so much blood in him?" (V.i.44-45). The blood was

real, not paint.[15] In her madness, her kindness emerges
—literally against her will: "The thane of Fife had a wife/
Where is she now?" (V.i.42-43). The Geneva gloss on Genesis
2 defines her inability to see soon enough the difference between the painted devil that might be scorned and the father
murdered, as captured by the child's eye within her: "This is
Satans chiefest subtiltie, to cause us not to feare Gods
theatenings."

The contradictory character of Lady Macbeth, the elements
of Lilith and Eve within her, can best be summarized by
examining one of the play's most controversial moments
—her feint-faint (II.iii.124). The arguments on each side of
the debate are familiar. Those who claim that the feint is
merely another improvisation by the skillful tactician, another
masking of reality with appearance by the originator of fair
façades, see it drawing attention away from Macbeth's suspicious rhetoric and from his questionable killing of the
grooms, and claim that it represents her effort to react as a
woman should (an "innocent flower"), that it atones for the
blunder she has already made (II.iii.92-93),* that the woman
who could take the knives back into the murder chamber
would hardly collapse at the mere mention of blood, and that
Macbeth's unconcern for her "faint" shows that he, at least,
knows she is in no danger. These arguments are persuasive.
Most critics believe, however, that she does faint.[16] They suggest that the murder has been a great strain on her, that she
has been active for many hours, making certain that everything is "In every point twice done and then done double"
(I.vi.15), that she has been drinking as well (II.ii.1-2), that, as
her mad scene proves, Duncan's blood made a frightful impression on her, and that the faces of the group suddenly as-
sembled on the cold stones of morning reflect to her for the
first time the heinousness of her deed. These, also, are persuasive arguments. We have such a perfect moment in am-

---

* Lady Macbeth's, "What, in our house?" *can* be read in the light of Banquo's rebuke, "Too cruel anywhere" (II.iii.92-93). It is also masterfully "natural." Lady Macbeth knows that Duncan is dead, yet she reacts with the "hostess's first thought," a
concern for the reputation of her "house" and hospitality. Such a response is typical
of a stress situation as a defense against "full recognition." Her faint would either
be, then, her simulation of full recognition—or its actuality.

biguity, in fact, that the strength of one case tends to cancel the other out. One must, perhaps, admit the validity of *each* case, move into the zone of negative capability, and recognize that this moment combines *two* Lady Macbeths. The feint suggests the scheming plotter of the early scenes; the faint predicts the sin-haunted woman of Act Five. If we do not insist on one interpretation or another, the moment points backward and forward, accomplishing the impossible by capturing the contradictory aspects of Lady Macbeth's career within a single instant. Such ambiguity is appropriate to a play in which fair and foul elements are blended inextricably at the outset. *Macbeth* is another play in which time must arbitrate. Lady Macbeth's subsequent history—the belated emergence of the woman beneath the kindless surface —increases our appreciation of the feminine power that helped persuade her husband to kill the king.

Any analysis of Lady Macbeth's role in encouraging Macbeth's crime must recognize that she, like the Witches, is not the *initiator* of evil. Lady Macbeth defines the Witches best:

> You murd'ring ministers
> Wherever in your sightless substances
> You wait on nature's mischief.

(I.v.49-51)

Lady Macbeth and the Witches are attendants and abettors—but the evil they encourage is already *within* Macbeth. West's analysis of the Witches emphasizes both their power *and* its limitations. Their "evil, in the play as in demonology, manifests itself in ways that are obscure and marvelous to man. . . . It is personal and acts against man with jealousy and hatred. . . . Fearsome as it is, it appears not absolute in power; it moves the human will only indirectly and knows the future only conditionally. . . . Traffic with it comes from evil in man and is itself evil and leads to evil and inevitably to ruin. Finally, the worldly compensation for this ruin turns out to be only a frantic emptiness."[17] Proof of Macbeth's frantic loss of reason and human contact is that, after leaving Lady Macbeth "innocent of the knowledge" of

Banquo's murder (III.ii.45), he goes to the Witches, elements of the unnatural, to reassure himself of his own role within the natural order he has already subverted, which order he further rebuffs in seeking them out:

> our high-plac'd Macbeth
> Shall live the lease of nature, pay his breath
> To time and mortal custom.
>
> (IV.i.98-100)

While the retribution Lady Macbeth experiences is defined by the Doctor as "a great perturbation in nature" (V.i.10), it is personal and internal. Nature's perturbation in *Macbeth,* however, is limitless, in Henry Adams's phrase "an insanity of force."[18] Nature's outrage in *Macbeth* swells to the proportions of an anti-Creation.[19]

Duncan represents God, the creative principle; he is the architect of Scotland's garden. What L. C. Knights calls the "holy supernatural"[20] aspect of *Macbeth* is best articulated by Banquo and Duncan as they approach Inverness:

Duncan. This castle hath a pleasant seat. The air
         Nimbly and sweetly recommends itself
         Unto our gentle senses.
Banquo.   This guest of summer,
         The temple-haunting martlet, does approve,
         By his lov'd masonry, that the heaven's breath
         Smells wooingly here. No jutty, frieze,
         Buttress, nor coign of vantage, but this bird
         Hath made his pendant bed and procreant cradle.
         Where they most breed and haunt, I have observ'd
         The air is delicate.

(I.vi.1-10)

Although fallen, this world, like Eden, exists in harmony with Heaven; it is creative; nests find the constructions of man hospitable; the delicate air of Heaven at once encourages new life into being and is re-created by that new life. The link between Duncan and the martlet is suggested by Robert Speaight: "Both are guests and both are innocent; it is no accident that the King is seen in relation to uncorrupted nature."[21] But this glimpse of Eden, a metaphor for Scotland

under Duncan, is deceptive; the external atmosphere of Inverness belies the duplicity of its internal preparations. With
the murder of Duncan, the "temple-haunting martlet" is
forced to flee before the "most sacrilegious murder" committed upon "the Lord's anointed temple" (II.iii.68-69).
Macbeth's memorial of "another Golgotha" (I.ii.40) enunciates an anti-Creation. The first verses of Genesis, of course,
suggest order—the distinction between light ("that it was
good") and darkness, heaven and earth, sea and land, day
and night, seasons, years, sun and moon. The opening verses
of Genesis emphasize growing things:

> Then God said, let the earth budde forth the fruit of the
> herbe, that seedeth seed, the fruitfull tree, which bareth fruit ac-
> cording to his kinde, which hath his seed in itselfe upon the
> earth.

With the murder, distinctions merely blurred in the opening
scenes become obliterated. The owl, normally the foe of field
mice, rises up to down a falcon (II.iv.12-13). Horses, "Con-
tending 'gainst obedience," turn wild, eat each other and
issue forth "as they would make/ War with mankind"
(II.iv.14-18). Night and morning "at odds" lose their distinc-
tive identities (III.iv.127). The well-planned garden of God
and Duncan becomes a kingdom of "weeds" (V.ii.30). "Answer me," Macbeth shouts at the Sisters with a rage of
thwarted will equaling (and echoing) Lear's, "Though bladed
corn be lodg'd and trees blown down. . .though the treasure/
Of nature's germens tumble all together,/ Even till destruction sicken" (IV.i.51-60). God's first *fait lux* is refuted. The
world has heeded Macbeth's "Stars, hide your fires!" (I.iv.50),
Lady Macbeth's "Come, thick night" (I.v.51), and Macbeth's
"Come, seeling night,/ Scarf up the tender eye of pitiful day"
(III.ii.46-47). The command is, "Let there be darkness."
Banquo's words, like Othello's on putting out the light,[22]
create an appropriate echo to the Tenebrae:

> There's husbandry in heaven;
> Their candles are all out.

> (II.i.4-5)

Macbeth discovers that "time and the hour" do *not*
"run. . .through the roughest day" (I.iv.146). A "rough night"
(II.ii.66), on which "the earth/ Was feverous and did shake"
(II.ii.64-65), shakes Scotland loose from the rhythms of
order, from time itself:

> By th' clock 'tis day,
> And yet dark night strangles the travelling lamp.
> Is't night's predominance, or the day's shame,
> That darkness does the face of earth entomb,
> When living light should kiss it?
>
> (II.iv.6-10)

A personified earth is denied light, love, and life. "It cannot/
Be called our mother, but our grave" (IV.iii.165-66). Once
wooed by "heaven's breath," the land now rejects the source
of life: "Each new morn. . .new sorrows/ Strike heaven on the
face" (IV.iii.4-6). Now, "both the worlds suffer" (III.11.16).
"How could it be," asks the Homily on Rogation Week, "that
the elements, so divers and contrary as they be among themselves, should yet agree and abide together in a concord
without destruction one of the other to serve our use, if it
came not onely of God's Goodness so to temper them?"

The sterile principle is concentrated, of course, in Macbeth:

> Upon my head they plac'd a fruitless crown
> And put a barren sceptre in my gripe.
>
> (III.i.61-62)

Again the lines echo the Geneva gloss on Genesis: "So that
we see it is the onely power of Gods word that maketh the
earth fruitful, which els naturally is baren." Duncan had said
as much long before. Macbeth finds ultimately only "The
sear, the yellow leaf" (V.iii.23), as opposed to the faithful
man described in the Homily on Faith, the man Duncan
would have made of Macbeth: "he is like a tree set by the
water side, and spreadeth his roots abroad toward the moys-
ture, and feareth not heate when it commeth, his leafe will
bee greene, and will not cease to bring foorth his fruit: even
so, faithfull men (putting away all fear of adversitie) will

shew foorth the fruit of their good workes, as occasion is offered to doe them." Having suspended the rules of nature,
Macbeth finds that they cannot be reinstated. Like the rebuffed Lear, Macbeth cries for the destruction of the universe
and of the internal microcosm of will and soul, whose conflict
tortures him:

> But let the frame of things disjoint, both the worlds suffer,
> Ere we will eat our meal in fear and sleep
> In the affliction of these terrible dreams
> That shake us nightly.
>
> (III.ii.16-19)

He would summon darkness not merely to obliterate the
judging eye of God but to cancel his *contact* with God, which
has developed, like that of Dante's damned, into absolute torture:

> Come, seeling night,
> Scarf up the tender eye of pitiful day,
> And with thy bloody and invisible hand
> Cancel and tear to pieces that great bond
> Which keeps me pale!
>
> (III.ii.46-50)

"That great bond" is that which makes him man, his bond to
nature. He would, as Coriolanus would, become a force independent of nature. But he cannot—he carries his humanity
within him, no matter how perverse or bestial it may become.
He calls for the universal cessation of time, the medium
within which he is tortured:

> I 'gin to be aweary of the sun,
> And wish th' estate o' the' world were now undone.
>
> (V.v.49-50)

He cannot escape, of course, as St. Bernard suggests: "The
ills the soul now suffers after sin do now replace that native
goodness and distort it, deforming an order they can in no
wise destroy."[23] The first Thane of Cawdor "set forth a deep
repentance" (I.iv.7) and so regained at the last the unity between will and soul he had lost. Macbeth's insistence on will
drives him deeper and deeper into his self-made trap:

And be these juggling fiends no more believ'd
That palter with us in a double sense,
That keep the word of promise to our ear,
And break it to our hope.

(V.viii.19-22)

As Walter C. Curry says, "Irrational acts have established habits tending to further irrationality and one of the penalties exacted is dire impairment of the liberty of free choice."[24]

The play's supreme example of nature's denial of Macbeth is the great banquet scene (III.iv). The new *Book of Common Prayer*, which King James issued on "the 5 day of March [1605], in the first yeere of our Reigne of England," contained a new prayer in the Communion Service:

> Almightie God, whose kingdom is everlasting, and power infinite, have mercie upon the whole congregation, and so rule the heart of thy chosen servant James, our King and governour, that he (knowing whose minister he is) may above all things seeke thy honour and glory, and that we his Subjects (duely considering whose authority hee hath) may faithfully serve, honour, and humbly obey him, in thee, and for thee, according to thy blessed worde and ordinance.

The only new element, of course, was the substitution of King for Queen, his for her, James for Elizabeth. To the Jacobean ear—that ear so much more finely tuned than the "modern" ear—the change would have been significant, since it had heard "Elizabeth" for almost fifty years. The prayer would have been heard anew and the lines of authority from God to King to subject would have been reemphasized. Whether *Macbeth* "honours" King James or not is irrelevant. What it does do is show a king attempting to establish precisely the lines of authority defined by the prayer, and failing. Nor is the Communion allusion merely topical; Macbeth's failure occurs within a Communion context, at what he calls a "solemn supper" (III.i.14) and Lady Macbeth a "great feast" (III.i.12) and a "good meeting" (III.iv.109).

G. Wilson Knight has termed "feasting" in Shakespeare a symbol of the "life-force."[25] Following Knight, J. P. Dyson calls "banquets and feasting. . .traditional symbols of harmony, fellowship, and union. They are dramatic symbols of life-forces, a fulfillment of nature."[26] The central feast, of course, is the Eucharist, celebrating union at the most profound level, and, if imitated in a play, creating deep possibilities for response within its audience:

> We dwell in Christ and Christ in us, wee be one with Christ and Christ with us. . . . Graunt us therefore gracious Lord, so to eate the flesh of thy deare Sonne Jesus Christ, and to drink his blood, that our sinful bodies may be made clean by his body, and our soules washed through his most precious blood, and that we may evermore dwell in him and he in us. . . . Almighty and ever-living God, we most heartily thanke thee, for that thou dost vouchsafe to feed us which have duely received these holy mysteries, with the spiritual food of the most precious body and blood of thy Sonne, our Saviour Jesus Christ, & dost assure us thereby of thy favor & goodness towards us, and that we be very members incorporate in thy mysticall body, which is the blessed company of all faithfull people and be also heires through hope, of thy everlasting kingdome.

Clearly, the emphasis is upon communion with the intangible element represented by the bread and wine. The same emphasis pertains to Macbeth's banquet:

>   My royal lord,
> You do not give the cheer. The feast is sold
> That is not often vouch'd, while 'tis a-making,
> 'Tis given with welcome. To feed were best at home;
> From thence, the sauce to meat is ceremony;
> Meeting were bare without it.
>
> (III.iv.33-37)

In the Homily on the Sacraments, the participants in Communion are compared to those who "sitteth at an earthly king's table." The difference, however, between the two tables is precisely that pointed at by Lady Macbeth's plea to Macbeth which, translated into the Communion context becomes, according to the Homily, "no vaine ceremonie, no bare signe, no untrue figure of a thing absent. . . ." But in Macbeth's banquet the elements of unity are horribly split. Macbeth neglects his guests because of his conference with the murderer at the door:

Be large in mirth; anon we'll drink a measure
The table round. [Approaching the door.]—There's blood upon
    thy face.

(III.iv.11-12)

The promise of a toast—itself a sacramental action*—is interrupted not by a reminder of "the Blood of our Lord Jesus Christ which was shed for thee," but by the sight of Banquo's blood, sacrificed to the will of Macbeth, to his frantic effort to thwart the very future he had once raced to attain. *That* blood (and Duncan's, of course) puts Macbeth on the wrong side of nature. His first effort at a toast ("Now, good digestion wait on appetite,/ And health on both": III.iv.38) is interrupted by the Ghost's first appearance. After the Ghost departs, the King tries again:

  Come, love and health to all;
Then I'll sit down. Give me some wine; fill full.
I drink to th' general joy o' th' whole table. . .
And all to all.

(III.iv.87-92)

This effort at a version of Communion and community is broken again by what Knight calls "a ghost, smashing life-forms with fantasies of evil and guilt."[27] Macbeth cannot participate in the sacraments, cannot say "Amen" (II.ii.29), because he continues to reject the preconditions for the "blessing" he so badly needs (II.ii.31-33), refuses to wade back through his self-created and deepening red sea (III.iv.136-38). The priest can admit to Communion "the penitent person. . .and not hym that is obstinate." In planning Banquo's murder, Macbeth sneers explicitly at the Gospels (III.i.88).[28] Like Faustus, Claudius, and Beatrice Joanna, Macbeth is barred, by his insistence upon will, from any contact with the positive life-giving elements of the supernature:

Ross.   Pleas't your Highness
          To grace us with your royal company?

---

* Cf. Charles Harris, D.D.: "Not only are the religious associations of the Chalice of a most moving kind, but the common cup powerfully suggests human fellowship of an intimate unselfish, generous, and uplifting nature (cf. the institution of 'the loving cup')." "Communion of the Sick," *Liturgy and Worship*, ed., W. K. Lowther Clarke, D.D. (London, 1932), pp. 614-15.

Macbeth.   The table's full.
Lennox.   Here is a place reserv'd, sir.
Macbeth.   Where?

(III.iv.44-48)

The Communion Service opens with a prayer to "Almighty
God. . .from whom no secrets are hid," and moves through
the Ten Commandments: "Thou shalt do no murther." The
Priest is instructed not to permit a "notorious evil liver, so
that ye congregation by him is offended" or "those betwixt
whom he perceiveth malice and hatred to reigne. . .to be partakers of the Lordes Table." Later, the Priest admonishes
those who do *not* take Communion: "But when you depart I
beseeche you ponder with your selves, from whom ye depart.
Yee depart from the Lords table, yee depart from your breth-
ren, and from the banquet of most heavenly food." Macbeth has thus exiled himself from the "gentle weal," by violating the "humane statute" (III.iv.76), which is, probably, the
Sixth Commandment, and is excommunicated from his own
"table" by an image of his own evil. His own guilt performs
the function of the Priest prescribed by the opening rubrics
of the Communion. Shakespeare underlines the exclusion of
Macbeth from the table by having Lady Macbeth keep "her
state" (III.iv.5). She never gets to the table either. Macbeth
and Lady Macbeth can sit on the throne, but are denied access to the spiritual mysteries that would make their throne
meaningful. Macbeth merely commends the ingredients of
his poisoned chalice to his own lips. His defiled mind
(III.i.65) and the rancors in the vessel of his peace (III.i.67)
contaminate the heart of his ceremony, regardless of his protestations to the contrary, words playing across a surface
through which notorious evil explodes:

Lady Macbeth.   For my heart speaks they are welcome.
Macbeth.   See, they encounter thee with their hearts' thanks.

(III.iv.8-9)

To call the banquet scene the climax of the play, as Dyson
does ("in this scene. . .the whole play turns over"),[29] is as in-
accurate as Kermode's judgment that the escape of Fleance is
"the turning point of the play."[30] The entrance of the Ghost

and the escape of Fleance are no doubt elements of Macbeth's *anagnorisis,* but the murder of Duncan, as Macbeth tells us (I.vii.1-28), is the moment of tragic choice.

Macbeth slips away from the banquet celebrating Duncan's coming, another feast of fellowship and unity: "In his commendations," says Duncan of Macbeth, "I am fed;/ It is a banquet to me" (I.v.55-56). Outside the chamber, Macbeth measures the "consequence" (I.vii.3) of the murder, both for this world ("We still have judgement here": I.vii.8) and for the world to come ("deep damnation": I.vii.20). Lady Macbeth interrupts:

> Macbeth.   Hath he ask'd for me?
> Lady Macbeth. Know you not he has?
>
> (I.vii.29-30)

God walked through Eden calling "Where art thou?" to Adam. The Geneva gloss on God's search gives context to Macbeth's departure from the banquet: "The sinnefull conscience fleeth God's presense."* Macbeth's departure reverberates not only against the Genesis story (like Wendoll's hiding from Frankford in *A Woman Killed with Kindness* [II.iii.70-74])[31] but, with equal appropriateness for this play, against the priest's exhortation to those who refuse Communion: "If any man say, I am a grievous sinner, and therefore am afraid to come: wherefore then do you not repent and amend? When God calleth you, bee you not ashamed to say you will not come?" Proper ritual in Scotland is overturned, the virtuous "communicant" refusing an invitation to a perverted ceremony, rather than the priest excommunicating the evil liver. Macbeth makes this clear in remarking Macduff's absence at the banquet:

> How say'st thou that Macduff denies his person
> At our great bidding?
>
> (III.iv.128-29)

Were Macduff to attend the banquet, he would be confirming an allegiance to the *negative* invisible powers represented

* Cf. Claudio: "God saw him when he hid in the garden" (*Much Ado About Nothing,* V.i.181).

by Macbeth's crown, the anti-sacramental elements of nature's dark underside. The banquet breaks up, of course, but Macduff's refusal signals the withdrawal from Macbeth of those who would align themselves with Edward's holy court and with the positively endowed crusade that will flow back into Scotland and which will culminate in Malcolm's invitation "to see us crown'd at Scone" (V.viii.75). We assume that no one will refuse *this* "great bidding."

The old morality pattern—good and evil angel—coheres in Macbeth. The good angel speaks truth, and Macbeth is persuaded: "We will proceed no further in this business" (I.vii.31), he tells his wife. But he does not base his argument on the theological issue he has been debating. Instead, like any man embarrassed at making a "moral" decision, he rationalizes:

> I have bought
> Golden opinions from all sorts of people,
> Which would be worn now in their newest gloss,
> Not cast aside so soon.
>
> (I.vii.32-35)

His argument is conditioned, perhaps, by her inability to see beyond the tangible.[32] He cannot speak of "double trust" to someone who understands only duplicity ("All our service/ In every point twice done and then done double" [I.vi.15]) or of Duncan's clarity in office to someone who will soon ask, "What do you mean?" as Macbeth waxes hyperbolic about the sleep he will never know again (II.ii.40). But to employ a materialistic excuse for not pursuing a materialistic course is to open oneself up to counterattack. Lady Macbeth retorts, implying with a sneer that cowardice lurks beneath the thane's new clothes: "When you durst do it, then you were a man" (I.vii.49). As Dr. Johnson says, with the certainty of the eighteenth-century critic, "Courage is the distinguishing virtue of a soldier, and the reproach of cowardice cannot be borne by any man without great impatience."[33] Lady Macbeth's skillful blend of scorn and sex—the primordial feminine weapons—upsets the precarious balance within Macbeth. She has played the evil angel, acted both witch and woman, yet the decision is Macbeth's: "I am settled, and bend up/ Each corporal agent to this terrible feat" (I.vii.79-80).[34] This is the play's climax. Macbeth has placed himself irredeemably on the wrong side of nature. He must act like a natural man, but the role mocks nature and himself, as his next words prove:

> Away, and mock the time with fairest show;
> False face must hide what the false heart doth know.
>
> (I.vii.81-82)

Macbeth now resembles the Claudius who rose unsuccessfully from prayer, as the "Homily that all good things commeth from God" suggests: "There can be none other end of such as draweth nigh to God by knowledge, and yet depart from him in unthankfulnesse, but utter destruction."

The banquet scene represents the political echo of the killing of Duncan and could be called a kind of judgment day for Macbeth. An explicit Judgment Day occurs, however, immediately after Duncan's murder. Macduff commands Malcolm, Donalbain, and Banquo to rise "As from your graves. . .and walk like sprites" to view "the great doom's image" (II.iii.83-84). Lady Macbeth asks on entering, "What's the business/ That such a hideous trumpet calls to parley/ The sleepers of the house" (II.iii.86-88). The judgment theme is extended by Banquo, who likens the scene to that in which a naked Adam and Eve stood ashamed just after the Fall: "And when we have our naked frailties hid. . ." (II.iii.132). The scene fulfills Macbeth's prediction that "we still have judgement here" (I.vii.8). And it is after the murder of Duncan that the wine-blood equation is most explicit, Macbeth seeing Duncan, rightly, as an embodiment of the sacraments:

> The wine of life is drawn, and the mere lees
> Is left this vault to brag of. . .
> The spring, the head, the fountain of your blood
> Is stopp'd; the very source of it is stopp'd.
>
> (II.iii.100-105)

Macduff's inability to articulate the magnitude of the crime ("Tongue nor heart/ Cannot conceive nor name thee!"

[II.ii.69-70]) echoes the Homilies on the coming of Christ *and* the life after death of the Saved Soul, suggesting, by contrast, the absolute horror of the murder of Duncan and of the world that the play has entered—a zone lower than that of merely a fallen world, hell itself, where the gracious Duncan has been replaced by the murderous Macbeth:

> Neither tongue can well express it [i.e. God's "sending downe a Saviour from heaven"], neither heart thinke it, much lesse give sufficient thanks to God for it.

> For death shall bee to him [who is saved] no death at all, but. . .a tasting of heavenly pleasures, so great, that neither tongue is able to expresse, neither eye to see, nor eare to heare them: no, nor any earthly mans heart to conceive them.

While Macbeth's decision to murder Duncan is the play's climax, the banquet scene is the tragedy in microcosm—a gathering that begins with promises of health for subject and state but breaks up before Macbeth's vision of yet another "sacrilegious murder" (II.iii.72). The "good meeting" is "broke" (III.iv.109) as "The Lord's anointed temple" was "broke ope" (II.iii.72-73). The banquet scene demonstrates how guilt—what has happened to Macbeth's body natural, his soul—can destroy the body politic, both king and kingdom. The scene represents an extension of the tragic choice Macbeth has already made, showing how the terrible split between will and virtue, ambition and conscience can rend society asunder, if that person be a king. As Delora G. Cunningham says, "the human person, like the human society, cannot function effectively without sharing in the supernatural energy which is grace."[35] The medium for the transmission to his subjects of that energy is, of course, the king. *Macbeth* demonstrates the dramatic economy of Shakespeare's plays—when a great general like Othello loses control as a man, riots spread wildly to the streets. And when a great king—a Lear—surrenders control, chaos extends automatically to every corner of the kingdom and poisons all rituals of unity.[36] It should be noted that not only Macbeth and Lady Macbeth are denied the table, but the guests as well:

At once, good-night.
Stand not upon the order of your going,
But go at once.

(III.iv.118-20)

The guests scramble out, an anti-ceremony destroying the "degrees" (III.iv.1) which had dictated their places at the table. Lady Macbeth's pathetic "A kind good-night to all!" (III.iv.121) gives way to Macbeth's perpetuation of unkindness, a weary metaphor of continued bloodshed:

I am in blood
Stepp'd in so far that, should I wade no more,
Returning were as tedious as go o'er.

(III.iv.136-38)

The banquet scene reflects Macbeth's exile from the feast of life. He has "supp'd full with horrors" (V.v.13), must "eat [his] meal in fear" (III.ii.17), has "commend [ed] th' ingredients of [his] poison'd chalice/ To [his] own lips" (I.vii.11-12), and has "put rancours in the vessel of [his] peace" (III.i.67). He cannot enjoy sleep, "great nature's second course,/ Chief nourisher in life's feast" (II.ii.39-40), "the season [phase of day, as of year, but primarily *flavor*] of all natures" (III.iv.141).

The banquet's emphasis on feeding (III.iv.34,58), "meat" and "sauce" (III.iv.36), "digestion" and "appetite" (III.iv.38), the scattering of the thanes to find what nourishment they may, focuses the play's reiterated emphasis on feasts, a motif G. Wilson Knight has discussed at length.[37] Duncan made a "banquet" (I.iv.56) of Macbeth's valor (I.v.54) and "commendations" (I.v.55). His feast promised plentiful return based on the reciprocity he felt toward "all deservers" (I.v.42). Contrasted against the feast of Duncan's positive ethic is the excessiveness, appetite, and unnatural feeding of the Scotland of Macbeth. Food itself is an emanation of God's order, as the Homily on Rogation Week makes clear:

Hee is therefore invisible everywhere, and in every creature and fulfilleth both heaven and earth with his presence. In the fire, to give heat, in the water to give moisture, in the earth to give fruit, in the heart to give his strength, yea in our bread and drinke is hee, to give us nourishment, where without him the bread and drinke cannot give sustenance, nor the hearbe health.

Without God, eating itself must be anti-sacramental.

The First Witch parodies Macbeth's coming crime in demanding food of a well-fed woman:

> A sailor's wife had chestnuts in her lap,
> And munch'd, and munch'd, and munch'd. "Give me!" quoth I.
> "Aroint thee, witch!" the rump-fed ronyon cries.
>
> (I.iii.4-6)

The hours surrounding the murder display several examples of excessive or unnatural drinking. Lady Macbeth accuses Macbeth's "hope" of being "drunk" and awakening with a sickly hangover, "to look so green and pale/ At what it did so freely" (I.vii.35-38). Her own drinking makes her "bold" and gives her "fire" (II.ii.1-2), yet the humanity she helps repress with wine will awaken in her, even as in her fragments of memory she chides Macbeth: "look not so pale" (V.i.70). Her "rooted sorrow" (Vi.ii.41) is a psychic answer to Banquo's question:

>   have we eaten on the insane root
> That takes the reason prisoner?
>
> (I.iii.84-85)

In her case, reason finally takes prisoner of will, but the struggle has destroyed both, leaving her traumatized at the moment of Duncan's murder, the night on which she "with wine and wassail so convince[d]" Duncan's guards (I.vii.64) that they became "slaves to drink" (III.vi.13), their "drenched natures" lying "as in a death" (I.vii.68), the night on which she "drugg'd their possets" (II.ii.6), possets being a combination of the two liquids, besides blood and water, most prominent in the play, namely milk and wine. The Porter's comments on drinking provide a comic counterpoint to the fatal excess of Duncan's "spongy officers" (I.vii.71):

> Macduff. I believe drink gave thee the lie last night.
> Porter.   That it did sir, i' the very throat on me. But I requited

> him for his lie; and, I think, being too strong for him,
> though he took up my legs sometime, yet I made a
> shift to cast him. (II.iii.41-46)

But, as the Porter's immoderation suggests, the positive values of wine drain out of the world with the shedding of
Duncan's "golden blood" (II.iii.118):

> renown and grace is dead;
> The wine of life is drawn, and the mere lees
> Is left this vault to drag of.
>
> (II.iii.99-101)

Replacing the positive banquet Duncan enjoyed is an appetite worse than drunkenness. Macbeth would have the world
believe that Malcolm and Donalbain preyed upon their
father, a version of cannibalism Ross rejects:

> 'Gainst nature still!
> Thriftless ambition, that would ravin up
> Thine own life's means.
>
> (II.iv.27-29)

Yet, after the murder, after wine drains to lees and milk
sours to gall, elements of nature *do* rebel against themselves.
The Old Man's speculation about Duncan's horses, "the min-
ions of their race" (II.iv.15), is corroborated by Ross:

> Old Man. 'Tis said they eat each other
> Ross.   They did so, to th' amazement of mine eyes
>   That look'd upon 't.
>
> (II.iv.18-20)

The Witches' broth is composed of predators like "the
ravin'd salt-sea shark" (IV.i.24), which is apparently, like the
sharks in *Moby Dick,* a victim of its own ravenous appetite,
only its "maw and gulf" (IV.i.23)—mouth and gullet
—remaining for the caldron, the rest possibly self-consumed.
The brew includes the victims of doubly unnatural
acts—"Finger of birth-strangled babe/ Ditch-delivered by a
drab" (IV.i.30-31) and the cannibalistic perpetrators of such
acts:

> Pour in sow's blood, that hath eaten
> Her nine farrow.
>
> (IV.i.64-65)

The "sow's blood" and the "baboon's blood" (IV.i.37) signify an anti-eucharistic ceremony providing Macbeth with "Sweet bodements" (IV.i.96) that ultimately will destroy his "hope" (V.viii.22), rather than fulfill it through the agency of elements whose efficacy is rooted in the communicant's faith in Christ. The Witches' elements, collected from nature's underside, "poison'd entrails" (IV.i.5), "digg'd in the dark" (IV.i.25), dragged forth from ditches, "grease that's sweaten/ From the murderer's gibbet" (IV.i.65-66), feed Macbeth's will, driving whatever vestiges of faith he might retain further downward. He can threaten the hags, as he demands to know of Banquo's issue, with a sentence they live under already, then damn time itself, after what he has demanded has enraged him:

> Deny me this
> And an eternal curse fall on you!
>
> (IV.i.104-5)

> Let this pernicious hour
> Stand aye accursed in the calendar!
>
> (IV.i.133-34)

But he also utters a larger truth: "And damn'd all those that trust them!" (IV.i.139). His own trust in them is absolute, but it has plunged his kingdom into such deep distrust that even Malcolm in England must lie about his appetite, simulating the "Macbeth ethic" and employing the unnatural ravenousness of Scotland as a device against betrayal. Macduff dismisses the lust and the avarice Malcolm imputes to himself:

> there cannot be
> That vulture in you to devour so many
> As will to greatness dedicate themselves.
>
> (IV.iii.73-75)

> Scotland hath foisons to fill up your will,
> Of your mere own.
>
> (IV.iii.88-90)

Of his avarice, Malcolm suggests that his "more-having would be as a sauce/ To make [him] hunger more" (IV.iii.81-82). The wine of life was drawn with Duncan's death; Malcolm would "Pour the sweet milk of concord into hell" (IV.iii.98), as Macbeth has done in poisoning his "milk of human kindness" (I.v.18), his "chalice" (I.vii.11) and "vessel" (III.i.67), and as Lady Macbeth has in vowing to destroy the "babe that milks" her (I.vii.55) and in trying to exchange her "milk for gall" (I.v.59). But Malcolm's detractions comment ironically on Macbeth's Scotland, are merely a prelude to his crusade, which "with Him above to ratify the work," will "give to our tables meats, sleep to our nights,/ Free from our feasts and banquets bloody knives" (III.vi.32-35). Malcolm's coronation, promised in the play's last lines, will be a ceremony infused with "the grace of Grace" (V.iii.72), not a ritual feast undermined and finally shattered by its celebrant's own notorious evil.

The banquet scene confirms Macbeth's movement toward inauthenticity. He has lost reality as man and king, seeing only those horrible images—bloody daggers, bloody ghosts, green seas turned red at his touch—which conscience forces through his clenched will. The scene is adumbrated in Macbeth's colloquy with the living Banquo. Macbeth gathers intelligence ("Ride you this afternoon?" "Is't far you ride?" "Goes Fleance with you?" [III.i.19,24,36]) while admonishing his "chief guest" (III.i.11) to attend that evening's banquet: "Tonight we hold a solemn supper, sir,/ And I'll request your presence" "Fail not our feast" (III.i.14-15, 28). The contrast will explode into the banquet—the effort at royalty undercut by the more comprehensive *effect* of will. An irony surrounds the suspicious Banquo, of course, but the larger irony grasps Macbeth. The scene's many references to time (III.i.25-28, 37, 41-42) remind us that Macbeth anticipated time, one of nature's rhythms, and that he is on the wrong side of nature. "Let every man be master of his time/ Till seven at night" (III.i.41-42), he says, believing that *he* is—until, at shortly after seven, Banquo keeps his promise:

> The time has been,
> That when the brains were out, the man would die,

> And there an end; but now they rise again,
> With twenty mortal murders on their crowns,
> And push us from our stools.
>
> $$(III.iv.78-82)^{33}$$

Banquo's rising again is a measure not of any resurrection, of course, but an image of Macbeth's damnation, a more dramatic version of Richard III's nightmare before Bosworth Field, the deepest contrast possible to the Eucharistic archetype of his royal feast. Macbeth challenges the tardy guest "for unkindness" (III.iv.42) and is himself "quite unmann'd" (III.iv.73) by the ghost's unkindly—unnatural—arrival. Macbeth commits the suicide of the unimpeded will, becoming as he says, "strange/ Even to the disposition that I owe" (III.iv.112-13). To know his deed is to know himself, but, like the damned's knowledge of God, only negatively. "His pester'd senses," Mentieth observes, "recoil and start/. . .all that is within him does condemn/ Itself for being there" (V.ii.22-25). Finally, a crusade comes to restore inner reality to the sacraments:

> That by the help of these—with Him above
> To ratify the work—we may again
> Give to our tables meat, sleep to our nights,
> Free from our feasts and banquets bloody knives,
> Do faithful homage and receive free honours.
>
> (III.vi.32-36)

"A moving grove" (V.v.38)—emblem of fertility, of nature itself—closes in finally to revenge itself upon him, a possibility he predicts even before his visit to the witches:

> Stones have been known to move and trees to speak.
>
> (III.iv.123)

The banquet scene ends with another of the analogies with which Shakespeare subtly underlines dramatic meanings, making his scenes not separate events but impulses of a single motive force. Banquo appeared unannounced at Macbeth's supper. Macduff refused, as he had avoided Macbeth's coronation (II.iv.36):

> How say'st thou that Macduff denies his person
> At our great bidding?
>
> (III.iv.128-29)

Duncan had asked for Macbeth even as Macbeth contemplated the king's murder. Now Macbeth demands the presence of the man who *also* will kill the king. The difference between Duncan's request and Macbeth's summons is well expressed in the Priest's Communion Exhortation: "[I] beseech you for the Lord Jesus Christes sake, that yee will not refuse to come thereto, being so lovingly called and bidden of God himselfe [to come to] his holy Supper."

Duncan was "clear in his great office" (I.vii.18), and Banquo wished to "keep/ [his] bosom franchis'd and allegiance clear" (II.i.26-27). Such clearness was fouled by Lady Macbeth's admonition to belie reality with appearance, to "look up clear" (I.v.72), and by Macbeth's demands for a craftsmanlike "clearness" from his hired swords (III.iii.133), whose "spirits shine through" them (III.iii.128), an antithesis to Duncan's clarity. Lady Macbeth felt that "a little water clears us of this deed" (II.ii.67), but Macbeth could not "sleek o'er [his] rugged looks" (II.ii.27) at the banquet, nor could the Doctor "Raze out the written troubles of the brain" (V.iii.42) of Lady Macbeth. Macduff's grief for Scotland's plight, however, could "wipe. . .the black scruples" of suspicion from the "soul" of Malcolm (IV.iii.115-16), but it is Macbeth's own doctor who suggests who is the purged and who the purgative:

> Were I from Dunsinane away and clear,
> Profit again should hardly draw me here.
>
> (V.iii.61-62)

Macbeth's ultimate damnation is implied in an eerie little scene that goes almost unnoticed between his somber soliloquies and the sweep of the final action. Having dismissed a pale messenger, Macbeth begins a soliloquy:

> Seyton!—I am sick at heart,
> When I behold—Seyton, I say!
>
> (V.iii.12-20)

What was to be the object of "behold"? Since the rest of the soliloquy concerns what Macbeth has lost, it may be that he was about to mention the soul he has lost. But, perhaps unwilling to confront that loss, he interrupts himself with another shout to his armor-bearer, a shout exhibiting the will's interruption of the impulses of guilt. But does his call check the thoughts that may be flowing toward damnation? Perhaps it echoes the same theme—the eventuality that must be always lurking on the borders of Macbeth's consciousness. "Seyton," after all, sounds almost like "Satan."[38] Macbeth continues:

> I have liv'd long enough. My way of life
> Is fallen into the sear, the yellow leaf.
>
> (V.iii.22-23)

His fall is linked to images of a faded Eden. The alternative, of course, was to accept Duncan's nurture of Scotland's garden and realize the promise of the First Psalm: "For he shalbe like a tree planted by the rivers of waters, that will bring forth her fruit in due season; whose leafe shall not fade." He goes on with a barren list of all that he cannot look to have: "honour, love, obedience, troops of friends" (V.iii.24-25). "Deep damnation" has become "Curses, not loud but deep" (V.iii.27). The soliloquy closes with another shout of "Seyton!" The cry has been repeated three times, linking Seyton with the rhythm of the Weird Sisters.

Seyton enters, and with what would seem Mephistophelian irony asks, "What's your gracious pleasure?" (V.iii.29). Few words could be more inappropriate to Macbeth than "gracious pleasure." Duncan was "gracious," as Lennox says (III.iv.3) and as Macbeth recognizes after the murder ("Renown and grace is dead": II.iii.99):

> For them the gracious Duncan have I murder'd;
> Put rancours in the vessel of my peace
> Only for them, and mine eternal jewel
> Given to the common enemy of man.
>
> (III.i.66-69)

This speech, resembling that on which Seyton enters, is explicit about the soul he has tossed away like a careless trifle (the earlier Thane of Cawdor knew that his *life* was not "the dearest thing he ow'd" [I.iv.10]). And Macbeth knows no pleasure; his speeches list the joys of life he has forsaken——not the least being the unity of Communion, "the vessel of [his] peace"—the joys Duncan had in abundance and offered to Macbeth, which Duncan retains ("he sleeps well" [III.ii.23]) and which Macbeth will never know again. As Seyton uses it, "pleasure" is doubly ironic; a King's pleasure is translated immediately into reality. Royal pleasure means control, and this Macbeth is losing also:

1 Witch. [to Macbeth about the First Apparition]
He will not be commanded.

(IV.i.75)

He cannot buckle his distemper'd cause
Within the belt of rule.

(V.ii.15-16)

Now minutely revolts upbraid his faith-breach.

(V.ii.18)

The richness of Seyton's irony suggests that he may be more than a mere armor-bearer.

Macbeth demands more news of him. Seyton tells him that "All is confirm'd, my lord, which was reported" (V.iii.31). All?—perhaps all that the Sisters reported to Macbeth on his second encounter with them. The line suggests more than a mere military report; it conveys a strange and encompassing knowledge of the movement of Birnam Wood and the approach of the untimely-born Macduff. Macbeth demands his armor. Seyton tells him that " 'Tis not needed yet" (V.iii.34), implying again a knowledge of the future appropriate to a play in which prophecies echo through the air. In Act Five, of all those who appear in Dunsinane before invading forces break in—the Doctor and the Gentlewoman, Macbeth and Lady Macbeth, the two pale messengers—Seyton alone displays no sign of fear. His attitude is almost complacent.

Later, as the enemy pushes closer, Macbeth hears a shriek and demands, "What is that noise?" (V.v.7). Seyton replies, "It is the cry of woman, my good lord" (V.v.8). Again, irony rings in the terms of address. Seyton leaves and returns with

word that "The Queen, my lord, is dead" (V.v.16). Within
the message of death, Seyton places yet another term of
preeminent position. Macbeth's last link with this world is
snapped. Such crushing news is appropriately delivered by a
Seyton-Satan, representative of absolute loss. Seyton, the
ironic armor-bearer, exists between two barren soliloquies; he
enters and departs to words that define Macbeth's meaning-
lessness. Seyton's presence implies that death is not all that
awaits Macbeth. The man who bears the illusory hope of an
external armor that can in no way save Macbeth's soul reinforces the rhythms of damnation with which Macbeth has
been merging from the first. We see Lady Macbeth in Hell;
we see Macbeth on the way.[39]

Macbeth had tried to emulate the abundance of Duncan.
At his banquet, he exorts his guests to "Be large in mirth"
(III.iv.11) and requests that his own cup be "fill[ed] full"
(III.iv.88), even after he has viewed the bloody face of his
cutthroat and the oozing ghost of Banquo, who, in Macbeth's
partial recognition, has made the "table. . .full" (III.iv.46).
Like his wife, he has been filled "top-full/ With direst cruelty"
(I.v.43-44), finds that his hands will "the multitudinous seas
incarnadine," making the "green one" red, or, in a preferable
reading, suggesting the horrible fullness he has achieved,
making the green "one red" (II.ii.61-63). In "expectation of
plenty" (II.iii.5-6), he discovers instead that his mind is "full
of scorpions" (III.ii.36). He can talk of "bounteous nature"
(III.i.98) even while plotting Banquo's murder, but he is on
the wrong side of bounty, and can be "perfect" only in
Banquo's death (III.i.108), "perfect" and "Whole" in the
death of Fleance (III.iv.21-22): "As broad and general as the
casing air" (III.iv.23). His "perfection," however, involves a
Scotland whose "Each minute teems a new [grief]"
(IV.iii.175). His future is nonexistent in this world. Indeed,
the line extending from his rival seems to "stretch out to th'
crack of doom" (IV.i.117). The "swelling act/ Of th' imperial
theme" (I.iii.128-29) becomes a mind swollen with scorpions,
a future blank in this world, "no son of [his] succeeding"
(III.i.64), himself headed, he believes, for damnation in the
world to come.

Macbeth had been like a "cannon. . .over charg'd with double cracks" (I.ii.37), had "Doubly redoubled strokes upon the foe" (I.ii.38). His praises had, "as thick as hail" (I.iii.97), been "pour'd down before" Duncan (I.iii.100). But the duplication of the warrior for his king becomes the duplicity of the man for the crown. He imitates finally the Witches' version of "double" (IV.i.35). His murderers exceed his own prowess; Banquo bides "safe in a ditch. . ./ With twenty trenched gashes on his head/ The least a death to nature" (III.iv.26-28). In response to his crimes, Caithness promises to "pour we in our country's purge/ Each drop of us" (V.ii.28-29). "Or," replies Lennox, "so much as it needs/ To dew the sovereign flower and drown the weeds" (V.ii.29-30). Blood becomes redemptive, sacramental, for the first time since Duncan's wine drained out of his body and his kingdom, and Scotland returns to the positive fullness of "Grace" (V.iii.72).

Unlike *King Lear, Macbeth* occurs within a clearly defined hierarchical framework. Macbeth's crime violates an existing order and is explicable only in relationship to that order—a mousing owl attacks a falcon (II.iv.11-13), Duncan's horses issue forth "as they would/ Make war with mankind" (II.iv.14-18). The "unruly" night and "feverous" earth reported by Lennox (II.iii.59, 66) are not manifestations of order's disintegration, but negative evidence of an order superior to man's efforts to pervert it. Like Milton's Satan, Macbeth only destroys himself.

Yet, like Satan, heroic qualities accrue to Macbeth even after his fall. And, unlike Satan, Macbeth's final moments reassert an almost buried heroism. Macbeth reduces himself to bestiality, but he rises from it at the end. He is not stretched and compressed to involuntary serpenthood on the stones of Dunsinane. West is correct to suggest that "Macbeth. . .keeps his human image to our sight, or else the end would not move us."[40] Regardless of his clearly graphed descent into bestiality, Macbeth is heroic at the end. As he throws his "warlike shield" (V.viii.33) in front of his body and clenches his sword for a final time in his right hand to "try the last" (V.viii.32), he battles not only Macduff but the *fear*

that has been his chief personal antagonist from the first. He
has tried to "outrun the pauser, reason" (II.iii.117), has tried
to usurp time itself, *and* he has consistently been afraid—but
obviously not of man. His heroism in the opening battle, his
challenge to Banquo's ghost to "dare [him] to the desert with
[his] sword" (III.iv.104), and his defeat of Young Siward
—although there his confidence is buoyed by the witches'
assurance—suggest that mortal fear, fear of physical pain
and death, are not within him. What he fears is the imagery
of his imagination, the pictures projected into his mind by
conscience, the *un*natural acts dictated by his will, the fear
generated by his own virtuous nature. His questions signal
the nature of his fear:

> I know I am thane of Glamis;
> But how of Cawdor?
>
> (I.iii.71-72)

> why do you dress me
> In borrowed robes?
>
> (I.iii.108-9)

> If ill,
> Why hath it give me earnest of success,
> Commencing in a truth?
>
> (I.iii.131-33)

> If we should fail?.
>
> (I.vii.59)

> Is this a dagger which I see before me,
> The handle toward my hand?
>
> (II.i.33-34)

> or art thou but
> A dagger of the mind, a false creation,
> Proceeding from the heat-oppressed brain?
>
> (II.i.37-39)

> But wherefore could not I pronounce "Amen"?
>
> (II.ii.31)

> Will all great Neptune's ocean wash this blood
> Clean from my hand?
>
> (II.ii.61)

Ride you this afternoon?

(III.i.19)

Is't far you ride?

(III.i.24)

Goes Fleance with you?

(III.i.36)

Which of you have done this?

(III.iv.49)

  shall Banquo's issue ever
Reign in this kingdom?

(IV.i.102-3)

Then live, Macduff: what need I fear of thee?

(IV.i.82)

What is that noise?

(V.v.y)

Wherefore was that cry?

(V.v.15)

These are not the questions of an Othello, weaving himself into a web of doubt and error spun by a Iago, but those of a man moving deeper into a *self*-dictated evil. Macbeth's questions relate primarily to externals, although some are projected from his vividly visual mind. Othello's questions move him deeper and deeper inside himself, into a mind seething finally with exclusively *internal* imagery of "horrible imaginings."

The Witches make Macbeth "start and seem to fear" (I.iii.51)—the first of the several shudders he involuntarily experiences during his movement deeper into fear. He fears the unnatural desire that has already shaped within him,

  that suggestion
Whose horrid image doth infix my hair
And make my seated heart knock at my ribs
Against the use of nature.

(I.iii.134-37)

His own nature rebels against the profound *un*kindness of "that suggestion." His is the fear of the forbidden, of the un-

natural world he knows he must explore if the "suggestion'
is pursued, the world whose pathway leads downward to a
second meeting with the Witches demanded by Macbeth,
downward toward his bestial nature, to which his better nature can respond only with the horror of the internecine self.
His perverse heroism at the outset, when he decides to murder Duncan, involves his willingness to thrust knowingly in a
direction against nature, and is effectively contrasted to Lady
Macbeth's willful suppression of the consequences ("What do
you mean?" [II.ii.40]). Macbeth moves against the order of
the world and, inevitably, against that of his own being,
which manifests horror in startled hair and pounding heart,
quite against his will, even before he has acted, which
"Shakes" his "single state of man" (I.iii.140) even as his
career of crime will continue to "shake" (II.iii.66) his realm,
until he himself is "ripe for shaking" (IV.iii.238). "Present
fears/ Are less than horrible imaginings" (I.iii.137-38), because his "murder yet is but fantastical" (I.iii.139), a murder
of the mind whose imagery, however horrifying, has yet to
develop into a guilt so powerful that it will become a visual
reality for him, projections of a dagger on the air, a ghost
upon a stool. If Macbeth were not a man fearful of the unnatural, whose fear, in sin's proliferating effect, did not
produce "horrible imaginings," his tragedy would hardly be so
vivid, nor his heroism in bending "up each corporal agent"
(I.vii.80) against his incorporeal fears so great. "Yet let that
be," he tells himself in heroic abandonment to consequences,
"Which the eye fears, when it is done, to see" (I.iv.52-53).

Macbeth knows that he must subvert his nature to an unnatural act, must hold his humanity still as, "towards his design [he]/ Moves like a ghost" (II.i.55-56), like an agent
beyond or below humanity, whose volition is controlled by
rhythms partaking of neither conscience nor fear. Nature itself must suspend its function, must silence itself to create a
medium "appropriate" to Duncan's murder:

    Thou sure and firm set earth,
  Hear not my steps, which way they walk, for fear
  The very stones prate of my whereabout

And take the present horror from the time,
Which now suits with it.

(II.i.56-50)

Macbeth's fear, positively interpreted, is his "human kindness," the natural bond he shares with humanity in general
and with Duncan in particular, as king, kinsman, and guest,
the bond whose observance is, for better or for worse, the
basis both of "judgement here" and "the life to come." Macbeth is full of the "sweet milk of concord" (IV.iii.98), yet it is
that nurturing liquid which Lady Macbeth would deny "the
babe that milks" her (I.vii.55). She "fear[s]" Macbeth's "nature" (I.v.17), not because it emphasizes the horror of the
deed, but because it inhibits its execution. But she knows her
man, even if she cannot glimpse the ultimate periphery of his
cosmic awareness, and she echoes him, talking of "That
which rather [he] dost fear to do/ Than wishest should be
undone" (I.v.25-26). She will "chastise" "Valour's minion"
"with the valour of [her] tongue," will "pour [her] spirits in
his ear" (I.v.27)—another version of archetypal poisoning.
Yet she, too, must pray that knowledge and will be divorced,
must, in another of her psychic translations of herself, *become*
a part of Macbeth to subvert him and herself, "that [her]
keen knife see not the wound it makes" (I.v.53). She calls
upon

> murd'ring ministers
> Wherever in your sightless substances
> You wait on nature's mischief

(I.v.59-51)

willfully blotting from her awareness other ministers who also
"wait on nature's mischief," as Macbeth knows—"heaven's
cherubin hors'd/ Upon the sightless couriers of the air"
(I.vii.22-23). Lady Macbeth's invisible agents of mischief defeat Macbeth's divine wind of heavenly outrage, as she completes the inversion of virtue and will within Macbeth:

> Art thou afeard
> To be the same in thine own act and valour
> As thou art in desire? Wouldst thou have that
> Which thou esteem'st the ornament of life,

> And live a coward in thine own esteem,
> Letting "I dare not" wait upon "I would,"
> Like the poor cat i' the' adage?
>
> (I.vii.39-45)

His courage, once the servant of "justice. . .with valour armed" (I.ii.29), is for her an indivisible quality, virtually a *quantity*, not to be measured against the use to which it is put. His "morality," as in the line from *Hamlet* about "conscience" (III.i.83), makes him a "coward." He responds correctly, rebuffing her equation between him and "the cat i' the' adage." The emphasis is on "man":

> I dare do all that may become a man;
> Who dares do more is none.
>
> (I.vii.46-47)

Who dares do more in none because he violates his own humanity, he "unbecomes" himself, becomes less than a man. He will prove his prediction accurate when Banquo creates "a gap in our great feast. . .and all-thing unbecoming" (III.i.12-13).

Lady Macbeth's scorn emerges from a verbal irony wrapped within a more comprehensive dramatic irony:

> What beast was't, then,
> That made you break this enterprise to me?
> When you durst do it, then you were a man;
> And, to be more than what you were, you would
> Be so much more the man.
>
> (I.vii.47-51)

You were a beast *then,* she sneers, according to your own definition of manhood. She does not, of course, account for Macbeth's deeper perception of the sources of true manhood since "then," but employs the contrast between his former "bestiality" (courage in her lexicon) and his present "manhood" (cowardice). She skillfully subordinates herself to the role of accomplice in what evolves under her persuasion as Macbeth's "terrible feat" (I.vii.80). The larger irony, of course, is that she marshals Macbeth to bestiality and will herself suffer horribly when her buried nature emerges from its shallow grave within her, as she repeats the verb so often used by herself and her husband—"to do"—too late: "What's done cannot be undone" (V.i.75). The only issue met in their confrontation before the murder is that of aligning Macbeth's predisposed will to her determined one. The issues of nature, "judgement," and "damnation" become sound waves radiating outward from his soliloquy and touching only the ears of the audience.

The full flood of Macbeth's fear would seem to come at the moment immediately after the murder, a "present horror" (II.i.59) where "every noise appals" him (II.ii.58), where his hands are "hangman's hands" (II.ii.28), where he cannot "pronounce 'Amen'," conceives of his murder as that of sleep itself (II.ii.35-40), and refuses to return the daggers to the murder room:

> I'll go no more.
> I am afraid to think what I have done;
> Look on't again I dare not.
>
> (II.ii.50-52)

He is accused of fearing a "painted devil" (II.ii.55), as Lady Macbeth will later chide him for starting (III.iv.63) at "the very painting of [his] fear" (III.iv.61), "Impostures to true fear" (III.iv.64), Banquo's ghost. There he repeats his assertion of normal manhood:

> What man dare, I dare.
> Approach thou like the rugged Russian bear,
> The arm'd rhinoceros, or th' Hyrcan tiger;
> Take any shape but that, and my firm nerves
> Shall never tremble. Or be alive again,
> And dare me to the desert with thy sword;
> If trembling I inhabit then, protest me
> The baby of a girl.
>
> (III.iv.99-106)

But he has gone beyond what man dares, has invited precisely the "horrible imaginings" that emerge from the negative area of nature, the unnatural underside within him that he has chosen to explore and cannot now escape. Once, like Othello, he could fight external monsters; now not only are they, as with Othello, inside of him (his mind is "full of scorpions" [III.ii.36]), but he projects them from the theaters of his guilt before his own external vision as well. As the ghost disappears he claims to be "a man again" (III.iv.108), but he is now in combat with something "more strange" (III.iv.82), "Strange images of death" (I.iii.97) beyond the boundaries of positive nature, outside the perimeters of normal manhood, inside the zone to which his will has pushed him, where "terrible dreams. . .shake [him] nightly" (III.ii.18-19), "and wicked dreams abuse/ The curtain'd sleep" (II.i.50-51). His "fears in Banquo/ Stick deep" (III.i.49-50). He has ignored Banquo's warnings of betrayal "In deepest consequence" (I.iii.126) and must "consider it. . .so deeply" (II.ii.30) because the nature he would destroy remains within him to rebel against his actions: "His pester'd senses. . .recoil and start" and "all that is within him does condemn/ Itself for being there" (V.ii.22-24).

His "fears in Banquo" stick so deep that his face is "blanch'd with fear" (III.iv.116). The "natural ruby" of Lady Macbeth's "cheeks" makes him "strange/ Even to the disposition that" he owns (III.iv.112-15). His fear is natural, he asserts; her calmness before "such things" (III.iv.110), unnatural. And he is right—the release he gives his fears in "fit[s]" (III.iv.21) preserves his sanity, uneven though it be to a victim of hallucination, of images sent before his own guilt-conditioned eyes, to a man whose initial "present horror" (II.i.59) develops, in an ironic reflection of positive nature, into a horror of the future and of time itself. Like Gertrude, Lady Macbeth cannot see the ghost, because, like Gertrude, she is conditionally "innocent of the knowledge" (III.ii.45) of the murder from which a ghost returns. Lady Macbeth will echo her scorn of Macbeth in her madness: "Fie, my lord, fie! A soldier and afeard?" (V.i.41), but she will not understand the nature of his fears. "What need we fear who knows it, when none can call our pow'r to account?" (V.i.42-44). She knows it, her own humanity calls her to account, the "milk" she would transmute to "gall" remains within her, but *has* become a kind of gall, as the superb control of the surface surrenders to the deep kindness that has been within her all along. As the Doctor says, "unnatural deeds/ Do breed unnatural troubles" (V.i.79-80)—the obsession of Lady Macbeth with the murder night, when each event and word printed itself indelibly upon her repressed nature, and the more immediate and therefore temporary startings of Macbeth.

Macbeth must continue his fight with fear—his link with nature, humanity, and with the manhood he carries with him through his descent to bestiality. Lady Macbeth expresses her inextinguishable humanity only after she has sunk beneath nature to madness. Confident because of the Witches' prophecies, Macbeth can scorn fear:

Bring me no more reports; let them fly all;
Till Birnam wood remove to Dunsinane
I cannot taint with fear. What's the boy Malcolm?
Was he not born of woman? The spirits that know
All mortal consequences have pronounc'd me thus:
"Fear not, Macbeth; no man that's born of woman
Shall e'er have power upon thee." Then fly, false thanes,
And mingle with the English epicures!
The mind I sway by and the heart I bear
Shall never sag with doubt nor shake with fear.

(V.iii.1-10)

He can chide the messenger telling of Malcolm's approach, as Lady Macbeth once scorned his "heart so white" (II.ii.65):

Go prick thy face, and over-red thy fear,
Thou lily-livered boy. . .those linen cheeks of thine
Are counsellors to fear.

(V.iii.14-17)

He can command his soldiers to "Hang those that talk of fear" (V.iii.36) and can shout, "I will not be afraid of death and bane,/ Till Birnam forest come to Dunsinane" (V.iii.59-60). At the screams of his wife's ladies-in-waiting, he can assert that he has "almost forgot the taste of fears" (V.v.9).

While the confidence is false, while the frenzy resembles that of a trapped animal, Macbeth's reiterated claims of freedom from fear are merely preludes to his final test, when he will face Macduff, the product of an unnatural birth, the man to whom Macbeth has been radically unkind:

> Of all men else I have avoided thee.
> But get thee back; my soul is too much charg'd
> With blood of thine already.
>
> (V.viii.4-6)

Macbeth's confidence is crumbled by the fulfillment of the Witches' prophecies. Yet he meets the first reality—the "moving grove" (V.v.38)—with a frantic fatalism:

> Blow wind! come, wrack!
> At least we'll die with harness on our back.
>
> (V.v.51-52)

The second revelation of truth—Macduff's nativity—"cow[s] [his] better part of man" (V.viii.18). His warrior's courage faces its most profound test. Now he fights no mere man, but a man not of woman born, an emblem of his own "untimely" and unnatural act in leaping toward his future—as Macduff was plucked to life before *his* time. Macduff had already been the source of words from Macbeth that defined the duality he has embraced, the whiteness of his fear, and the insomnia produced by the cosmic disturbance he has encouraged:

> Then live, Macduff: what need I fear of thee?
> But yet I'll make assurance double sure
> And take a bond of fate. Thou shalt not live;
> That I may tell pale-hearted fear it lies,
> And sleep in spite of thunder.
>
> (IV.i.82-86)

Regardless of his timing in entering the world, Macduff's coming was a moment of creativity. Macbeth is the killer of "babes" (IV.i.152), an anti-creator. Now he must discover whether any last vestiges of his original valor remain. His fear—a consistent element even in his bravado before his final battle, a "bravery" undercut by his *preoccupation* with fear—has kept him before our own humanity as a man, someone more sympathetic than merely the "butcher" Malcolm would make of him (V.iii.69). His final overcoming of that fear confirms his "better part of man"—the heroism that

sets him *apart* from our humanity—his valorous deeds for
Scotland, his willingness to drive his will past his conscience
in spite of his knowledge of the consequences, and, finally,
his courage in disproving Macduff's taunt of "coward"
(V.viii.23):

> Though Birnam wood be come to Dunsinane,
> And thou oppos'd, being of no woman born,
> Yet I will try the last. Before my body
> I throw my warlike shield. Lay on, Macduff,
> And damn'd be him that first cries, "Hold, enough!"
>
> (V.viii.30-34)

He dies fighting against Scotland as, long before, he had
lived fighting for her. But he rises from the caged monster
Macduff would make of him to the warrior he had been. His
fear has confirmed his manhood for us and his final overcoming of it represents the only victory he can achieve, the
isolated moral triumph of the single man gleaming like a
brief candle against the "deep damnation," "destruction,"
"darkness," and "deed[s] of dreadful note" he has perpetrated. Heroism emerges at the end from bestiality; the man
who was flashes fitfully forward from the black background
of his own evil.

Malcolm's manipulation of Macduff represents, as Theodore Spencer says, "a reversal of the usual situation in the
play and instead of the appearance being good and the reality evil, it is the other way around, for the appearance is evil
while the reality is good."[41] Instead of masking murderous
intentions with innocence, Malcolm stains himself with his
own detractions the better to prove Macduff a friend. He
shows that he has learned what his sainted father did not
know—how to discover the mind's construction, how to deliver "the child of integrity" (IV.iii.115). Malcolm's manipulation reveals his virtue as a concomitant to his political skill,
not, as with Henry VI, a detriment to kingship. Una Ellis-
Fermor commiserates with "the unfortunate Malcolm, en-
cumbered as he is by the third scene of the fourth act."[42]
There can be no denying the awkwardness of the scene. Malcolm does not announce his rationale to us, nor has he been
clearly enough established for us to guess it. Our experience

coincides with Macduff's and, like his (IV.iii.138-39), it may
come confusedly. Our awareness of Malcolm's fitness to be
king, morally and politically, dawns with Macduff's, and,
after that, we, like him, are prepared to participate in
Malcolm's triumphant sweep toward the throne. If Malcolm's
production seems awkward beside the silken machinations of
Lady Macbeth, it is the awkwardness of virtue groping back
into a world where evil has been temporarily dominant. Unlike Duncan, Malcolm has learned caution. "Devilish Macbeth," he tells Macduff; "By many of these trains hath sought
to win me/ Into his power. . ." (IV.iii.116-18). Though
"Angels are bright still" (IV.iii.22), the Homily on the comming downe of the holy Ghost, defines the necessity of
Malcolm's restraint against "over-credulous haste"
(IV.iii.120): "Many shall come in my name (saith Christ) and
shall transforme themselves into Angels of light, deceiving (if
it bee possible) the very elect."

In addition to reversing the play's appearance-and-reality
pattern, the scene reasserts a just cosmos and aligns Malcolm
with it. Macduff speaks of "Heaven" resounding "As if it felt
with Scotland" (IV.iii.6-7). Malcolm assures him that "Angels
are bright still, though the brightest fell" (IV.iii.22). The
scene is England, where the "gracious" (IV.iii.43, 189) and
"good king" (IV.iii.147) is not a Macbeth, whose crimes
"Strike heaven in the face" (IV.iii.6), but a healer: "Such
sanctity hath Heaven given his hand" (IV.iii.144). Macbeth,
like Faustus ("Physic, farewell" [I, 28]), spurns medicine (and,
ironically, confirms his bestiality): "Throw physic to the dogs;
I'll none of it" (V.iii.47). Edward, "full of grace" (IV.iii.159),
is a medium between man and supernature:

> How he solicits Heaven,
> Himself best knows; but strangely-visited people,
> All swoll'n and ulcerous, pitiful to the eye,
> The mere despair of surgery, he cures,
> Hanging a golden stamp about their necks,
> Put on with holy prayers.
>
>   (IV.iii.149-54)

This "supernatural soliciting," clearly, is good. Malcolm himself will translate Macduff's sorrow at the murder of his family into "med'cines. . . To cure this deadly grief"

(IV.iii.214-15). Caithness marches to meet Malcolm, "the med'cine of this sickly weal" (V.ii.27). Rather than heed the ambiguous predictions of "instruments of darkness" (I.iii.124), King Edward "hath a heavenly gift of prophecy" (IV.iii.157). England ånd its King are the spiritual antithesis of Scotland and Macbeth. Malcolm's return to Scotland at the head of "goodly thousands" (IV.iii.44) will be a crusade endorsed not only by England but by the "powers above" that "Put on their instruments" (IV.iii.238-39), and are a combination of might and right, as contrasted with poor Richard's "God for his Richard hath in heavenly pay/ A glorious angel; then, if angels fight,/ Weak men must fall, for Heaven still guards the right" (III.ii.60-62). Malcolm's crusade embodies abstract virtues moving against a king who had once represented similar values. The crusade is enhanced by the presence of Old Siward, "An older and a better soldier none/ That Christendom gives out" (IV.iii.191-92).[43] "The night is long," says Malcolm, "that never finds the day" (IV.iii.239-40). As a "hideous trumpet" (II.iii.87) had signaled Duncan's death, Malcolm announces a Last Judgment for Macbeth:

> Make all our trumpets speak; give them all breath,
> Those clamorous harbingers of blood and death.
>
> (V.vi.9-10)

While Malcolm's scene in England is an ironic reflection of the situation in Scotland, a masking of virtue with rhetoric, rather than a concealing of a false heart beneath a false face, Malcolm cleverly enunciates the "Macbeth ethic," imputing to himself the perverse fullness of Macbeth's Scotland. His "confineless harms" (IV.iii.55), he claims, would bring Scotland "more vices than it had before" (IV.iii.47):

> your wives, your daughters,
> Your matrons, and your maids could not fill up
> The cistern of my lust.
>
> (IV.iii.61-63)

Malcolm insists that his is a "stanchless avarice" (IV.iii.78) and that he "abound[s]/ In the division of each several crime,/ Acting it many ways" (IV.iii.95-97). He lacks the "king-becoming graces" (IV.iii.91), particularly that displayed by his "sainted" father (IV.iii.109) and "good king" Edward (IV.iii.147), namely, "Bounty" (IV.iii.93). King Edward, "pious" (III.vi.27) and "holy" (III.iv.30), had not greeted Malcolm in proportion to the prince's fallen estate, but "receiv'd" him "with such grace/ That the malevolence of Fortune nothing/ Takes from his high respect" (III.vi.26-29). The infinitude of Malcolm's pretended evil shrinks before Macduff's bewildered ears to the dimensions of Malcolm's first lie: "my first false speaking/ Was this upon myself" (IV.iii.130-31), and we find Malcolm at the end fulfilling his father's role, measuring value in his kingdom and bestowing appropriate rewards. Ross suggests that the loss of Young Siward "must not be measur'd by his worth, for then/ It hath no end" (V.viii.45). Old Siward's immediate acceptance of his son's death draws from Malcolm a promise of kingly generosity: "He's worth more sorrow,/ And that I'll spend for him" (V.viii.50-51). Malcolm's largess soon moves beyond sorrow:

> We shall not spend a large expense of time
> Before we reckon with your several loves
> And make us even with you.
>
> (V.viii.60-62)

Immediately, he elevates his "thanes and kinsmen" to earldoms (V.viii.62-63), and promises not only the return of such essential elements of order as "time and place" (V.viii.73) to Scotland, but "measure" as well (V.viii.73). His "confineless harms" were fictional; the meting out of positive bounty becomes his kingly function, as it has been his father's. Malcolm completes the restitution prescribed for the "notorious evil liver" in the Communion rubrics. His evil was in words only, but he eradicates the evil Macbeth has neither repented nor lived to "have recompensed the parties, whom he hath done wrong unto, or at the least declare him selfe to be in full purpose so to doe, as sone as he conveniently may."

While no one can deny the authenticity of the anarchy that boils over Scotland during Macbeth's term, it has been limited in space (as the scene in England suggests) and in time (as Malcolm's restoration proves); *Macbeth*'s final scene, unlike

King Lear's, shows order convincingly restored. Macduff summarizes the reestablishment of relationships with a magnificent metaphor:

I see thee compass'd with thy kingdom's pearl.

(V.viii.56)

He sees a crown—a circle of nobles encompassing the central jewel, the King. With a pun on "pearl," Malcolm enhances the value of the metaphorical crown:

My thanes and kinsmen,
Henceforth be earls, the first that ever Scotland
In such an honour nam'd.

(V.viii.62-64)

"The time is free" (V.viii.55), returned to its natural sequence. Macbeth, who tried to twist time to his own design, who waged war with the future, is finally defeated by that future. ("Time," he had said, "thou anticipat'st my dread exploits" [IV.ii.144]). Malcolm reiterates the principle of growth once asserted by Duncan (I.v.39-40) and interrupted by Macbeth. Scotland's garden will be "newly planted with the time" (V.viii.65). No longer will innocent flowers shelter serpents. Appearance will be attuned again with reality:

this, and what needful else
That calls upon us, by the grace of Grace
We will perform in measure, time, and place.

(V.vii.71-73)

God and the crown—Grace and the graceful circle newly alighted on Malcolm's head—are reunited; the harmonious relationship between heaven and the state of man, the alignment of God's will and the king's, so apparent in England, is restored to Scotland. The stately cadence of Malcolm's speech, reinforced by rhymes that until now have echoed ominously (I.ii.64-65, I.vii.81-82, II.i.63-64, III.ii.54-55), underlines the order defined by the words. Like Satan's, Macbeth's rebellion has been a partial evil within a more comprehensive good. Macbeth's reign becomes the memory of a nightmare, scarcely disturbing Scotland's serene new dawn.

NOTES TO CHAPTER 5: *Macbeth*

1. Auerbach, *Mimesis*, p. 279.
2. W. C. Curry, *Shakespeare's Philosophical Patterns*, p. 67.
3. Nevill Coghill, "Listening to Shakespeare," *Stratford Papers on Shakespeare*, 1962 (Toronto, 1963), p. 23.
4. D. A. Traversi, *An Approach to Shakespeare*, p. 154.
5. The parallel was noted by Coleridge, whom A. C. Bradley quotes as saying, "It is a fancy; but I can never read this [Duncan's succession speech: I.iv.35-43], and the following speeches of Macbeth, without involuntarily thinking of the Miltonic Messiah and Satan": *Shakespearean Tragedy*, p. 433. Another version (simply the notation "Messiah-Satan") appears in *Coleridge's Writings on Shakespeare*, ed. Terrence Hawkes, p. 192. The parallel is developed in greater detail by John W. Hales, "Milton's *Macbeth*," *Nineteenth Century* 30 (Dec. 1891): 919-32. Hales examines the thematic links between *Macbeth* and *Paradise Lost:* "No other of Shakespeare's plays comes so near dealing with the very subject of *Paradise Lose* or. . .does in fact so fully deal with it, as *Macbeth.*" Macbeth's is the "disobedience of a remote son of Adam. . .he too plucked forbidden fruit and was expelled from his Eden—expelled from the state of happiness, honor, and peace." See also Paul Siegel, *Shakespearean Tragedy and the Elizabethan Compromise* (New York, 1957), pp. 142-60 (in which the Eve-Lady Macbeth equation is noted, pp. 143-44); M. D. H. Parker, *The Slave of Life* (London, 1953), pp. 162-64; J. Dover Wilson, *Macbeth* (Cambridge, 1947), pp. lxiv-xvi; and Helen Gardner, "Milton's 'Satan' and the Theme of Damnation in Elizabethan Tragedy," p. 6.
6. On the infinitive phrase *to outrun the pauser reason* as an expression of the action imitated in *Macbeth*, see Francis Fergusson, "*Macbeth* as the Imitation of an Action," *The Human Image in Dramatic Literature*, pp. 115-25.
7. Shakespeare's constant equation of Macbeth with bestiality in Act Five suggests the tradition that both the fallen angels and the titans were transformed into monsters after their falls, and thus creates another link between the epic and the tragic Macbeth.
8. Yet some critics see Macbeth as, somehow, a "tragedy of salvation." Cf. J. A. Bryant, Jr., *Hippolyta's View* (Lexington, Ky., 1961), p. 172: "Nothing in Macbeth's life became him quite like the leaving it; he died cleaner than he began, and he died with his manly readiness still about him. Undoubtedly this, too, was part of the providential plan," and G. Wilson Knight, *The Imperial Theme* (London, 1961), p. 128: "Macbeth at the last, by self-knowledge, attains grace." Mary McCarthy strikes a middle ground, finding Macbeth a man of "unimaginative mediocrity," a victim of "know-nothing materialism," "timorous, unimaginative." She suggests that "Macbeth does not fall; if anything, he somewhat improves as a result of his career in crime." "General Macbeth," *Harper's* (June 1962), pp. 35-39. Miss McCarthy seems intent on using Macbeth to attack the American middle-class male, who no doubt merits attack but might be attacked more directly. Suffice it that were Macbeth as stultified as Miss McCarthy claims, the play that bears his name would not have survived for her to distort. For more positive feminine reactions to *Macbeth* (if not necessarily to Macbeth), see Margaret Webster, *Shakespeare Without Tears* (New York, 1955), pp. 169-74, and Dame Edith Sitwell, *A Notebook on William Shakespeare* (London, 1948), pp. 24-46. For a more persuasive version of the materialist argument, see Walter C. Curry, *Shakespeare's Philosophical Patterns*, pp. 112-19. A

further negative opinion is that of G. B. Harrison, who says that *"Macbeth* has been extravagantly overpraised. . .it is the weakest of Shakespeare's great tragedies. . .," *Shakespeare's Tragedies* (New York, 1956), p. 184. Alfred Harbage disagrees, seeing the power of the play in the humanity of Macbeth: "If Macbeth were other than he is, less like ourselves, he would be a less powerful symbol of our own worst potentialities and the abyss we have escaped." *Macbeth* (Baltimore, Md., 1956), p. 19. Francis Fergusson says that *Macbeth* "takes possession of the mind and the imagination directly." *"Macbeth* as the Imitation of an Action," p. 179. And Dover Wilson sees it as "a gigantic reflexion of our sinful selves thrown upon the immeasurable screen of the universe." *Macbeth*, p. lxviii.

9. Particularly lucid discussions of the play's pattern of appearance and reality are Theodore Spencer, *Shakespeare and the Nature of Man*, pp. 153-62, and L. C. Knights, *"King Lear* and the Great Tragedies," *The Age of Shakespeare*, pp. 241-45.

10. Cf. Hardin Craig: "He is seduced by the witches, clearly powers of evil, who exemplify the morality doctrine that Satan is a deceiver." "Morality Plays and Elizabethan Drama," *SQ* 1 (April 1950): 64-72. Professor Craig's neglect of Macbeth's spiritual struggle keeps Macbeth in line with the morality hero, who "lacks personal motivation or any inward struggle," but such a view results in a vast oversimplification of Macbeth's movement toward evil. A more qualified view is that of Willard Farnham: *"Macbeth* is a morality play written in terms of Jacobean Tragedy. Its hero is worked upon by forces of evil, yields to temptation in spite of all that his conscience can do to stop him. . .and is brought to retribution by his death." *Shakespeare's Tragic Frontier* (Berkeley, Calif., 1950), p. 79. Certainly Macbeth suffers from the overconfidence and ignorance of the morality hero (cf. Everyman's self-deceptive nature in the first half of the play, and Faustus's "Learn thou of Faustus manly fortitude"). Like Everyman, Macbeth exhibits (when he cannot say "Amen") what Van Laan calls "a felt need to pray. . .inhibited by excessive worldliness," *"Everyman,"* p. 467. The Macbeth-Claudius relationship is also enhanced by Macbeth's inability to say "Amen."

11. Macbeth himself engages in some significant echoing: " 'Glamis hath murder'd sleep, and therefore Cawdor/ Shall sleep no more! Macbeth shall sleep no more' " (II.ii.40-41). The final step in the sequence should be *King;* instead Macbeth recoils in horror at himself, at the humanity he has lost in becoming King.

12. Quoted in Donald Nugent, "The Renaissance and/of Witchcraft," *Church History* 40, no.1 (March 1971): pp. 69-78.

13. Nugent, "Renaissance and/of Witchcraft."

14. Cf. Fergusson, "Introduction" to *Macbeth, Shakespeare's Tragedies of Monarchy* (New York, 1962), p. 178, on V.i: "In her nightgown, alone, she would look less like the power-mad woman of Act I than like a little girl lost in the dark."

15. Dr. Johnson's question on II.ii.54-55, "Could Shakespeare possibly mean to play on the similitude of *gild* and *guilt?*" (William Wimsatt, *Johnson on Shakespeare*, p. 103) is pursued by Cleanth Brooks, who says, "for [Lady Macbeth] there is no moral order: *guilt* is something like *gilt*—one can wash it off or paint it on." "Shakespeare as a Symbolist Poet," *The Yale Review* 34 (June 1945): 660. For a response to Professor Brooks's new-critical approach, see Dame Helen Gardner, "A Reply to Cleanth Brooks," *Approaches to Shakespeare*, pp. 90-98.

16. See the Variorum Edition, pp. 161-64, for a summary of the debate. Among those who believe that Lady Macbeth really faints are Bradley, *Shakespearean*

Tragedy, pp. 394-95; Edward Dowden, *Shakspere: His Mind and Art* (New York, 1962), p. 254; Edmund Chambers, *Shakespeare: A Survey,* p. 236; G. Wilson Knight, *The Wheel of Fire,* p. 152; G. L. Kittredge, *Macbeth* (Boston, 1939), p. 146, W. A. Neilson, *Shakespeare,* p. 1182; Thomas M. Parrott, *Shakespeare,* p. 826; and Irving Ribner, *Patterns of Shakespearian Tragedy,* p. 162.

17. West, *Shakespeare and the Outer Mystery,* p. 77.

18. Henry Adams, *The Education of Henry Adams* (New York, 1931), p. 228.

19. Cf. G. Wilson Knight: "The whole play may be writ down as a wrestling of destruction with creation." *The Imperial Theme* (Oxford, 1931), p. 153: and G. R. Elliott, who compares the "dreadful disorder" to "that of primal chaos." *Dramatic Providence in "Macbeth"* (Princeton, N.J., 1958), p. 104, n36. Another analogue, perhaps *the* analogue to *Macbeth*'s storm, is Matthew's version of the aftermath of the Crucifixion (27:51): "And beholde, the vaile of the Temple was rent in twayne, from the top to the bottome, and the earth did quake, and the stones were cloven." Cf. "Where we lay,/ Our chimneys were blown down; and, as they say,/ Lamentings heard i' the' air; strange screams of death,/ . . .some say, the earth/ Was feverous and did shake" (II.iii.59-66) and "Most sacrilegious murder hath broke ope/ The Lord's anointed temple, and stole thence/ The life o' the' building!" (II.iii.72-74).

20. L. C. Knights, *Explorations* (New York, 1964), p. 37. G. W. Knight shares these sentiments in *The Wheel of Fire,* p. 149.

21. Robert Speaight, *Nature in Shakespearian Tragedy* (New York, 1962), p. 61. On the Raven-Martlet contrast in *Macbeth,* see J. P. Dyson, "The Structural Function of the Banquet Scene in *Macbeth,*" *SQ* 14, no. 4 (Autumn 1963): 369-71.

22. Roy W. Battenhouse, "Shakespearean Tragedy: A Christian Approach," *Approaches to Shakespeare,* p. 210.

23. E. Gilson, *The Spirit of Mediaeval Philosophy,* p. 295.

24. Walter C. Curry, *Shakespeare's Philosophical Patterns,* p. 134.

25. G. Wilson Knight, *The Imperial Theme,* p. 136. See also *The Crown of Life* (Oxford, 1947), pp. 214-16.

26. J. P. Dyson, "The Structural Function of the Banquet Scene in *Macbeth,*" p. 371. For other useful discussions of the banquet scene, see Miguel A. Bernad, S.J., "The Five Tragedies in *Macbeth,*" *SQ* 13 (Winter 1962): 49-61, and L. C. Knights, *Explorations,* pp. 36-41.

27. G. Wilson Knight, *The Imperial Theme,* p. 137.

28. Cf. George L. Kittredge: " 'so gospell'd': so tamely submissive to the gospel precept to 'love your enemies, bless them that curse you, do good to them that hate you, and pray for them which despitefully use you and persecute you' (*Matthew,* v, 44)." *Macbeth* (Boston, 1939), p. 158, n88.

29. J. P. Dyson, "The Structural Function of the Banquet Scene," p. 371.

30. Quoted in Muir, New Arden Edition of *Macbeth,* p. 91, n18.

31. Mr. Frankford is also betrayed by "a gentlemen on whom [he] built an absolute trust." Mrs. Frankford, like Lady Macbeth, acts in ignorance, or at least in defiance of, her intrinsic nature. Mrs. Frankford repents. Lady Macbeth's "kindness" repents for her, forcing its way through the layers of will she tried to place between her nature and her crime.

32. Miss McCarthy contends that Macbeth says this "to himself" ("General Macbeth," p. 37). I have not seen a text that supports this contention; it is convenient, however, in view of her thesis of Macbeth's "know-nothing materialism."

33. *Johnson on Shakespeare,* ed. Wimsatt, p. 103.

34. That the witches have only reminded him of previous thoughts is implied even before Lady Macbeth's suggestion that the murder was conceived originally by Macbeth (I.vii.47-52). When Banquo interrupts Macbeth's speculations about murdering Duncan (I.iii.152), Macbeth apologizes, saying, "My dull brain was wrought with things forgotten" (I.iii.154). The apology suggests that the witches have merely reminded Macbeth of murderous thoughts suspended amid the hurlyburly of battle. Curiously, Coleridge calls Macbeth's excuse a "lie" (*Coleridge's Writings on Shakespeare*, p. 191).

35. Cunningham, *"Macbeth:* The Tragedy of the Hardened Heart," p. 46.

36. Cf. Rosencrantz (III.iii.11-23) and Octavius (*Antony and Cleopatra*, V.i.14-19).

37. G. W. Knight, *The Imperial Theme*, particularly pp. 134-41. See also Knight, *The Crown of Life*, pp. 212-13.

38. Kokeritz says that "Hodges (1643) lists *say* and *sea* as homonyms." *Shakespeare's Pronunciation* (New Haven, 1953), p. 144.

39. Kenneth Muir suggests in the New Arden Edition that "one critic suggests wildly that Shakespeare intended [in 'Seyton'] a quibble on Satan." P. 152, n29. I have been unable to identify this antic critic. At least one director, Mr. Donald McWhinnie, has seen the possibilities in Seyton's part, as indicated in this review by J. C. Trewin: "Seyton in his revival became a character of some consequence. Just as Catesby must be always with Richard III, so Seyton was always with Macbeth. He was the mysterious third murderer at Banquo's ambush." "The Old Vic and Stratford-upon-Avon, 1961-1962," *SQ* 13 (Autumn 1962): 516.

40. West, *Shakespeare and the Outer Mystery*, p. 181.

41. Theodore Spencer, *Shakespeare and the Nature of Man*, p. 161.

42. Una Ellis-Fermor, "Shakespeare the Dramatist," *Modern Writings on Major Authors*, ed., James R. Kruezer and Lee Cogan (Indianapolis, Ind., 1963), p. 182.

43. Cf. John of Gaunt's "God's is the quarrel. . ." (I.ii.36-41) and the Homilies (1852 edition): "But we must refer all judgment to God, to kings and rulers and judges under them, which be God's officers to execute justice, and by plain words of Scripture, have their authority and use of the sword granted from God." "We must in such case patiently suffer all wrongs and injuries, referring the judgment of our cause only to God," pp. 102 and 107.

6

The Tempest

Thou seest with what wyndes, with what waves, with what stormes thy sele shyp is tossed, thy ship wherein thi litle flock is in peril to be drouned. And what is nowe lefte, but that it utterly synke and we al perish: Of this tempest & storme we may thanke our owne wickednes and sinful livying, we espy it wel & confesse it, we espy thy righteousnes, & we bewaile our unrighteousness; but we appeale to thy mercy. . .without whiche neither the angels in heaven can stand sure before the, muche lesse we sely vessel-les of clay.

— Henry VIII, "Prayer for Peace in the Church"

Therefore I will, in all the haste,
Have a reckoning of every man's person;
For, and I leave the people thus alone
In their life and wicked tempests,
Verily they will become much worse than beasts;
For now one would by envy another up eat;
Charity they all do clean forget.

— God, in *Everyman* (45-51)

And behold, there arose a great tempest in the sea, in so muche as the ship was covered with waves. . . . Then he arose & rebuked the windes & sea & there followed a great caulme. But the men merveiled saiyng: what maner of man is this, that bothe wyndes and sea obeye hym.

— Matthewe, VIII

If, as Henry VIII suggested in the preface to his Primer of 1545, all creation moves toward salvation,[1] Shakespeare's

374

tragedies suggest a counter-movement, the exploration of a dimension insisted upon by the will of man, an impulse of the individual that interferes with or contradicts the striving of all creation. Macbeth explicitly rejects the creative swelling of nature and the invisible pressure of supernature toward fulfillment. Nature and supernature reject him, in turn, as he has rejected his place within their positive frame. The world of *King Lear* struggles to the brink of redemption, but at the ultimate moment hope is stillborn, the world is thrust back into a "cheerless, dark, and deadly" zone as empty of meaning as the storm from which it has seemingly emerged was full of sound and fury. Creation and any hope for salvation lie "dead as earth." Hamlet sets in motion a creative work of art designed to sweep past Claudius's defenses and, with the sightless couriers of guilt, penetrate his very soul. But Hamlet interrupts his play before it can explore the opportunity for salvation it represents for the "mighty opposites." However opposite, each is bound to the other in the same movement toward an eternity, where, as Claudius recognizes and the Homily reiterates, "at the last daye. . .the secretes of all mennes hartes shalbe manifest to all the worlde. And then the truth shal appere, and accuse them and their owne conscience. . . . And Christ the righteous judge, shal then justly condempne them to everlasting shame and death." Whatever the fate of Hamlet's and Claudius's souls, redemption for the king is forestalled by the prince. Prospero also catches the conscience of a king, by echoing his guilt back to him, but Prospero's choice is for "virtue," not "vengeance" (V.i.28). His manipulation provides perhaps as profound a commentary on *Hamlet* and, indeed, on Shakespeare's tragic world, as anything written since. The application of grace is neither interrupted, delayed, nor denied. It flows at last from *within* Prospero and with its coming he redeems himself as well as Alonso. Prospero achieves victory in the ultimate struggle defined by Thomas a Kempis in *The Imitation of Christ*: "[No one] hath a harder conflict to endure than he who labours to subdue himself."[2] Prospero explicitly embraces a crucial tenet in the "imitation" Kempis describes: he turns his "eye inwardly upon himself, and [is wary] of judging the actions of others." At the end of the play, Prospero extends the injunction about judging to his audience.

The final plays of Shakespeare, *Pericles, Cymbeline, The Winter's Tale,* and *The Tempest,* move from initial discord and alienation to ultimate harmony and reconciliation. Chaos, whether a husband's conviction of a wife's infidelity or a storm at sea, gradually dissipates during the play; it does not develop into the violent darkness of Scotland under Macbeth or culminate in the murder of a Desdemona or a Cordelia. The timely application of grace modulates the plays into the rhythms of comedy. *The Tempest* imitates the comic action described by Northrop Frye, which parallels "the central myth of Christianity. . . . The framework of the Christian myth is the comic framework of the Bible, where man loses a peaceable kingdom, staggers through the long nightmare of tyranny and injustice that is human history, and eventually regains his original vision. Within this myth is the corresponding comedy of the Christian life. We first encounter the law in its harsh tyrannical form of an external barrier to action, a series of negative commands, and we are eventually set free of this law, not by breaking it, but by internalizing it: it becomes an inner condition of behavior, not an external antagonist as it is to the criminal."[3] With mild qualifications, this description applies to Ferdinand, Alonso, and, particularly, to Prospero.

Prospero attempts to put Alonso and the other conspirators through a penitential experience, to evoke within each a "heart's sorrow" leading toward redemption—"a clear life ensuing" (III.iii.81-82). The alternative to a clarifying contrition is the process of damnation Ariel describes:

> Ling'ring perdition, worse than any death
> Can be at once, shall step by step attend
> You and your ways.
>
> (III.iii.77-79)

The banquet spread before the sinners disappears, a Communion Feast deferred "until," in the words of *The Book of Common Prayer,* "[the sinner] have openly declared him self to have truely repented, and amended his former naughty lyfe."[4]

The conspirators are excommunicated from what the stage directions describe as a "banquet," accompanied by "Solemn and strange music," and by "gentle actions of salutation" from "several strange shapes" who invite "the King, etc., to eat." Alonso describes the music as "harmony" and Gonzalo as "Marvellous sweet" (III.iii.18-19). Gonzalo notes that the "manners" of the shapes "are more gentle, kind, than of/ Our human generation you shall find/ Many, nay almost any" (III.iii.32-34). Alonso "cannot too much muse/ Such shapes, such gesture, and such sound, expressing,/ Although they want the use of tongue, a kind/ Of excellent dumb discourse" (III.iii.35-38). However strange the shapes and music are, the emphasis is on solemnity, ceremony, harmony, kindness, on a communication that resonates without words on the inner natures of Gonzalo and Alonso. (Sebastian and Antonio, although impressed, place the dumb-show into the contexts of antique fable and current fashion respectively [III.iii.21-27]). The central visual interest of the scene, once the shapes vanish, focuses on the waiting table. The treatment of the banquet in the play is consonant with the words of the Communion Service describing the Eucharist as "the banket of most heavenly food" and as "a moste godly and hevenly feast."

But, clearly, Sebastian and Antonio are disqualified from partaking of the feast. Immediately before its appearance they have reconspired against Alonso and Gonzalo (III.iii.13-17). They are excluded not only by the opening rubrics prohibiting "open and notorious evil liver[s]" and those guilty of "malice and hatred" from the table, but by Prospero himself: "some of you there present/ Are worse than devils" (III.iii.35-36). Alonso is disqualified by his despair:

> Even here I will put off my hope and keep it
> No longer for my flatterer.
>
> (III.iii.7-8)

> I will stand to and feed.
> Although my last. No matter, since I feel
> The best is past.
>
> (III.iii.49-51)

None of the three can partake, "because it is requisite that no man shoulde come to the holye Communion, but with a full trust in goddes mercy, and with a quiet conscience." That they are excommunicated, however, is not merely punishment for transgression, but a removal of the possibilities for damnation and an encouragement toward qualification for Communion, as the *Book of Common Prayer* makes explicit:

> For as the benefyte is greate, if wyth a trulye penitente herte and lyvely faith we receive that holy sacrament (for then we spiritually eate the fleshe of Christ, and drincke his bloude, then we dwell in Christe and Christe in us, we be one wyth Christ, and Christe with us) so is the daunger great, if we receyve the same unworthely. For then we be gilty of the body and bloud of Christ our saviour. We eate and drincke our owne dampnation, not considering the lordes bodye. We kindle gods wrath against us, we provoke him to plague us with divers diseases, and sundrye kyndes of death. Therfore if any of you be a blasphemer of god, an hinderer or slaunderer of his worde, an adulterer, or be in malyce or envye, or in anye other grevous crime, bewaile your Sinnes, and come not to this holy table, lest after the taking of that holy sacrament, the devil enter into you, as he entred into Judas, and fil you full of al iniquities, and bring you to destruction both of bodye and soule. Judge therefore your selves (brethren) that ye be no judged of the Lord. Repent you truly for your sinnes past, have a lively and stedfast faithe in Christ our saviour. Amende your lives, and bein perfect charitie wyth all men, so shal ye be mete partakers of those holy misteries.

Ariel condemns the conspirators in words which reverse the psalmist's pattern:

> for which foul deed
> The powers, delaying, not forgetting, have
> Incens'd the seas and shores, yea, all the creatures
> Against your peace.
>
> (III.iii.72-75)

Instead of all the elements praising God (as, for example, in the Benedicte), all nature attacks the ungodly. Macbeth, of course, suffers a more profound retribution; his communion is destroyed (he has "Put rancours in the vessel of [his] peace" [III.i.67], and "broke the good meeting,/ With most admir'd disorder" [III.iv.109-10]). Alonso's Communion will occur, literally, at the marriage that the play promises just

beyond the Fifth Act, a nuptial that will observe "All sanctimonious ceremonies" "with full and holy rite" (IV.i.16-17).
Ariel's angry speech to the "three men of sin" (III.iii.53)
echos the Homily of the Passion, which asks witnesses of
Christ's sacrifice to respond as Ariel suggests the conspirators
should: "But to these and many other such extremities, was
hee driven by thy sinne, which was so manifold and great,
that God could bee only pleased in him and none other.
Canst thou thinke of this O sinfull man, and not tremble
within thyself? Canst thou heare it quietly without remorse of
conscience, and sorrow of heart?" Alonso cannot "heare
it"—the story of Prospero, "Him and his innocent child"
(III.iii.72), the story of his own "foul deed" (III.iii.72), which
has "bereft" him of his own "son" (III.iii.76-77)—without remorse. "I' the name of something holy, sir, why stand you/ In
this strange stare?" Gonzalo asks (III.iii.94-95). And then he
answers his own question:

> All three of them are desperate: their great guilt,
> Like poison given to act a great time after,
> Now gins to bite the spirits.
>
> (III.iii.104-6)

The interrupted banquet has activated guilt to take what
course it will within each of the three. Unlike Hamlet's interruption of his play, however, the disappearance of Prospero's
table is, as he makes clear (III.iii.83-91), a phase within a
deeper pattern, not the destruction of the pattern itself.
Alonso, a guilty creature sitting at a play, is struck so to the
soul that presently he proclaims his malefactions:

> Oh, it is monstrous, monstrous!
> Methought the billows spoke and told me of it;
> The winds did sing it to me, and the thunder,
> That deep and dreadful organ-pipe, pronounc'd
> The name of Prosper; it did bass my trespass.
> Therefore my son i' th' ooze is bedded, and
> I'll seek him deeper than e'er plummet sounded
> And with him there lie mudded.
>
> (III.iii.95-102)

Here "heart's sorrow" is a precondition not for salvation but
for suicide. Alonso's reason *will* be obliterated (it will, in

Prospero's metaphor, lie "foul and muddy" [V.i.82]). But
Alonso, like Lear, will awaken on the far side of annihilation.
The repentance speech contradicts the impulse toward
suicide by implying the essential rhythm of *The Tempest*—the
transition from storm ("billows," "wind," "thunder") to harmony ("sing," "organ-pipe," "bass").[5] Alonso's potentially
soul-destroying despair and Prospero's role in translating it
into positive value are described by the Homily on Repentance: "Although we be never so earnestly sorie for our sinnes, acknowledge and confesse them: yet all these things shall
bee but meanes to bring us to utter desperation, except wee
doe stedfastly beleeve that God our heavenly father will for
his Sonne Jesus Christs sake, pardon and forgive us our of-
fenses and trespasses, and utterly put them out of remem-
brance in his sight." Only through Prospero's imitation of God's
pardoning action can Alonso move into the fourth and final
phase of repentance: "an amendment of life, or a new life."

Prospero's manipulation of the shipwreck victims is an admittedly imperfect device; it suffers from the shortcomings
of those it would redeem. Not all can achieve the "inner condition" Frye describes. Prospero's effort is partial; the marriage at the play's end, idyllic as it seems, occurs within a
world from which the negation of the tragedies can never be
wholly dispelled. But if the limitations of man and his world
have been exposed in the tragedies, the *significance* of man
has deepened. In the early comedies, the manipulation of
Biron and his mates, of Beatrice and Benedick, and of Orlando aimed at the exposure of foolish attitudes and the reformation of their possessors. Religious terms were *metaphors*
for change. These plays usually ended with good-natured
laughter all around and the inevitable marriages beyond.
Prospero's play exposes not folly but sin, and aims at repentance. In *The Tempest*, religious terms are *symbolic* of change;
manipulations have deepened from the rituals that awakened
Biron, Beatrice and Benedick, and Orlando to the sacrament
that moves Alonso. Manipulation does not merely educate
the self in *The Tempest*, it redeems the soul. The play ends
solemnly; its experience has been too deep for laughter. The
marriage that the play promises beyond itself is merely a

symbolic token of what Prospero's manipulation has hoped to achieve. It is not, as in Rosalind's effort with Orlando, the goal for which the entire dramatic movement has been striving. In *The Tempest* that goal has been either reached or not reached within the heart of each character before he begins the speedy voyage back to Naples.

The Tempest is largely, as D. G. James says, "a story issuing from the commanding magic of Prospero."[6] This discussion will center, as the play does, on Prospero, on his awareness of what he is attempting and on his control of the production that brings harmony out of discord. Prospero's initial approach to his production is primarily intellectual; the results of his play, however, force his human feelings to catch up with his understanding. The feeling of charity at last coincides with the concept of charity, and the fusion occurs, appropriately, at the moment when Prospero discards his role as God and submits to the limitations of mankind.[7]

While Prospero's "project" (V.i.1) brings himself as well as Alonso to harmony, it is not true, as James suggests, that "nothing can resist the power of Prospero."[8] The play surrounding Prospero's manipulation reveals clearly the limitations of his effort at redemption. The play imitates one of the central tenets of Protestant theology—the "inward man" is, finally, the only one who can change himself. No amount of external manipulation can coerce a hardened heart; some men, like Antonio, choose not to be redeemed. As Auden suggests, Prospero's "all is partial"; Antonio remains "by choice myself alone."[9] If the comic vision is exposed by the shallowness of a Claudio on whom it cannot function, it is questioned more profoundly by the defiance of the Antonio who refuses to permit it to function. At the same time, however, those who have been moved by Prospero's play have reached awarenesses more significant than that of a courtly lover stripped of his affectations. *The Tempest,* then, is about the extent and limits of man's control over the inner lives of other men.

Even more basically, perhaps, *The Tempest* explores the nature of freedom, and concludes that freedom and responsibility are linked, that freedom without responsibility is license

and, ultimately, bondage.[10] Prospero's Epilogue imposes on
the spectator the test to which the characters have been subjected, asking the spectator to make the experience of the
play *his* experience and to decide whether he stands with
Alonso and Prospero inside the circle of reconciliation, or
with Antonio willfully beyond it. Appropriately, at the end of
his comedy, Prospero asks the spectator to consider the play
on a level deeper than that of entertainment. The play occurs, as James Russell Lowell says, "in the soul of man, that
still vexed island hung between the upper and the nether
world, and liable to incursions from both."[11] Unless the spectator experiences it this way, the play means nothing. As Jan
Kott says, "the island is a stage on which the history of the
world is being acted and repeated,"[12] and the spectator is invited through the medium of Prospero's play to participate in
that reenactment. The island is like the earth of *Paradise Lost,*
a meeting place of two competing visions, the first represented by Caliban, a "thing of darkness" (V.i.275), and by
what Knight isolates as the "*Macbeth* rhythm,"[13] the suggestive
patterns of conspiracy and treason in Antonio, Sebastian, *and*
Caliban: "for I know thou dar'st/ But this thing dare not"
(III.ii.63-64), by cursings, drunkenness, and treachery. The
second is the "majestic vision" (IV.i.118) of fertility and increase presented by Ariel for the young lovers, but emerging
from the imagination of Prospero:

> Spirits, which by mine art
> I have from their confines call'd to enact
> My present fancies.

(IV.i.120-22)

Yet even the Masque contains within it, in the plot of Venus
and Cupid (IV.i.94-101), an analogue to the competing visions, and in their rebuff an analogue to *The Tempest.* Cupid
amends his ways, returning from "wanton" mischief (IV.i.95)
to a recognition of his own nature:

> Her waspish-headed son has broke his arrows,
> Swears he will shoot no more, but play with sparrows
> And be a boy right out.

(IV.i.99-101)

Forces that would destroy "full and holy rite" and "sanctimonious ceremonies" (IV.i.16-17) are forestalled and transformed. The Masque represents a projection into mythological symbols of Prospero's admonitions to Ferdinand about chastity. The problem is "solved" within the Masque, where Cupid experiences a transformation from manipulative deity to human, predicting Prospero's "return to humanity." For Ferdinand, perhaps, the Masque represents something like a dream, in which his desires are projected into symbolic form and "worked out" through the dream process. The Masque itself, with its harmonies and images of abundance, is produced by a mere "rabble" (IV.i.37) controlled by the power of Prospero's art, whose primary property is to transform.* But it is not that one vision triumphs outright at the end of the play. Where it cannot be translated into repentance, the evil is subdued and controlled. The idyllic stands on the edge of its meeting with a clearly less than perfect world. The ending is a harmonizing of conflict best represented by the reconciliation of Alonso and Prospero, the one repentant, the other forgiving, each surrendering the will's control to meet on a level of mutual kindness.

Act One is *The Tempest* in microcosm. Its dominant figure is Prospero, presiding over its stormy opening and prompting its harmonious close, pointing to Miranda as a product of his education, but acknowledging the limits of education, personified by Caliban, who has learned language only to curse (I.ii.363-64). The sojourn on the island has educated Prospero himself; he has learned something more basic than meteorological control. While his problem is similar to Hamlet's—to revenge or not to revenge—he has had the crucial advantage of viewing it from the objective stance of time and distance. Hamlet loses himself amid the complexities of his emotional interaction with his situation. Prospero controls himself *and* his island and, when he has done all he can do,

---

* The transformation of the "meaner fellows" (IV.i.35), "the rabble" (IV.i.37), into pagan goddesses represents yet another of the play's "sea changes." The transformation also comments wryly on Caliban's traffic with Stephano and Trinculo: "What a thrice-double-ass/ Was I to take this drunkard for a god/ And worship this dull fool" (V.i.294-96).

his emotions emerge, and he integrates himself into the society from which he had held himself aloof.

Prospero raises a tempest to re-create for those aboard the ship his own sea experience, which began with the treachery of Antonio, who cast them adrift "To cry to the sea, that roar'd to us" (I.ii.149). Like Hamlet, Prospero redepicts the conspirators' guilt, forcing them to imitate it in their own *experience,* however, rather than as spectators at a play. The sea did Prospero and Miranda "but loving wrong" (I.ii.151), and their "sea sorrow" (I.ii.170) terminated in proof of "Providence divine" (I.ii.159), as will Ferdinand's experience: "by immortal Providence she's mine" (V.i.189). The sea brought Prospero and Miranda to the island, where he has had time to come to terms with the wrong done him, to achieve calmness where rage had been, to harmonize an experience that began discordantly. In losing himself, he has found himself. The crucial thing he has learned, as Margaret Webster says, is "that freedom often turns out to be different from what he had imagined, involving responsibility and not merely license, and that each of us must find his own way to the resolution of the conflict within himself."[14] Although they cannot know it yet, some of the passengers bound back from Tunis to Naples will reenact Prospero's voyage, the archetypal voyage of Jonah, Odysseus, the Ancient Mariner, Ishmael, and the *Narcissus,* into zones having no geography or chronology, into the tempestuous darkness of the self, and from thence to rebirth.

The opening tempest symbolizes the spiritual storm of its victims. Their turmoil is greater, in fact, than that around them, as the Boatswain suggests:

A plague upon this howling! They are louder than the weather or our office. (I.i.39-40).[15]

Ferdinand's cry as he leaps from the sinking ship applies both to the fury of the storm and to the guilty passengers:

Hell is empty
And all the devils are here.

(I.ii.214-15)

That his words apply to some of the passengers is confirmed later by Prospero, who says, "some of you there. . .are worse than devils" (III.iii.35-36). Prospero parallels inner and outer weather again in explaining to Miranda:

> I have with such provision in mine art
> So safely ordered that there is no soul—
> No, not so much perdition as an hair
> Betid to any creature in the vessel
> Which thou heard'st cry, which thou saw'st sink.
>
> (I.ii.28-32)

With the interlocking construction he employs occasionally,[16] Shakespeare makes "cry" the verb of "creature" and "sink" the verb of "vessel." The ship in the storm symbolizes souls in torment. Three times in the first thirty lines of scene two, the people on the ship are called "souls," an emphasis suggesting the area with which Prospero is most concerned. Although, admittedly, Shakespeare often uses "souls" without religious overtones (cf. Ariel in I.ii.208), here the religious sense is enforced by the word "perdition."

The storm is more, of course, than a projection of damnation. It suggests man's frailty in the face of superhuman power, like the storm in *King Lear:* "What cares these roarers for the name of king?" (I.i.17-18). Even the Mariners break and throw themselves upon forces beyond their own skills and strengths: "All lost! To prayers, to prayers! All lost!" (I.i.55). This abandonment of man's effort, of individual will, is the play in microcosm, a moving into a situation "When no man [is] his own" (V.i.212)—as no man in this world, as in the storm, *is* his own. The storm reminds us of the "wicked tempests" God promises at the beginning of *Everyman* (l. 48) and coincides with Prospero's reiterated suggestion that "The hour's now come" (I.i.36), as it had for Everyman, although he, like the souls bound from Africa to Italy, could not know it. Prospero tells Miranda their story because the future has suddenly become possible and must be linked with the vector of the past, particularly if Miranda is to play her role in Prospero's project, which itself is carefully patterned to coincide with the natural rhythm of time. With the coming of the ship, timelessness gives way to sequence. The world of the island has suddenly become dynamic. For the first time, "now" becomes an operative word, as the present suddenly intersects the moment connecting the past and the future:

> 'Tis time
> I should inform thee farther.
>
> (I.ii.22-23)

Thou must now know farther.

>
> (I.ii.33)

> Miranda.   You have often
> Begun to tell me what I am, but stopp'd
> And left me to a bootless inquisition.
> Concluding, "Stay not yet."
> Prospero.   The hour's now come;
> The very minute bids thee ope thine ear.
> Obey and be attentive. Canst thou remember
> A time before we came unto this cell?
>
> (I.ii.33-39)

Prospero's repetition of past history brings him "to the present business" (I.ii.136), to a "zenith" that

> doth depend upon
> A most auspicious star, whose influence
> If now I court not but omit, my fortunes
> Will ever after droop.
>
> (I.ii.181-84)

His story finished, Miranda sleeps, and Prospero calls for Ariel: "Come away, servant, come; I am ready now" (I.ii.187).

The storm has clear analogues with biblical descriptions of the World's End:

> There shalbe signes in the Sonne, & in the Moone, and in the Starres, & in the yearth, the people shalbe at their wittes ende, through dispayre. The sea, and the water shall roare, and mennes hartes shall fayle them for fear, and for looking after those thynges whiche shal come in a cloude, with power and great glory. When these thinges begin to come to pass, then looke up, and lift up your heddes, for youre redempcion draweth nygh. (Luke 21)

And there folowed voyces, thundringes, and lightnynges: and there was a great earthquake, and as was not since men were upon the earth. (Revelation 16:18)

The Tempest, however, reverses the order of events in *King Lear:*

> If that the heavens do not their visible spirits
> Send quickly down to take these vile offences,
> It will come,
> Humanity must perforce prey on itself,
> Like monsters of the deep.
>
> (*King Lear,* IV.ii.46-50)

> What foul play had we, that we came from thence?
> Or blessed was't we did?
>
> (I.ii.60-61)

Unlike *Lear,* good *follows* evil in *The Tempest:*

> Both, both, my girl.
> By foul play, as thou say'st, were we heav'd thence,
> But blessedly holp hither.
>
> (I.ii.61-63)

Like that of the opening storm, the sea "roar'd," but, like the tempest of the first scene, nature's seeming malevolence hid benign purpose: "th' winds whose pity, sighing back again,/ Did us but loving wrong" (I.ii.150-51). As Miranda has reminded Prospero of the "virtue of compassion" (I.ii.27) after the opening storm, she had educated him to strength during their initial sea sorrow:

> Oh, a cherubin
> Thou wast that did preserve me. Thou didst smile,
> Infused with a fortitude from heaven,
> When I have deck'd the sea with drops full salt,
> Under my burden groan'd; which rais'd in me
> An undergoing stomach, to bear up
> Against what should ensue.
>
> (I.ii.152-58)

The predictive content of their previous experience implies the comedy of the play itself—grace will be applied in time.

If the storm is for the passengers the first movement in a reenactment of the sea sorrow of Prospero, the First Act provides further comments on the storm and anticipations of its ultimate result. The stories of Ariel, Caliban, and Ferdinand and Miranda reflect the themes of freedom and bondage, of losing oneself to find oneself.

Ariel's career parallels what Prospero hopes will be the experience of those arriving on the island; it begins in confinement and pain, but ends in freedom:

> Thou best know'st
> What torment I did find thee in; thy groans
> Did make the wolves howl and penetrate the breasts
> Of ever-angry bears. It was a torment
> To lay upon the damn'd, which Sycorax
> Could not again undo. It was mine art,
> When I arriv'd and heard thee, that made gape
> The pine, and let thee out.
>
> (I.ii.286-93)

Those who roared while caught in the power of the storm have been brought safely to land. The storm represents the torment of the damned ("All the devils are here"), which Prospero will attempt to subdue as he did the spell of Sycorax (who also had an intimate connection with the devil [I.ii.319-20]).[17] The tree in which Ariel was imprisoned (a "cloven pine" [II.ii.27]) suggests the world, the flesh, and the devil, which have trapped the guilty passengers. Only a higher power can triumph over these forces, as Prospero did over Sycorax and her god, Setebos. Ariel is a subordinate commander, in charge of "all his quality" (I.ii.193) by explicit directive of Prospero (IV.i.37-38). Yet regardless of what Ariel is—and West is again right to suggest that he and Prospero's magic cannot be pressed to a per se definition[18]—Ariel is equal or superior to the pagan gods:

> On the topmast,
> The yards and bowsprit, would I flame distinctly,
> Then meet and join. Jove's lightnings, the precursors
> O' the' dreadful thunder-claps, more momentary
> And sight-outrunning were not; the fire and cracks
> Of sulphurous roaring the most mighty Neptune
> Seem to besiege, and make his bold waves tremble,
> Yea, his dread trident shake.
>
> (I.ii.199-206)

Prospero, Ariel's commander, has also shaken the provinces of the pagan gods with their own weapons:

> I have bedimm'd
> The noontide sun, call'd forth the mutinous winds,
> And 'twixt the green sea and the azur'd vault
> Set roaring war; to the dread rattling thunder
> Have I given fire, and rifted Jove's stout oak
> With his own bolt; the strong-bas'd promontory
> Have I made shake.
>
> (V.i.41-47)

Such power carries with it, as West suggests, "its never-eluded shadow of moral and metaphysical uncertainty."[19] Prospero's surrender of his magic will be crucial to the return to humanity he achieves at the play's end. But before he can reach that moment he must educate Ariel, an essential actor and stage-manager within the drama being produced on various parts of the island by and for various segments of the original shipboard community.

When Ariel proves moody, agitating for freedom, Prospero threatens to "rend an oak/ And peg thee in his knotty entrails till/ Thou hast howl'd away twelve winters" (I.ii.294-96). Ariel immediately begs for "pardon" (I.ii.297), and his submission brings a prompt promise of freedom. Not only in the account of Ariel's previous history but in the scene itself, we observe a movement from pain (or the threat of it) to freedom. The threat is followed by a successful plea for pardon. The episode anticipates the pattern Prospero hopes to impose on those now placed about the island—the movement from torment to a recognition of the need for pardon, the need to submit to a power greater than that of their own wills, the submission that becomes freedom, a movement paralleling the comedy of the Eucharist. Freedom, even for the spirit Ariel, is a product of the individual's acceptance of the discipline of natural rhythms:

> Pros. What is't thou canst demand?
> Ari. My liberty.
> Pros. Before the time be out? No more!
>
> (I.ii.244-46)

Ari.   I will be correspondent to command
        And do my spiriting gently.
Pros.   Do so, and after two days
        I will discharge thee.
Ari.   That's my noble master!
        What shall I do? Say what? What shall I do?

                                            (I.ii.297-300)

Ariel's freedom depends upon his ability to subordinate himself to Prospero's design. His service is analogous to that
which, in the "Collecte for Peace," becomes "perfect freedom":

Pros.   Thou shalt be as free
        As mountain winds; but then exactly do
        All points of my command.
Ari.   To th' syllable.

                                            (I.ii.498-500)

Pros.   Shortly shall all my labours end, and thou
        Shalt have the air at freedom. For a little
        Follow, and do me service.

                                            (IV.i.265-67)

Pros.   My Ariel, chick
        That is thy charge. Then to the elements
        Be free, and fare thou well!

                                            (V.i.316-18)

A contrast to the confrontation between Prospero and
Ariel and a comment on it is the ensuing one with Caliban,
who represents the willful refusal to be free. Although he
knows Prospero to be stronger than his "dam's god, Setebos"
(I.ii.373), he curses Prospero in the name of his mother:

    All the charms
    Of Sycorax—toads, beetles, bats, light on you!

                                            (I.ii.339-40)

He receives not a promise of freedom, but threat of more
pain:

    I'll rack thee with old cramps,
    Fill all thy bones with aches, make thee roar
    That beasts shall tremble at thy din.

                                            (I.ii.369-71)

Like those howling in the storm, Caliban is captive not of external agents but of his inward refusal to yield to powers greater than those either of his own will or that of his discredited god. Prospero defines this condition when he calls Caliban "slave," as he does five times in the scene.

Walter C. Curry's description of Macbeth applies equally to Caliban: "Irrational acts have established habits tending to further irrationality and one of the penalties exacted is dire impairment of the liberty of free choice."[20] That Caliban is a self-made slave accounts for Prospero's otherwise excessive anger at Ariel in the previous scene. His anger does not necessarily prove that Prospero is a "crusty and irascible old pedant";[21] this is to define a symptom and ignore the cause. Prospero does not wish Ariel to become a slave to self-will, particularly since Ariel is so crucial an instrument in Prospero's project to free others from self-will. Caliban's disordered nature demands the retribution with which Prospero threatened Ariel. Even though Caliban knows that Prospero's "spirits hear [him]," he "needs must curse" (I.ii.3-4). Caliban represents the lower limits of Prospero's efforts at education, a warning built into the play that we must not expect too much of Prospero's redemptive drama. Caliban is

> A devil, a born devil, on whose nature
> Nurture can never stick! on whom my pains,
> Humanely taken, all, all lost, quite lost!
> And as with age his body uglier grows,
> So his mind cankers. I will plague them all,
> Even to roaring.
>
> (IV.i.188-93)

Prospero can produce the roar of torment induced by the spirits pinching Caliban. He can thwart the several plots hatching malignantly on his island. He cannot change the nature of the plotters. Disordered and disorderly elements *can* be controlled, however, as Edmund had been for nine years during the reign of King Lear. Prospero admits of Caliban,

> But, as 'tis,
> We cannot miss him. He does make our fire,
> Fetch in our wood, and serves in offices
> That profit us.
>
> (I.ii.310-13)

Antonio cannot, apparently, discover the "deity" (II.ii.278) of
conscience in his bosom, yet he *must* surrender to external
compulsion, whether the possibilities of inward repentance
reside within him or not:

> [I] require
> My dukedom of thee, which perforce, I know,
> Thou must restore.
>
>   (V.i.132-34)

Certain elements of humanity, or subhumanity, must be
coerced into a merely formal integration with society. There
be those, as Prospero says of Caliban, "Whom stripes may
move, not kindness!" (I.ii.344).

A comic analogy to the Communion denied the "noble"
characters (III.iii) is Caliban's initiation to wine. On discover-
ing the two-voiced monster, Stephano describes the healing
powers of his bottle:

> He shall taste of my bottle; if he have never drunk wine afore,
> it will go near to remove his fit. (II.ii.77-79)

> If all the wine in my bottle will recover him, I will help his
> ague. Come. Amen! I will pour some in thy other mouth.
> (II.ii.97-99)

The promise echos derisively against the Communion's
Prayer "for the whole estate of Christes Church": "And we
moost humbly beseache the of thy goodnes (O Lord) to comfort and succoure all theyme whyche in thys transitory lyfe
bee in trouble, Sorowe, nede, sicknes, or any other adversity." Twice Caliban is asked to "Kiss the book" (II.ii.134,
145), like Julia in *The Duchess of Malfi,* who kisses the
Cardinal's poisoned Prayer Book and dies (V.ii.320-37). As
the wine invades him, Caliban comes to believe that Stephano
has "dropped from heaven" (II.ii.140), that he is "a brave
god and bears celestial liquor" (II.ii.121). Caliban kneels to
Stephano, like Milton's intoxicated Eve, who inclines to a
subordinate power in eating the fruit and captures the posture of her surrender in bowing to the tree. To aspire is to
fall. Caliban swears allegiance to the self-destroying ethic of
will and becomes a slave again, surrendering his "rights" in

the island if only Prospero can be destroyed. Having kissed the book, Caliban debases even himself by bending to "kiss [Stephano's] foot" (II.ii.156). The anti-sacrament plays against the "lifting up" of the Communion. Caliban claims that Stephano's "liquor is not earthly" (II.ii.130) and, in an ironic fulfillment of his statement, is reduced to a "howling monster" (II.ii.183), repeating the sound of the play's spiritually tormented characters. Caliban's deification of Stephano derives from his desire to partake of the wine *per se,* not of any power the wine symbolizes—other than the physical intoxication Caliban mistakes for the gift of a "brave god" (II.ii.121). "When's god's asleep," says Trinculo, "he'll rob his bottle" (II.ii.154-55). Caliban takes Stephano's "celestial liquor" (II.ii.121) for his Communion, contradicting that which the Homily concerning the Sacraments calls a "celestiall banket and feast." The ritual with Stephano's bottle merely drives Caliban downward to deeper servitude, disrupting further an already deranged nature. "Here is that which will give language to you, cat," Stephano says, introducing the bottle to Caliban's lips (II.ii.86). Caliban's profit on it is to learn further "how to curse" (I.ii.364).

The wine, instead of symbolizing the spiritual cleansing of the Communion, merely extends the characteristics of the *ethos* of each character, as Gilbert Harrison astutely suggests: "Shakespeare had an acute knowledge of the effects of liquor. Stephano is suffering from illusions of grandeur; Trinculo has become more cynical; Caliban more savage and revengeful."[22] And, as the *Book of Common Prayer* suggests, it is better not to celebrate Communion at all than to do so "unworthely":

> Then ye shal reconcyle youre selves unto them, ready to make restitucion & satisfaction according to the uttermost of your powers for all the injuries and wronges done by you to any other, and likewise being ready to forgive other than offended you, as you would have forgeveness of your offences at Goddes hande. For otherwyse, the receiving of the holy Communion doth nothing els, but encrease your dampnation. . . For then we be gilty of the body & Bloud of Christ our saviour. We eate and drinke our own dampnation, not considering the lordes bodye. We kindle Gods wrath against us. We provoke hym to plague us with diverse diseases.

Caliban's encounter with Sephano begins the last episode in his effort at revenge against Prospero. For such compulsive rebellion against order, Caliban (and later his confederates) receives precisely the punishment prescribed by the Prayer Book:

> For this, be sure, to-night thou shalt have cramps,
> Side-stitches that shall pen thy breath up.
>
> (I.ii.325-26)

>   I'll rack thee with old cramps
> Fill all thy bones with aches, make thee roar
> That beasts shall tremble at thy din.
>
> (I.ii.369-71)

> I will plague them all,
> Even to roaring.
>
> (IV.i.192-93)

> Go charge my goblins that they grind their joints
> With dry convulsions, shorten up their sinews
> With aged cramps, and more pinch-spotted make them
> Than pard or cat o' mountain.
>
> (IV.i.259-62)

> Sebastian.   Why, how now, Stephano!
> Stephano.   O, touch me not; I am not Stephano, but a cramp.
> Prospero.   You'd be king o' the isle, sirrah?
> Stephano.   I should have been a sore one then.
>
> (V.i.285-88)

The drunken plotters, who parody Antonio's original conspiracy against Prospero and that of Antonio and Sebastian against Alonso, realize a punishment similar to that which Dante assigns the Gluttons: "I' the' filthy-mantled pool. . ./ There dancing up to the chins, that the foul lake/ O'erstunk their feet" (IV.i.182-84), and similar to that the Homily concerning the Sacrament assigns to those who "cannot attaine unto [the taste of the sundry graces of God]": "Who be drowned in the deepe durtie lake of blindness and ignorance." At the end, however, Caliban seems to have begun a positive education, leaving Antonio more profoundly alone in his self-chosen isolation.

While Ariel and Caliban comment on the ultimate hopes and limitations of Prospero's project, the most complete exemplification provided by Act One of Prospero's purpose is the relationship of Ferdinand and Miranda. It is an idyllic and allegorical version of what is to happen to Alonso, idyllic and allegorical because the lovers represent a pre-lapsarian perfection not to be found in their world-stained elders. The love story begins stormily, involves a test (largely external, but not without significance), and ends in harmony and fair weather. The story illustrates explicitly one of the themes of *The Tempest* and *the* theme of Prospero's manipulation—that one must lost himself to find himself.

Having leaped in frenzy from the sinking ship, Ferdinand enters, drawn by Ariel's song suggesting reconciliation:

> Come unto these yellow sands
> And then take hands.
>
> (I.ii.376-77)

The music soothes Ferdinand as later it will soothe Alonso (V.i.58-60). Ferdinand reiterates the equation between inner and outer weather:

> Sitting on a bank
> Weeping again the King my father's wrack,
> This music crept by me upon the waters,
> Allaying both their fury and my passion
> With its sweet air.
>
> (I.ii.389-93)

Here the storm is analogous not to souls gripped by damnation but to Ferdinand's grief. His concern for another is, in *The Tempest*, an essential precondition for his *own* redemption. His grief for his father wins him a vision of "the goddess/ On whom these airs attend" (I.ii.421-22). Later, his father's grief for him will precede Alonso's beatific "vision of the island" (V.i.176), where he will also take Miranda for a controlling deity:

> Is she the goddess that hath sever'd us,
> And brought us thus together?
>
> (V.i.187-88)

In her concern for those aboard the sinking ship, Miranda has already fulfilled this condition. The storm makes her suf-

fer "with those that [she] saw suffer" (I.11.6) and has
"touch'd/ The very virtue of compassion in [her]" (I.ii.27).
Later, she extends the compassionate principle to nature itself: when the wood Ferdinand collects "burns,/ 'Twill weep
for having wearied" him (III.i.18-19). One reason why *The
Tempest* has the *feeling* of comedy is that the compassionate
principle dominates its world as it does not, for example, in
King Lear. There compassion is finally ineffectual and is not
so deeply visualized *in* nature—except by Cordelia—as it is in
The Tempest:

> Th' winds whose pity, sighing back again,
> Did us but loving wrong.
>
> (I.ii.150-51)
>
> Though the seas threaten, they are merciful.
>
> (V.i.178)

The competing versions of nature in *King Lear* ultimately
cancel each other out. At the end of *The Tempest,* Prospero
can "promise. . .calm seas, auspicious gales,/ And sail so expeditious that shall catch/ Your royal fleet far off"
(V.i.314-16).

Although Prospero's soul prompts their love, (I.ii.420) he
devises a harsh playlet designed to educate Ferdinand some-
what as Biron and Orlando were educated, but more deeply.
As with Ariel, Prospero imposes bondage on Ferdinand. The
Prince responds not with the self-punishing defiance of a
Caliban but with submission and expressions of freedom:

> My father's loss, the weakness which I feel,
> The wrack of all my friends, nor this man's threats
> To whom I am subdu'd are but light to me,
> Might I but through my prison once a day,
> Behold this maid. All corners else o' the' earth
> Let liberty make use of. Space enough
> Have I in such a prison.
>
> (I.ii.487-93)

Prospero's harsh control of Ferdinand as of Ariel is a way to
freedom. His irascibility is that of a man with a master plan
in mind, which others cannot understand until they have
experienced it. While it could be explained it would then have

no meaning except in the mind, and it is not with the mind
that Prospero hopes to work. His anger also derives from the
fact that it is primarily in *his* mind that Prospero understands
his production. His emotions have yet to coincide with his intellectual conception. One of the reasons for his tardiness of
emotion is the *precision* he must exercise:

> Hast thou, spirit,
> Perform'd to the point the tempest that I bade thee?
>
> (I.ii.193-94)

> Ariel, thy charge
> Exactly is perform'd; but there's more work. . .
>   The time 'twixt six and now
> Must by us both be spend most preciously.
>
> (I.ii.237-41)

> Prospero.   Thou shalt be as free
>   As mountain winds; but then exactly do
>   All points of my command.
> Ariel.   To th' syllable.
>
> (I.ii.498-500)

We see the positive results of Prospero's test of Ferdinand
in the first scene of Act Three. Ferdinand enters "bearing a
log" (s.d.), but not complaining because "sweet thoughts" of
Miranda "refresh [his] labours" (III.i.14). Miranda enters, her
compassion aroused by Ferdinand's exertions. She bids him
rest and offers to assume his task. For Ferdinand, unlike
Caliban, slavery is a way to freedom: "most poor matters/
Point to rich ends" (III.i.3-4). Yet his will is not quite aligned
to the goal conceptualized in Prospero's mind. Miranda's
offer makes the point clear:

> It would become me
> As well as it does you; and I should do it
> With much more ease, for my good will is to it,
> And yours is against it.
>
> (III.i.28-31)

The image of Miranda bearing logs awakens him to the
larger truth beyond the mere logs he has carried all day. He
refuses, with a metaphor suggesting how much his inner
weather has changed since his arrival on the island:

No, noble mistress. 'Tis fresh morning with me
When you are by at night.

(III.i.33-34)

They exchange vows, each pledging service to the other:
"The very instant that I saw you," says Ferdinand, "did/ My
heart fly to your service; there resides,/ To make me slave to
it; and for your sake/ Am I this patient log-man"
(III.i.64-67). "To be your fellow/ You may deny me,"
Miranda replies, "but I'll be your servant,/ Whether you will
or no" (III.i.84-86). Ferdinand accepts her as his wife, "with
a heart as willing/As bondage e'er of freedom" (III.i.88-89).
The reiteration of the freedom-bondage theme suggests
again that voluntary service for another constitutes freedom,
that while the lovers have lost their individual selves, they
have found themselves in each other. Prospero's blessing on
the exchange makes yet another meteorological reference:

> Fair encounter
> Of two most rare affections! Heavens rain grace
> On that which breeds between 'em.

(III.i.74-76)

The gentle and nourishing rain is reminiscent of the tears
Ferdinand shed for his father, and which Miranda dropped
at the sight of the shipwreck and of her lover's labors, tears
now translated to emblems of happiness:

> I am a fool
> To weep at what I am glad of.

(III.i.73-74)

Later, speaking directly to Ferdinand, Prospero repeats the
suggestions of a blessed rain, but in a negative context:

> If thou dost break her virgin-knot before
> All sanctimonious ceremonies may
> With full and holy rite be minist'red,
> No sweet aspersion shall the heavens let fall
> To make this contract grow; but barren hate,
> Sour-eyed disdain, and discord shall bestrew
> The union of your bed with weeds so loathly
> That you shall hate it both.

(IV.i.15-20)

The words do not prove that Prospero is an "irritable old man,"[23] but assert his belief that responsibility is the concomitant of freedom, that value emerges from submission to control, in this case, self-control. As Frye suggests, "The chastity of Miranda is a controlled energy that must develop from virginity to marriage by observing the proper rhythms of time and of ritual, otherwise the whole order of nature will go out of alignment."[24] To harmonize himself with the rhythms of nature, man must yield to rituals like matrimony, which, in turn, coincide with the elements of nature *and* intersect the supernature that includes and exceeds nature's visible and invisible components. If a man seeks his will *outside* of the context of God, which is reflected in the sacraments, time becomes his enemy, as it was for the early Everyman, for Dr. Faustus, Beatrice-Joanna, and Macbeth. A contrast to Ferdinand and Miranda is Edmund, who means to do "Some good" (V.iii.243). That his "repentance" does not completely align him with natural rhythms is suggested by his accepting lust for love ("Yet, Edmund was belov'd!" [V.iii.239]). His will still interprets events to *its* satisfaction, thus his "Nay, send in time" (V.iii.247) and "Haste thee" (V.iii.251) cannot affect events positively. His "humaneness" (if that is what it is) does not coincide with the natural rhythms that only the uncorrupt will can realize. The formal rites of marriage will have meaning only if the partners accept a law higher than that of their individual wills, only if their spiritual reality coincides with the words of the ceremony coupling them. Else would the world be peopled all with Calibans.

Prospero's talk of beneficent rains from heaven anticipates the "fellowly drops" (V.i.64) that finally will fall from his own eyes. When this occurs, *The Tempest* will have reached its climax, for it will show that while he may have *thought* the concept of forgiveness all along, his heart has at last consented. The education of Prospero constitutes the central drama of *The Tempest*.

While Prospero has hardly exhibited the willful blindness of King Lear, he *has* perpetrated a version of Lear's defection, abandoning the duties of his office for personal pursuits:

The government I cast upon my brother
And to my state grew stranger, being transported
And rapt in secret studies. . .my library
Was dukedom large enough.

(I.ii.75-110)

Like Lear, Prospero surrenders "revenue" (I.ii.98) and
"power" (I.ii.99), but not his title. As in *King Lear,* the result
is predictable; Prospero solicited the response he got by
wholly neglecting his ducal "body politic":

I, thus neglecting worldly ends, all dedicated
To closeness and the bettering of my mind,
With that which, but by being so retir'd,
O'er-prized all popular rate, in my false brother
Awak'd an evil nature; and my trust
Like a good parent, did beget of him
A falsehood, in its contrary as great
As my trust was.

(I.ii.89-95)

Prospero tried to arrange for himself the career denied
Hamlet, and, like Hamlet, was saved by "the love [his] people
bore" him (I.ii.141). While he deplores the "most ignoble
stooping" of "poor Milan" (I.ii.115-16) to the crown of Naples, his own neglect has created Antonio's thirst "for sway"
(I.ii.112). Like Lear, Prospero is exiled into a storm
(I.i.148-49). He takes "a cherubin" (I.ii.152), Miranda, however, and his magic. That magic now will not merely be employed in private study, but in Prospero's project of redemption. Instead of leading Prospero away from man, as it had
been doing, his magic will become the vehicle of his return to
"kindness."

   While Prospero clings to the original conception of his project without intruding to destroy it, he is not at peace with
himself. While his anger at Ariel can be described as the impatience of a master-planner with the quibblings of a subordinate, the vehemence of it and the tone of his words to
Caliban and Ferdinand suggest a source deeper than mere
impatience—the struggle, perhaps, of the man who is "with
their high wrongs. . .struck to the quick" (V.i.25) against the
god attempting to abstract himself from the human desire

for vengeance; or, more basically, the conflict between his godlike hopes for his manipulation and his human awareness that it may fail. The conflict is clearest as he breaks up the Masque; the harmony is achieved soon after, as Ariel reports the pitiable condition of Prospero's enemies. Prospero's godlike conception of his manipulation surrenders to his human experience of it. He is freed of the necessity of playing god, and as he releases the role, he finds his humanity again; the tears springing suddenly to his eyes are a product of something other than his will. His manipulation succeeds most profoundly within himself, and its success there, of course, is essential to his permitting it to have its way with the others.

Prospero's Masque is, for Ferdinand, such a "majestical vision" (IV.i.118) that he thinks himself in "Paradise" (IV.i.125).[25] This is precisely where he is not; "Caliban and his confederates" (IV.i.140) are approaching to murder Prospero, an event the Masque warns about in depicting the disruptive plans of Venus and Cupid. In the midst of his Masque, Prospero remembers the imminent incursion of the real world and interrupts the performers, who "to a strange, hollow, and confused noise. . .heavily vanish" (s.d.). Here, discord supplants harmony. The discord emerges from Prospero's inner state; he is "distemper'd" (IV.i.145), "vex'd" (IV.i.158), "troubled" (IV.i.159). Caliban's pathetic conspiracy alone could not evoke such distress. But Caliban represents the uneducable element, the factor that casts doubt on the potential success of Prospero's project. Perhaps the play "reminds him of the trials of the past twelve years, which are now being rapidly reenacted;"[26] if so, the petty incursion reminds him of the reiterated perfidy of Antonio, of the world's inherent disorder, of the dark zones that must remain ever unilluminated. Caliban represents unredeemable anarchy, the "born devil." When Prospero warns Ariel that they "must prepare to meet with Caliban" (IV.i.166), he means not merely with an entity but with a principle—of unregeneracy and compulsive rebellion. Prospero is disturbed also that he "forgot the foul conspiracy" (IV.i.134) in presenting his Masque. The prospective father-in-law produces a trifle at the potential expense of the grand design of the god.

He has ignored his own injunctions about control, demonstrating the lack of awareness he has admonished in Ariel, chastised in Caliban, and refined away in Ferdinand. At this point, he not only despairs at those his project may never touch, he is also angry at himself. As Van Doren says, "Prospero to his own confusion forgets for a moment when he loses himself in a certain 'vanity' of his art. . . ."[27] His negligence has almost permitted a repetition of the original crime against him (after he became "transported/ And rapt in secret studies": I.ii.76-77). He has already averted another version of that crime by dispatching Ariel to rouse the slumbering Alonso and Gonzalo (II.i).

Prospero's magnificent speech ("Our revels. . .") must be read in the context of his disturbed state. The speech is perhaps the most important in the play; Brower has shown that it expresses almost all of the play's key metaphors, and when we hear it we feel that it is Prospero's mature pronouncement on life. (Some productions place it at the end of the play, making it refer to *The Tempest* itself.)[28]

The speech seems to say several conflicting things at once. Harbage interprets it as saying that "our lives are not the final reality, anymore than stage representations are our lives."[29] This view could make the speech an affirmation of immortality. Halliday, however, sees it as referring to "the oblivion that lies beyond life's dream."[30] The thrust of the present discussion would make the speech mean that recognition of the world's transience is the beginning of freedom. To be free one must recognize that the things of this world are nothing. As Auden has Prospero say, "I am glad I did not recover my dukedom till/ I do not want it."[31] Prospero himself says at the end, "Every third thought shall be my grave" (V.i.311).

Life then, is no more than a dream; but what lies beyond that dream? Prospero could be suggesting that "our revels"—the Masque we have witnessed—are meaningless compared to the redemptive drama he is producing, and that *that* play, in turn, fades to insignificance before the goal of that redemption. Our little lives, then, are the stuff of eternity. What dreams come *then* must give us pause, for they will be the sweet dream of salvation or the eternal nightmare of damnation. Our lives decide what our souls will be once all material things have dissolved. Prospero could be suggesting, however, that *all* man's efforts fade finally to insignificance. As Walter Kaufmann says, the speech can mean "that man is thrown into the world, abandoned to a life that ends in death, with nothing after that."[32] The speech does not hint strongly of an afterlife, particularly if we remember the equation between sleep and death employed by such seventeenth-century figures as Lady Macbeth, John Donne, and Octavius Caesar. James suggests that "there is no need to assume that 'rounded' means 'finished off'; it may equally well be taken to mean 'encompassed by' and therefore 'occurring within' a 'sleep'—'we are such stuff as dreams are made on.' "[33] Life becomes, then, a dream within a dream, a moment of partial wakefulness within oblivion. "We are such stuff as dreams are made on"—we are no more substantial than dreams and are doomed to be flicked out as quickly as the Masque, or, we are the basis of dreams, of greater realities beyond this insubstantial life.[34]

Which is the correct reading? Probably neither. The speech emerges from two Prosperos, hence carries traces of each. He is the god carrying on a project that the man, thinking of Caliban, knows may fail. He is the god calling down blessings on the marriage of Ferdinand and Miranda, and the man who knows well that the world poses deep threats to such beginnings. In context, the speech is bound to convey contradiction; it is a product of a divided man, expressing pessimism and affirmation, encompassing Caliban and Ferdinand, unredeemed darkness, and potential illumination. Between the Masque and the conspiracy, between appearance and reality, between dream world and fact, Prospero touches two worlds in his speech, seeming to say two things at once. It is a moment modeled on that instant of awakening in which the waker balances between the symbols of his dream and the realities of his diurnal world. Majestic and impressive as the speech is, Prospero's vision as he utters it is not clear—nor can it be, for he is not God, as he is coming to admit. But his speech is profoundly Shakespearean; it can be read in two ways; it throws back an image not of its creator but of its interpreter.

The climax of Prospero's redemptive drama and of *The Tempest* comes once each of his enemies "Lies at [his] mercy" (V.i.264). It may be, as Kenneth Muir suggests, that "when he has his enemies in his power Prospero has to overcome again the natural desire towards vengeance."[35] It is tempting to believe that Prospero has struggled all along with his inclination to revenge, that his outbursts have been signs of the inner conflict between potential tears or possible blood. In the absence of much solid evidence for this view, however, it is safer to suggest that Prospero finally experiences the truth of what until now has been an intellectual conception. His decision is better described as between the alternatives of judging and not judging. On returning from where Prospero's enemies stand spellbound, Ariel poses a crucial question:

> Ariel.   the good old Lord Gonzalo['s]
> . . .tears run down his beard like winter's drops
> From eaves of reeds. Your charm so strongly works 'em,
> That if you beheld them, your affections
> Would become tender.
> Prospero. Dost thou think so, spirit?
> Ariel.   Mine would, sir, were I human.
>
> (V.i.15-20)

Ariel asks, "Are you human, Prospero? Or have you removed yourself so far into your godlike role that you have lost the ability for compassion?" Ariel hints that thus far Prospero's affections have *not* been tender. Ariel's is another of the analogues of compassion presented to Prospero—Miranda's for those on the ship and later for Ferdinand, Ferdinand's for his father, Alonso's for Ferdinand, Gonzalo's for his companions, and now Ariel's.[36]

Compassion, in *The Tempest,* relates directly to the theme of control and freedom. Compassion, in fact, is a kind of *self*-control. It represents the suspension of self-will. Self-will, of course, is the opposite of self-control (a contradiction resolved by the freedom-service equation of the New Testament). Compassion represents an alignment of the individual with the supernature presiding over him. If dormant traces of this supernature reside within the conspirators, Prospero's production will activate them.

Now his manipulation brings his own humanity out from behind the godlike façade:

> Hast thou, which art but air, a touch, a feeling
> Of their afflictions, and shall not myself,
> One of their kind, that relish all as sharply
> Passion as they, be kindlier mov'd than thou art?
>
> (V.i.21-24)

Prospero, in the words of David Horowitz, "is moved to mercy by the image of himself, suffering in their agony."[37] Prospero has already recognized that nature *per se* embodies the principle of compassion: "to sigh/ To th' winds, whose pity, sighing back again/ Did us but loving wrong" (I.ii.149-51). Any thoughts of revenge he might entertain would be in conflict with a basic element he perceives in nature, a principle that finally kindles itself within him. Having himself achieved complete "kindness" and compassion, he reasserts the concomitant—control, applying the principle appropriately to himself as he had earlier applied it to Miranda, Ferdinand, Ariel, and more harshly, to Caliban:

> with my nobler reason 'gainst my fury
> Do I take part. The rarer action is
> In virtue than in vengeance. They being penitent,
> The sole drift of my purpose doth extend
> Not a frown further. Go, release them, Ariel.
> My charms I'll break, their senses I'll restore,
> And they shall be themselves.
>
> (V.i.26-32)

In breaking his charms, he becomes himself. Prospero the god has accomplished all he can and the need for the role is over. He frees himself, achieving the harmony he hopes to have encouraged in his enemies. He throws over the magic, which " 'twixt the green sea and the azur'd vault/ Set roaring war" (V.i.43-44), in favor of "heavenly music" (V.i.52), the last outward manifestation of his potent art. He had been like the Christ who stilled the "greate tempest in the sea, in

so muche as the ship was covered with waves" (Matthew 8:
24); and when he said "not so much perdition as an hair/
Betid to any creature in the vessel," he echoed the Apostle
Paul, who had said "there shall not an haire fall from the
head of any of you" to a group of frightened men on a
tempest-tossed boat (Acts 27: 34).[38] His words to the "spell
stopp'd" (V.i.61) royal party:

> The charm dissolves apace,
> And as the morning steals upon the night,
> Melting the darkness, so their rising senses
> Begin to chase the ignorant fumes that mantle
> Their clearer reason.

(V.i.64-67)

echo the Preface appointed in the Communion Service for
Whitsunday:

> we are brought out of darkenesse and errour into the clear
> light and true knowledge of thee, and of thy Sonne Jesus Christ.

Prospero's metaphor, of course, could relate to many similar
passages in biblical or liturgical literature. It has its deepest
analogue in God's original *fiat lux.* Clearly, Prospero is imitating the rhythms of Genesis:

> Pros. How's the day?
> Ari.   On the sixth hour; at which time, my lord,
>   You said our work should cease.

(V.i.3-5)

Prospero is most Christlike, however, as he descends from
the remote reaches of godhead to rejoin humanity as healer
and man of compassion:

> A solemn air, and the best comforter
> To an unsettled fancy, cure thy brains,
> Now useless, boil'd within thy skull!. . .
> Holy Gonzalo, honourable man,
> Mine eyes, ev'n sociable to the show of thine,
> Fall fellowly drops.

(V.i.26-64)

As Theodore Spencer says, "Prospero is purged, but his
purgation is exactly opposite to the purgation of Alonso:

Alonso sinks *below* reason before returning to it; before Prospero returns to the rational human level, he has lived for a time above it. The important thing to notice is his return."[39] Alonso had threatened to "seek [Ferdinand] deeper than ever plummet sounded" (III.iii.101). His emergence from despair is paralleled by Prospero's return to humanity, signaled by his abandonment of magic:

> I'll break my staff,
> Bury it certain fathoms in the earth,
> And deeper than did ever plummet sound,
> I'll drown my book.

(V.i.54-57)

A passage from Pascal's *Pensées* suggests the contrast *and* similarity between the restorations of Alonso and Prospero—although *The Tempest* exhibits their return to humanity dramatically, not within the precisely defined theological context Pascal provides:

> He makes the soul feel that its peace lies wholly in him, and that it has no joy save to love him. To know God after this fashion one must know first one's own misery and worthlessness and the need of a mediator in order to approach God and be united with him. The knowledge of God without the recognition of our misery engenders pride. The recognition of our misery without the knowledge of Jesus Christ produces despair. But the knowledge of Christ frees us alike from pride and despair, because here we find conjoined God and our misery in which it can be repaired.

The "fellowly drops" shed by Prospero for "Holy Gonzalo" are reminiscent of Cordelia's tears, "holy water" (IV.iii.32), which she hopes will restore Lear:

> All blest secrets,
> All you unpublish'd virtues of the earth,
> Spring with my tears! Be aidant and remediant
> In the good man's distress.

(IV.iv.15-18)

While the situations are similar, the primary restoration occurring with Prospero's tears is his own. As Horowitz says, "compassion is a self-preserving force. It is putting oneself in

the place of others, seeing oneself as one of their infirmity
and imagining their sufferings as possible to oneself; it is the
recognition of an essential humanity, despite all apparent differences, in which one shares."[40]

Significantly, Prospero does not provide the rationale behind his production until Act Five. (Ariel, of course, has
done so earlier: "Heart's sorrow/ And a clear life ensuing"
[III.iii.81-82]). Prospero's explanation coincides with his return to humanity from the remote and lofty plane he had
inhabited. Appropriately, we are invited to identify with him
at this "sociable" moment; as he finally takes us into his confidence, we experience his return to humanity. The moment
represents a perfect coalescence of a character's awareness of
himself and the spectator's awareness of the character. His
abandonment of magic combines, as Daniel C. Boughner
suggests, with his "modulation of feelings from wrath to forgiveness," to release "the audience from its uncertainty and
fear and prepares for a comic *catastrophe*."[41] The comedy has
been predictable, of course, but Prospero's abandonment of
his role of god constitutes its climax.

Prospero recognizes that the quality of redemption is not
strained. Were he to continue playing god, he might destroy
whatever his production may have accomplished *within* its
participants. He might be able to assert coercion, as he must
with Antonio, but be *unable* to embrace compassion, as he can
with Alonso. Instead, he surrenders his role and frees himself from the bondage of his own will, becoming a humble
exemplification of the theme of his play, of *The Tempest,* and
of The Sermon on the Mount, forgiving others as a precondition to his own suit for grace. He recognizes the potential
irony of his position (Ariel points it out clearly), and in surrendering one of his roles, he eliminates the ironic possibilities inherent in the dichotomy between man and god.
He recognizes that the injunction about judging applies to
himself; instead of judging, he forgives and submits to the
judgment of the God whose role he had temporarily assumed, becoming, like Christ, a man who exemplifies the
doctrines of that God. Many earlier elements of the play,
particularly the persistent analogies of harmony following

storm and of pain evoking compassion, suggest that this play is to be a comedy. We cannot be certain, however, as Boughner suggests, "whether the wronged Duke may rise to his capacity for forgiveness,"[42] until, as West neatly says, "Ariel's superiority to passion matched with passion's superiority to Ariel [moves] Prospero to take part with his nobler reason against his fury."[43] By surrendering his role as a god, with its dangerously *hubristic* potentiality, Prospero steps *down* to the role of man but achieves the highest status that man can reach. To maintain the role of God would be to destroy his humanity, and the spectator should feel the possibility strongly in the instant before its resolution. His "I'll drown my book" is a freely chosen, uncoerced decision compared to Faustus's desperate "I'll burn my books!" Prospero recognizes in time, as Faustus does not, the potentiality ascribed to the tragic hero by Northrop Frye: "In many tragedies, he begins as a semi-divine figure, at least in his own eyes, and then an inexorable dialectic sets to work, which separates the divine pretence from the human actuality."[44]

Gonzalo's "all of us [found] ourselves/ When no man was his own" (V.i.212-13) is obviously optimistic—but typical of the old man's tendency toward over-generalization. The success of Prospero's drama is measured by its effect on those who have acted in it. Ferdinand has "Receiv'd a second life" (V.i.195); Alonso obviously has been deeply affected; Antonio watches the ending with a sneer. Alonso expresses his guilt in a speech which, like Prospero's adjuration speech, moves from storm to music (III.iii.95-102). Immediately upon his return to sanity, he matches the amendment of his mind with that of his crime:

> Th' affliction of my mind amends, with which,
> I fear, a madness held me. . .
> Thy dukedom I resign and do entreat
> Thou pardon me my wrongs.
>
> (V.i.114-19)

His repentance is met with the sight of Miranda and Ferdinand, an explicit reward for his amendment of life:

My dukedom since you have given me again,
I will requite you with as good a thing.

(V.i.168-69)

Like Lear at the end ("she's gone forever" [V.iii.270]), Alonso
had been convinced that Ferdinand was "gone" (II.i.122).
Now, like Ferdinand, Alonso receives a second life:

    If this prove
A vision of the island, one dear son
Shall I twice lose.

(V.i.175-77)

His reunion with Ferdinand is obviously reminiscent of
Lear's with Cordelia:

    But, O, how oddly will it sound that I
    Must ask my child forgiveness.

(V.i.197-98)

Unlike Lear's, Alonso's redemption is not a prelude to
deeper anguish. Those most profoundly affected by the production, Prospero and Alonso, are rewarded for their reunion with mankind by the union of Ferdinand and Miranda.

Some see Caliban as unregenerate. "What. . .does
Prospero's art finally accomplish?" asks Rose A. Zimbardo; "it
had never been able to fix form on Caliban."[45] The ending,
however, suggests that Caliban is not "the begged question"
Auden makes of him,[46] but has begun to free himself of his
compulsive and self-punishing defiance. While Prospero calls
him a "Demi-devil" (V.i.271) and a "thing of darkness"
(V.i.275), Caliban calls himself a "thrice-double ass. . .to take
this drunkard for a god/ And worship this dull fool!"
(V.i.291-97). While Caliban never exhibits the compassion so
often in The Tempest, the beginning of freedom, he begins to
respond to Prospero at the end. "How fine my master is!"
(V.i.262) he exclaims on seeing him in his ducal robes. His
only previous use of "master" for Prospero had been
"Farewell, master" (II.ii.182). He uses the word for Stephano,
of course, along with "lord" and "king." Ariel uses "master"
some nine times, once, significantly, after Prospero's promise

of freedom (I.ii.299). Perhaps Caliban glimpses the equation between service and freedom; when Prospero promises Caliban "pardon" (V.i.293) for the trimming of his cell, Caliban leaps off with the alacrity of an Ariel:

> Ay, that I will! and I'll be wise hereafter,
> And seek for grace.
>
> (V.i.294-95)

That he can say "grace" suggests that he now grasps concepts unphrasable in his former vocabulary.

Antonio remains. He has not felt "This deity [conscience] in his bosom" (II.ii.277-78), and has apparently felt none since, in spite of Prospero's effort. He stands forgiven but not accepting that forgiveness; his only response to the "high miracle" (V.i.177) of the ending is a sneering comment on Caliban:

> one of them
> Is a plain fish, and, no doubt, marketable.
>
> (V.i. 265-66)

His comment places him squarely in the company of Shakespeare's other calculator-villians—Richard III, Don John, Iago, Edmund, Iachimo, *et al.* Antonio remains unredeemable, refusing to participate in the symbolic taking of hands of the ending ("Come unto these yellow sands/ And then take hands"), preferring like Milton's Satan to know God only as pain. His "inward pinches therefore are most strong" (V.i.77). As Robert Hunter says, "More than any other of Shakespeare's plays, *The Tempest* insists strongly upon indestructibility of evil. . . . Antonio, in some form, will always exist and can only be forgiven for existing."[47] As Frank Kermode suggests, however, "A world without Antonio is a world without freedom."[48] In choosing the freedom of self-will, Antonio chooses slavery, of course, but helps emphasize the freedom the others have won by submitting to a mastery more encompassing than that of their own wills. Ariel's final mission before he merges with the Mediterranean sky is to provide weather symbolic of the inner harmony achieved by most of the characters in Prospero's production, weather leading back toward mankind. "[I] promise you," says Prospero to Alonso, "calm seas, auspicious gales,/ And sail so expeditious that shall catch/ Your royal fleet far off" (314-16). For this final service, Ariel is enlarged at last.

Prospero can be said to continue Hamlet's play from the point at which the Prince interrupted it. As Francis Fergusson says, "[Prospero] has a ripeness and a clarity and a power which Hamlet lacks, but for that very reason he helps one to see what Hamlet, with his play, was trying to do."[49] The ripeness is all. Prospero comes to recognize during his long exile that revenge is worse than meaningless—it reduces the revenger to the level of the criminal's corruption. Unlike Hamlet, Prospero allows his production to find its meaning in the characters manipulated. His magic is primarily external; it can achieve no inward changes unless its participants have the capacity for change. It is this magic, this method of reaching the spirit, that Hamlet gets hold of and fails to recognize. Hamlet defines himself as modern man,[50] oppressed and isolated, seeing the sacraments as a convention finally irrelevant to the soul of man. He is wrong about their power, as Claudius's efforts at prayer prove. Prospero recognizes that a reenactment of guilt *may* evoke a penitential response from guilty creatures and that it is the only method worth trying. He defines himself as servant of forces larger than himself. He experiences at the end what he has known all along—that, regardless of his godlike command, he is subject to those forces. Hamlet could not retain the conception of his play that he himself had expressed—that "guilty creatures" can be "struck so to the soul" that they will "proclaim their malefactions." Hamlet destroys his play before it can explore this possibility. Prospero does not. "The rarer action is in virtue than in vengeance" because it can achieve a restoration to self and humanity not only for the guilty participant in a penitential drama, but for the dramatist as well.

NOTES TO CHAPTER 6: *The Tempest*

1. Quoted in H. Maynard Smith, *Henry VIII and the Reformation* (London, 1948), p. 398.
2. Thomas a Kempis, *The Imitation of Christ* (London, 1910), p. 2.

3. Northrop Frye, *A Natural Perspective* (New York, 1965), p. 133. I take mild exception to Professor Frye's description of man's regaining "his original vision." The emphasis of C. S. Lewis is, to my thinking, more accurate: *"Paradise Lost* records a real, irreversible, unrepeatable process in the history of the universe; and even for those who do not believe this, it embodies. . .the great change in every individual soul from happy dependence to miserable self-assertion and thence either, as in Satan, to final isolation, or as in Adam, to reconcilement and a different happiness." *A Preface to* Paradise Lost (New York, 1961), p. 133.

4. The relationship of the Communion to Ariel's feast has been suggested by Robert G. Hunter, *Shakespeare and the Comedy of Forgiveness* (New York, 1965), pp. 227-41.

5. On the poetry of *The Tempest,* particularly on the way poetic emphasis underlines dramatic movement, see Reuben Brower's superb essay in *The Fields of Light* (New York, 1951), pp. 95-122.

6. D. G. James, *Scepticism and Poetry* (London, 1937), p. 238.

7. This interpretation of Prospero places him closer to Marston's Altofronto than to the self-deposed Vincentio. In donning a disguise to discover "what our seemers be" (I.iii.55), Vincentio *becomes* a seemer. We are invited, as we watch him pull his monk's hood over his head, to watch as well the revelation of what *he* is. He insists on controlling his manipulation to the very end and produces not a redemptive drama but a self-vindication. He is finally exposed by his production. As D. R. C. Marsh suggests, "The shifting vision of the play, which has exposed the pretensions of all the characters, in turn, is turned in the final scene back on the Duke, showing how even his justice is rooted in the concerns of the self." "The Mood of *Measure for Measure,"* SQ 14 (1963): 37. For another negative view of Vincentio, see Rebecca West, *The Court and the Castle,* pp. 44-48. Most critics, of course, equate Vincentio and Prospero. See Harold S. Wilson, "Action and Symbol in *Measure for Measure* and *The Tempest,"* SQ 4 (1953): 375-84; G. Wilson Knight, *The Wheel of Fire,* pp. 76 and 79; C. J. Sisson, "The Magic of Prospero," *Shakespeare Survey* 11 (Cambridge, 1958): 70-77; and Francis Fergusson, Introduction to *The Tempest* (New York, 1961), p. 14. For a contrast between Vincentio and Prospero as dramatic devices, see Bertrand Evans, *Shakespeare's Comedies* (Oxford, 1960), p. 332.

8. D. G. James, *Scepticism and Poetry,* p. 239.

9. W. H. Auden, "The Sea and the Mirror," *Collected Poetry* (New York, 1945), p. 361.

10. Cf. Dowden: "A thought that runs through the whole of *The Tempest*. . .is the thought that the true freedom of man consists in service." *Shakspere: His Mind and Art,* p. 419, and Fergusson: "'Freedom' in many different ways is the main motive of the play." Introduction to *The Tempest,* p. 9.

11. Quoted in *Shakespeare's Critics,* ed. A. M. Eastman and G. B. Harrison (Ann Arbor, 1964), p. 305.

12. Jan Kott, *Shakespeare: Our Contemporary* (New York, 1964), p. 180.

13. G. W. Knight, *The Crown of Life* (London, 1948), pp. 212-13.

14. Margaret Webster, *Shakespeare Without Tears* (New York, 1961), p. 215.

15. The opening scene, with its emphasis on the equation between controlling a ship and controlling oneself and on the contrast between the rules of the sea and the land, is remarkably Conradian. Cf. *The Nigger of the Narcissis, Typhoon, Youth, Shadowline, The End of the Tether, Lord Jim,* and *The Secret Sharer.*

16. Cf. Polonius: "This must be known, which, being kept close, might move/ More grief to hide than hate to utter love" (II.i.118-19), and Banquo: "Speak then to

me, who neither beg nor fear/ Your favours nor your hate" (I.iv.60-61), and Leontes: "though I with death and with/ Reward did threaten and encourage him."

17. Prospero is, in the Old Testament sense, a "type of Christ." His defeat of Setebos is analogous to Samson's of Dagon (in Judges)—a contest in Miltonic terms to determine "whose god is God"—and to Elijah's victory over Baal (I Kings). In Milton, Christ chases away the pagan gods in "On the Morning of Christ's Nativity," defeats, the rebel angels in *Paradise Lost* and Satan in *Paradise Regained.*

18. West, *Shakespeare and the Outer Mystery,* pp. 80-95.

19. *Ibid.,* p. 87.

20. Curry, *Shakespeare's Philosophical Patterns,* p. 134.

21. Rose A. Zimbardo, "Form and Disorder in *The Tempest,*" *SQ* 14 (1963): p. 55.

22. G. B. Harrison, *"The Tempest,"* *Stratford Papers on Shakespeare,* 1962 (Toronto, 1963), p. 231.

23. Bernard Knox, "The Tempest and the Ancient Comic Tradition," English Institute Essays, 1954 (New York, 1955).

24. Northrop Frye, *A Natural Perspective,* p. 136. On the function of time in Shakespeare, see, in addition, Professor Frye's *Fools of Time: Studies in Shakesperian Tragedy* (Toronto, 1967), and Wolfgang Clemen, "Past and Future in Shakespeare's Drama," British Academy Lecture, 1966 (Oxford, 1967), pp. 231-52.

25. Ferdinand thus creates a strange parallel between this scene and that in Dr. Faustus, where Faustus views the Seven Deadly Sins and thinks *himself* in Paradise: "That sight will be as pleasing unto /Me as paradise was to Adam, the/ First day of his creation" (VI.128-30). In each case, the character is transported from reality—Faustus by distorting the vision of his own evil into a metaphor for his own depravity, Ferdinand by extending his happiness in Miranda to an idyllic conclusion that the facts of the world will not support.

26. Frank Kermode, ed., *The Tempest* (Cambridge, Mass., 1958), p. 104, n159.

27. Mark Van Doren, *Shakespeare* (New York, 1939), p. 285.

28. See, for example, Margaret Webster, *Shakespeare Without Tears,* p. 214.

29. Alfred Harbage, *Shakespeare: A Reader's Guide,* p. 478.

30. F. E. Halliday, *The Poetry of Shakespeare's Plays* (New York, 1964), p. 52.

31. W. H. Auden, "The Sea and the Mirror," p. 352.

32. Walter Kaufmann, *From Shakespeare to Existentialism,* p. 3.

33. D. G. James, *Scepticism and Poetry,* p. 241.

34. Cf. Leslie Fiedler, "The Defense of the Illusion and the Creation of Myth," p. 82: "The world *does* decay, and only the individual, in his moment of discovery or passion or tragic insight, is forever. In this sense the apparent contradiction between our being immune to death ('Not a hair perished') and yet 'such stuff as dreams are made on' is reconciled." Fiedler, I take it, would equate Prospero's speech with the fusion of contradictions in "Kubla Khan."

35. Kenneth Muir, *Last Periods of Shakespeare, Racine, and Ibsen* (Detroit, Mich., 1961), p. 52.

36. Gonzalo, responding with the "kindness" he possesses with a fullness lacking in the other members of his party, predicts Ariel's intimation of "kindness": "though they are of monstrous shape, yet not,/ Their manners are more gentle, kind, than of/ Our human generation you shall find many, nay, almost any" (III.iii.31-34). Gonzalo's response is a reversal of Ariel's, that of a human for spirits. The response comes, appropriately, as the table stands before the

group, and draws praise from Prospero: "Honest lord,/Thou hast said well; for some of you there present/ Are worse than devils" (III.iii.34-36). Prospero's words underline the suggestion that the "three men of sin" are denied the Eucharist.

37. David Horowitz, *Shakespeare: An Existential View* (New York, 1965), p. 87. For a constrasting version of Prospero's control over his inclination toward revenge, see Bertrand Evans, *Shakespeare's Comedies*, pp. 333-37. For criticism that tends from other points of view to support the present analysis, see Frye, *A Natural Perspective*, pp. 118-59; David William, *"The Tempest* on the Stage," *Jacobean Theater* (Stratford-upon-Avon Studies I, 1960), pp. 133-57; and Nevill Coghill, "In Retrospect," *Stratford Papers on Shakespeare* (Toronto, 1963), pp. 175-99.

38. Paul's ship, like Alonso's is bound to Italy from Asia Minor, when it is "tossed with an exceeding tempest." An angel appears before Paul, telling him that the ship's passengers "must be cast into a certaine Iland." Paul promises the passengers that "there shall not an haire fall from the head of any of you." The voyage ends as "some on boardes, and some on certaine pieces of the shippe...they came all safe to land" (Acts 37). For an illuminating demonstration of how Shakespeare expands his sources into *The Tempest,* see Phillip Brockbank, *"The Tempest:* Conventions of Art and Empire," *Stratford-upon-Avon Studies* 8 (New York, 1967): 183-201. For other useful discussions of *The Tempest*'s relation to its sources, see Frank Kermode's Introduction to the New Arden Edition (New York, 1964), pp. xxv-lxxi, and G. B. Harrison, *"The Tempest,"* *Stratford Papers on Shakespeare* (Toronto, 1963), pp. 212-38.

39. Theodore Spencer, *Shakespeare and the Nature of Man*, p. 198. See also Henri Fluchère, *Shakespeare and the Elizabethans* (New York, 1956), pp. 248-49. For an illuminating discussion of music as a restorative power in *The Tempest,* see Catherine M. Dunn, "The Function of Music in Shakespeare's Romances," *SQ* 20 (Autumn 1969): pp. 400-405.

40. David Horowitz, *Shakespeare: An Existential View*, p. 82.

41. Daniel C. Boughner, "Jonsonian Structure in *The Tempest,"* *SQ* 21 (Winter 1970): 9.

42. Boughner, "Jonsonian Structure," p. 9.

43. West, *Shakespeare and the Outer Mystery,* p. 94.

44. Frye, *An Anatomy of Criticism* (Princeton, 1957), p. 217.

45. Rose A. Zimbardo, "Form and Disorder in *The Tempest,"* p. 55.

46. W. H. Auden, "The Sea and the Mirror," p. 374.

47. R. G. Hunter, *Shakespeare and the Comedy of Forgiveness*, pp. 240-41.

48. Frank Kermode, Introduction to *The Tempest,* p. lxii.

49. Francis Fergusson, *"Hamlet:* the Analogy of Action," p. 52.

50. Very much as D. G. James describes him in *The Dream of Learning.* The paralyzed Hamlet that James describes is *not* the Hamlet who plans the play for Claudius, however.

Conclusion

The Tempest is Shakespeare's final commentary on the world of his tragedies, incorporating, as G. Wilson Knight points out, "the *Macbeth* rhythm,"[1] and creating a contrast to Hamlet's decision. "The rarer action," Prospero decides, "is/ In virtue than in vengeance" (V.i.27-28). *The Tempest* includes an interrupted banquet, the feast Ariel quaintly whisks away because its would-be partakers are "three men of sin" (III,iii 53) who must feel "heart's sorrow," beyond which expands "a clear life" (III.iii.81-82). The alternative to contrition is the process of damnation Ariel describes:

> Ling'ring perdition, worse than any death
> Can be at once, shall step by step attend
> You and your ways.
>
> (III.iii.77-79)

The banquet disappears, deferred "until [the sinner] have openly declared him self to have truely repented, and amended his former naughty lyfe." Alonso, the "King Lear" of this play, emerges from his despair to accomplish this progress. Stephano, Trinculo, and Caliban contribute an anti-sacrament, kissing the book (II.ii.134, 145), translating "celestial liquor" (II.ii.121) into enslavement in drink and into their self-defeating plot to supplant Prospero. For Caliban, insistence on freedom becomes a compulsive movement

416

represented by the folded arms, rigid back, and sneer of Antonio, however surrounded he is by benign control. Man *can* refuse to be saved. That is the choice offered by the Reformation to a Dr. Faustus as it never was to an Everyman. In Shakespeare, the choice is echoed constantly against the perfect model of Christian experience and action available to the tragic hero and deeply familiar to the spectator—the Eucharist, whose redemptive rhythms become increasingly unavailable to the tragic hero, for whom it expresses itself only negatively within the tragic world. Richard must unking and unmarry himself; Hamlet must force poisoned wine down the throat of his dying foe, hoping Claudius will find his "union" in hell; Othello must marry Iago, having divorced himself by his radically misguided will from Desdemona; Macbeth must be denied his ceremonial table by the image of his own "notorious evil"; King Lear rejects Cordelia within a ritual whose rubrics are dictated by his absolute will. Lear journeys to a reconciliation that resonates outward from archetypes of baptism and resurrection, but, as with his kingdom, is denied the benefits of his profound education. Grace might have been applied in time. But once Richard conspires against Gloucester and compounds his crime by seizing Bolingbroke's inheritance; once Hamlet destroys his play; once Othello yields to a superhuman conception of self-hood; once Lear disinherits himself from the context that would make his insights operative in his kingdom; once Macbeth cancels his virtue with his will, the opportunity for any paralleling of the comic rhythm of the Eucharist is gone.

Tragedy demonstrates the difference between what a man might have been and what he becomes. The comic progress of King Lear, of King Alonso, and Duke Prospero shows man merging with an essential self, with his kindness, with an awareness of the humanity he shares with others, purging his error and his potentiality for further error, not, as in Hamlet, Othello, and Macbeth, divorcing his virtue gradually from his will until that isolated half of his personality drives toward further errors, which insist on death as an inevitable consequence of the acts the character has performed within his tragedy. By reversing tragic choice, Prospero focuses the potential comedy that is latent in Shakespeare's tragedies, and that, indeed, in *King Lear,* emerges as a profound pattern within the dramatic shaping of the play, which presses an even more profound tragedy beyond the comedy. But Lear has made his tragic choice already. Prospero refuses to yield to the godlike temptations that ensnare Lear in his opening scene and Othello as he lands on Cyprus, and thus encourages the comic ending. Prospero cannot save Richard, Hamlet, Othello, Lear, or Macbeth, but he does save himself. His redemptive drama is qualified and imperfect, but, for Alonso and himself, it is the ultimate that can be requested of the sacraments designed to imitate the lifting up to God of the human heart from this fallen earth.

NOTES TO CONCLUSION

1. G. Wilson Knight, *The Crown of Life,* p. 215.
2. Theodore Spencer, *Shakespeare and the Nature of Man,* p. 198.
3. A similar use of an epilogue as an *extension* of a play's meaning is that of Pandarus at the end of *Troilus and Cressida.* That he should have the last word suggests the degradation into which the world of that play has fallen. Thersites has fled the battle, suggesting that "if the son of a whore fight for a whore, he tempts judgement" (V.vii.21-22). Hector has killed a pocky coward in sumptuous armor. Achilles has treacherously slain Hector. Pandarus's last word, appropriately is "diseases" (V.x.57). The rottenness of the Trojan world is extended by Pandarus to London ("Some galled goose of Winchester" [V.x.55]), a disjunctive analogue to Prospero's application of the hope for grace encompassed within *The Tempest* to his seventeenth-century audience.
4. Northrop Frye, *A Natural Perspective,* p. 159.
5. *The Tempest* may, of course, have been performed at Blackfriars. See Bernard Beckerman, *Shakespeare at the Globe: 1599-1609* (New York, 1962); G. E. Bentley, *The Jacobean and Caroline Stage* (Oxford, 1941) and "Shakespeare at the Blackfriars Theater," *Shakespeare Survey* I (1948); and E. K. Chambers, *The Elizabethan Stage,* vol. 2 (Oxford, 1923).

Bibliography

Works Cited and Consulted

Abel, Lionel. *Metatheater*. New York, 1963.

Adams, Henry. *The Education of Henry Adams*. New York, 1931.

Alexander, Peter. *Hamlet: Father and Son*. Oxford, 1955.

————. *Shakespeare's Life and Art*. New York, 1961.

Allen, J. W. *A History of Political Thought in the Sixteenth Century*. New York, 1960.

Altick, Richard. "Symphonic Imagery in *Richard II*." *PMLA* 62 (1947).

Armstrong, Edward. *Shakespeare's Imagination*. Lincoln, Neb., 1963.

Auden, W. H. "The Sea and the Mirror." *Collected Poems*. New York, 1945.

————. "The Christian Tragic Hero." *The New York Times Book Review,* December 16, 1945.

Auerbach, Erich. *Mimesis*. Garden City, N. Y., 1957.

Babcock, Weston. *Hamlet: A Tragedy of Errors*. Lafayette, Ind., 1961.

Baldwin, T. W. *Shakespeare's Small Latine and Lesse Greeke*. Urbana, Ill., 1944.

Barber, C. L. *Shakespeare's Festive Comedy*. Princeton, N. J., 1959.

Barnet, Sylvan. "Some Limitations of a Christian Approach to Shakespeare." *ELH* 22 (1955).

Battenhouse, Roy W. "*Measure for Measure* and Christian Doctrine." *PMLA* 51 (1946).

———. "Shakespeare's Moral Vision." *Stratford Papers on Shakespeare: 1964.* Toronto, 1965.

———. *Shakespearean Tragedy: Its Art and Its Christian Premises.* Bloomington, Ind., 1969.

Beckerman, Bernard. *Shakespeare at the Globe: 1599-1609.* New York, 1962.

Aiken, William, and Henning, Basil, eds. *Conflict in Stuart England.* New York, 1960.

Benson, Carl, and Littleton, Taylor, eds. *The Idea of Tragedy.* Glenview, Ill., 1966.

Bentley, Gerald. *The Jacobean and Caroline Stage.* Oxford, 1941.

———. "Shakespeare and the Blackfriars Theater." *Shakespeare Survey* 1 (1948).

Bernad, Miguel. "The Five Tragedies in *Macbeth.*" *SQ* 13 (1962).

Bethel, S. L. *Shakespeare and the Popular Dramatic Tradition.* Durham, N. C., 1944.

———. "Shakespeare's Imagery: The Diabolic Images in *Othello.*" *Shakespeare Survey* 5 (1962).

Bevington, David. *From Mankind to Marlowe.* Cambridge, Mass., 1962.

Black, J. B. *The Reign of Elizabeth.* Cambridge, Eng., 1936.

Black, Matthew, ed. *Richard II.* New Variorum Edition. Philadelphia, Pa., 1955.

Bloom, Edward, ed. *Shakespeare: 1564-1964.* Providence, R. I., 1964.

Bodkin, Maud. *Archetypal Patterns in Poetry.* Oxford, 1948.

Boughner, Daniel. "Jonsonian Structure in *The Tempest.*" *SQ* 21 (1970).

Bowers, Fredson. *Elizabethan Revenge Tragedy.* Princeton, N. J., 1941.

———. "Hamlet as Minister and Scourge." *PMLA* 70 (1955).

———. "Dramatic Structure and Criticism: Plot in *Hamlet.*" *SQ* 15 (1964).

Bradbrook, M. C. *Themes and Conventions of Elizabethan Tragedy.* Cambridge, Eng., 1960.

———. *The Growth and Structure of Elizabethan Comedy.* Baltimore, Md., 1963.

———. *Elizabethan Stage Conventions.* Cambridge, Eng., 1968.

Bradley, A. C. *Oxford Lectures on Poetry.* London, 1909.

———. *Shakespearean Tragedy.* New York, 1949.

Brockbank, Phillip. *"The Tempest:* Conventions of Art and Empire." *Stratford-upon-Avon Studies* 8. New York, 1967.

Brook, Peter. *Thomas Cranmer's Doctrine of the Eucharist.* London, 1965.

Brook, Stella. *The Language of the Book of Common Prayer*. New York, 1965.

Brooke, Nicholas. *Shakespeare: King Lear*. New York, 1963.

Brooks, Cleanth. "Shakespeare as a Symbolist Poet." *Yale Review* 34 (1945).

————, ed. *Tragic Themes in Western Literature*. New Haven, Conn., 1956.

Brower, Reuben. *The Fields of Light*. New York, 1951.

Brown, John Russell. *Shakespeare and His Comedies*. London, 1957.

Bryant, J. A., *Hippolyta's View*. Lexington, Ky., 1961.

Bultmann, Rudolph. *Existence and Faith*. Cleveland, Ohio, 1960.

Burckhardt, Sigurd. *Shakespearean Meanings*. Princeton, N. J., 1958.

Byrne, M. St. Clare. "*King Lear* at Stratford-on-Avon." *SQ* 11 (1960).

Calderwood, James, and Toliver, Harold, eds. *Essays in Shakespearean Criticism*. New York, 1970.

Cam, Helen. *England Before Elizabeth*. New York, 1960.

Campbell, L. B. *Shakespeare's Tragic Heroes: Slaves of Passion*. Cambridge, Eng., 1930.

————. "Theories of Revenge in Elizabethan England." *MP* 28 (1931).

Campbell, O. J. "The Salvation of Lear." *ELH* 14 (1947).

Chambers, E. K. *The Elizabethan Stage*. Oxford, 1923.

————. *Shakespeare: A Survey*. New York, n.d.

Chambers, R. W. "The Jacobean Shakespeare and *Measure for Measure*." British Academy Lecture, 1937.

Chaplin, William. "Form and Psychology in *King Lear*," *Literature and Psychology* 29 (1969).

Charlton, H. B. *Shakespearian Comedy*. London, 1938.

————. *Shakespearian Tragedy*. Cambridge, Eng., 1948.

Clarke, W. K. L., ed. *Liturgy and Worship*. London, 1932.

Clebsch, W. A. *England's Earliest Protestants: 1520-1535*. London, 1964.

Clemen, Wolfgang. *The Development of Shakespeare's Imagery*. New York, n.d.

————. "Shakespeare's Soliloquies," The Presidential Address of the Modern Humanities Research Association. Cambridge, Eng., 1964.

————. "Past and Future in Shakespeare's Drama." British Academy Lecture, 1966. Oxford, 1967.

Cogan, Lee, and Kreuzer, James, eds. *Modern Writings on Major Authors*. Indianapolis, Ind., 1963.

Coghill, Nevill. "In Retrospect," and "Listening to Shakespeare." *Stratford Papers on Shakespeare: 1962*. Toronto, 1963.

Columbia Encyclopedia. New York, 1947.

Coursen, Herbert. "In Deepest Consequence: *Macbeth.*" *SQ* 18 (1967).

———. "Malcolm and Edgar." *Discourse* 11 (1968).

———. *'The Rarer Action':* *Hamlet's Mousetrap.* Madison, Wis., 1969.

———. "Prospero and the Drama of the Soul." *Shakespeare Studies* 4 (1969).

———. "*Love's Labour's Lost* and the Comic Truth." *Papers on Language and Literature* 6 (1970).

———. "Shakespeare: A Single Vector." *British Studies Monitor* 1 (1970).

———. "Henry V and the Nature of Kingship." *Discourse* 13 (1970).

———, ed. *Henry IV,* Part II. Blackfriars, Dubuque, Iowa, 1971.

Cox, Roger. *Between Earth and Heaven.* New York, 1969.

Craig, Hardin. *The Enchanted Glass.* New York, 1936.

———. *An Interpretation of Shakespeare.* New York, 1948.

———. "Morality Plays and Elizabethan Drama." *SQ* 1 (1950).

Crane, Milton, *Shakespeare's Prose.* Chicago, 1963.

Cunningham, Dolora. "*Macbeth:* The Tragedy of the Hardened Heart." *SQ* 14 (1963).

Curry, W. C. *Shakespeare's Philosophical Patterns.* Baton Rogue, La., 1937.

Danby, John. *Shakespeare's Doctrine of Nature.* London, 1961.

Dean, Leonard, ed. *Shakespeare: Modern Essays in Criticism.* New York, 1961.

———. *A Casebook on Othello.* New York, 1961.

Dickens, A. G. *The English Reformation.* London, 1964.

Dorius, R. J. "A Little More than a Little." *SQ* 11 (1960).

———. ed. *Shakespeare's Histories.* Boston, 1964.

Dowden, Edward. *Shakspere: His Mind and Art.* New York, 1962.

Draper, John. "Political Themes in Shakespeare's Later Plays." *JEGP* 35 (1936).

Dunn, Catherine. "The Function of Music in Shakespeare's Romances." *SQ* 20 (1969).

Dyson, J. P. "The Structural Function of the Banquet Scene in *Macbeth.*" *SQ* 14 (1963).

Eastman, A. M., and Harrison, G. B., eds. *Shakespeare's Critics.* Ann Arbor, Mich., 1964.

Eliot, T. S. "Shakespeare and the Stoicism of Seneca." *Selected Essays.* London, 1932.

———. *Essays on Elizabethan Drama.* New York, 1956.

———. "Hamlet and his Problems." *The Sacred Wood.* London, 1960.

Elliott, G. R. *Dramatic Providence in 'Macbeth'*. Princeton, N. J., 1958.

Ellis-Fermor, Una. *The Jacobean Drama*. New York, 1964.

Elton, William. *King Lear and the Gods*. San Marino, Calif., 1966.

Empson, William. *Some Versions of Pastoral*. New York, 1960.

————. *Seven Types of Ambiguity*. Cleveland, Ohio, 1963.

Evans, Bertrand. *Shakespeare's Comedies*. Oxford, 1960.

————, ed. *The College Shakespeare*. New York, 1973.

Farnham, Willard. *The Medieval Heritage of Elizabethan Tragedy*. New York, 1936.

——. *Shakespeare's Tragic Frontier*. Berkeley, Calif., 1950.

Fergusson, Francis. *The Idea of a Theater*. Garden City, N. Y., 1953.

————. *The Human Image in Dramatic Literature*. Garden City, N.Y., 1957.

————. "Introduction," *The Tempest*. New York, 1961.

————. "Introduction," *Macbeth*, New York, 1962.

Fiedler, Leslie. "The Defense of the Illusion and the Creation of Myth." *English Institute Essays: 1948*. New York, 1949.

Fluchére, Henri. *Shakespeare and the Elizabethans*. New York, 1949.

Ford, Boris, ed. *The Age of Shakespeare*. Baltimore, Md., 1960.

Forker, C. R. "Shakespeare's Theatrical Symbolism and its Function in *Hamlet*." *SQ* 14 (1963).

Forster, E. M. *Aspects of the Novel*. New York, 1954.

Frost, William. "Shakespeare's Rituals and the Opening of *King Lear*." *Hudson Review* 10 (1957).

Frye, Northrop. "The Argument of Comedy." *English Institute Essays: 1948*. New York, 1949.

————. *An Anatomy of Criticism*. Princeton, N. J., 1957.

————. *Fables of Identity*. New York, 1963.

————. *A Natural Perspective*. New York, 1965.

————. *Fools of Time*. Toronto, 1967.

Frye, R. M. *Shakespeare and Christian Doctrine*. Princeton, N. J., 1963.

————. "Theological and Non-theological Structures in Tragedy." *Shakespeare Studies* 4 (1969).

————. Review of *Fools of Time*. *SQ* 20 (1969).

Gardner, Dame Helen. "Milton's 'Satan' and the Theme of Damnation in Elizabethan Tragedy," *Essays and Studies* 1 (1948).

————. *The Business of Criticism*. Oxford, 1963.

————. *"King Lear."* The John Coffin Memorial Lecture. London, 1966.

Gilson, Etienne, *The Spirit of Mediaeval Philosophy*. New York, 1936.

————. *A History of Christian Philosophy in the Middle Ages*. New York, 1955.

Gittings, Robert, ed. *The Living Shakespeare.* New York, 1960.

Goddard, Harold. *The Meaning of Shakespeare.* Chicago, 1951.

Granville-Barker, Harley. *Prefaces to Shakespeare.* Princeton, N. J., 1946.

————, and Harrison, G. B., eds. *A Shakespeare Companion.* Garden City, N. Y., 1960.

Grebanier, Bernard. *The Heart of Hamlet.* New York, 1960.

Green, Andrew. "The Cunning of the Scene." *SQ* 4 (1953).

Griffin, Alice. *Pageantry on the Shakespearean Stage.* New Haven, Conn., 1951.

Hales, John. "Milton's *Macbeth.*" *Nineteenth Century* 30 (1891).

Halio, Jay. "Hamlet's Alternatives." *Texas Studies in Literature and Language* 8 (1966).

Halliday, F. E., ed. *Shakespeare and his Critics.* New York, 1963.

————. *The Poetry of Shakespeare's Plays.* New York, 1964.

Hankins, John. *The Character of Hamlet and Other Essays.* Chapel Hill, N. C., 1941.

————. Review of *Shakespeare and Christian Doctrine. SQ* 15 (1964).

Harbage, Alfred. *Shakespeare's Audience.* New York, 1941.

————. *As They Liked It.* New York, 1961.

————. *William Shakespeare: A Reader's Guide.* New York, 1963.

————, ed. *Shakespeare: The Tragedies.* New York, 1964.

Hardison, O. B. *Christian Rite and Christian Drama in the Middle Ages.* Baltimore, Md., 1965.

————. "Three Types of Renaissance Catharsis." *Renaissance Drama,* n. s. 2 (1969).

Harrison, G. B., *"The Tempest," Stratford Papers on Shakespeare: 1962.* Toronto, 1963.

————, ed. *Shakespeare: The Complete Works.* New York, 1953.

Hawkes, Terrence, ed. *Coleridge's Writings on Shakespeare.* New York, 1959.

Haydn, Hiram. *The Counter-Renaissance.* New York, 1950.

Hazlitt, William. *Characters of Shakespear's Plays.* New York, 1845.

Heilman, Robert. "The Lear World." *English Institute Essays: 1947.* New York, 1948.

————. *This Great Stage.* Baton Rogue, La., 1948.

————. *Magic in the Web.* Lexington, Ky., 1956.

————. " 'Twere Best Not Know Myself'." *SQ* 15 (1964).

Hibbard, G. R. "The Year's Contributions to Shakespearian Studies." *Shakespeare Survey* 23 (1970).

Holland, Norman. "Shakespearean Tragedy and The Three Ways of Psychoanalytic Criticism." *Hudson Review* 15 (1962).

————. *Psychoanalysis and Shakespeare.* New York, 1966.

Holloway, John. *The Story of the Night.* Lincoln, Neb., 1961.

Horowitz, David. *Shakespeare: An Existential View.* New York, 1965.

Hoy, Cyrus. *"Love's Labour's Lost* and the Nature of Comedy." *SQ* 13 (1962).

Hubler, Edward. "The Damnation of Othello: Some Limitations of the Christian View of the Play." *SQ* 9 (1958).

Hughes, P. E. *Theology of the English Reformers.* London, 1965.

Hunter, G. K. *"Othello* and Colour Prejudice." British Academy Lecture 53 (1967).

Hunter, R. G. *Shakespeare and the Comedy of Forgiveness.* New York, 1965.

James, D. G. *Scepticism and Poetry.* London, 1937.

————. *The Dream of Learning.* Oxford, 1951.

Jayne, Sears. "Charity in *King Lear." SQ* 15 (1964).

Jenkins, Harold. "The Tragedy of Revenge in Shakespeare and Webster." *Shakespeare Survey* 14 (1961).

Johnson, S. F. "The Regeneration of Hamlet," *SQ* 3 (1952).

Johnston, Arthur. "The Player's Speech in *Hamlet." SQ* 13 (1962).

Jones, Emrys. "Othello, Lepanto, and the Cyprus Wars." *Shakespeare Survey* 21 (1968).

Jones, Ernest. *Hamlet and Oedipus.* New York, 1949.

Jorgensen, Paul. *Shakespeare's Military World.* Berkeley, Calif., 1956.

————. *Lear's Self-Discovery.* Berkeley, Calif., 1967.

Joseph, Bertram. *Conscience and the King.* London, 1953.

Joseph, Sister Miriam. *Shakespeare's Use of the Arts of Language.* New York, 1947.

————. *"Hamlet:* A Christian Tragedy." *SP* 59 (1962).

Jowett, Benjamin, and Twining, Thomas, eds. *Aristotle's Politics and Poetics.* New York, 1957.

Kantorowitz, Ernst. *The King's Two Bodies.* Princeton, N. J., 1957.

Kaufmann, Walter. *From Shakespeare to Existentialism.* Garden City, N. Y., 1960.

Kaula, David. "Othello Possessed: Notes on Shakespeare's Use of Magic and Witchcraft." *Shakespeare Studies* II (1966).

Keast, W. R. "Imagery and Meaning in the Interpretation of *King Lear." MP* 57 (1949).

Kermode, Frank, ed. *The Tempest.* Cambridge, Mass., 1958.

Kernan, Alvin. "Introduction" to *Othello.* New York, 1963.

Kettle, Arnold, ed. *Shakespeare in a Changing World.* New York, 1964.

Kirshbaum, Leo. *Character and Characterization in Shakespeare.*

Detroit, Mich., 1962.

Kitto, H. D. F. *Form and Meaning in Drama.* New York, 1960.

Kittredge, George, ed. *Hamlet.* Boston, 1939.

————. *Macbeth.* Boston, 1939.

Knight, G. Wilson. *The Shakespearian Tempest.* London, 1932.

————. *The Wheel of Fire.* New York, 1957.

————. *The Crown of Life.* London, 1958.

————. *The Imperial Theme.* New York, 1961.

————. *The Christian Renaissance.* New York, 1962.

————. *Shakespearian Production.* Evanston, Ill., 1964.

Knights, L. C. "On Historical Scholarship and the Interpretation of Shakespeare." *Sewanee Review* 63 (1955).

————. *Some Shakespearean Themes.* London, 1959.

————. *Explorations.* New York, 1964.

Knox, Bernard. "The Tempest and the Ancient Comic Tradition," *English Institute Essays: 1954.* New York, 1955.

Kokeritz, Helge. *Shakespeare's Pronunciation.* New Haven, Conn., 1953.

Kott, Jan. *Shakespeare: Our Contemporary.* Garden City, N. Y., 1964.

La Guardia, Eric. "Ceremony and History: The Problem of Symbol from *Richard II* to *Henry V.*" *Pacific Coast Studies in Shakespeare* (1965).

Lawlor, John. *The Tragic Sense in Shakespeare.* London, 1960.

————. "The Tragic Conflict in *Hamlet.*" *Review of English Studies* 1 (1960).

Leech, Clifford, *Shakespeare's Tragedies and other Studies in Seventeenth-Century Drama.* London, 1950.

————. *The Duchess of Malfi.* New York, 1963.

————, ed. *Shakespeare: The Tragedies.* Chicago, 1965.

Lerner, Laurence, ed. *Shakespeare's Tragedies.* Baltimore, Md., 1963.

Levenworth, Russell, ed. *Interpreting Hamlet.* San Francisco, Calif., 1960.

Levin, Harry. *The Question of Hamlet.* New York, 1959.

Levin, Richard, ed. *Tragedy.* New York, 1960; alternate edition, 1965.

Levinson, J. C., ed. *Discussions of Hamlet.* Boston, 1960.

Le Winter, Oswald, ed. *Shakespeare in Europe.* Cleveland, Ohio, 1963.

Lewis, C. S. "Hamlet: The Prince or the Poem." British Academy Lecture 28. London, 1942.

————. *A Preface to* Paradise Lost. New York, 1961.

Lucas, F. L. *Tragedy.* New York, 1962.

Lyons, Clifford. " 'It Appears so by the Story.' " *SQ* 9 (1958).

Mack, Maynard. "The World of *Hamlet.*" *Yale Review* 41 (1952).

———. *King Lear in Our Time.* Berkeley, Calif., 1965.

Maclean, Hugh. "Disguise in *King Lear:* Kent and Edgar." *SQ* 11 (1960).

Mahood, M. M. *Poetry and Humanism.* New Haven, Conn., 1950.

Madariaga, Salvador de. *On Hamlet.* London, 1948.

Main, William, ed. *King Lear.* New York, 1962.

——— *Hamlet* New York, 1963.

——— *Macbeth.* New York, 1964.

Mandell, Oscar. *A Definition of Tragedy.* New York, 1961.

Marsh, D. R. C. "The Mood of *Measure for Measure.*" *SQ* 14 (1963).

Maxwell, J. C. "The Technique of Invocation in *King Lear.*" *MLR* 45 (1950).

McCarthy, Mary. "General Macbeth." *Harper's* (June, 1962).

McFarland, Thomas. *Tragic Meanings in Shakespeare.* New York, 1966.

McKeon, Richard, ed. *Introduction to Aristotle.* New York, 1947.

McKernan, Maureen. *The Amazing Crime and Trial of Loeb and Leopold.* New York, 1957.

McNeill, John T., ed. *John Calvin; Institutes of the Christian Religion.* Translated by F. L. Battles. Philadelphia, 1960.

Mendonca, Barbara de. "The Influence of *Gorboduc* on *King Lear.*" *Shakespeare Survey* 13 (1960).

Michel, Laurence. "The Possibility of a Christian Tragedy." *Thought* 31 (1956).

———. "Hamlet: Superman, Subchristian." *Centennial Review* 6 (1962).

———, and Sewell, Richard, eds. *Tragedy: Modern Essays in Criticism.* New York, 1963.

Morris, Christopher. *Political Thought in England: Tyndale to Hooker.* Oxford, 1953.

Morris, Harry. "No Amount of Prayer Can Possibly Matter." *Sewanee Review* 77 (1969).

Muir, Edwin. "The Politics of *King Lear.*" *Essays in Literature and Society.* London, 1949.

Muir, Kenneth. *Last Periods of Shakespeare, Racine, and Ibsen.* Detroit, Mich., 1961.

———, ed. *Hamlet.* New York, 1963.

———, ed. *King Lear.* Cambridge, Mass., 1964.

———, ed. *Macbeth.* Cambridge, Mass., 1964.

Murray, Henry, ed. *Myth and Mythmaking.* New York, 1960.

Murry, J. M. *Shakespeare.* London, 1936.

Myrick, Kenneth. "The Theme of Damnation in Shakespearean Tragedy." *SP* 38 (1941).

Neale, J. E. *Queen Elizabeth I.* Garden City, N. Y., 1957.

Neilson, W. A., and Hill, C. J., eds. *The Complete Works of Shakespeare.* Cambridge, Mass., 1942.

Nugent, Donald. "The Renaissance and/of Witchcraft." *Church History* 15 (1971).

Ornstein, Robert. "Historical Criticism and the Interpretation of Shakespeare." *SQ* 10 (1959).

——. *The Moral Vision of Jacobean Tragedy.* Madison, Wis., 1960.

Oxford English Dictionary

Palmer, John. *Political and Comic Characters of Shakespeare's Plays.* London, 1961.

Parker, M. D. H. *The Slave of Life.* London, 1955.

Paterson, John. *"Hamlet."* *SQ* 2 (1952).

Paris, Jean. *Shakespeare.* New York, 1960.

Parrott, Thomas, ed. *Shakespeare.* New York, 1931.

Peter, John. *Complaint and Satire in Early English Literature.* Oxford, 1956.

Polanyi, Karl. *"Hamlet."* *Yale Review* 43 (1954).

Prosser, Eleanor. *Hamlet and Revenge.* Palo Alto, Calif., 1967.

Rabkin, Norman, ed. *Approaches to Shakespeare.* New York, 1964.

Ranald, Margaret. "The Indiscretion of Desdemona." *SQ* 14 (1963).

Raysor, Thomas. *Coleridge's Shakespearean Criticism.* London, 1930.

Reese, M. M. *The Cease of Majesty.* New York, 1961.

Reid, B. L. "The Last Act and the Action of *Hamlet.*" *Yale Review* 54 (1964).

Ribner, Irving. *The English History Play in the Age of Elizabeth.* Princeton, N. J., 1947.

——. " 'The Gods are just': A Reading of *King Lear.*" *Tulane Drama Review* 2 (1958).

——. *Patterns of Shakespearian Tragedy.* London, 1960.

Righter, Anne. *Shakespeare and the Idea of the Play.* London, 1962.

Robertson, D. W. *Preface to Chaucer.* Princeton, N. J. , 1962.

Rogers, Robert. "Endopsychic Drama in *Othello.*" SQ 20 (1969).

Rosen, William. *Shakespeare and the Craft of Tragedy.* Cambridge, Mass., 1960.

Rosenberg, Marvin. "In Defense of Iago." *SQ* 6 (1955).

Rosier, James. "The Lex Aeterna and *King Lear.*" *JEGP* 53 (1954).

Rossiter, A. P. *Angel With Horns.* London, 1961.

Rowse, A. L. *The England of Elizabeth.* New York, 1961.

Sacks, Claire, and Whan, Edgar, eds. *Hamlet: Enter Critic*. New York, 1960.

Santayana, George. *Interpretations of Poetry and Religion*. New York, 1957.

Saunders, Norman, and Thaler, Alwin, eds. *Shakespearian Essays*. Knoxville, Tenn., 1964.

Schoff, Francis. "Hamlet and His Critics: A Series." *Discourse* 4 (1961).

———. "King Lear: Moral Example or Tragic Protagonist?". *SQ* 13 (1962).

Schucking, L. L. *Character Problems in Shakespeare's Plays*. London, 1922.

———. *The Meaning of Hamlet*. Oxford, 1937.

Scragg, Leah. "Iago—Vice or Devil?" *Shakespeare Survey* 21 (1968).

Sen Gupta, S. C. *Shakespearian Comedy*. Oxford, 1950.

Sewell, Arthur. *Character and Society in Shakespeare*. Oxford, 1951.

Sewell, Richard. *The Vision of Tragedy*. New Haven, Conn., 1962.

Seznec, Jean. *The Survival of the Pagan Gods*. New York, 1961.

Shaffer, Elinor. "Iago's Malignity Motivated." *SQ* 19 (1968).

Siegel, Paul. "The Damnation of Othello." *PMLA* 68 (1953).

———. "Adversity and the Miracle of Love in *King Lear*." SQ 6 (1955).

———. "The Damnation of Othello: An Addendum." *PMLA* 71 (1956).

———. *Shakespearean Tragedy and the Elizabethan Compromise*. New York, 1957.

———. Letter to the Editor. *SQ* 9 (1958).

———, ed. *His Infinite Variety*. Philadelphia, Pa., 1964.

Singer, Irving, ed. *Essays in Literary Criticism of George Santayana*. New York, 1956.

Sisson, C. J. "The Magic of Prospero." *Shakespeare Survey* 11 (1958).

Sitwell, Dame Edith. *A Notebook on William Shakespeare*. Boston, 1961.

Smith, H. Maynard. *Henry VIII and the Reformation*. London, 1948.

Speaight, Robert. *Nature in Shakespearian Tragedy*. New York, 1962.

Spencer, Theodore. *Shakespeare and the Nature of Man*. New York, 1942.

Spivack, Bernard. *Shakespeare and the Allegory of Evil*. New York, 1958.

Spurgeon, Caroline. *Shakespeare's Imagery*. Boston, 1958.

Stampfer, J. "The Catharsis of *King Lear*." *Shakespeare Survey* 13 (1960).

Stauffer, Donald. *Shakespeare's World of Images.* New York, 1949.

Stempel, Daniel. "The Silence of Iago." *PMLA* 84 (1969).

Stirling, Brents. *Unity in Shakespearian Tragedy.* New York, 1956.

Stoll, E. E. *Art and Artifice in Shakespeare.* New York, 1951.

Strathmann, Ernest. "The Devil Can Cite Scripture." *SQ* 15 (1964).

Tate, Allen, ed. *The Language of Poetry.* Princeton, N. J., 1942.

Tillich, Paul. *Love, Power, and Justice.* New York, 1954.

Tillyard, E. M. W. *Shakespeare's Last Plays.* London, 1938.

———. *The Elizabethan World Picture.* London, 1943.

———. *Shakespeare's Problem Plays.* London, 1950.

———. *Shakespeare's History Plays.* New York, 1962.

Traversi, D. A. *Shakespeare: The Last Phase.* New York, 1955.

———. *An Approach to Shakespeare.* Garden City, N.Y., 1956.

———. *Shakespeare: From "Richard II" to "Henry V."* Palo Alto, Calif., 1957.

———. *"King Lear," Stratford Papers on Shakespeare: 1964.* Toronto, 1965.

Trewin, J. C. "The Old Vic and Stratford-upon-Avon, 1961-1962." *SQ* 13 (1962).

Trimble, W. R. *The Catholic Laity in Elizabethan England.* London, 1964.

Van Doren, Mark. *Shakespeare.* New York, 1939.

Van Laan, Thomas. "*Everyman:* A Structural Analysis." *PMLA* 78 (1963).

Vyvyan, John. *The Shakespearian Ethic.* New York, 1959.

Walker, Roy. *The Time is out of Joint.* London, 1948.

Webber, Joan. "The Renewal of the King's Symbolic Role: From *Richard II* to *Henry V.*" *Texas Studies in Literature and Language* 4 (1962).

Webster, Margaret. *Shakespeare Without Tears.* New York, 1961.

West, Rebecca. *The Court and the Castle.* New Haven, Conn., 1961.

West, Robert. *Shakespeare and the Outer Mystery.* Lexington, Ky., 1968.

Wheelwright, Philip. *The Burning Fountain.* Bloomington, Ind., 1954.

Whitaker, Virgil. *Shakespeare's Use of Learning.* San Marino, Calif., 1953.

———. *The Mirror Up To Nature.* San Marino, Calif., 1965.

William, David. "*The Tempest* on the Stage." *Stratford-upon-Avon Studies* 1 (1960).

Wilson, Harold. "Action and Symbol in *Measure for Measure* and *The Tempest.*" *SQ* 4 (1953).

————. *On the Design of Shakespearian Tragedy*. Toronto, 1957.

Wilson, J. D., ed. *Macbeth*. Cambridge, Eng., 1947.

————. *What Happens in Hamlet*. Cambridge, Eng., 1961.

Wilson, Mona, ed. *Johnson*. Cambridge, Mass., 1951.

Wimsatt, W. K. *Samuel Johnson on Shakespeare*. New York, 1960.

Woodard, Charles. "The Archetype of the Fall." *College English* 38 (1967).

Zimbardo, Rose. "Form and Disorder in *The Tempest*." *SQ* 14 (1963).

Index